PAY FOR PLAY

Sport and Society

Series Editors
Benjamin G. Rader
Randy Roberts

*A list of books in the series
appears at the end of this book.*

PAY FOR PLAY

A HISTORY OF BIG-TIME COLLEGE ATHLETIC REFORM

RONALD A. SMITH

University of Illinois Press

Urbana, Chicago, and Springfield

Library of Congress Cataloging-in-Publication Data
Smith, Ronald A. (Ronald Austin), 1936–
Pay for play : a history of big-time college athletic reform /
Ronald A. Smith.
p.   cm. — (Sport and society)
Includes bibliographical references and index.
ISBN 978-0-252-03587-6 (cloth : alk. paper)
ISBN 978-0-252-07783-8 (pbk. : alk. paper)
1. College sports—United States—History.
2. College sports—Moral and ethical aspects—United States—History.
3. College sports—Law and legislation—United States—History.
4. National Collegiate Athletic Association—History.
I. Title.
GV347.S65   2010
796.04′30973—dc22   2010024102

This book is dedicated to the North American Society for Sport History, the oldest and the most important organization promoting the research and writing of sport history.

Contents

Preface

Woodrow Wilson, as an undergraduate at Princeton University in the 1880s, was an athletic "cheerleader" for his beloved Princeton Tigers. Later, when he was a professor of political economy at Wesleyan University, he helped coach the football team in its competition against the likes of Yale and Harvard. When he took a position in jurisprudence and politics at Princeton, he again assisted with the football team and was chair of the Committee on Outdoor Sports. Only a few years before he became president of the United States, he was president of Princeton University, where he tried unsuccessfully to help reform big-time college sport, against the wishes of his governing board and other universities. By then, Wilson believed, the students were preoccupied with nonacademic activities; or as he said, "The sideshow has swallowed up the circus." Wilson was symbolic of the reformers and cheerleaders who have often been at variance on the direction that college sport has taken since Yale and Harvard inaugurated American intercollegiate sport nine years before the American Civil War. Others who have become university leaders repeatedly have been as conflicted as was Wilson. More often than not they have played the role of cheerleader for their own institutions while calling for reform of the system for all the others. Cheerleading has generally won the day, whereas reforming the system has generally been subscribed to by word but not by action. *Pay for Play* recounts the yin and yang (dark and cold, bright and hot) of the various players in the attempts to reform intercollegiate sports. It traces the history of those who have made attempts to reform big-time athletics that students unaided created and the institutions that took them over for a variety of reasons. The harmony sought by the balance of yin and yang of college athletics has been an elusive feature of big-time athletics.

The writing of this volume was first suggested by Sandy Thatcher, then director of the Penn State University Press, while we were involved in a series of interdisciplinary discussions about sport sponsored by Stephen Ross, a professor of law at Penn State. I had circulated a timeline on the history of intercollegiate athletic reform to the group, and Thatcher proposed creating a history of athletic reform, something that he was deeply interested in since his competitive swimming days at Princeton University. I had personally been studying athletic reform since writing my PhD dissertation in the 1960s at the University of Wisconsin–Madison on the history of the Wisconsin State University Athletic Conference, but not before. At my undergraduate institution, Northwestern University, I was a history major on an academic scholarship, but I was recruited for both the basketball and baseball teams. I did not know of scholarship athletes who were given special academic privileges, and I knew of only one particular course that some athletes took because it was supposed to be easy: The History of Greek Literature. I was probably naive, coming from a rather sheltered life on a dairy farm in southern Wisconsin and long before we could learn of all the problems in college athletics on ESPN.

Later, when I was interviewed for a position in the prestigious department of Physical Education at Penn State University in 1968, I asked two important individuals in the interview process whether any pressure was ever placed upon university professors at Penn State to change or raise grades of athletes. Knowing that it was not unusual in institutions of higher education, I did not want to be placed in that situation. During the discussion, I was then told the story of Joe Paterno when he was an assistant football coach early in his coaching career. What was told to me is that Paterno had gone to see a professor about a football player's grade in an effort to keep the player eligible. When Dean of the College Ernie McCoy was informed of this indiscretion, he called Paterno into his office. The straight-shooting McCoy told the coach that if he ever heard of him putting pressure on a professor in the future, Paterno would no longer be at Penn State. In my twenty-eight years at Penn State, with several all-Americans and a Heisman Trophy winner in my classes, I was never approached or called by any coach or member of the Athletic Department about grades. Penn State may not be pure in athletics or in any other area of higher education, but its integrity in intercollegiate athletics is high on my ladder of athletic ethics.

In this volume, I have attempted to trace the history of individuals, inside groups, and outside entities that have influenced the reformation of intercollegiate athletics since they began in the 1850s. These include the most visible: students, faculty, presidents, governing boards, the NCAA, private agencies, legislators, and courts. Presidents, for well over a century, have been called upon to reform athletics. However, after four decades of research, especially in university archives, I have come to the conclusion that it is not likely that presidents of institutions of higher learning will be successful in reforming college athletics. I have never found a president who was naive about college athletics, and I have looked at hundreds of presidential records dating back to the last half of the nineteenth century. Presidents are knowledgeable about the problems in athletics, but they are often the chief cheerleaders for their institution, and though they often offer high-sounding words about reform, their actions do not always coincide with their rhetoric.

Presidents, though, probably should be understood more for the difficult situation they encounter relative to athletics, for they are torn between what they know is needed to bring athletics more in line with existing academics and the supporters of the status quo of highly commercialized and professionalized "amateur" sport. The latter group often includes alumni, students, trustees, athletic directors, coaches, media, and the interested public. A former president of the University of Michigan, James Duderstadt, may be correct when he stated in the early twentieth-first century: "As long as higher education continues to allow the networks, the media, the sporting apparel companies, and the American public—not to mention celebrity coaches and ambitious athletic directors—to promote and pressure college sports to become an entertainment industry, there will be little progress toward true reform within the athletics programs." Because the entertainment industry and athletics have been tied together since the Rowing Association of American College Regattas of the 1870s and the New York City Thanksgiving Day Football Championships of the 1880s and 1890s, it is not likely that this aspect of college athletics will disappear with mere presidential reform efforts. What may be needed is for governing boards, faculty, and students to join with the reform-minded presidents to bring about lasting reforms. If that does not happen, it may very well be outsiders, especially national legislators and the courts, who will make reforms in a number of areas of intercollegiate athletics.

This volume is based to a great extent on the university and other archives that I have perused since the 1960s. For this book, I have been influenced and directed by materials found in the following archives: Arizona State, Association of Intercollegiate Athletics for Women, Atlantic Coast Conference, Brown, Bucknell, Butler, Cambridge, Clemson, William and Mary, Columbia, Cornell, Dartmouth, Dickinson, Drake, Duke, Eastern College Athletic Association, Georgetown, Georgia Tech, Harvard, Library of Congress, Manhattan, Mary Baldwin, National Collegiate Athletic Association, New York City Public Library, Northwestern, Ohio State, Oxford, Penn State, Princeton, Rutgers, Smith, Southern Methodist, Stanford, State Historical Society of Wisconsin, Swarthmore, Todd-McLean Collection, Tulane, U.S. Military Academy, U.S. Naval Academy, Alabama, California, Chicago, Colorado, Georgia, Illinois, Maryland, Michigan, Minnesota, Nebraska, New Mexico, North Carolina, Notre Dame, Oklahoma, Pennsylvania, Southern California, Tennessee, Virginia, Wisconsin, Wisconsin State University System, Vassar, Wesleyan, Western Maryland, and Yale.

I am indebted to a number of individuals who have contributed by providing information or reading sections of the manuscript. Included are William Bowen, Princeton University; Bob Eno, Indiana University; Scott Kretchmar, Penn State University; John Nichols, Penn State University; Jim Odenkirk, Arizona State University; Allen Sack, University of New Haven; Sandy Thatcher, Penn State University; Nathan Tublitz, University of Oregon; and John Watterson, James Madison University. No one spent more time reading the manuscript than my wife and friend, Susan Fernald Smith.

I was fortunate to have Carol Burwash as a freelance copyeditor, for she showed perspicacity in her editorial judgments throughout the manuscript. A thank you to in-house editor Jennifer Clark, who saw the book through to publication, and to Bill Regier, director of the University of Illinois Press, who proposed that I publish with the University of Illinois Press.

Introduction

A resort steamer, *Lady of the Lake,* lay on the calm waters of Lake Winnipesaukee, New Hampshire, on a fine day in August 1852, while the excited passengers listened to martial music of the Concord Mechanics Brass Band. They all awaited the beginning of competition between the crews of Harvard and Yale as they took in the view of the Red Hills behind the village of Centre Harbor at the northern end of the lake.[1] As a purely commercial venture of the newly opened Boston, Concord, and Montreal Railroad, the first intercollegiate athletic contest in America[2] was secondary to the promotional wishes of what would be the dominating industrial success of the nineteenth century: the railroad industry. To James Elkins, the superintendent of the Boston to Montreal rail line, it was a business deal, and he would "pay all the bills" for an eight-day rowing vacation if Yale and Harvard athletes would agree to put on several rowing exhibitions. But to the crews of the two most prestigious institutions of higher learning in America, this was merely a "jolly lark."[3] Following a Harvard victory over Yale, before possibly a thousand cheering spectators, including Democratic presidential candidate Franklin Pierce, a second contest scheduled for the following day was canceled due to the weather. Nevertheless, when the conditions cleared somewhat, the Harvard and Yale crews rowed on the lake "for the gratification of the townspeople."[4] In the intervening century and a half, athletics continued to serve as a gratification for those both inside and outside institutions of higher learning. Athletics also have provided ample cause for reformers to try to bring college sports into a role complementary to the academic goals of higher education.

Although a New York City newspaper predicted that the Harvard-Yale crew meet and intercollegiate athletics in general would "make little stir in a busy world," they did just that.[5] Nearly as soon as intercollegiate athletics were introduced, questions demanding reform arose. The first came about when Yale and Harvard renewed their athletic competition in 1855, a half-dozen years before the American Civil War. Immediately a problem arose. Harvard decided that the coxswain who led the Harvard crew to victory in 1852 would again be the leader in the boat despite having graduated two years before. He participated, and Harvard won again. The eligibility of graduates and especially graduate students would remain on the reform agenda for the next half century. Early on, most of the questions of eligibility reform were left to students to resolve, for students alone had created intercollegiate athletics, and students negotiated not only the schedules of competition but also the terms under which the competitions would be held. There were no athletic conferences at first and no national organizations, such as the National Collegiate Athletic Association, to determine the conditions around which the contests would be conducted.

There were only five logical groups that could reform athletics either at individual institutions or among a number of colleges in the early years. First, the students acted in their own self-interest to create competitive sports that would serve them, but they had little need of or interest in reforming what they had constructed. Second, the faculty had a direct interest in reforming athletics, because athletics came to dominate the extra curriculum of most colleges and affect the academic side of higher education during the second half of the nineteenth century. Third, presidents were often concerned about the domination of such intercollegiate sports as crew, baseball, track and field, and football in the late 1800s and the impact they had, both negative and positive, on their colleges. Fourth, governing boards, which were formed to create college policy, had a direct interest in the value of college athletics to their institutions. Fifth, graduates of institutions, who were often crucial to the financial success of colleges, had a keen interest in how athletics were used to the benefit of the institution. Reform efforts, then, could come from a variety of interest groups, but because four of the five groups were led principally by cheerleaders, not reformers, significant reforms were difficult to achieve over a century and a half.

In almost all cases, reform efforts over the first century and a half of intercollegiate sports were brought about for one of four reasons: (1) to create competitive equity, the "level playing field"; (2) to bring about financial solvency; (3) to consider banning or restricting brutal or unsavory practices; or (4) to achieve academic integrity. Competitive equity issues have dominated reform efforts. Nearly all eligibility issues have been fought to prevent a school or schools from gaining competitive advantages on the playing field. These issues include prohibiting the participation of graduates or graduate students, setting limits on how much money an athlete may be paid to attend college, limiting the number of years a person may compete, determining what academic credentials an individual must have to be admitted to college, controlling the minimum number of credits and academic achievement an athlete must attain while attending college, and restricting the participation of an individual who transfers from one institution to another.

Over the years, reform efforts have been attempted to keep intercollegiate athletics financially solvent. Financial stress is a major reason why alumni came to dominate college athletics in the nineteenth and early twentieth centuries, and alumni continued to be a controlling factor for a number of schools into the twenty-first century. When students did not or could not finance their own contests without going into debt, to the detriment of the college image, outside forces came into play. Alumni were there to help financially, and where financial support was introduced, power over the program often came with it. Presidents and governing boards also came into the equation, generally at first to prevent financial abuses and later to use athletics for their own purposes such as advertising their institutions, bringing a virile image to colleges, raising money, and increasing enrollment.

Reform of brutal or unethical practices was not usual in college athletics, but reform of violence and unsavory practices was the principal reason for the creation of the National Collegiate Athletic Association (NCAA) during the 1905–6 crisis in football. The brutal nature of football, with a few deaths and many severe injuries, was reformed through major changes by the football rules-making body, which prevented mass-momentum plays and opened up the game with the forward pass in the years between 1906 and 1910. A half century later, the death of a University of Wisconsin boxer, Charlie Mohr, and the opinion that boxing was a brutal sport, led the NCAA to ban boxing as a championship sport in colleges. Hardly anyone referred to the banning of boxing as a reform measure, but it surely was.

Nearly always, a stated reason for reform has been to further academic integrity. Seldom has this been the primary accomplishment of reform. From early on, when a Harvard student publication admitted in 1880 that "some students come to college for the avowed purpose of engaging in athletic contests," noting that "the object of their college course is quite as much college sports as college studies," there has been a question of academic integrity in college athletics.[6] Not much later, a Princeton athletic advisory group noted: "We all know athletic supremacy is more highly esteemed by many young men than intellectual culture, and it seems to us that the duty of the college authorities in the case of such men is to see that they maintain their standing in their studies."[7] Yet a century later the prestigious Knight Foundation's Commission on Intercollegiate Athletics report emphatically stated: "The root difficulty is not creating a 'level playing field.' It is insuring that those on the field are students as well as athletes."[8] It was the same problem with no easy solution whether in the 1880s or the 1990s. Unfortunately for needed reforms, the Knight Commission and other reform agencies for more than a century have often pursued the wrong solution to accomplish meaningful reform.

The Knight Commission still existed well into the twenty-first century, and its solution was no more commendable or attainable as it was when the Knight Commission was established in 1989. In bold letters, the Knight Commission report of 1991 stated that its "bedrock conviction is that university presidents are the key to successful reform."[9] "Poppycock." Charles W. Eliot, president of Harvard University from 1869 to 1909, knew better than either former presidents William C. Friday of the University of North Carolina and Theodore M. Hesburgh of the University of Notre Dame, who cochaired the Knight Commission report. President Eliot, who was a senior at Harvard when the first intercollegiate contest took place on a New Hampshire lake in 1852, made a prescient comment in 1905 at the height of the most important athletic reform opportunity in higher education history. "College presidents," he said when asked to head a conference for football reform, "certainly cannot reform football, and I doubt if by themselves they can abolish it."[10] Eliot, after three and a half decades of leading Harvard, knew that college presidents did not have the power to reform or abolish intercollegiate athletics. More than a century later, the Knight Commission and college presidents had less insight than President Eliot, though they had a century of experience from which to profit.

The Knight Commission, however, was only one of many reform units whose members believed college athletics could be reformed only by presidents. In 1905, at the same time President Eliot sagely announced that presidents could not reform football, President Schurman of Cornell declared: "Presidents have it in their power to abolish the evils of the game. All that is needed is action."[11] Two decades later, the *American College Athletics* report of the Carnegie Foundation for the Advancement of Teaching concluded that "college presidents have left the shaping of athletic policies to conferences, committees, or specialists," and their lack of attention contributed to the major problems in intercollegiate athletics.[12] A generation after the Carnegie Report, a special committee of the American Council on Education, led by Michigan State University President John Hannah, reinforced the presidential theme. "Presidents of colleges," Hannah noted, "must assume all responsibility for the conduct of athletics at their institutions." Item number one of Hannah's 1952 "Report of the Special Committee on Athletic Policy" recommendation was for presidential control of athletics and the needed reforms.[13] Two decades later, another study by the American Council on Education reported the belief that presidents have "within their power to take corrective action."[14] By the 1980s, the president of the American Council on Education, J. W. Peltason, described his organization as believing "in athletics, there is no substitute for presidential involvement and leadership" when raising eligibility standards and other reforms needed in college athletics.[15] By the time of the Knight Commission report of the 1990s, little had changed. Presidents, the report stated emphatically, "are the linchpin of the reform movement."[16]

Ten years later, as the twenty-first century moved college athletics into their third century, the Knight Commission, composed principally of college presidents, knew that its reform movement led by college presidents was a failure.[17] Only minimal reforms had been instituted under college presidents, and things had gotten worse. The Knight Commission conducted a survey of college faculty about college athletics and then called a meeting, the Knight Commission's Faculty Summit on Intercollegiate Athletics in late 2007.[18] If there had been any group that had been overlooked by reform presidents and other reformers, it was the faculty. Rarely since the 1800s had faculty been brought fully into the reform efforts. It is true that faculty members had been put on athletic committees, been faculty representatives to the NCAA, and served on committees dealing with athletics on university faculty senates, but they had seen nearly all power stripped from them by presidents and governing boards for more than a century. For once, the individuals who had the most to gain from having athletics meet some criteria of academic integrity on college campuses—faculty members—were listened to with some attention.

This may have occurred because faculty members nationally were beginning to move into the power equation, something that had been missing for generations. In 1999, a new faculty organization was founded, the Drake Group. Jon Ericson, a professor of rhetoric and communication studies at Drake University, decided to hold a national conference on restoring academic integrity to college athletics. From the first meeting, no consensus was attained about reform, but some of the more radical faculty reformers were energized, including William C. Dowling, a professor of literature at Rutgers; Allen Sack, a sociologist from the University of New Haven; Murray Sperber, a professor of English and American studies at Indiana; Ellen Staurowsky, a professor of sports studies from Ithaca College; and Andrew Zimbalist, an economist from Smith College. Larry Gerlach, a history professor at the University of Utah and an athletic reform skeptic, said after the original Drake Group meeting that faculty must be given stronger voices if reform is to succeed.[19] The Drake Group continued to meet, to discuss and draw up reform proposals, but it showed little power to exact change.

Another faculty group, which appeared to know better the importance of power in creating athletic reform, was created out of a faculty discussion at the University of Oregon, expanded to the PAC-10 Conference, and finally spread nationally as the Coalition on Intercollegiate Athletics (COIA). Unlike the Drake Group, COIA was not a group of individuals who sought reform but consisted of a number of faculty senates across the nation's big-time NCAA Division I-A institutions. COIA worked with the NCAA, the Association of Governing Bodies, College Sports Project,

Division I-A Faculty Athletic Representatives Association of the NCAA, Division I-A athletic directors, and the Knight Commission. After widespread consultation, COIA in 2007 constructed a white paper, "Framing the Future: Reforming Intercollegiate Athletics." Later that year, it partnered with the Knight Commission to organize a Faculty Summit on Intercollegiate Athletics.[20] The president-led Knight Commission may have learned what President Charles Eliot believed more than a century ago: Presidents alone, especially those who are primarily cheerleaders for their own institution, cannot or will not reform athletics.

Those who have academic integrity most in mind—faculty—could be successful if given the power to act with others. That was a big if. "Faculties have not a single vote on National Collegiate Athletic Association matters," stated a former leading athletic director, Don Canham of the University of Michigan.[21] Retired Michigan President James Duderstadt wrote a book condemning the commercialism and professionalism in big-time college sport, *Intercollegiate Athletics and the American University: A University President's Perspective,* after his presidency, though he accomplished little to reform his own tainted institution while he was president. When his 2000 book came out in paperback three years later, he wrote an epilogue in which he admitted: "Few contemporary university presidents have the capacity, the will, or the appetite to lead a true reform movement in college sports." He noted, however, "there is one important ally remaining that could challenge the mad rush of college sports toward the cliff of commercialism: the university faculty."[22] After more than a century of the faculty being buried under the dictates of presidents and governing boards, their involvement appeared to be the last best hope of reforming intercollegiate athletics from within institutions of higher learning. If that were to occur, then the policies could be designed not only to create a level playing field for the competitors and result in greater financial stability, but more important the reform could bring about a greater degree of academic integrity to institutions of higher learning.

To understand how college faculties have been removed from the academic integrity equation, it is helpful to look back over a century and a half of big-time intercollegiate athletics and the place of students, faculty, presidents, governing boards, alumni, general public, federal legislature, courts, commercial concerns, and the media in creating the highly commercialized and professionalized sports at all divisional levels of the National Collegiate Athletic Association. For the most part, the differences between Division I (big-time) and Division III (small-time) are ones of degree, not generally of kind.[23] With a few notable exceptions, the form of Division III athletics is similar to those of Division I. That is, there are professional coaches, professionalized recruiting, and professionalized advising; commercialized stadiums and arenas; lengthy schedules; prolonged training periods both daily and seasonally; play-offs and national championships; lowering of standards to bring less academically gifted athletes into the schools; "arms races" to build enticing athletic facilities; and a sports publicity office to carry the word to the alumni and general public. It might be suggested that if athletic reform is desired, it should be for all colleges, large and small. Yet for all big-time institutions or for many of those not so big-time, a dilemma exists, which may be why few reform solutions have been achieved in more than a century and a half. It is difficult, if not impossible, to attempt to create athletic programs that are educationally sound and based on principles of amateurism when the historical model for well over a century is professional in most respects and generally financed commercially.[24]

The history of big-time athletic reform in American institutions of higher learning is generally one of failure and not inspiring. The possibilities of reform may seem more difficult than eliminating slavery, but that was accomplished in America shortly after intercollegiate athletics came into being. The abolition of slavery, however, took a civil war to accomplish. Athletic reform could be as difficult as extending the right to vote to women in America, but that came about early in the previous century. Nevertheless, it took years of organized protests to achieve. It may be as challenging as reforming the medical and insurance industries to provide affordable medical care for all Americans. In all three cases—rights of African Americans, rights of women, and rights to medical care—it took national legislation and court cases to help reform the system. Reform of college athletics is a daunting task, and it may require additional action from court cases and laws to achieve. It is a problem worthy of exploring historically. Those in position to reform college athletics could use the perspective that history can provide. College presidents as well as faculty, students, governing boards, legislators, and judges could use such insights.

1

Student-Controlled Athletics and Early Reform

Walter Camp, often called the "Father of American Football," may have stated best the role students played in creating American intercollegiate athletics. "Neither the faculties nor other critics assisted in building the structure of college athletics," Camp noted, three years after completing his six-year football career at Yale, "it is a structure which students unaided have builded."[1] Camp did not claim, however, that students were unaided in the efforts to reform the student games. Students, nevertheless, started the process of reform following the second intercollegiate contest. Several years after Yale's defeat in the first intercollegiate crew meet, Yale men challenged Harvard to another vacation-time meet. This time it was held on the Connecticut River at Springfield, an 1855 race of one-and-a-half miles downstream and back. The new boat purchased by the Yale crew was not enough to beat the Harvard eight, led by Joseph Brown, a Harvard graduate who had been coxswain of the winning crew in 1852.[2] Bringing a graduate back in a successful effort to beat Yale did not seem fair to the Yale undergraduates. They protested Brown's participation, and Harvard agreed not to compete with its own graduates in future contests. One should note, though, that Harvard and many other universities used graduates of other institutions, who were in professional schools or graduate schools, on their athletic teams into the twentieth century.

Students continued to run their own programs, often making dual agreements with another college when they participated in the first intercollegiate sports. Students organized their own sports, and in the second half of the nineteenth century there was a rapid growth of sporting events, generally originating in the eastern colleges and spreading to the West and South. The first six were (1) a crew meet between Harvard and Yale in 1852; (2) a baseball game between Amherst and Williams in 1859; (3) a cricket match between Haverford and Penn in 1864; (4) a football (soccer-like) game between Princeton and Rutgers in 1869; (5) a track meet between Amherst, Cornell, and McGill in 1873; and (6) a football (rugby) game between Harvard and McGill in 1874. By 1900, there were intercollegiate contests in rifle, lacrosse, bicycling, tennis, boxing, polo, cross-country, fencing, ice hockey, basketball, golf, trapshooting, water polo, swimming, and gymnastics.[3] Because students originated these contests, they created the rules that attempted to level the playing field between contestants, without giving thought to any academic integrity issues that participation in these contests might create.

Several examples of disputes leading to competitive changes in the early period of intercollegiate athletics confirm the control of reform by students. By 1870, Harvard and Yale had been rowing dual meets for a number of years, but an incident took place that year in a meet on Lake Quinsigamond near Worcester, Massachusetts. The Lake Quinsigamond site was not long enough for a straightaway race, so the two schools agreed to a turning stake, around which the two crews would negotiate and return to the starting line. At the turning stake, Harvard was leading by about a boat length. As both crews were making the turn, Harvard's rudder broke, disabling it and allowing Yale to take the lead and the victory. Harvard then protested to the regatta committee, claiming that the Yale boat caused the accident, while Yale believed that the rudder had been broken by the turning stake and not by the Yale shell. After several hours, the judges ruled the victory would go to Harvard. The Yale crew was indignant over the decision and immediately challenged Harvard to row again the next day. Harvard refused, claiming that one of its rowers could not remain. Yale then resolved that "No Yale crew should be allowed to challenge any Harvard crew, except for a straight-away race."[4] After a winter and spring of dispute, played out in the newspapers by students of the two schools, Yale students refused to capitulate to Harvard. Yet Harvard was conscious of its superiority over Yale both as an institution and in crew and called for a convention to create rules and regulations for an open regatta of eastern colleges. Harvard continued to criticize Yale's conditions: "If Yale refuses to take part in the annual regatta of American colleges, Harvard insists on the right of the challenged party to name the time and place of the race, and Yale can only row for the championship a race similar to the one in which she was last year defeated."[5] Yale refused and declined participation in the inclusive regatta. This was the kind of reform one could expect from student-run athletics: discussions of a level playing field and nothing more.

The new Harvard-initiated Rowing Association of American Colleges existed for six years, beginning in 1871, with participation first on the Connecticut River at Springfield, Massachusetts, and later at the summer vacation spot, horse racing center, and gambling resort at Lake Saratoga, New York. Prior to the 1873 regatta, students began a reform effort to determine who was eligible to compete. Should students from Yale Scientific School, considered inferior by Yale College students, be allowed to compete? Should Harvard be allowed to use graduate students in the Harvard law, medical, and divinity schools? Should students in undergraduate professional schools such as law be allowed to participate? Should graduates of one institution be allowed to compete for another university? Should professional coaches be allowed to coach the various teams? The student representatives decided that any undergraduate in a bachelor degree program could participate, but not graduate students. No graduates of another institution would be allowed to row for another college. In the future, no professional coach would be allowed to prepare crews, only a graduate of that institution could do so.[6] To Harvard, this allowed an uneven playing field, for "the equality between colleges can only be established by allowing each to enjoy its fullest resources." Professional students studying law, Harvard students argued, should be allowed to row in the regatta.[7]

In baseball, most rules were created between the two schools after a challenge for a contest was made. Prior to the first intercollegiate baseball game, two years before the American Civil War, the senior class president at Amherst College, at the conclusion of morning prayers, brought up the question of challenging Williams College, and the students voted overwhelmingly to do so. Williams accepted, and the rules were agreed to. None had to do with whether freshmen would be eligible, if a certain grade point average had been attained, or if everyone who only played for the love of the game was an amateur. What the two schools agreed to was that each team would use its own ball on defense, the ball could be batted in any direction as in cricket, a fly out could be made only by catching the ball on the fly rather than on the usual first bounce, and the team that garnered sixty-five runs would be victor. A neutral site, Pittsfield, was chosen as it was accessible by a new rail line. Amherst won 73–32.[8]

Following the Civil War, baseball rapidly spread across America, but the leadership was still in the East. Harvard first played Yale in 1868 as part of a Worcester Regatta. Yale challenged Harvard for a game in which members would be "selected only from the academic departments of either college." Thus professional schools, such as law schools, would be excluded. Three years later, two Harvard players and one from Yale were eliminated from their teams because they were in professional schools. Both schools then made an agreement that in the future "the selection of the College Nine should be made from any department of the University."[9] By the mid-1870s, colleges were playing both noncollege amateur teams and professionals. They won occasionally when competing against teams of the first professional major leagues, the National Association of Professional Base Ball Players and, later, the National League when it was formed in 1876. But mostly college teams wanted to compete against other college teams for the prestige and bragging rights that the contests brought. By the end of the 1870s, a group of eastern colleges, consisting of Amherst, Brown, Dartmouth, Harvard, Princeton, and Yale, was playing regular home and away series of games. The teams with the best record in this informal arrangement would claim the championship. The number of games scheduled and played by each college was not clearly stated, nor was it clear if the number of games won or the number of series between teams won was the determining factor. This led to claims and counterclaims during and following the 1879 season. In addition, there were two questionable issues of eligibility that contributed to the boiling of tempers.

The 1879 season was key to questions of eligibility. Harvard, which had won the mythical championship in 1878, lost an early-season game in 1879 to Brown by the embarrassing score of 21–5. A week later, Harvard was beaten by its archrival Yale. Humbled and humiliated, the Harvard captain prevailed upon two former Harvard players of the class of 1876, Harold Ernst and James Tyng, who had pitched and caught with uncommon success for the Crimson the past several years. Ernst at the time was in his last year at the Harvard Medical School, while Tyng was in the Harvard Law School. These four- and five-year veterans agreed to help Harvard in its quest for continued glory. The other colleges were understandably angry. A writer for a Princeton paper was incensed. "It is a blot on the fair name of Harvard that she descends to such tricks to obtain the championship."[10] Nevertheless, with no written eligibility rules, the two Harvard alums continued to participate. Not to be outdone, Brown, with possibly the best amateur or professional pitcher in baseball, Lee Richmond, met the Harvard team. Brown's return game against Harvard, with Richmond pitching, resulted in 6–2 Brown victory. Richmond followed with a masterpiece in beating Yale 3–2 for the "championship." But by that time, Richmond had become a professional, pitching for the Worcester team in the National League. In his professional debut against the Chicago White Stockings, prior to the Yale victory, the Brown left-hander threw a no-hitter, including shutting down Cap Anson, the best-known nineteenth-century ballplayer, and Abner Dalrymple, the National League leading hitter of 1878. Richmond had brought his college catcher, Bill Winslow, to battle against the best professionals.[11] The question of player eligibility was ablaze, and the students of the six schools tried to agree on common eligibility rules.

In December 1879, a baseball conference of the eastern schools met in Springfield, Massachusetts. The issues of graduate student and professional participation were the major agenda items. After arguing for more than two hours whether Brown's Richmond and his catcher Bill Winslow should be eligible the following year, they finally agreed to prevent future professional players from participating. When they would not make it ex post facto, Yale walked out of the meeting, but not before attacking the Ernst-Tyng duo from Harvard for playing as alumni and members of professional schools. Yale had proposed a rule to prevent professional school students from participating but withdrew it when Harvard agreed not to play Ernst and Tyng in the future. Another Yale motion to prevent players from participating more than five years was defeated. The acrimonious meeting ended, but not before students had created a new Baseball Association in which each of the five colleges (Yale refused) agreed to play two-game, home and away series with the other schools.[12] The reform in banning the playing of professionals was significant, but in the future there would be major questions of playing ball during the summer for money and returning to college and participating as an amateur.

Student-controlled football had some similar problems. After intercollegiate football originated, with soccer competition between Rutgers and Princeton in 1869, Harvard refused to be drawn into soccer football, electing to play its own brand of football, something more akin to rugby than soccer. Harvard's refusal to draw up common soccer rules caused soccer to die within a few years. Yale wanted to play against Harvard, who had by 1874 accepted rugby rules after competing against McGill University of Montreal, Canada. Soon Yale agreed to play a rugby game against Harvard, and Princeton then knew that it must adopt rugby in order to play Yale. All other schools accepted the leadership of key eastern schools after a convention was called to ratify rugby rules and create a Thanksgiving Day championship game in New York City beginning in 1876. The student-run Intercollegiate Football Association had reformed football to its liking, and within six years it had changed the rules of play and had Americanized rugby into what became the most popular game on American campuses.[13]

The annual Thanksgiving Day game in New York City for the two decades following the formation of the Intercollegiate Football Association promoted football as the beacon of commercialized athletics a half century before radio gave it additional promotion in the 1920s and television by the 1940s and 1950s. By taking the game to the financial and fashion center of America, football had joined the academically select colleges of the East with the social elite of America's largest city. By the 1890s, as many as 40,000 spectators, with many upper-class leaders, viewed the Thanksgiving Day classic. Having been taken away from the college campus, football was much more than a college game played for the students and a growing group of alumni. Football had become a social event, expanding it beyond just an athletic contest. The attraction of elite eastern institutions playing before tens of thousands moved football to a national stage as newspapers everywhere reported on the annual contest. As Michael Oriard has pointed out, "football's emerging audience discovered football not from the grandstand but from the daily press."[14] The expansion of football in the late 1880s and early 1890s made it college's most prestigious sport by the 1890s. The new celebrity led football not only away from the college campus but also away from the eyes of the educational establishment—the presidents and faculties. If college athletics and college football in particular had remained solely a campus activity, it could have been controlled more fully by university administrators and faculty. Alumni and the general public did not wish for this to occur, and certainly many students saw that the excitement of a football game was far greater than anything that took place in the classroom.

While alumni and the general public were taking a greater part in collegiate athletics, an eligibility incident in 1889 showed that students were still in control of much of the athletic scene prior to the turn of the century. Students at the time were concerned about reforming eligibility rules relative to the level playing field, not about furthering academic integrity. Eligibility rules that gave any kind of advantage to other schools were challenged by their competitors. In the midst of the 1889 football season, before the big games between Harvard, Princeton, and Yale, a convention, prompted by Yale's Walter Camp, one of a new group of alumni advisors, was called by leaders of the student-led Intercollegiate Football Association. The students chose their more experienced alumni advisors to represent them as they met to hear claims about amateurism and possible ineligible players from several teams.[15] Yale charged Harvard and Princeton not only with playing athletes who had received money for participating and for recruiting athletes from prep schools, offering them inducements by paying tuition, board, and other costs, but also with bringing back older players who had graduated, entering them in professional schools and allowing them to continue competing. Yale's alumni advisor, Walter Camp, introduced a resolution on eligibility prohibiting any student from participating unless he was attending a set number of class recitations each week and banning any student who had participated in athletics for pay. A Princeton representative then proposed that all students in professional departments and all postgraduates be banned from participation. This was aimed principally at Harvard and Penn, who had a number of athletes in professional and postgraduate programs. However, because this proposal by Princeton was not part of the conference agenda, it was rejected.[16]

The dispute, however, that played out then and for the next year was primarily between Harvard and Princeton. When the convention was called two weeks before the Harvard-Princeton game, Harvard claimed that a dozen Princeton players should be ineligible for not being either full-time students or amateurs. The most important challenges were to the participation of E. O. Wagenhurst and Knowlton "Snake" Ames, the Princeton captain, who at season's end was chosen on Walter Camp's first All-American team at fullback.[17] Wagenhurst had graduated from

Princeton in 1888, played professional baseball, and then returned to Princeton to play football in the fall of 1889.[18] Ames had played baseball for money in his hometown, Chicago, in the summer of 1889. Princeton immediately dropped Wagenhurst. However, Ames was a different case. When challenged, a Princeton professor rationalized: "Although we deplore Ames' receipt of money on this occasion, this fact does not constitute professionalism which is a habit."[19] Immediately Princeton retaliated, claiming that four of the Harvard men should be ineligible. Two players, Princeton said, were being paid to attend Harvard, both of whom had left for Harvard after having planned to attend Princeton that fall. Another had left Harvard following graduation, got married, and then returned to play football while attending a professional school. A fourth Harvard player had toured England playing baseball during the summer of 1889 and was charged with having been paid during the tour. Harvard denied all allegations.

A second meeting to hear from all the charged players was held only two days before the important Harvard-Princeton game. When the delegations met, however, Princeton moved to table the protests, and in a 3–2 vote, Princeton, Penn, and Wesleyan voted to table while Harvard and Yale opposed the motion. The protest was tabled—killed—and the delegates returned home. Princeton officials, including the dean of the college, the registrar, and Professor William Milligan Sloane of the Committee on Outdoor Sports, signed a statement that all twelve protested athletes were bona fide undergrads (including special students) or graduate students in the Theological Seminary.[20] Two days later, play would go on. Harvard lost 41–15 to Princeton, and almost immediately the Harvard captain called a meeting of Harvard students to not only withdraw from the Intercollegiate Football Association, formed in 1876, but also to begin negotiations with Yale for a Dual League. The students overwhelmingly took action on both accounts, not to reform football but to punish Princeton.

Harvard's Athletic Committee, formed of three students, three alumni, and three faculty, was somewhat more circumspect but nevertheless voted to abandon the Intercollegiate Football Association. The Harvard Athletic Committee originally had been formed in 1882 by the Harvard faculty to resist the encroachment of athletics upon the life of the institution. At first it was formed only of faculty members, but when its decisions, such as banning football one year, were so antithetical to the wishes of the students and alumni, a new committee of students, alumni, and faculty was formed in 1888.[21] The next year, the Athletic Committee joined with the students in backing the withdrawal from the Intercollegiate Football Association. The members claimed that the withdrawal was due to "the intense competition within the league" leading to "objectionable practices in all the colleges." College athletics, Harvard claimed, "have been infected with professionalism." Rules agreed upon, the Committee said, "are the best evidence of the sincerity of our students in their efforts for reform."[22] It was obvious by then that students were not the only group involved in reform, probably not even the most important. Not only had the Harvard Athletic Committee, of which only one-third were students, joined the fray, but the alumni Advisory Committee to the Intercollegiate Football Association took a central role. The Advisory Committees were becoming more than advisory, for its members had been the chief negotiators prior to the withdrawal of Harvard from the Association. Student control at the major big-time athletic schools of Harvard, Yale, and Princeton was beginning to slip away as athletics became more prominent.

The Harvard situation at the time of its withdrawal from the Intercollegiate Football Association is a case in point. Prior to the split after the 1889 game with Princeton, a Harvard alumnus, Harry Crocker, unfolded a Harvard plan to withdraw from broad intercollegiate competition and form an all-sports league only with Yale. A Dual League plan was hatched, but Harvard felt the need to first defeat its chief non-Yale football rival, Princeton. Harvard did not want to appear to slink away from a competitor it could not defeat. During the 1880s, Harvard had won only two of its nine football games with Princeton. In addition, and probably more important, Harvard authorities, including the faculty, president, and governing boards, wanted to impose more control than students were willing to provide over the expanding athletic program. For instance, during the 1886–87 academic year, there were ninety-four Harvard intercollegiate contests, including thirty-four away games. The faculty, president, and Board of Overseers were concerned that such a heavy load of sports activities was diverting students from their academic responsibilities, exposing them to unhealthy moral influences at away contests, and tending to make athletics into a business rather than a gentlemanly contest. The Board of Overseers' advisory committee on athletics recommended in a 4–1 vote to ban all intercollegiate sports while expanding intramural sports and athletic facilities. Even the one Overseer who opposed this drastic measure favored limiting competition only with Yale and limiting contests specifically to New England.[23]

The eligibility controversy with Princeton, rather than a victory over Princeton, provided Harvard the justification of a Dual League with Yale. Many at Harvard wanted to isolate Princeton, which Harvard believed was a bandit school that would do anything, including paying its athletes to come to Princeton. When Highland Stickney decided to attend the Harvard Law School in the fall of 1879 rather than go to Princeton, Stickney kept his letter from the Princeton football captain, Knowlton "Snake" Ames. "I will tell you plainly," Ames wrote Stickney prior to the football season, "I will do all I can for you in every way. . . . I can get your board, tuition, etc., free. The athletic men at Princeton get by all odds the best treatment in any of the colleges."[24] Of course, Princeton believed that Stickney, a starting tackle for Harvard that fall, had likely gotten a better deal from Harvard. A Dual League, with Princeton on the sidelines, would allow the two most prestigious colleges in America, Yale and Harvard, to rise above the rest, some believed, and set a reform standard that others might emulate. One Harvard alumnus, however, believed that Princeton should be included in a triple league. He argued that Princeton would agree immediately to a league of only Harvard, Yale, and Princeton, for it was "especially sensitive about being classed among secondary colleges." Therefore Princeton would join the tripartite league and accept needed eligibility reforms if it wanted to compete against Harvard and Yale.[25] This idea was rejected, for eligibility reforms seemed less important than the relationship between Harvard and Yale.

For a half decade, Harvard and Yale worked on and off toward a Dual League with little success. Each made demands upon the other that were refused. Then, in 1894, almost five years to the day after the disruptive Princeton-Harvard game, Yale and Harvard competed in a game filled with brutal play. Relations were broken between the two schools, not only in football but also in all sports for a short period.[26] The Harvard-Yale Dual League proposal was not really as much a reform measure as it was a social class ploy, an attempt by the two most elite educational institutions in America to remain athletically, and therefore socially, separate from the others. Even if Harvard and Yale had succeeded in the joint plan and created an uplifting reform in college athletics, it would likely have failed. Attempting to realize a Dual League in a highly competitive society, which proclaimed its dedication to equality and freedom of opportunity for all, it was almost surely doomed from the start. If Harvard and Yale remained aloof, they could not prove their superiority; if they participated with others and lost, the proof was even stronger that their status was diminished. Real athletic reform in America could not come from two institutions standing alone, or for that matter by a reform conference such as the creation of the Ivy League a half century later, no matter what their status in society. The two "superior" institutions would soon be left behind athletically in the less stratified social system in America relative to the aristocratic, stratified system that allowed Oxford and Cambridge to continue their English "Dual League" well into the twentieth century.[27] Reform would come neither from a "Dual League" nor from students acting alone. Students and their organizations attempting to reform athletics were not principally interested in how their reforms would impact academic concerns, for their considerations were aimed at creating competitive equity on the field of play. And then the individual institutions wanted to turn any reform to their competitive advantage. Meaningful reform, if it would ever occur, would not come from students who created intercollegiate athletics. The push for meaningful reform, however, might come from the actions of faculties.

2

Faculty, Faculty Athletic Committees, and Reform Efforts

The Harvard Athletic Committee in 1889, with a strong faculty hand, stated: "We are entirely in accord with the effort made by the students of [Harvard] to reform college sports." The Committee anticipated "that they shall hereafter be played under rules which will limit participation in them to bona fide members of the University."[1] This response to the Intercollegiate Football Association crisis following the Harvard-Princeton game was mostly wishful thinking, for there was little evidence that students were interested in their own athletes being bona fide students, only those of other institutions. Faculty members, on the other hand, were little interested in bona fide students in other institutions, but they wanted their own to be principally interested in academics, not athletics. This was generally true for at least a century at Harvard and elsewhere, beginning well before athletic committees were organized by faculties on nearly all university and college campuses across America to address growing problems created by intercollegiate athletics. Faculties traditionally promoted the policy of in loco parentis, for they were often acting as moral and religious guardians in the place of the students' parents. From colonial times well into the nineteenth century, colleges had lists of things forbidden at each institution, so faculties were generally in command of refusing a variety of activities thought to be harmful to moral character, learning, or safety. These would include such activities as card playing, drinking, smoking, leaving the college campus without permission, and throwing snowballs and baseballs, or kicking footballs, on campus and thus endangering buildings.[2] At Yale just prior to the American Revolution, students were prohibited from fishing or sailing unless permission was obtained from a tutor or president.[3] Only a few years after the Americans defeated the British at Yorktown, ending the Revolutionary War battles, the Princeton faculty banned field hockey as "low and unbecoming gentlemen and scholars."[4] At about the same time, a student at King's College in New York (Columbia) was punished for swimming off campus and sentenced to confinement to his room and commanded to translate Latin for a week.[5] In the South, a student at Virginia's William and Mary in 1795 found the faculty lenient in allowing "a game of fives [handball] against the old House." He said, "If a person comes here for improvement, he must study hard, but if pleasure be his object, it is a fine place for spending money as ever I saw."[6] In the intervening hundred years, faculty at most institutions were ready either to ban sport, and intercollegiate sports when they began, or to reform them to comply with what they considered educational and moral aims of the institutions.

Well before intercollegiate sport began with a crew meet between Harvard and Yale, college faculties were banning sports, especially football. At a number of schools, the kicking game of soccer-like football was prohibited by faculty, including Brown, West Point Military Academy, Williams, Yale, and Harvard. At Harvard, students had a tradition of playing a freshman-sophomore football game dating back to at least the early 1800s. It was called "Bloody Monday" because it was played the first Monday of the fall term as a way to initiate freshmen into being subservient to upperclassmen. The hazing object was not so much for the sophomores to beat the freshmen, for that was nearly a foregone conclusion, but to physically punish the newcomers, who, new to the college, hardly knew their teammates. It was so brutal and unsavory that the Harvard faculty banned future contests in 1860.[7] Football was not reintroduced at Harvard for a decade, and by then other colleges were playing the kicking game. Princeton and Rutgers began intercollegiate football when they played two soccer-type games in the fall of 1869, each under slightly different rules. Despite twenty-five Princeton players taking the train to New Brunswick for the first game and Rutgers making the trip to Princeton for a return game, neither faculty protested the team actions or banned future contests.[8] By the early 1870s, a number of colleges with on-campus football began to take up the game intercollegiately, following the 1869 Princeton-Rutgers contests. Columbia, Cornell, Michigan, Pennsylvania, and Yale were some of the larger institutions playing intercollegiately. Harvard students had their own game, a contest with running of a ball, somewhat akin to rugby, but when invited to play in Montreal against McGill University, they declined, indicating that the Harvard faculty would not allow the team to travel to Montreal during the term.

Faculties elsewhere acted in response to particular events once intercollegiate contests began. Generally speaking, faculties had laissez-faire attitudes toward the student-run athletics unless they had deleterious effects upon academic interests or the good name of the institution. Paternalism, in the form of in loco parentis, was slowly breaking down in most institutions of higher learning in the second half of the nineteenth century, but it still existed. When faculty members believed that students were spending too much time and money on athletics, were hiring professional and often unsavory coaches to lead the teams, were paying athletes to attend college, or were acting dishonorably, they were prone to step in and stop what they considered abuses. After the first intercollegiate cricket match, in which Haverford College beat the University of Pennsylvania 89–60 in only one inning because of darkness, the Haverford players entertained Penn at a local tavern, bringing about a Pennsylvania faculty rebuke.[9] Yale's faculty forbade its baseball team to play three away games in 1868, for it was impacting class recitations for both players and student spectators.[10] Following a forty-four-game baseball schedule in 1870, the Harvard faculty limited games to Saturdays and holidays in 1871 for similar reasons.[11] Faculties elsewhere began to limit students' freedom to engage in a rapidly growing number of athletic events and other extracurricular activities, including bands and orchestras, dramatic clubs, and student publications. The entire faculty often met to discuss these activities, and it became a burden on their time. By the 1880s and 1890s, faculties began to create specific committees to deal with the problems, especially those dealing with athletics.

The creation of faculty athletic committees began at Princeton in 1881, when the athletic teams and the Princeton Glee Club were increasingly missing class time and, possibly more important to the Presbyterian-led Princeton leaders, being absent from mandatory chapel. The Glee Club was absent even more than any Princeton athletic team in the early 1880s, and the faculty formed a Committee on Athletics and the Musical Clubs, the first such committee in higher education.[12] Reform was on the minds of the three-member committee, including historian William Milligan Sloane, who fifteen years later would be the key American involved in sending athletes (during term time) to the first modern International Olympic Games in Athens, Greece. The first Princeton committee reform was to limit the amount of time away from classes. Athletes could be absent from Princeton no more than eight days each term, and then only if they were on the baseball and football teams. Other teams could be out of town only during vacations or on Saturday afternoons, and all students needed parental permission to be absent from campus.[13] The Princeton committee then moved to fix dates for the baseball team and to approve who the students could choose to be their coach. Obviously both policies ran into opposition by the students, who had previously set the schedule and decided who they would hire to be their coach or trainer. Within three years, the faculty committee ruled that no professional athlete, oarsman, or baseball player could be employed to coach or to practice with the team.[14] What the Princeton faculty was attempting to do was to keep athletics amateur and to protect them from the perceived evils of professionalism.

Harvard faculty members, too, found the growth of athletics to be academically disturbing. Within five years of Harvard founding a baseball club, the team, with essentially no faculty constraints, concluded a forty-four-game schedule, twenty-six of which were during term time in the spring of 1870. The team lost only ten games, but nine of them were to professional teams. The next year, the Harvard team continued a lengthy schedule, including a number of games against professionals. The Harvard faculty then ruled that in the future all games must be played on Saturdays and holidays, the result being an eleven-game season in 1872. Within a couple of years, the faculty eased the restrictions by allowing four games on weekdays.[15] By the early 1880s, like the situation at Princeton, the number of away games was a major concern. Of Harvard's twenty-eight-game schedule, nineteen were away contests, and a disturbingly large number, according to the faculty, were against professional teams. The Harvard faculty decided to form an athletic committee to deal with the increasing time commitment competitive sports were demanding of the entire faculty.[16]

Professionalism and the atmosphere surrounding athletics at Harvard were on the agenda when the Harvard Athletic Committee of three first met in the spring of 1882. Two members of Harvard College, a professor of fine arts and another of Greek, along with a medical doctor in charge of the Harvard gymnasium, adopted rules for the conduct of Harvard athletics, reforming the hiring of coaches and the playing against professionals. The committee prohibited the baseball team from playing against pro teams while demanding that the hiring of coaches by students be done only with the consent of Dr. Dudley A. Sargent. At the same time, the committee made a decision to build a fence around the athletic field to protect the grounds and to "exclude objectionable persons" from the games.[17] The committee gave little thought to competitive equity in making its decisions, and this disturbed the student athletic leaders. A faculty ban on games with professional teams would make the Harvard baseball team less competitive against Yale, its chief rival, for Yale had no restrictions against playing professionals. It created tension between the students and the faculty committee.

The hiring of professionals to coach both the crew and the baseball team was also a concern of the Harvard Athletic Committee. It fired the professional baseball coach in 1882, much to the consternation of the students.[18] The faculty committee favored the British upper-class concept of amateurism, always looking down upon the professional, who often needed financial support to maintain his involvement with sport rather than being from the elite who did not require additional money.[19] The next year, the committee sent Dr. Sargent to visit five colleges to find out what other faculties felt about professional coaches. Most professors at Amherst, Columbia, Princeton, Williams, and Yale opposed professional coaches, but obviously the students did not.[20] Harvard students were incensed the following year when the Harvard Athletic Committee dismissed the highly successful paid crew coach, William Bancroft. They wanted an explanation for the firing, and the Committee replied: "To the Public we have given no reason, and have none to give." The Athletic Committee took its authoritarian stand one step farther when it pressured the editorial staff of the *Harvard Crimson* to not publish the negative letters of former crew captains regarding the dismissal of Bancroft.[21] The feud between faculty and students continued as students fought to maintain control of their athletic program. Circumventing the faculty committee, the crew privately hired another professional to aid the rowers the next spring. Yet in the long run the faculty made some inroads against professionalism, and not surprisingly the Harvard crew won only once in the next dozen years against Yale, whose faculty generally had a hands-off policy regarding athletics.[22] In the previous twenty-five contests with Yale, Harvard had won eighteen crew meets.

The most controversial decision of the faculty Athletic Committee, however, was to prohibit football, while the entire faculty attempted to do so on several occasions.[23] While the committee was dealing with pro coach issues with the crew team, the brutality and ungentlemanly behavior of the football team irritated the faculty and caused the group to take action. One of the rules of the student-led Intercollegiate Football Association (IFA) stated that a player would not be disqualified until he was guilty of "striking with closed fist" for the third time in a game. Following the 1883 Yale game in which slugging was exhibited, the Athletic Committee ruled that there would be no more football until the rules were changed. Though the IFA changed the rule, the committee watched game conduct carefully the next year and concluded at the season's end that football as then played was "brutal, demoralizing to players and spectators, and extremely dangerous." As a result, the Athletic Committee asked the faculty to prohibit the game. The faculty concurred.[24] At that point, the students and alumni strongly criticized the action of the faculty, and the faculty agreed to change the composition of the Athletic Committee to reflect the interests of both students and faculty.[25] The new committee was composed of two students and one alumnus with an interest in athletics, the director of the gymnasium, and a medical doctor from the Cambridge area, but this lasted only a couple of years when the faculty complained, and the Harvard governing board set up its own committee to investigate the abuses and excesses of athletics at Harvard.

Out of the turmoil over athletic control came the prototypical athletic committee often copied by other colleges. Beginning in 1888, the Harvard Athletic Committee was composed of three faculty, three alumni, and three students, often the captains of teams. The Committee was no longer under faculty control, as was the original committee, for it was created by the recommendation of the Overseers, part of the governing structure of Harvard. The Overseers had asked the Corporation, the official policy makers at Harvard, to create a new Athletic Committee and at the same time to allow contests to be played only in New England. The Harvard faculty's recommendation of a return to a committee of three faculty members was not followed by the Corporation. Rather, the Corporation accepted the 3–3–3 system, with the supervision of athletics coming under the control of the Athletic Committee and not the faculty.[26] The fact that the Harvard faculty no longer had control of athletics was seen in 1895, following a particularly brutal football game between Harvard and Yale. The faculty voted by a 2–1 margin to abolish football, but the Athletic Committee voted unanimously to continue the game if it were reformed. The question was resolved, at least for the time being, when the Corporation sided with the Athletic Committee, and the faculty then rescinded its resolve to ban football.[27]

The power struggle involving faculty was not over at Harvard or at other colleges in the late 1800s and early 1900s. In 1903, the Harvard faculty asked the Athletic Committee to once again abolish football. The Committee refused, indicating that "football is only one of many distractions in college life."[28] Three years later, in the midst of the national football crisis of 1905–6, the faculty voted to ban football, and the Overseers, with the blessing of the Corporation, voted to do away with football as then played. At that time, all elements of the athletic power equation became involved, including faculty, students, alumni, president, and governing board. Indeed, a Harvard alumnus, President Theodore Roosevelt, was a key player in the reform of football at the national level and helped prevent the abolition of football at Harvard. When new reform rules were created for 1906, including the introduction of the forward pass, the Overseers and Corporation agreed to allow football to continue at Harvard.[29] The following year, a committee report of the Harvard faculty indicated that the Athletic Committee of students, alumni, and faculty did not "represent the Faculty point of view sufficiently, and that athletics are too strongly represented."[30] The Harvard situation had clearly shown the conflict between faculty and students over the control of athletics. Indeed, it was also clear that the faculty was shown to have both proathletic sentiments seeking reform as well as antiathletic beliefs of those who felt athletics were anathema to the intended purposes of institutions of higher learning.

The Harvard faculty may have been the leader in attempting to reform athletics, but it was not alone. By the turn of the century, committees of athletic control had been created by the faculties of most colleges and universities in America. In actuality, athletic committees had become buffers between the students, who wanted a laissez-faire policy, and the faculty, who often wanted to eliminate troublesome athletics or at least to have severe restrictions. If athletic committees were at first formed of only faculty members, they soon came to include students and alumni. Students were needed for their technical knowledge of athletics. They also needed to be pacified through some type of representation, to nullify to some extent the belief that the faculty committees had been formed originally because students could not be trusted to manage their own affairs. Alumni were brought into athletic committees because their influence was being felt in all aspects of governance of higher education in the second half of the nineteenth century. When intercollegiate athletics grew, alumni influence became important, because alums were a major financial source of support of athletics in building facilities, paying for equipment and travel, and supporting athletes who wished to attend the alum's institution. In addition, most colleges hired former athletes from their particular institution to become coaches of various teams.

Students often resented the loss of freedom, usually to faculty, to run their own extracurricular programs such as athletics. Northwestern University's president reflected this feeling, writing in his 1896 annual report. Students, he said, "seemed to think that the University was meddling with matters that did not properly come with its jurisdiction."[31] At Cornell, a professor, Burt Wilder, wanted his faculty to create "a declaration of independence [from] the existing athletocracy" of students by passing one faculty rule: No student may be absent for any athletic contest. Wilder believed this would help restore the educational mission of higher education. When this proposal did not pass, students at Cornell thanked the faculty for its "refusal to introduce . . . an element of paternalism into . . . athletic interests."[32] Wilder, like many faculty members at other institutions, experienced the loss of control over the educational mission of higher education as athletics and other extracurricular activities appeared to dominate the curriculum as the focus of college life.

When alumni were increasingly added to athletic committees, faculty members felt an erosion of their power over the growth of athletics. In addition, alumni financial support of athletics brought about alumni control in many cases. Dartmouth College is a clear case of this phenomenon. After a series of poor athletic teams at Dartmouth, the alumni association in 1892 asked the Board of Trustees to place athletics in the hands of the association. The trustees agreed by creating an alumni athletic committee. With alumni control, Dartmouth's athletic fortunes rose. The alumni took over the operation of the gymnasium from physical educators, and they built a new athletic field. One member of the original Alumni Committee on Athletics, William Tucker, became president of the college. By the early 1900s, President Tucker looked with pride at the success of Dartmouth athletics and the general growth of Dartmouth College. Alumni, Tucker said, contributed much to athletics with its "distinct and well organized movement."[33] Tucker, like many presidents throughout the century, was more of a cheerleader for athletics than a reformer. A year later, a battle erupted between Dartmouth's faculty and alumni over athletic governance during the football crisis of 1905–6. The faculty petitioned the Board of Trustees to restore a wider control over athletic affairs to the faculty. The Board, however, rejected the faculty's desire, concluding that the Alumni Committee on Athletics should continue to "determine the athletic policy of the College."[34] Many college faculties, including Dartmouth, experienced the loss of significant opportunities to reform college athletics at the individual institutional level. Dartmouth symbolized the significant demise of power of faculty to reform athletics, but faculty members continued to discuss, if not influence, its direction. As educational and societal critic Thorstein Veblen stated in the early twentieth century: "The faculties have become deliberative bodies charged with power to talk."[35]

The Dartmouth situation was repeated at many other institutions by the early 1900s. As the twentieth century progressed, students lost complete control over the games they created, and faculties were generally impotent when important decisions were made in the direction taken. Decisions made that generally excluded faculty and students included such areas as the admittance to college of students who were athletes, the hiring of professional coaches, the beginning of preseason practice and length of the season, the number of games to be played and where they would be contested, and whether enormous sums of money would be used to build stadiums and other athletic facilities. By the early 1900s, athletic committees, no matter what their composition, could not independently solve major problems of athletics in higher education. In the early twentieth century, philosopher and dean of Brown College, Alexander Meiklejohn, believed that only through cooperation and mutual understanding of the colleges could athletics be reformed to meet the needs of higher education. He, like many others before him, stated that students could "not be trusted to manage their own contests." In addition, Meiklejohn wrote that athletic committees could not solve athletic problems because there was "no provision for intercollegiate cooperation in the management of athletics."[36] Until colleges were willing to relinquish some of their independence to a larger body could a semblance of order be brought to intercollegiate athletics. Individual colleges increasingly lost control of their individual autonomy over athletics to the collective action of groups of colleges. Early reform efforts came when interinstitutional control expanded.

3

Early Interinstitutional Reform Efforts

Reform efforts by students, who created intercollegiate athletics, and those of athletic committees were not substantial in the latter years of the nineteenth century. The students who controlled athletics had a desire for equitable rules to create a level, competitive playing field, but they were little concerned with the influence athletics had on the quality of education for the student or the institution. Faculty athletic committees were much more concerned about athletics and education than were the students, but from an early period these committees were principally interested in only their own institutions and not how their decisions impacted the athletic relations with other schools. Athletic committees were reluctant to give up individual institutional autonomy over college sports in favor of greater outside control and the collective good. In this respect, colleges acted somewhat similarly to the larger America where the individual states knew what was best for them and resisted federal legislation. The nineteenth and early twentieth centuries could be considered the period of "states' rights" for college athletics, and not until much later did individual colleges give up their rights to either regional or national authority. As could be expected, collective reform was generally unsuccessful at first, and only in a period of crisis did the laissez-faire attitudes of colleges give way to collective legislation.[1]

The first efforts of interinstitutional reform came through the work of President Charles W. Eliot of Harvard. Eliot had been active in the early 1880s in attempting to reduce the number of games being played and in eliminating professional coaching and participation against professionals. In 1882, he wrote letters to other New England college presidents to see if united action among colleges could help reform intercollegiate athletics. "Our Faculty," Eliot wrote to other eastern college presidents, "wishes me to inquire if your Faculty would think it expedient first to prohibit your baseball nine from playing with professionals and secondly to limit the number of matches."[2] Eliot's concern over professionalism had evidently been sparked by Harvard's hiring of a professional baseball coach in 1881 and the number of games Harvard was playing against professional players, whom he considered the lower-class elements competing on major-league teams. Eliot believed that his faculty was ready to take action against professionalism but felt that common action would be more effective than Harvard acting alone. The faculty of Harvard's chief rival, Yale, considered Eliot's proposal but refused to act.[3] The Yale faculty inaction was the first of more than two decades of a hands-off policy in most aspects of athletics at Yale. Yale's refusal to consider interinstitutional control of athletics was likely the result of Yale's athletic superiority during the latter years of the nineteenth century and into the twentieth century under the leadership of Walter Camp, the dominant figure in intercollegiate athletics for a generation and more. Why should we reform, Yale reasoned, when we are successful in all the favored sports?

The next year, the Harvard faculty Athletic Committee requested Yale's faculty to call a meeting of leading colleges in a joint reform effort. The Yale faculty again declined. The Harvard Athletic Committee then called for a late December 1883 conference, principally to discuss professionalism, especially of professional coaches. The first faculty conference on athletic reform consisted of eight institutions meeting in New York City, where Yale was represented but soon withdrew. The remaining seven faculty members represented Harvard and Princeton and five lesser athletic institutions: Columbia, Penn, Trinity, Wesleyan, and Williams. Among the resolutions passed by the conference were the following: (1) no professional athletes should coach any team, (2) no team should compete against a professional team or noncollege team, (3) participation should only be on a college's home grounds, (4) no student should participate more than four years, (5) all colleges should form faculty athletic committees to approve rules and regulations, and (6) colleges should compete only against others who passed the resolutions.[4] Once passed, the resolutions were sent to twenty-one eastern institutions with the condition that when five colleges adopted them, they would become binding. Only two faculties adopted them: Harvard by a 25–5 vote and Princeton unanimously. No other colleges supported the resolutions.[5] The result of the first conference attempt at institutional reform was unsuccessful.

That nineteen of twenty-one institutions' faculties failed to support the reform measures was to a great extent due to individual college faculties opposing a specific resolution, while students from all campuses opposed the resolutions in general. For instance, the Harvard Athletic Committee debated whether colleges should be able to participate against noncollegiate amateur teams and whether some contests might be played on neutral sites rather than on home grounds. Stated Harvard's Dr. Dudley Sargent: "If the rules could not be accepted as they were," he would "vote to abandon joint action entirely and let each college fall back upon its own regulations."[6]

Students, however, not only opposed individual resolutions but also, more importantly, objected to any faculty incursion into their games. The student-controlled track-and-field organization, the Intercollegiate Association of Amateur Athletes of America, was nearly unanimously opposed to the faculty resolutions. Columbia students called for an intercollegiate student convention to oppose faculty interference. Princeton students passed a satirical circular protesting the action of faculty. A Harvard senior commented that the resolutions were "objectionable in themselves and objectionable on the grounds that we were not consulted, but mainly objectionable on the principle they violated, that of non-interference." Yale was delighted in the opposition to the resolutions, and math faculty member Eugene L. Richards wrote to Princeton historian William Milligan Sloane, chairman of the faculty conference, suggesting "the management of athletic sports might wisely be left to the students."[7] The popular journal *Spirit of the Times* summed up the stalemate between faculty desires and student responses to the first faculty attempt at interinstitutional reform: "Students and professors look at athletics from totally different standpoints, . . . [professors believing] that between them is a chasm which affords no tenable middle ground; that the students are unwisely stubborn in support of their own ideas; and that this obstinacy will, sooner or later, drive the strong arm of authority to attain by harsh action, what might have been done by timely concession and compromise.[8]

Faculty interinstitutional reform efforts, while unsuccessful, had only begun. Students would eventually lose all control over their own sports, and the faculty involvement would be diminished so as to be nearly nonexistent. But this would not occur before several more reform efforts took place.

Complaints about the student games continued with faculties and presidents becoming involved. Following the 1886 football season, President James McCosh of Princeton sent a circular to other eastern college presidents urging intercollegiate cooperation to reform athletic abuses.[9] McCosh believed that Harvard should lead the reform as America's oldest and most prestigious college. After Harvard's Charles Eliot asked his faculty about another reform effort, the Harvard faculty replied that it would welcome a conference, but only if Yale were represented. Yet the Yale position had not changed in the preceding three years, and Yale agreed with its athletics leader, Walter Camp, who had earlier written that "college athletic organizations if left to themselves would soon work out their own salvation."[10] With

Yale's refusal to cooperate with any but student-led organizations, the proposal for interinstitutional faculty reform by President McCosh of Princeton died.

As initial interinstitutional reform efforts failed in the East, an important reform conference was created in the Midwest. In little more than a decade of the initial football competition for most midwestern colleges, the president of Purdue University, James H. Smart, urged the presidents of six other institutions—Chicago, Illinois, Lake Forest (soon replaced by Michigan), Minnesota, Northwestern, and Wisconsin—to join with Purdue to reform intercollegiate athletics under closer faculty supervision. The purpose of the Big Ten Conference (then called the Western Conference or the Intercollegiate Conference of Faculty Representatives) was to establish common eligibility rules, curb practices detrimental to amateur sport, and maintain the positive values of college sport. The presidents met in early 1895 and determined that each institution should have an athletic committee to control athletics. Furthermore, athletic participants could only be bona fide students and certified by the institution, students delinquent in studies were not eligible, transfer students had to matriculate for a half year before participation, all games had to be played on college grounds, student managers and captains of team had to be approved by the athletic committee, athletes paid for participation were not eligible, and no contests with professional teams were allowed.[11] To a great extent, what the reform elements of eastern colleges had attempted and failed to accomplish, the Big Ten had achieved at its first meeting.

The new conference continued for a decade under faculty control when demands for additional reforms in the Big Ten came with the national football crisis at the end of the 1905 season. The University of Wisconsin faculty, led by frontier historian Frederick Jackson Turner, wanted to ban football. Turner's ringing denunciation of football rings true to some more than a century later: "Football has become a business carried out too often by professionals, supported by levies on the public, bringing in vast gate receipts, demoralizing student ethics, and confusing the ideals of sport, manliness, and decency."[12]

The Northwestern faculty actually abandoned the game for two years. Nevertheless, the faculty representatives of the Big Ten met, after a call by Michigan's president, James Angell, in what has become known as the "Angell Conferences" in early 1906, to hammer out new reform measures. The Big Ten adopted the freshman ineligibility rule, no participation by graduate students, elimination of training tables and athletic dorms, limits on ticket prices (50 cents), shortened football seasons (five games), and appointment of coaches by the university officials at modest salaries.[13] So by the early twentieth century, the Big Ten was considered the reform conference in the nation, and for most of the century it was the conference many others looked to for guidance.

Meanwhile in the East, faculties at the leading institutions were attempting to come together to reform what they considered the wrongs in intercollegiate athletics. With the failed attempts at reform in the 1880s, eastern institutions found troubling problems of professionalism and questionable ethics continuing to plague many schools. While each college set its own standards of eligibility and athletic conduct, there were often acrimonious charges that one institution's rules gave it advantages over another in the quest for victory. The idea of a permanent organization of colleges working cooperatively to reform rules was not new when it was suggested toward the end of the century by chairmen of athletic committees of several eastern colleges. Many problems had arisen since the previous 1886 attempt at mutual rules, primarily for football and baseball, the two leading sports at most eastern universities in the 1890s. The question of "tramp athletes," who moved from one college to another primarily to participate in football, was particularly troubling. One example was Fielding H. Yost, later a well-known football coach at Michigan. Yost was a solid, six-foot, 195-pound tackle playing for West Virginia University in 1896 when he "transferred" to Lafayette College in Pennsylvania just prior to Lafayette's contest with the University of Pennsylvania. Penn had been undefeated for thirty-six games when Yost made his appearance in one of the great games of the nineteenth century. Lafayette upset Penn 6–4 with "freshman" Yost playing left tackle. Almost immediately, Yost transferred back to West Virginia University to complete work on a law degree, which he received half a year later.[14]

Tramp athletes were only a symptom of a myriad of problems in need of reform. Athletes at many institutions grew old competing far longer than four years, often playing as students in professional schools such as law, medicine, or seminary. The scene of Walter Camp competing into his seventh year at Yale in the 1880s was duplicated at many other institutions. A six-year player at Fairmount College in Wichita, Kansas, Graham Foster, competed an additional three years at Yale.[15] Carl Johanson had an eight-year football career at Williams College and Cornell University.[16] Whether students were competing for three or eight years, most colleges had no rules for making normal progress toward a degree. In addition, students were often paid in one form or another to play football and baseball. Payment of college baseball players to compete for town teams or at summer resorts was common practice, and there was no agreed upon definition of being an amateur. The hiring of professional coaches had not been resolved, and increasingly pro coaches were able to produce winners over amateur coaches or alumni coaches, whether paid or not. Especially for football, there was a growing question of how much preseason practice should be allowed and whether spring football practice should be permitted. There were also issues of commercialization that were considered ripe for reform.

On February 18, 1898, all the colleges of the present-day Ivy League, with the conspicuous exception of Yale, met in Providence, Rhode Island, for a reform conference hosted by Brown University. Only four days after the battleship *Maine* was sunk in Havana Harbor, faculty, alumni, and undergraduate athletic representatives met to battle with questions that were nearly as inflammatory for colleges as was the question of possible war with Spain over Cuba. Each of the seven colleges— Brown, Columbia, Cornell, Dartmouth, Harvard, Penn, and Princeton—sent three delegates, faculty, alumni, and student, to meet in an attempt to find joint answers to vexing athletic questions of the latter years of the nineteenth century. The so-called Brown Conference was important for the three groups that were pivotal in the early development of college sport. All the major issues were thrashed out into the wee hours of the morning: eligibility of undergrads and graduate students, scholarships for athletes, contests held on grounds other than the college campus, summer baseball for pay, professional coaches, excessive gate receipts, and faculty control of athletics.[17] No decisions were reached, but a special committee of seven professors was created to conclude the work of the conference.

The seven faculty members, led by Brown's Wilfred Munro, had a faculty agenda. It probably was a mistake to not include representatives of the students and alumni to draw up a reform report. Wilfred Munro, a professor of European history, was a graduate of Brown and was captain of his class team, which defeated the New England baseball champion Lowells of Boston in 1868.[18] He did not detest athletics as did some professors of the era, but he wanted them to be played by amateurs who were gentlemen. The results of the interinstitutional faculty committee in the spring of 1898 reflected his attitudes. An early draft of the Brown Conference report likely showed truer feelings of the faculty members than did the published document. The first draft charged that many of the abuses in athletics were due to "athletics being vested solely in undergraduates," while "most of the quarrels are due primarily to the actions of graduates." The faculty, according to a pre-published outline, desired to "weed out" any "student who has entered the university for athletic purposes solely." The first document called the student games "gladiatorial contests" but was later changed to "public spectacles."[19] Even with editorial changes, probably made to make the document appear less antagonistic to students and alumni, the final 1898 "Report on Intercollegiate Sports" was a strongly worded document.

The Brown Conference Committee report, written by the leading athletic and educational leaders in America sans Yale, stands out as a potent call from faculty for institutional cooperation to cure the evils of intercollegiate athletics. "We are not engaged," the final report asserted, "in making athletes." What the committee wanted to accomplish was to prevent college athletics "from interfering with the mental and moral training of the students." The committee also knew what it did not want in college sports, and that was any taint of professionalism and commercialism. The Brown Conference report spoke out for the upper-class British sport model found at Oxford and Cambridge, where a gentlemanly game of enjoyable competition transcended "victory at all costs."[20]

The attainment of excellence in athletics through victory, favored by students and alumni, was not a high priority of the faculty-controlled Brown Conference. "We should not seek perfection in our games, but, rather, good sport," the report emphasized.[21] But seeking perfection, or at least excellence, was exactly what college athletes desired in the 1890s. Because college students desired to beat other college teams, they had already developed an elaborate, rationalized system of rigid practice schedules and training systems, had hired coaches and recruited athletes, and had created methods of raising revenue to meet their needs.[22] Historically, American college athletics had been commercialized from the first railroad-sponsored contest between Harvard and Yale in 1852. Athletics had been professionalized by the next decade when the first coach was hired by Yale in 1864 during the American Civil War to enable the Yale crew to defeat Harvard for the first time.

There is a touch of irony in the issue of excellence and winning, which students and alumni stood for, and the Brown Conference faculty report's concern for gentlemanly participation. Harvard's president, Charles W. Eliot, a leading advocate of the British model of gentlemanly moderation in sports, had been, nevertheless, one of the college spokesmen for attaining preeminence in athletics at Harvard. In Eliot's 1869 inaugural address upon assuming the Harvard presidency, he stated: "There is an aristocracy to which sons of Harvard have belonged, and, let us hope, will ever aspire to belong—the aristocracy which excels in manly sports."[23] Eliot had challenged Harvard students to be the best not only in intellectual concerns but also in athletics, a statement made less than a month before the first intercollegiate football game between Princeton and Rutgers. The statement was not lost upon the ears of those who loved sports at Yale, including some members of the faculty. One, Professor Thatcher of Yale, later quoted Eliot, saying that he and Harvard had "expressed a desire to win in athletics; that Harvard had set the pace for Yale and drawn them into it."[24]

Harvard's premier philosopher, George Santayana, might have challenged the Brown Conference report on philosophical grounds. Writing in the 1890s on the topic "Philosophy on the Bleachers," Santayana captured the spirit in American college sports better than did the faculty at the Brown Conference. Santayana called for an athletic aristocracy similar to that of Eliot a generation before. Athletics, said Santayana, at a highly competitive level were for the few who could excel, were played as a "dire struggle" in a situation analogous to war, and were valued by society because of the degree of perfection attained. College students who played in the contests might never have thought about it, but they would likely have agreed with the philosopher; it was Santayana who said that in athletics, as in all performances, "The value of talent, the beauty and dignity of positive achievements depend on the height reached, and not on the number that reach it. Only the supreme is interesting: the rest has value only as leading to it or reflecting it."[25]

College students would almost certainly have ridiculed the early Brown Conference report draft, which claimed that "there is very little fun in watching a college team which has been so trained and perfected that it can win every game during the season."[26] Both the students and Santayana would likely have agreed that intercollegiate contests in America did not have the tradition of gentlemanly play for recreation and fun, for they had been contested for more than a generation emphasizing excellence and winning.[27] The Brown Conference report would not change the thrust of sport in American colleges, though that was exactly what it attempted to do.

The Brown Conference report is the most thorough analysis of the attitudes of faculty toward college athletics in the nineteenth century. Coming from prestigious eastern colleges, it gave guidelines for faculty athletic control not previously given such clarity. It wanted an athletic committee with faculty representation in each college that would approve all coaches, trainers, captains, and team managers in addition to all athletic competition, and all athletes would be certified as bona fide students, while participation by athletes in more than one sport would require committee approval. The report required that all athletes be in good academic standing, and students deficient academically in one department could not participate if they transferred to another department in the same university. Further, special or part-time students could not participate until they attended college for one year, and no student admitted without passing the university entrance examination, or convincing governing authorities that he was capable of doing a full year's work, would be athletically eligible. The Brown Conference report limited the length of athletic eligibility to four years. Freshmen were only allowed to participate on freshmen teams, and transfer students could participate only after one year in residence. The report addressed the control of practices and contests. No teams could practice during college vacation, except for ten days before the fall term to allow football teams a preseason to prevent injuries. All contests would be held on college grounds, and students would be given priority in the allotment of seats to these contests. The report also called for amateurism in the fight against professionalizing the contests. No athlete who had ever participated for financial gain or had earned money teaching sports would be eligible. Financial gain included receiving board free at special dining facilities or training tables for athletes.

What the Brown Conference report of 1898 favored was faculty influence to maintain truly amateur contests, competed in by bona fide students, and without excessive commercialization. While the goals of the report were exemplary for the upper-class ideals of nineteenth-century, British-like amateur sport, the attempt by the eastern faculty group to foster these ideals on a fiercely competitive, win-oriented, and less class-restrictive American society would prove to be unsuccessful. The reform report did have some effect, for there were college athletic committees who accepted a number of the specific reforms as their own, and in so doing moved colleges closer to uniform eligibility rules.[28] However, individual colleges refused to take collective action on the reform measures. The Brown Conference recommendations for yearly conferences "to consider regulations and the proper development of the athletics sports" did not bear fruit at this time. Colleges were still reluctant to commit the direction of athletic programs to an annual conference in which faculties would have a strong influence. Faculties, nevertheless, were reluctant to have the extracurriculum taken away from student management. Harvard, the leading institution desiring reform, favored student management, and it was a policy of the governing board. A year before the Brown Conference, the Harvard Corporation recognized that "the undergraduates, under careful general restriction, ought to be given so far as possible a *free hand* in the management of their sports."[29] The "free hand" would continue uneasily, if it ever truly existed, until a crisis of major proportions erupted in the early 1900s and brought college presidents more fully into the discussion of athletic control and reform.

4

Presidents

Promoters or Reformers?

The satirist and playwright George Ade wrote a popular comic play in 1904, *The College Widow*, catching the spirit of college presidents as promoters of intercollegiate athletics. "Do you know, Mr. Bolton," President Witherspoon of Atwater College said to the star Atwater football player, "this craze for pugilistic sports is demoralizing our institutions." Replied Billy Bolton, "Oh I hardly think so. Do you know I never heard of Atwater until it scored against Cornell two years ago?" The president rejoined, "Oh, my dear young friend, you, too, are possessed of this madness. Well, come along, Mr. Larrabee [the football coach], I suppose we shall have to give the team whatever it wants."[1] College administrators, more than the faculties, appreciated the popularity of football and other sports among the students, alumni, and the general public and how the spectacles brought recognition to their institutions of higher learning. College presidents were constantly looking for both private and public support—scouring their regions on speaking tours, asking the state legislators to generate money, and allying themselves with the influential individuals, often members of the rising business class, who were being placed on governing boards. Presidents found that athletics lent them a vehicle for advertising their institutions with little cost. One keen observer noted this, believing that it was a "crude confusion of the methods of business with the aims of education that drove many a college president to justify professional sports by their advertising value."[2]

College presidents were often athletic promoters, acting more like cheerleaders than reformers, and to this end contributed significantly to the failure of intercollegiate athletic reform. From that perspective, not much changed from the time of President Charles W. Eliot's inaugural address at Harvard in 1869 to the twenty-first century. When President Eliot spoke of Harvard's "aristocracy which excels in manly sports," he was setting a standard not only for the most important institution of higher education in America but also for other colleges that followed where Harvard led. Only months before his inauguration, Eliot could have (but did not) condemned the Harvard baseball team for playing against the first all-professional team, the Cincinnati Red Stockings; for scheduling an eleven-day trip into New York to play Yale at a neutral site in Brooklyn; and for completing a lengthy thirty-three-game schedule.[3] The Harvard president could have (but did not) bemoaned the decision of the Harvard crew to travel to London, England, in 1869 to row on the Thames River against Oxford University. The first international collegiate contest was held before a crowd estimated to be about one million spectators, the largest crowd ever to watch a university contest firsthand.[4] Less than a week before Eliot's famous inaugural address, the Harvard baseball team agreed to play what was traditionally considered the strongest team in New England, the Boston Lowell Club, in a fund-raising event for the Harvard University Boat Club.[5] Eliot, at the beginning of his presidential career, was acting as a promoter and not a reformer. He would later change his mind, favoring many changes to intercollegiate sport, while many other presidents continued the cheerleading role as promoters.

For more than a century, university presidents often have been singled out as having the greatest opportunity to reform any evils that may have entered the intercollegiate athletic scene. Presidents have also been criticized historically for seldom attempting to reform athletics. By 1905, in the midst of football's major crisis, one individual remarked that President Charles Eliot of Harvard, probably the best-known educator in the history of American higher education, was the only president who was attempting to rid college athletics of abuses. The individual said that for the previous twenty years President Eliot "protested without the seconding voice of any other college president."[6] Though that was a slight exaggeration, most presidents were hesitant then, as today, to attempt to reform athletics.

An important question is raised: Why have presidents traditionally been unwilling to reform or why have they been unsuccessful in reforming athletics? There are several reasons for this. First, in the second half of the nineteenth century, there was a perception that the virile features of American society were disappearing as the nation urbanized and the tough frontier mentality faded away. Theodore Roosevelt was the most visible individual in the pursuit of manliness in American society even before he became president in 1901. Writing in the 1890s, he feared national decay, suggesting that America would "reach a condition worse than that of ancient civilizations in the years of decay."[7] In a country experiencing the decline of manly virtues at the end of the nineteenth century, there was a call for concrete and symbolic forms of manhood.[8] Nowhere was this more apparent than on the eastern college campuses dominated by the collegiate sons of both middle-class and more socially elite parents. Football became a concrete form of manliness for a small group of athletes, but it became the major symbolic form for the institution. Presidents and others interested in higher education were keenly aware that colleges and universities were considered effete and lacking virile characteristics. Thus, when student-led intercollegiate athletics arose, presidents often embraced the increased masculinity that vigorous athletics brought to the image of their institutions. Even President Eliot, who eventually came to oppose both baseball and football and who on several occasions voted to ban football, stated publicly a number of times: "Effeminacy and luxury are even worse evils than brutality."[9] He was not alone.

A second reason for the failure of presidential support of athletic reform was that presidents headed individual institutions, and because achieving reform of intercollegiate athletics necessitated interinstitutional agreements, full athletic cooperation among the institutions was generally unsuccessful. This is natural because each institution was constantly competing for resources and enrollment for its own survival, growth, and prestige. The desire to cooperate was limited when the need to compete for survival and growth was so apparent. This was, after all, the period of Darwinian thought in which the strong would survive and the weak would perish. It was applied not only to the animal and plant world but also to social institutions such as colleges. With the fierce independence of American colleges, presidents may have spoken out for athletic reform in general terms, but when collective action to implement reform was suggested, they seldom took leading positions. That was true in the 1880s and 1890s, and it was true a century and more later.

However, a third reason for presidents' impotence in reforming athletics appears to be more important. Each university president was caught between at least two power groups that have traditionally been important in the athletic equation: the faculty and the governing board. Faculties have appeared to be concerned principally about academics and about the academic integrity of their institutions, and they would reform (or abandon) intercollegiate athletics in short order. Governing boards, on the other hand, have been concerned about the image, financial stability, and growth of their institutions. The two groups have often differed on the value of athletics. Presidents were caught between these two groups but were beholden only to one: the governing board. Presidents were hired and, more importantly, fired by boards, and it has been a rare president who has taken a stance on athletics that differs from that of the board (at least not for long). Presidents, however, often opposed the faculty on athletic issues. As educational historian Laurence Veysey has noted, college administrators were by the 1890s already more dedicated to the public image than to an academic philosophy.[10] Henry S. Pritchett, the early 1900s president of the Carnegie Foundation for the Advancement of Teaching, noted the ineffectiveness of presidents, especially those who stood for sound educational goals. Some of the presidents with solid educational policy, Pritchett said in 1911, were dismissed because of "the popular cry for greater numbers or winning athletic teams."[11] Presidents were, then, cautious about making waves with the commercialized and professionalized athletics that developed soon after the start of intercollegiate athletics. They still are.[12]

From early on, the presidential athletic promoters were in ascendancy. This was not illogical, for in the more or less free-market economy of institutions of higher learning in the United States, each president had been on the lookout for any way to raise the visibility or money for the institution. In the nineteenth century, most colleges were private, and if athletics provided an inexpensive means of advertising the institution, then it was logical for the president to welcome athletics. Obviously, winning athletics provided more visibility than losing. Advertising through athletic contests provided visibility within the first couple of decades of intercollegiate sports. In 1874, Columbia won the most prestigious event in college sport at the time, the intercollegiate regatta, beating both Harvard and Yale. Following the victory upon the waters of Lake Saratoga, the crew was transported back to New York City in a Palace car, the most stylish of Pullman's railroad cars, and given a parade up Fifth Avenue to a tremendous welcome at the gates of the college. President Frederick Barnard spoke in glowing terms of the triumph, congratulated the crew, and pronounced "that in one day or in one summer, you have done more to make Columbia College known than all your predecessors have done since the founding of the college." President Barnard did not stop there. "I assure you in the name of the Faculty and the Board of Trustees, whom I represent," he told the crew, "that whatever you ask in the future you will be likely to receive."[13] It was not surprising that Columbia soon built a rowing tank in the basement of the library for year-round crew training.

The next year, Cornell College rose to heights in promotion that it had never reached before in nearly ten years of existence. President Andrew D. White had rowed for Yale in the early 1850s, and he helped the Cornell crew, not only by assisting the crew to establish a University Boat Association but also by his purchase of a new rowing shell prior to its first college regatta competition in 1873. President White knew the promotional value of the most esteemed Cornell sport at the time. In two years, Cornell showed what a "boat load of mechanics from Ithaca" could do by besting Columbia, Harvard, and Yale at their game. The president wired the victorious crew: "The University chimes are ringing, flags flying and cannons firing," and wrote in his diary that "Everybody is ecstatic here. No end of demonstrations and joy."[14] Shortly thereafter, recognizing that the victories did more to publicize Cornell than if the governing board had spent $100,000, the president absorbed the $1,100 debt of the crew and charged it to college advertising. Yet, paradoxically, President White two years earlier had reacted negatively to a challenge from Michigan to play a game with Cornell's new football team. "I will not," White telegraphed forcefully to Michigan, "permit thirty men to travel four hundred miles merely to agitate a bag of wind."[15] The president did not know then that football would become the most popular college sport or that to allow it would improve the visibility of Cornell to unprecedented levels.

Most presidents were acting as cheerleaders for athletics, and it was most pronounced for football, the dominant sport in colleges by the 1890s. This is not surprising for alumni, who began to dominate governing boards and who helped make presidents more responsive to the times.[16] Presidents, thus, were more apt to support the desires of alumni and governing boards than they were to back faculty calls for reforming the excesses of athletics. Francis Patton, president-elect of Princeton, remarked in an 1888 talk before Princeton alumni that in "brawny contests" of football "some of the very best elements of manhood may emerge."[17] While Princeton was in its third decade of intercollegiate football, the game was just being launched to the West and South. In 1888, the presidents of Trinity College (now Duke University) in North Carolina and Miami College of Ohio organized football teams in an effort to publicize their schools. After defeating the University of North Carolina, Trinity President John Franklin Crowell, who coached the Trinity team, said that the victory over its neighbor "gave the College an indefinable prestige of a general but most effective kind."[18] At Miami of Ohio, President Ethelbert Warfield not only organized the first football team, but he also played on it, probably being the first president to incur an injury while playing for a college team. Warfield had insisted that all able-bodied men at Miami play on the team, a means, in part, to publicize the institution.[19] In a similar way, President William Slocum of Colorado College gave a pep talk to his 1898 football team, stating that Colorado College could "never gain the recognition that it deserves until it has a winning football team."[20] Other presidents used football in similar ways to promote their institutions.

At the University of Chicago, President William Rainey Harper moved from his position as chair of Semitic languages at Yale to lead the new university in Chicago funded by John D. Rockefeller's oil millions. Harper wanted Chicago to be the best university in America, and he paid highly in the early 1890s for department heads to make it so. One position was the Director of the Department of Physical Culture and Athletics, a position offered to Yale's Amos Alonzo Stagg. The former Yale all-American end and baseball pitching star was recruited by Harper "to develop teams which we can send around the country and knock out all the colleges. We will," Harper offered, "give them a palace car and a vacation too." Harper, an intellectual who graduated from college at age fourteen and concluded his Yale doctorate in linguistics at age eighteen, believed that football was the "great American college game." To lead football at Chicago, Harper made Stagg the first tenured professor in physical education and thus the first tenured football coach anywhere, paying him the fine salary of $2,500 in 1891.[21] Harper gave his athletic teams financial and moral support. During one football game in the 1890s, Chicago was behind 12–0 at halftime to Wisconsin. The president walked into the dressing room and delivered a stirring speech to the Chicago players. "Boys," he said, "Mr. Rockefeller has just announced a gift of $3,000,000 to the University." Rockefeller, Harper said, believes "the University is to be great. The way you played in the fist half leads me to wonder whether we really have the spirit of greatness in ambition. I wish you would make up your minds to win this game and show that we do have it." Chicago won 22–12 with the help of a cheerleading president.[22]

Like Harper, President Charles F. Thwing of Western Reserve in Cleveland praised football. Football, Thwing said at the close of the century, is "a game of hearts" in which gritty play characterizes the Anglo-Saxon race. Recognizing some of the evils of the game, Thwing conducted a survey of college presidents, who generally favored football, as it was coming under strong criticism.[23] When one of the critics cited brutality in football, the president of the University of Notre Dame, John Cavanaugh, said in the early 1900s that he would rather see young men playing the dangerous game of football receiving "a broken collar bone occasionally than to see them dedicated to croquet."[24] In a similar way, President Edwin A. Alderman of Tulane University urged all students to participate on the Tulane football team in 1900, concluding that he would "rather see a boy of mine on the rush line, fighting for his team, than on the sideline, smoking a cigarette."[25] He was a promoter not a reformer. Writing in the early 1900s, historian Edwin Slosson, who personally opposed football, noted that not only did colleges often show a tendency toward femininity but college presidents also were nearly unanimously in favor of the virile game.[26]

Some of the presidents wanted to ban athletics, or at least football, or reform them to better meet the educational goals or in some cases the moral or religious goals of institutions of higher learning. Of the two presidents of eastern institutions who led two failed reform efforts in the 1880s, Charles Eliot of Harvard and James McCosh of Princeton, only Princeton's McCosh could be considered a religious reformer of athletics, as Princeton and McCosh were strict Presbyterians.[27] Eliot, a Unitarian who was concerned about the ethics of sport, was not one to consider reform in athletics as a religious issue. There were other presidents, though, who were at religiously oriented institutions at which denominational leaders saw sport and the environment surrounding it as sinful, for to play was to waste time, and to waste time was to sin. While attitudes in fundamentalist churches such as the Baptists and Methodists were changing in the second half of the nineteenth century, as late as the 1870s a Methodist church school could state that students should indulge in nothing that the world calls play.[28] Football contests were just beginning to attract attention in the West and the South when religious leaders looked to ban early football in those two regions, sometimes with the presidents in opposition to those religious leaders.

The predecessor to Duke University, Trinity College, hired a young, thirty-one-year-old president in 1888, John Franklin Crowell, a Pennsylvanian who attended Dartmouth before attaining his BA from Yale in 1883. At Yale he saw, though he did not participate, the dominating football team of early college football. He carried his enthusiasm for football to Durham, North Carolina, and helped form the first football team at that Methodist school. At the end of the year, little Trinity defeated the University of North Carolina in a Thanksgiving Day game. This victory, according to Crowell, gave status to Trinity, which had previously been looked down upon by the first state university in America. Trinity continued playing football for the next half-dozen years, and in 1893 it defeated North Carolina again to win the unofficial North Carolina state championship. However, the team, after playing and losing to Virginia, consumed a keg of beer on its trip back to Durham. This incident triggered a reaction by Methodist ministers, who were previously none too keen about the game of football. At two Methodist conferences held in late 1893, the ministers condemned football for being "dangerous to the health, life and morals of many of our young men." President Crowell soon resigned after his game was censured by the Methodist leaders.[29] Thus some presidents who favored football, and who might have reformed some of the perceived evils of the game, left when religious elements forced their hands. Football at Trinity remained a banned game until 1920, not too dissimilar to Wake Forest, a Baptist institution, where football was abandoned from 1895 to 1908.

In the West, a conference of ministers of the Methodist Episcopal Church met in Abilene, Kansas, in 1894. Their resolution requested Methodist colleges to ban, not reform, intercollegiate contests:

> Resolved: That as ministers of the Kansas conference, being more fully convinced than ever that intercollegiate games are dangerous physically, useless intellectually, and detrimental morally and spiritually, we respectfully request, with renewed emphasis, the trustees and faculties of our institutions of learning to do all in their power to abolish such games.[30]

This resolution came only months after Baker College, a Methodist institution, had just been crowned "Champions of the West" following the defeat of the University of Kansas in football. The young president of Baker College, W. A. Quayle, was a so-called Muscular Christian and very much in favor of vigorous athletics. Quayle polled a number of other presidents of Methodist schools, including Northwestern University, Syracuse University, Illinois Wesleyan, and Ohio Wesleyan, to get their views on athletics. He got a number of responses, from very supportive to highly critical, but the important reaction was from his Board of Trustees with the backing of the Methodist Board of Education to abolish football at Baker.[31] Quayle left Baker, and football did not return until 1908, when the next president decided that school spirit was needed at his institution.[32]

Northwestern was another Methodist institution in the 1890s presided over by a Methodist minister, Henry Rogers. Probably prompted by W. A. Quayle and Baker's recent inquiry about football, Rogers wrote to a number of major football-playing colleges of the East and Midwest, asking them to respond to the question of possible football abolishment. Could an institution acting alone, he asked, be successful in abolishing football? While several responded that eliminating football at a single school would be problematic, President Harper of Chicago rejected the idea, indicating that he would continue the game if only a couple of other schools kept the sport.[33] Rogers's negative feeling about football might have added to Purdue President James Smart's desire to reform football and other sports by creating an athletic conference. Within a year of Rogers's inquiry, Smart had contacted the presidents of seven schools in the midwestern states of Illinois, Indiana, Michigan, Minnesota, and Wisconsin and brought reform measures to a new athletic conference, eventually called the Big Ten. Northwestern was among them.

By the turn of the century, presidents were often involved in the direction being taken by intercollegiate athletics, but they were seldom the leaders as in the case of the Big Ten. There was ample reason for reforming the games that students had started only a generation or so before, but presidents either would not or could not be effective in reform efforts that were being called for by other presidents, by many faculty members, and increasingly by reformers in the media. When the journalist muckrakers of the late 1800s and early 1900s brought a focus to college athletics as an area in need of changes and a crisis in brutality and ethics came together in the football season of 1905, reform on a national level came to the fore for the first time. The football crisis of 1905–6 was the most important reform effort in collegiate history, and the organization it spawned, the National Collegiate Athletic Association, became the longest-standing alliance claiming athletic ideals in a national higher education setting.

5

Football, Progressive Reform, and the Creation of the NCAA

"In view of the tragedy on Ohio Field today," New York University Chancellor Henry M. MacCracken telegraphed Charles W. Eliot, requesting that the Harvard president call "a meeting of university and college presidents to undertake the reform or abolition of football."[1] Thus began a series of events addressing not only the death of a Union College football player in a pileup in a game against New York University, but also the larger question of brutality and unsavory practices in football that had been going on for several decades. The telegram at the conclusion of the 1905 college football season, to the president who was most identified with a desire to reform or abolish football, was answered almost immediately. "I do not think it expedient to call a meeting of college presidents about football," Eliot telegraphed MacCracken. "They certainly cannot reform football, and I doubt if by themselves they can abolish it. . . . Deaths and injuries are not the strongest argument against football. That cheating and brutality are profitable is the main evil."[2] Charles Eliot, the most imposing educator of the time and the one who attempted to reform athletics from the 1880s on, dropped out of the arena to reform athletics on a regional or national basis.

Chancellor MacCracken's involvement in athletic reform was an electrifying action that began with the death of a player his school was competing against, but it was only one of a series of events leading up to a major reform of football rules and the creation of the National Collegiate Athletic Association. Had it not occurred in the midst of the Progressive Movement in American history, the ensuing reform would likely not have taken place. With the issues raised about the industrialization and urbanization of America in the second half of the nineteenth century, a reform movement was born. The Progressive Movement of the late nineteenth and early twentieth centuries was based on the belief that society collectively could be cured of its ills through economic, political, and social reform.[3] There was a shift from a traditional laissez-faire policy to governmental activism in areas such as legislation to prevent corruption in politics, industrial monopolies, adulterated food and drugs, child labor and other worker exploitation, and abominable urban living conditions. The investigative journalists who exposed societal issues, such as corrupt political bosses, monopolistic industrialists, and fraudulent claims of patent medicines, were called muckrakers. Some of the leading muckrakers included Lincoln Stephens (corrupt politicians), Ida Tarbell (Rockefeller oil), Ray Stannard Baker (Pullman Strike), Jacob Riis (slums), and Upton Sinclair (meatpacking). It was Theodore Roosevelt, U.S. president in the early years of the twentieth century, who coined the term *muckraker,* based on the man with the muck-rake in John Bunyon's *Pilgrim's Progress* who raked up the muck of society. Those who raked the muck of intercollegiate athletics had a large impact upon the reform of football and the creation of the National Collegiate Athletic Association in 1905.

The ills of intercollegiate athletics were only a minor problem in industrial America in the early years of the twentieth century, but they attracted attention, particularly of the popular press. College athletics were covered intently both by newspapers and by periodicals of the time, and major issues were the violence and questionable ethics found in college sport, especially football. The muckrakers of athletics attracted national attention, significantly that of President Theodore Roosevelt in the summer of 1905. Of the periodicals publishing reform articles, such as *Cosmopolitan, Outlook, Nation,* and *The Independent,* none was more important in athletic muckraking than *McClure's.* Henry Beech Needham penned a two-part *McClure's* series in the spring and summer of 1905 that ran concurrently with Ida Tarbell's study of the oil monopolist, John D. Rockefeller, and Lincoln Steffens's piece on Ohio's political corruption.[4] These two articles on "The College Athlete" attacked the most prestigious eastern universities for what Needham called the "prostitution of college athletics." The articles condemned the win-at-all-cost behavior, including hiring tramp athletes, inducing athletes to attend college for financial advantage, paying baseball players during the summer, squandering athletic income, cheating in the classroom, collusion of faculty with athletes, unethical practices of professional coaches, building costly stadiums, commercializing college sports, and the continuing brutality of football.

Needham's condemnation of the athletic scene in preparatory schools, especially elite Andover and Exeter, caught the particular notice of headmasters of prep schools. Only two years before, a group of seventy headmasters asked the Intercollegiate Football Rules Committee to modify its rules to eliminate the dangerous mass plays. The headmaster of Groton Preparatory School, Endicott Peabody, was disturbed to the point that he requested his friend, President Theodore Roosevelt, in 1905 to invite the so-called Big Three universities—Harvard, Yale, and Princeton—to an early fall White House meeting to discuss football ethics and brutal play.[5] Roosevelt was already well aware of the problems, and, as a Progressive reformer, he was ready to enter the battle for athletic reform. At about the same time as the publication of Needham's first article, Roosevelt had given a commencement address at Harvard University, his alma mater, and spoke to the question of ethics and violent behavior. "Brutality in playing a game," Roosevelt told the Harvard gathering, "should awaken the heartiest and most plainly shown contempt for the player guilty of it; especially if this brutality is coupled with a low cunning."[6] Shortly after his address, Roosevelt invited Needham to his vacation home at Oyster Bay on Long Island.[7] Roosevelt was acting as he often did when he exchanged ideas with the muckrakers, and then, as historian Robert Wiebe has shown, he turned other's "contributions into dramatic personal victories."[8] Roosevelt tried to do this with college athletics.

Headmaster Endicott Peabody's letter, urging a White House meeting, pointed out the athletic dishonesty that was ruining intercollegiate sports. Peabody believed that if he could get the most prestigious colleges and their coaches together under Roosevelt's leadership, the president could "persuade them to undertake to teach men to play football honestly." If Harvard, Yale, and Princeton would take the leadership, he believed other colleges would soon follow, and football from the standpoint of rough and dishonorable play would be reformed. Roosevelt honored the request and held a Big Three White House discussion early in the football season of 1905.[9] Roosevelt invited two men from each of the schools: three head coaches (Bill Reid, Harvard; John Owsley, Yale; and Arthur Hillebrand, Princeton) and three representatives (Dr. Edward Nichols, Harvard team physician; Walter Camp, Yale; and Professor Henry B. Fine, Princeton Athletic Committee). The six met with Roosevelt and new Secretary of State Elihu Root at an early October luncheon, with Walter Camp, the "Father of American Football," appropriately seated at the President's right. Roosevelt discussed football in general and noted several unfair incidents that involved each of the three colleges. He emphasized the need for conducting football in the spirit of fair play. After the discussion, Roosevelt asked the three older men, none of whom were head coaches, to draw up an agreement for clean and ethical football. As the train carrying the six journeyed north from the nation's capital, a message intended for Roosevelt and the nation was constructed.[10]

The train-ride memorandum was telegraphed to Roosevelt, who approved of it, and it was soon publicly released by Walter Camp. It read, in full: "At a meeting with the President of the United States, it was agreed that we consider an honorable obligation exists to carry out in *letter* and in *spirit* the rules of the game of football, relating to roughness, holding and foul play, and the active coaches of our universities being present with us, pledge themselves to so regard it and to do their utmost to carry out that obligation."[11]

Had reform, as conducted by the Big Three, had a great impact, and had other institutions followed where Harvard, Yale, and Princeton believed they should, the reform effort might have solved many of the problems facing intercollegiate sport, especially football. But the trickle-down theory of sport reform had little effect among the nation's football-playing schools, and members of the Big Three soon broke their own pledge.

The nature of football as conducted by the colleges was such that questionable practices and serious injuries would continue despite the moral suasion of President Roosevelt and the three leading institutions. Sport as conducted in America was result oriented—victory was the one major objective, not the enjoyment of participation. Sports at the elite levels were hard work, not fun activities. It would be most difficult for the three signatories to carry out the spirit of the rules when football players, according to a Harvard athlete, had been taught for years the "tricks of the trade" in deceiving the officials.[12] If each of the three leading football powers distrusted the other two, it was not likely that a national call for upholding the spirit of the rules would be successful elsewhere. President Roosevelt, who won the Nobel Peace Prize for negotiating a peace treaty between Russia and Japan in September 1905, was unable to bring about a peaceful solution among three universities that same fall. It was much easier for the muckrakers to expose the problems than for the President of the United States to solve them. That would always be the nature of reform.

Harvard would be the center of any reform efforts as the football season progressed in the fall of 1905. Harvard's President Eliot wanted not to reform football, but rather to abolish it. When the Harvard coach, Bill Reid, was told that his president and the governing boards were considering banning football, he and the football advisors decided to use Eliot's previous concerns about the game and to concoct a letter for Reid to sign and send to the Harvard Graduates' Athletic Association. The letter coming from the Harvard football coach asking for the reform of football was more effective than any article a muckraker might have published. "I have become convinced that the game as it is played to-day," Reid's letter read, "has fundamental faults which cannot be removed by any mere technical revision of the rules." The letter went on to say that because of "brutality and the evasion of the rules" the game needs to be radically reformed.[13] He then asked the Harvard Graduates' Athletic Association to appoint a committee to make recommendations to drastically alter the game as then played. Those closely associated with football at Harvard had deceived the ruling authorities by this letter and had beaten Walter Camp and Yale to the reform punch. Coach Reid confirmed this when he confided in his diary: "By getting this letter printed now . . . Harvard will be in the front seat of the band wagon and some of Yale's fire will be stolen."[14]

Harvard athletic authorities, the president, and the governing boards were now in the forefront of any reform that might take place. The letter was released only three days before Harvard's important game with Penn. At Franklin Field, Penn's home field, the Pennsylvania athletic leaders had watered the field the night before the game, as they had done in 1900 and 1901. Penn came onto the field at game time with new, long cleats to enable the team to maneuver more effectively on the muddy field. Using regular cleats, the Harvard team fell and fumbled, losing for the first time under Coach Reid, following twenty victories. The game lacked both civility and sportsmanship, and slugging by a Harvard player brought a disqualification. That act of violence was brought to the attention of President Roosevelt, who called Coach Reid to the White House to explain the first major violation of the agreement Harvard signed only a month before. When Reid said that the disqualified Harvard player had slugged the Penn player only after he had been hit in the groin several times and the game official took no action, Reid asked the president what he would have done. The president looked at Reid, spoke vehemently through his teeth as he often did, and replied, "It wouldn't be good policy for me to state," agreeing that the Harvard man had some justification for this actions.[15]

Two weeks later, concluding the season, Yale journeyed to the new (1903) stadium in Cambridge, Massachusetts, with about 43,000 spectators jamming the arena. An incident occurred that once again led to charges of brutality and the need for reform. Francis Burr, Harvard's nearly 200-pounder awaited a punt from Yale, signaled a fair catch, and two Yale players hit him, one low and one high, striking him squarely in the face. With blood spurting from Burr's broken nose, the fans began a storm of hisses. Major Henry L. Higginson, an influential governing board member who had fifteen years before presented Harvard with thirty-one acres for an athletic field, charged onto the field and asked Coach Reid to remove his team. Reid refused, Harvard lost, and the brutal incident would not go away. Neither would Theodore Roosevelt. The president again called Reid to the White House, but Roosevelt was more upset with the umpire, Paul Dashiell, a faculty member at the Naval Academy and a member of the Football Rules Committee. At the time, Dashiell was up for promotion at the Naval Academy, and now the U.S. commander in chief could ruin his life. Dashiell wrote to Roosevelt regretting the incident and "the injury that it has done the game, now in so critical a condition." Roosevelt, probably more upset that his alma mater lost to Yale than about any lack of reform, held up Dashiell's appointment for a six-month period, and the president was probably happy that Dashiell never again officiated a Harvard-Yale game.[16]

The same day of the Harvard-Yale game, an even more important event took place in New York City, where a Union College football player, Harold Moore, was killed in a game with New York University. When President Eliot rebuffed the NYU chancellor's plea to call a conference either to reform football or to abolish it, Henry MacCracken decided to invite nineteen institutions against which NYU had competed for the past two decades to discuss abolishing or reforming the game. In his letter, MacCracken asked three questions, including his preference: "Ought the present game of football be abolished?"[17] "If not," MacCracken asked, "what steps should be taken to secure its thorough reform?" In the event it was voted to abolish football, what game or games should take its place?[18] In less than two weeks, on December 8, 1905, the MacCracken Conference took place in New York City's Murray Hill Hotel. Two-thirds of the institutions invited sent delegates, and five of thirteen institutions were represented by presidents: Lafayette, New York University, Rochester, Rutgers, and Wesleyan. One institution, Columbia, had just banned football, and others, including NYU and Union, were considering similar action and eventually did so.[19] Noticeably absent was one university that had competed against NYU, Princeton, as President Woodrow Wilson politely declined the invitation, stating, "We do not as yet feel prepared to take part in such a conference."[20] Yet five other presidents attended, while faculty members represented the other eight schools.

While no major football-playing school attended the conference, the MacCracken Conference nevertheless took decisive action that led to the creation of the National Collegiate Athletic Association within three weeks. Columbia and West Point came closest to being considered strong football schools. They stood on opposite sides of the issue of banning or reforming the game. President Nicholas Murray Butler's Columbia representatives wanted to end all football competition and asked the conference to vote to do so. West Point, led by a young Army captain, Palmer Pierce, came with its own agenda of saving football through reform. After a lengthy discussion, a resolution by Columbia to abolish football was favored by NYU and Union, the two schools involved in Harold Moore's death two weeks before, and they were joined only by Rochester and Stevens Institute. The majority, led by West Point and Wesleyan, favored reforming football to meet acceptable standards of play.[21]

The conference concluded, though not without rancor, by determining that it would meet on December 28, 1905, after inviting all football-playing institutions of higher learning to attend. The MacCracken group formed a special football rules committee to rid the game of dangerous, brutal, and mass plays. This group would naturally come in conflict with the Old Rules Committee, dominated over the years by Walter Camp of Yale. On the Old Rules Committee were representatives from the elite football schools of Chicago (Amos Alonzo Stagg), Cornell (L. M. Dennis), Harvard (Bill Reid), the Naval Academy (Paul Dashiell), Princeton (John B. Fine), Pennsylvania (John Bell), and Yale (Walter Camp). In terms of status, probably only Dr. Henry Williams of the New Rules Committee could compare favorably to most on the Old Rules Committee.[22] Williams had played football at Yale in the 1880s with the great William "Pudge" Heffelfinger and Amos Alonzo Stagg, eventually earning a medical degree from Penn and going on to coach at the University of Minnesota. When the late-December conference decided to have its rules committee consolidate with the Old Rules Committee, Williams was asked to be the negotiator. It was a difficult negotiation, for the Old Rules Committee was reluctant to give up any of its power over the game.

The December 28 conference at the Murray Hill Hotel in New York City was important for more than creating a second rules committee. The group, challenging the elite sport institutions, decided to form a permanent organization and elected Captain Palmer Pierce of West Point as its president. Representatives from Williams, Rutgers, Ohio Wesleyan, Vanderbilt, Western University of Pennsylvania (Pittsburgh), and Kenyon rounded out the Executive Committee of the new Intercollegiate Athletic Association of the United States, thus forming in 1905 rather than what the present-day National Collegiate Athletic Association (NCAA) believes was its founding in 1906.[23]

The NCAA really was an outgrowth of football rules reform and had almost nothing to do with how athletics fit into higher education. By 1905, athletics were entrenched into the American form of higher education, and Harvard's building of the first reinforced concrete stadium in the world in 1903 indicated that the commercialized form of football was likely to be a permanent fixture of colleges in America. The rule changes were needed, however, to prevent the brutal side of football from overwhelming the enormously popular side of America's favorite college game. What was needed, according to most of the influential leaders of football, was to curb the most blatant acts of violence so that the game would continue to attract large numbers of spectators and large gate receipts—something that would help pay for all the athletic teams colleges wished to sponsor. No other sport, including the next most popular sport, baseball, could provide that financial support. This was true at Harvard, and it was true at most other football-playing institutions.

Though Harvard did not attend the original December 1905 meeting of the NCAA, it became the most important institution in creating reform rules that came from an amalgamation of the two football rules committees. The Old Rules Committee, headed by Yale's Walter Camp, met in early December, but Bill Reid,

Harvard's representative, was asked by Harvard athletic authorities to not meet with the committee until the Harvard Graduates' Athletic Association Committee had drawn up what it considered were necessary rule changes for the Old Rules Committee to adopt. Meanwhile, on December 28, sixty-eight institutions met at the Murray Hill Hotel in New York, formed a permanent organization, and instructed its New Rules Committee to meet in Philadelphia the next day with the Old Rules Committee to amalgamate or merge the two rule-making bodies, if possible. If the Camp committee refused, the reform group would then form its own rules.[24] In Philadelphia, the New Rules Committee requested a meeting with the Old Rules Committee, which was granted. However, the Old Rules Committee of big-time football powers hesitated about cooperating with the newcomers, deciding that each committee member should return to his campus and get permission from athletic officials. They would then meet again and either reject or accept the amalgamation proposal.

By early January, the Harvard Graduates' Athletic Association Committee had drawn up its proposed rules and instructed Bill Reid to withdraw from the Old Rules Committee and support the reform group. Reid had informed Camp that the merger was necessary or the meeting of the Old Committee should be canceled. "If by having a meeting we can settle the question of amalgamation," he telegraphed Camp two days before the meeting, "I should advise having one, if not, it hardly seems worthwhile." He also told Camp that he would withdraw from the Old Rules Committee to join the new group and hoped that other members might do the same.[25]

As it turned out, Harvard did not act alone by withdrawing from the Old Rules Committee, for President Theodore Roosevelt had told Paul Dashiell of the Naval Academy to support the merger. Dashiell could hardly afford to go against his commander in chief. On the day of the meeting, the two groups met independently at the Hotel Netherland in New York City. After four hours of independent discussions, exchanging notes, and Reid's withdrawal to join the new group, the Old Rules Committee offered to merge, provided that its officers would be the officers of a new committee. This was rejected, and it was finally decided that the amalgamated committee be formed with the Old Rules Committee having the chairmanship and new group securing the position of secretary. L. M. Dennis of Cornell was chosen chair, and James Babbitt of Haverford was selected for the key position of secretary. However, a Machiavellian political move was accomplished by the reform group when Babbitt immediately resigned in favor of Harvard's Bill Reid. Harvard had outmaneuvered Yale by eliminating Walter Camp from the secretarial position of power that he had held for years. When Reid began using his new position to Yale's disadvantage, Yale President Hadley confided to Camp that the Harvard coach was "not playing fair [and] ought to be a lesson to us for the future."[26] Yale, always the reluctant reformer, had been duped by Harvard. Reform was not achieved without conflict among the older, elite institutions as well as with the new reformers.

The newly merged committee of fourteen, however, went to work on reforming the rules to bring about a more open game, one that might eliminate the violent side of football. Bill Reid brought the series of Harvard demands, rule changes that would be necessitated if the new ban on Harvard football by the Overseers would be abrogated. Reid told the potential reformers that if Harvard's proposed changes were not accepted, "there will be no football at Harvard; and if Harvard throws out the game, many other colleges will follow Harvard's lead, and an important blow will be dealt the game."[27] He asked other committee members to take the Harvard proposals as their own, for only two days before the conference, the Harvard Overseers voted that there should be no more football at Harvard until it had a report on the acceptance of the Harvard proposals by the national rule-making body.[28]

The conflict between Yale and Harvard over football rules, a half century after their first conflict over rowing eligibility, was played out in the new amalgamated rules committee. Yale's Walter Camp was unwilling to do anything that might mar the game he so remarkably influenced from the 1870s and 1880s. Yet Yale was in no position to stonewall major rule reform. At the time, an investigation of Yale athletic excesses was being carried out by Yale's faculty. It revealed that Yale athletics had a huge $100,000 secret fund that had been used to tutor athletes, give expensive gifts to athletes, purchase entertainment for coaches, and pay for trips to the Caribbean, as revealed by a former Yale athlete, Clarence Deming, in a muckraking article.[29] Walter Camp wanted only one major rule change: to increase the number of yards to be gained before relinquishing the ball from five yards to ten yards. This was an attempt to force wider runs and prevent mass plays in the center of the line of scrimmage. Harvard and others demanded more. After a series of meetings in the winter and spring of 1906, major rule changes, including the ten-yard rule, were agreed upon. Some of the more important changes involved creating a ball-length neutral zone between the two teams, prohibiting runners from hurdling the line, preventing tackling below the knees, increasing the number of officials to four, and adding heavier penalties for rule violations. The most controversial, because Camp was so opposed, was legalizing passing the ball forward. The forward pass was an attempt to spread players and avoid the bunching of both teams near the line of scrimmage. There were, however, major questions to be debated. Who could catch the ball, where could it be thrown from, where could it be caught, and what would be the result if the ball was not caught or touched? The final decision, after much discussion, was that one forward pass could be made from behind the line of scrimmage, if it was thrown at least five yards to either side of the center to an end or a back. A major limiting factor was that if the ball was not touched by a player on either side, the ball went to the opponent at the spot where the ball was thrown. Later rules would make less severe penalties for the forward pass, but the committee wanted to be cautious at first.[30]

The forward pass and other new legislation intended to eliminate mass plays and unethical physical contact helped convince a number of institutions and a majority of Harvard's Corporation and Overseers that the new game should be given one more year to prove its worthiness. President Eliot was not convinced and voted with the minority on the Harvard governing boards. Only a few other important colleges were in agreement with Charles Eliot. While Columbia, NYU, Union, Northwestern, California, and Stanford banned football, most colleges looked to the new football ruling body's reform measures as being satisfactory to continuing the game. While changing football rules was a major reform effort and it brought about the creation of the first national collegiate body for athletics, the NCAA, no other reforms beneficial to higher education came out of the 1905–6 crisis in intercollegiate athletics. The major big-time universities in competitive sports were unwilling to relinquish any of their accumulated power to the lesser schools that originally formed the NCAA.

6

The NCAA
A Faculty Debating Society
for Amateurism

For its first half century, the National Collegiate Athletic Association (NCAA) was principally a debating society for faculty representatives interested in amateur athletics. If the smaller schools that had founded the NCAA in December 1905 could have had their way, it would have been more than a debating society, but if it had been given power to legislate and enforce the legislation, few big-time institutions would have joined the organization. Harvard, Yale, and Princeton, the triad dominating college athletics throughout the nineteenth century and into the twentieth, refused to join the NCAA in its earliest years, and that was true of many of the larger colleges and universities. While the NCAA would eventually become extremely powerful, with money coming primarily from operating the NCAA men's basketball tournament, it began as a small group of colleges lacking status, unity, or real power to lead intercollegiate reform.

The weakness of the NCAA resulted from the reluctance of prestigious colleges and universities to give up the athletic leadership they had traditionally wielded for a generation and more. Of the institutions that had membership on football's Old Rules Committee, only Pennsylvania joined the NCAA in the first year. This left Harvard, Yale, Princeton, Cornell, the Naval Academy, and Chicago out of the new organization. Columbia, Brown, and every member of the Big Ten except Minnesota refused to join. Not one West Coast institution enrolled in the NCAA, and only a few southern schools—Missouri, North Carolina, and Vanderbilt—became members.[1] The less prestigious institutions that joined the NCAA attempted to bring the leading institutions into the fold by assuring that the established football schools would not lose power by joining the group. For instance, the NCAA president, West Point's Palmer Pierce, wrote to Princeton's president, Woodrow Wilson, stating that the NCAA "decided to give the greatest of independence to institutions."[2] This approach eventually appeased the leading institutions that favored athletic autonomy. The principle of institutional autonomy, something Pierce called the Home Rule principle, was agreed to from the first.[3] Paradoxically, the objective of the NCAA as stated in the new constitution was "the *regulation* and *supervision* of college athletics throughout the United States." Yet the bylaws would provide for no regulations and thus no national eligibility rules. The bylaws called for "each institution . . . to enact and enforce such measures as may be necessary to prevent violations of the principles of amateur sports."[4] Mandatory eligibility rules were "judged impracticable" by President Palmer Pierce and were left up to each institution.[5] A major part of the reasoning by Pierce and the small institutions was that they did not want to step on the toes of the important institutions remaining out of the NCAA, hoping they would soon join. There was also a historical sense of college independence, reflecting other American institutions. A keen spectator of America, Englishman James Bryce made an observation about the independence of Americans the same year the NCAA was created. Americans, Bryce said, were the most individualistic of all people, and "they are not the people whom the art of combination has reached its peak."[6] Bryce was certainly right relative to intercollegiate athletics. To make Home Rule clear, the NCAA amended the constitution in 1907 to read: "Legislation enacted at a conference of delegates shall not be binding upon any institution."[7] For the first half century of the NCAA's existence, Home Rule dominated. The colleges agreed collectively to act individually. There would be no national eligibility rules enacted and enforced by the NCAA for nearly a half century. The NCAA became a debating society, something akin to many high school student councils or university faculty senates—much discussion but little legislative impact.

Moral force, not political force, was the keystone of the NCAA's diluted power in the early years. Yet its lack of numbers at the first annual meeting in December 1906 made even moral suasion difficult. By then, only thirty-nine institutions had joined the NCAA, and only twenty-eight sent delegates to the first meeting in New York City. This was considerably fewer than the sixty-eight institutions that met in New York City the previous December when the NCAA was founded. After the first year closed, the financial situation showed the precarious nature of the organization as the treasurer reported a balance of $28.82.[8] Three years later, three of the original seven institutions represented on football's Old Rules Committee—Pennsylvania, Chicago, and Harvard—had joined the NCAA. By then, membership had grown to sixty-seven, including two-thirds of the Big Ten members. After Harvard and a number of the larger state universities joined the NCAA, it became a more stable organization.

Though the NCAA lacked power to legislate, its importance was in providing a national focus to intercollegiate athletic problems. Only in creating uniform rules for football and eventually other sports did it solve athletic problems. Nevertheless, the NCAA provided a forum for discussing a myriad of problems and produced guidelines for individual institutions and conferences to adopt. If an institution wanted to achieve faculty control of athletics, it had the voice of the NCAA behind that choice. If a college wanted to limit recruiting and providing athletic grants to athletes, the NCAA guidelines could be used. Similarly with guidelines for eliminating summer baseball for pay or opposing play by professional athletes in college sports, the NCAA could be helpful to institutions or conferences. The freedom of an individual institution to carry out its own athletic policy was not jeopardized by belonging to the NCAA.

The original constitution and bylaws were reform documents. The objective of the NCAA, according to the constitution, was the "regulation and supervision of collegiate athletics throughout the United States" so that they could be "maintained on an ethical plane in keeping with the dignity and high purpose of education."[9] Furthermore, the principles of amateur sport in the bylaws demanded that each member agree to prevent inducements to athletes to enter colleges for athletic purposes and to prohibit all but bona fide students in good academic standing from participating.[10] The bylaws also set standards that the individual colleges were expected to maintain. There should be no participation if the athlete was not taking a full schedule of classes, had ever received money for playing, had already participated for four years, and had transferred and not remained athletically inactive until he attended for one year. There was a specific rule that prohibited "any football player" from participating again if he left school without attending two-thirds of the previous year.[11] The original wording of the constitution and bylaws was a far cry from the principle of Home Rule that would allow institutions and conferences to set their own rules, yet it was understood that no legislation, only recommendations, would come from the annual meetings of the NCAA.

The NCAA, rather than legislating, studied the questions around which intercollegiate athletic reform could be addressed by individual institutions and conferences. In the first two years, the faculty representatives to the NCAA discussed, among other issues, amateurism, summer baseball for pay, freshman eligibility, graduate student eligibility, number of years of eligibility, entrance requirements, scholarship standards for athletes, progress toward graduation, recruitment of athletes, transfer of athletes, training table, preseason practice, professional coaching, the number of contests, betting at games, national rules of eligibility, basketball rules, working with the Amateur Athletic Union, and faculty control of athletics.[12] Next to anything to do with football, the question of amateurism and summer baseball was the NCAA's most vexing problem for its first decade. Despite West Point's Palmer Pierce's statement that "the effort to make college sport truly amateur has been successfully carried out" in his district, questions surrounding amateurism and summer baseball arose almost immediately.[13]

Of all the issues surrounding the question of amateurism, none was more volatile than the question of college baseball players leaving for summer vacation and playing baseball and earning money for their efforts.[14] Summer baseball was an issue as early as 1879 when Brown University's J. Lee Richmond played for Worcester of the National League of Professional Baseball and returned to Brown to play against and beat the likes of Harvard and Yale.[15] More often, though, college players were not good enough to play in the professional major leagues or even in the minor leagues. Other avenues for participation, however, arose. Mountain vacation destinations, first in New England and New York, and then summer seaside resorts in the East, sought entertainment for their wealthy guests. In the prosperity of the 1880s, mountain hotels and Eastern Shore resorts catered to a wealthy clientele who sought various kinds of amusements. Baseball, the "Great American Game," was part of the summer pleasure at many resorts. To fill the teams, resort owners sought physically and socially skilled athletes of the elite eastern institutions, both to play baseball and to carry out various tasks at the retreats. A hotel owner might offer room, board, and an allowance of possibly $5 or $10 or more per week for the summer. The players were thus paid for an enjoyable summer job, the patrons were entertained, and only the purity of amateurism was soiled. Yale's Eugene L. Richards, a baseball captain in the mid-1880s, warned: "Unless this tendency to professionalism is stopped, amateur athletics in this country will not amount to anything."[16] However, except for the amateur purists, few individuals would have complained if the playing field had not been unleveled. Playing baseball the entire summer gave players added expertise to lead them to collegiate victory the following spring.

A good but controversial example by the early 1900s was Harvard's Walter Clarkson, probably the best collegiate pitcher from 1901 to 1904. Clarkson was born into a well-to-do Cambridge, Massachusetts, family, one that enjoyed baseball. Two of Clarkson's older brothers played in the major leagues. Walter Clarkson loved baseball and apparently was keenly interested in following the path of his brothers. From the beginning of his highly successful Harvard career, he was held under suspicion of playing baseball under an assumed name at a summer hotel.[17] A private investigation carried out by the rival Yale athletic department showed that he was paid $15 per game in North Attleboro, Massachusetts. Because Yale could find no one at the resort to sign affidavits that Clarkson had been paid, he continued to participate on the Harvard varsity and, more importantly, helped beat Yale.[18] Only when Clarkson signed a bonus contract to play professional baseball in the major leagues during his last year at Harvard did the Harvard Athletic Committee gather clear evidence that he was ineligible to participate.[19] Even at Harvard, the American institution most closely identified with upholding the supposed virtues of amateurism given to America by Oxford and Cambridge in England, it was difficult to maintain strict amateur ideals.

To a number of reform-minded individuals, however, adhering to the ideal of amateurism was the most important reform needed in college athletics. The most outspoken was the American apologist for untainted amateurism, Caspar Whitney, long-time editor of *Outing* magazine. Whitney, the faux aristocrat, looked at the summer baseball player as soiled by being associated with professional athletes and others of the "great unwashed." To Whitney, "it is not easy to reconcile college-bred men with these positions," and he campaigned unceasingly for colleges to rid themselves of summer baseball.[20] One collegian in the late 1800s commented that Whitney's attitude reminded him "of the English rule that no amateur may perform manual labor." In America, the writer stated, "no American student who works honestly either with his head or his hands, need ever be ashamed."[21] When the NCAA was formed following the 1905 football crisis, a number of the reform group members tried to carry on the work of Caspar Whitney by forming the first nonfootball committee, the Committee on Summer Baseball. The committee soon concluded that "the playing of baseball in summer for gain is distinctly opposed to the principles of amateurism."[22]

Two vocal Muscular Moralists, Clark Hetherington of the University of Missouri and Amos Alonzo Stagg of the University of Chicago, were leaders in the NCAA pushing for pure amateur rules. Hetherington headed the Committee on Summer Baseball that wrote the resolutions condemning summer baseball. Hetherington was a physical educator, who, in the wake of early-twentieth-century Progressives, was more interested in the moral outcomes of physical activity than in the quality of the performance or in wins. He looked to the NCAA as a reform agency to eliminate the evils of athletics, summer baseball being a significant one. He believed in educational athletics, not commercialized athletics, which, so many Progressives believed, could be achieved with "proper administrative policies and adequate organization."[23] Many of the faculty representatives at the NCAA were in agreement with Hetherington. Stagg, the University of Chicago coach and athletic director, was one of them. He spoke at the first NCAA conference, asking for a national organization to regulate college sports and ban such activities as summer baseball. Stagg pointedly spoke in opposition to summer baseball that would "allow professionalism to creep into college sports."[24] Stagg spoke from high moral ground, though his athletic program at Chicago did not always meet the high standards he professed. Verging on hypocrisy in 1903, Stagg recruited the great high school quarterback Walter Eckersall to the University of Chicago. Eckersall had only recently been suspended by the Amateur Athletic Union for accepting money to play summer baseball. Later in Eckersall's career, Stagg should probably have been calling for eligibility reform at his own institution, for Eckersall had less than half the credits needed for graduation as he completed his four years of football eligibility with all-American status.[25] Stagg's dog-eat-dog, athletic survival-of-the-fittest policies were more Darwinian than Progressive, more pragmatic than moralistic. He was far more interested in winning and in his own survival and promotion than in defeating summer baseball and preserving amateurism.

Debating summer baseball and other reform issues continued in the faculty-controlled National Collegiate Athletic Association, but summer baseball remained the most controversial concern. Hetherington and Stagg were probably in the majority of the faculty representatives, but not all faculty representatives or presidents supported their position. The president of Clark University and noted psychologist G. Stanley Hall wanted to eliminate what he considered the summer baseball hypocrisy. "I'm not only saying that it is a right for a man to play summer ball for money," Hall said in a sermon, "but I'm going further than that. . . . He is failing in his duty to himself and to the world if he does not take advantage of it and use it to the best of his ability."[26] Penn State's J. P. Welsh, a faculty member, agreed. Speaking at an NCAA meeting, Welsh argued that a student in good standing "who earns money during the summer vacation . . . needs to be let alone in the full, free, untrammeled exercise of his American citizenship, which entitles him to 'life, liberty, and the pursuit of happiness,' which sometimes means money."[27] There were many other comments on both sides of the issue, including that of a University of Nebraska professor, R. G. Clapp, who in 1911 observed: "Like 'the poor,' the summer baseball problem is always with us [and] no satisfactory solution has been devised," noting that numerous college baseball players competed in the summer for pay.[28]

There was a conflict between those Progressive, reform-motivated members of the NCAA who wanted to paternalistically control athletes and amateurism and those who thought that directing athletes in their summer vacations was undemocratic, certainly not giving students freedom to pursue their own interests. Progressives have been noted for being controllers, especially control by "experts." The faculty members of the NCAA often believed they were the experts in athletics and therefore knew what was best for the less privileged athletes. Students, who had, from the beginning of intercollegiate athletics, complained of faculty interference were greatly opposed to controlling athlete's lives during summer vacation. Many felt there was nothing wrong with earning money during the summer, using their expertise in a way similar to a musician playing in a dance band or a theology major selling Bibles. The 1908 NCAA faculty representatives were informed that students from three eastern colleges—Amherst, Wesleyan, and Williams—voted overwhelmingly to oppose the curtailing of summer baseball.[29] This was the tenor of feeling of students whether in the East, the West, or the South. Don't interfere, don't restrict athletes from making money during the summer, and don't take away their freedom.

Amateurism was not an American concept, for it had been developed by nineteenth-century social elites in Britain as a way to separate the upper social classes from having to participate with the lower and working classes.[30] It was clearly a social class concept that did not make sense to many Americans who lacked the sharp social class divisions so clearly seen in British society. A French observer, Lucien Dubeck, contrasted American and British sport. "As long as sport remained British," Dubeck noted, "it was aristocratic, chivalrous, courteous, and organized as a hierarchy."[31] Americans, as far back as the writing of the Declaration of Independence, had rejected the British concept of a fixed status system based upon heredity, position, education, and wealth, and that is a major reason why the concept of amateurism in America had been modified. Collegians had cast off many of the British concepts of amateurism by the early 1900s, including competing against professionals, charging money at the gate, paying for food at the training table, paying for tutors, recruiting athletes, and hiring professional coaches.[32] As Francis A. March of Lafayette College stated, opposition to summer baseball was a borrowed affectation, "a bit of snobbishness from across the water, and totally opposed to the American theory of equality."[33] Because there was no unanimity about summer baseball in individual institutions and in conferences, players continued to participate during the summer, often earning money for their efforts. The NCAA never got a handle on summer baseball, but it continued to be a major point of reform on the national level.

By the time of World War I, the NCAA had been in existence for about a decade, and it was still the voice of athletic reform without legislative power. By then, a number of athletic conferences, usually on a regional basis, had been established, where legislation could be successful in directing individual colleges to follow collective rules and regulations. Prior to the creation of the NCAA, a number of single-sport conferences had been organized by students in the East and were spreading West and South. By the 1890s, multisport conferences became more common outside the East, some originated by students but a number of others by faculty. In 1894, the Southern Intercollegiate Athletic Association was the first noteworthy conference to be organized by faculty, initiated by a reform-minded medical doctor from Vanderbilt, William Dudley. It consisted of other important institutions, including the Agricultural and Mechanical College of Alabama (Auburn), University of Alabama, Georgia Tech Institute, University of South Carolina, and the University of the South. Eventually most of these institutions formed the heart of the Southern Conference in 1921 and the Southeastern Conference in 1932. The Southern Intercollegiate Athletic Association was soon followed by the Intercollegiate Conference of Faculty Representatives (Big Ten) in 1895, and it almost immediately became the leading conference in America. Others, often based on the leadership of the Big Ten, followed, including the Northwest Conference (1904), Missouri Valley Intercollegiate Athletic Association (1907), Rocky Mountain Faculty Athletic Conference (1909), Middle Atlantic Conference (1912), Inter-Normal Athletic Conference of Wisconsin (1913), Southwest Athletic Conference (1914), Minnesota-Dakota Athletic Conference (ca. 1915), and Pacific Coast Intercollegiate Athletic Conference (1915).[34] Conferences were the locus of reform if it were to be successful, setting standards of amateurism, freshman ineligibility, one-year residency rules, limits on training tables, length of seasons, and a variety of eligibility standards.

The NCAA continued to foster reform into the early years of World War I, before the United States was involved in the European battle. Just months prior to the 1917 U.S. declaration of war, the NCAA consisted of eighty-three individual colleges and universities, including every member school of the Old Rules Committee, which at first were reluctant to join, and all institutions of the Big Ten. The sixty-two member institutions that had delegates continued to discuss ways in which schools and conferences could create amateur sports and restrain commercialism, though one frustrated member admitted that it was still not possible to "induce institutions to adopt standards" of the NCAA. Another, on a more promising note, said that the NCAA was the "first organization . . . to attempt the direction in a large way of extra curricula activities for moral ends."[35] The NCAA was to a number of its representatives a moral force for good, and if it could influence conferences and individual institutions to reform athletics for the good of higher education, it could be considered a success. Whether in the long run that could be accomplished as a debating society could be questioned. In fact, a longtime representative of the NCAA, Amos Alonzo Stagg, thought that a national study was needed to investigate athletics from a moral standpoint. Stagg's motion to petition a foundation to do the study was passed, but not for another decade did action occur.[36] By then, intercollegiate athletics, especially football, was at a new level of commercialism and professionalism.

7

The 1920s and the Carnegie Report on College Athletics

Following America's entry into World War I, athletics in colleges had been reduced because of the war effort, but after the armistice there was a burst of sporting activity in the nation generally and most notably in intercollegiate athletics. In the colleges this included conducting the first national championships, increasing the hiring of professional coaches, intensifying the recruitment of athletes, and building massive arenas and stadiums. Progressive reform in America, at its height in the decade and a half prior to World War I, mostly collapsed with America's involvement in the war effort. Reform in intercollegiate sport also took a back seat, raising the ire of those who looked at college athletics as being out of balance with the goals of higher education. There were those, though, who kept alive a reform agenda, including a number of faculty members who dominated the proceedings during first few decades of the National Collegiate Athletic Association (NCAA). By the end of the 1920s golden age of sport, the Carnegie Foundation for the Advancement of Teaching, upon the recommendation of the NCAA, concluded a three-year study of college athletics, producing a 350-page document condemning the professionalized and commercialized athletics found across the country. The 1929 Carnegie Report on *American College Athletics* is often considered the most significant historical reform document in intercollegiate athletics.[1]

When the U.S. entered World War I in April 1917, West Point's Palmer Pierce, the president of the NCAA, asked President Woodrow Wilson and Secretary of War Newton D. Baker if continuing intercollegiate athletics was in keeping with the war aims of the Wilson administration. Wilson assured the nation that college and school sports would contribute to the national defense, and Secretary Baker said "there are not enough star athletes in the colleges to fill our armies." In response, the NCAA, in a special convention, resolved that athletics should be continued and even expanded to include more students. However, the reform-minded NCAA members made the war resolution into a reform document, calling for freshman ineligibility, elimination of training tables, professional coaching pay reduction, preseason practice elimination, and no lowering of eligibility standards for participation.[2] The faculty members of the NCAA hoped the war emergency would bring about reforms that previously had not been brought to fruition. None of the called-for reforms had much impact, but the war depleted the number of men available to participate in athletics, and the number of colleges dropping intercollegiate sports or reducing the emphasis on them was noticeable until after the armistice of 1918.

There were plenty of NCAA representatives, such as Frank Nicolson, the secretary-treasurer of the NCAA, who desired to use the present war moment "to place college athletics on a more sensible plane after the war."[3] Yet many of those associated with athletics had major concerns about the very people who were represented at the NCAA. The financial officer of the Harvard Athletic Association, Fred Moore, was one of them. Less than two weeks after the armistice ending the war, he wrote fearfully that the "radical reformers should not control in athletics any more than in government," hoping that a "sane and sensible course may be determined by Harvard, Yale, and Princeton, and if possible by the National Collegiate [Athletic] Association."[4] What Moore wanted was for Harvard and other big-time schools to continue the pragmatic commercialized and professionalized system that had been developed by the eastern elite for the past half century, not the pure and idealistic amateur model desired by a number of faculty representatives in the NCAA. Reform to achieve an amateur, noncommercial model, which never existed in American intercollegiate sport, was problematic at best, if not unreachable. The physical director at Brown University, F. W. Marvel, stated most clearly the dilemma of amateur-commercial sport: "We are told by the college officials that we must conduct our sports and play along amateur lines, but we must finance them along lines that are purely commercial and professional."[5] College administrators were unwilling or unable to finance sports, intercollegiate or intramural, by making them part of the overall institutional budget. Thus a commercial base was required to enable athletics to exist. The dilemmatic question, though simplistic, could be stated: How can amateur sports be achieved if one must pay highly for a professional coach who can bring in outstanding athletes and turn out winners to bring spectators into the stands to pay for the cost of teams? It wasn't possible then, and it wasn't possible in the next century.

Nevertheless, the NCAA recommended policies to make athletics more amenable to the goals of higher education just as the revival of sport following the war led to more intense commercialization and professionalism by the individual colleges. The lull in athletic competition for the year and a half that the United States was at war was replaced by a renewed intensity almost as soon as military veterans began returning home. Shortly after the war, there were complaints of recruitment and payment of players, tramp or transfer students, evasion of eligibility rules, summer baseball, training tables, lengthening of schedules, professional coaches, and crass commercialism. James Babbitt of Haverford College and a member of the Football Rules Committee believed "the general spirit among the colleges is not to conform to the advice of the Association."[6] A 1920 NCAA survey of all members indicated that "athletic standards have been growing steadily worse throughout the country since the war."[7] Most of the complaints were for violations of the spirit of amateurism. The NCAA's definition of an amateur, first placed in the constitution and bylaws in 1916, did not appear to produce amateur results: "An amateur athlete is one who participates in competitive physical sports only for the pleasure, and the physical, mental, moral, and social benefits directly derived therefrom."[8]

In an effort to curb athletic excesses, the NCAA produced nine fundamental principles that it urged member institutions and conferences to adopt. These 1922 principles included: (1) strict adherence to the NCAA's definition of amateurism; (2) organization of conferences to adopt rules; (3) adoption of the freshman ineligibility rule; (4) three years of eligibility; (5) opposition to athlete migrants; (6) no graduate participation; (7) participation only on the institutional team, even during vacations; (8) suppression of betting by the institution; and (9) "absolute faculty control." To gain acceptance, the NCAA asked for each NCAA district representative to visit all colleges in his district to advocate for these principles.[9] The two principles that were never instituted, except in name, were the upholding of amateurism and faculty control. While the concept of amateurism had been universally accepted by colleges and conferences, it had nearly universally been rejected in practice. Relative to faculty control, even with conferences such as the Big Ten being run by faculty representatives, the wishes of faculty could easily be trumped by presidents and governing boards, and they often were when important issues arose. To the credit of the NCAA representatives, more conferences were formed and most eventually eliminated graduate students while limiting freshman and migrant athletes (transfers) from immediate participation.

While the NCAA attempted reform through its principles, it promoted its first national competition by sponsoring a national championship in track and field in 1921. Amos Alonzo Stagg, the University of Chicago's representative to the NCAA and football and track coach at Chicago, organized the meet, held on Chicago's Stagg Field. It could be considered a success from several standpoints. Nearly half of the 102 NCAA member institutions were represented at the June competition with thirty-one of the forty-five teams gaining points, including institutions from all sections of the nation. One athlete, Earl Thomson of Dartmouth, tied a world record in the 120-yard high hurdles at 14.4 seconds even in wet conditions, one of fifteen events contested. The NCAA was pleased that the profits from the national championship paid for two-thirds of all travel expenses of the teams involved.[10] Track and field was the first of a number of championships sponsored by the NCAA, though none would be nearly as important as the national basketball championship first contested in 1939.[11] Only later did the commercial aspects of NCAA championships become a dominating factor in its sponsorship—and then only in men's basketball.

Far more important to the commercialization of college athletics than the promotion of national championships was the building of giant stadiums in the 1920s. Here was a situation the NCAA representatives did not try to reform. Though the stadium-building frenzy of the 1920s may have helped the decade to be identified as the golden age of sport, stadiums were the product of more than a half century of big-time athletics in American universities. Stadiums, to seat the increasing number of spectators who wanted to see the games, did not create the emphasis on commercialized college football; rather they were the logical result of student, alumni, and general public interest in the phenomenon. The largest buildings on college campuses, stadiums, were icons representing what universities recognized were important to their image building as institutions of higher learning—competing among themselves for honor and emulation.

It could be claimed that the origin of the intercollegiate stadium began with the first Harvard-Yale football game in 1875, more than a quarter century before Harvard constructed its stadium. It was the freshman class at Cambridge, Massachusetts, who saw this game and a generation later contributed the money needed to build the first reinforced-concrete stadium in history. The Harvard Class of 1879 saw the Crimson overwhelmingly defeat the blue-shirt-clad Yale team, four goals and four touchdowns to nothing in the new game of rugby, soon to be adopted and transformed into the American brand of football by colleges across the nation. Within a year, an Intercollegiate Football Association was created and the annual Thanksgiving Day game was born. In 1903, the Harvard Class of 1879 contributed a munificent $100,000 toward the new stadium.[12] Once constructed, the Greek-columned stadium was a marvel, but also a symbol of what to some was wrong with college athletics. "Harvard stadium," muckraker Henry Needham wrote in 1905, "stands before the college world today as a glorification of the gate money, the evil side of athletics."[13] Just over a decade later, Princeton and Yale built their large stadiums, with Yale's being 30 percent larger than the ancient Roman Colosseum and seating 70,000. Only World War I slowed the rush of colleges to imitate the Harvard, Yale, and Princeton stadium trinity.

The emulation of Harvard, Yale, and Princeton stadiums came to fruition in the 1920s. The Midwest and the Far West led the post–World War era in stadium building. By naming a number of the structures memorial stadiums to honor the war dead, football was tied to patriotism and in the process was important in helping to gain support and financing of the iconic structures.[14] Every member of the Big Ten Conference built a stadium during the golden age of sport. Ohio State was the first with a 61,000-seat stadium in 1922, temporarily expanded to 75,000 for the Michigan game. In short order, Illinois, Minnesota, Chicago, Northwestern, Michigan, and Iowa constructed stadiums holding 50,000 or more, while Purdue, Wisconsin, and Indiana put up new facilities of lesser size. Before the decade closed, Big Ten institutions could house more than a half-million spectators on any fall afternoon. On the West Coast, the two leading institutions, California and Stanford, had just reestablished playing American football after a decade-long ban following the 1905 football crisis. After hosting overflow crowds for the 1919 and 1920 games, Stanford and California agreed to build 60,000-seat stadiums.[15] In a rush to completion, Stanford built its stadium in less than five months, and in its first game against California brought in enough money to pay for the $200,000 structure.[16] Within a few years, Stanford could easily finance the stadium's expansion to nearly 90,000 seats, the largest stadium of any college. By 1930, there were seventy-four concrete stadiums in the United States, seven with seating capacities over 70,000.[17] Commercialization of football was rampant across the nation.

If commercialism was best seen in the construction of stadiums, professionalism was highlighted by the hiring of professional coaches in football, which helped produce winning teams to fill the stadiums. At war's end, the chairman of the Stanford athletic committee, Frank Angell, may have made the most derogatory statement about the professional coach when he stated that he "is by all odds the most sinister figure in amateur athletics."[18] However, the pro coach in colleges had a long history. Hiring professional coaches went back to the time of the American Civil War, when Yale students engaged William Wood as the first college coaching professional in a successful effort to beat Harvard in crew.[19] The hiring of professionals was unusual for the next generation because most colleges brought back graduates to coach, who, whether paid or not, were considered amateur coaches. Nevertheless, in the next couple decades, professionals were also employed in baseball, track and field, and football. By the turn of the century, football coaches in the East began to dominate the intercollegiate scene with pay equivalent to the highest-paid individuals in some universities. Columbia hired an ex-Yale athlete, George Sanford, paying him $5,000, more than double the salaries of college professors, while twenty-six-year-old Bill Reid at Harvard, with his $7,000 salary, was paid nearly as much as that of the longtime president, Charles W. Eliot.[20] The pro coach was beginning to appear in all regions to the South and West. An itinerant coach, such as John Heisman or Fielding H. Yost, would move quickly from place to place to the highest bidder in the early 1900s. John Heisman, whose name is attached to the Heisman Trophy, began at Oberlin in 1892 and moved to Akron, Auburn, Clemson, Georgia Tech, the University of Pennsylvania, Washington and Jefferson, and concluded his career at Rice with a salary of $12,000. At Georgia Tech, his best-known affiliation, his 1903 contract called for $2,250 plus 30 percent of the gate receipts after expenses.[21] Fielding H. Yost coached at Ohio Wesleyan in 1897, moving to Nebraska, Kansas, and Stanford before taking a long-term position at the University of Michigan in 1901, where he began at $2,000 plus living expenses.[22] So there was nothing new in the 1920s in paying dearly for the professional coach who could turn out winners.

What was peculiar to the 1920s was the expansion of professional coaches and the extraordinary efforts used to secure highly successful coaches to the

institutions most interested or most capable of affording the high-priced professionals. One might note Knute Rockne of Notre Dame, for he entertained offers
from a number of institutions, including the University of Iowa, the University of
Southern California, and Columbia University. In 1924, after an undefeated Notre
Dame season, Rockne signed a three-year, $8,000-a-year contract at Iowa, only to
renege and sign a ten-year, $100,000 contract to stay at Notre Dame. Rockne had
been angered by the Notre Dame Athletic Committee's decision to tighten one of
its eligibility standards that stated: "No student who has not already competed
in inter-collegiate athletics will be allowed to compete if he has any condition in
any previous [academic] work."[23] Two years later, after winning a total of seventy-
five games and losing six at Notre Dame, Columbia University offered a reported
three-year, $25,000-a-year position to Rockne if he would break the last eight
years of his contract with Notre Dame.[24] The motivation for Rockne, other than
money, was that the Notre Dame administration was dragging its feet in building
a stadium that Rockne had been campaigning for the previous four years. When
news of the contract was released to the press before Rockne could be freed from
his long-term contract, Rockne rejected Columbia's offer. In a bit of irony, the
longtime president of Columbia, Nicholas Murray Butler, who had banned football
at Columbia in 1905, stated that Rockne's hiring matter "is out of my line. It is a
matter for the students and alumni."[25] Rockne remained at Notre Dame until an
untimely airplane crash in 1931 ended his life.

Glenn "Pop" Warner was nearly as well known as Rockne in the 1920s. As a
wandering professional coach, he had tenures at Georgia ($340 for the season),
Cornell, Carlisle Indian School (where he coached the great Jim Thorpe), Pittsburgh, Stanford, and Temple. Warner's Stanford contract was probably the first to
offer a bonus if his team was successful and played in a postseason game. In the
twenty-first century, bonuses are common for about a dozen categories of success, such as finishing in the top twenty in a national poll or in achieving a 65
percent graduation rate. In 1922, Warner was invited to coach at Stanford while
he was under contract with the University of Pittsburgh, and Pittsburgh officials
would not release him from the two years left on his contract. The chief Stanford
negotiator was the cheerleading president, Ray Lyman Wilbur. He suggested to
Warner that he become the Stanford coach two years later, after the contract had
been satisfied. In the meantime, Warner would become Stanford's "advisory" football coach with a salary and expenses of $5,500, principally for coaching spring
practice. Beginning in 1924, the salary would be raised to $7,500 (the highest
salary of any Stanford professor), with $2,500 for expenses and, significantly, an

additional $2,500 if his team went to the Pasadena Rose Bowl.[26] Thus the bowl bonus was born, with nary a voice of protest, for the president kept the contract secret. Here again, a president was a sport promoter, not a reformer.

If there was any successful reform relative to professional coaching, it came about at the hands of the Big Three—Harvard, Yale, and Princeton—in 1925. From the time that Bill Reid received $7,000 for coaching football at Harvard in 1905 and 1906, to the $15,000 salary Tad Jones received at Yale in the early 1920s, there was continual upward pressure on football coaching salaries.[27] The Harvard coach, Robert Fisher, was paid $7,000, and Harvard authorities wanted to equalize the pay "to compete on even terms with Yale," its chief competitor. Pressure was coming from the Harvard Football Graduate Advisory Committee to purchase a better and more expensive football staff to keep up with Yale, asking that a new coach be paid $10,000. The Harvard Athletic Committee, however, wanted to limit coaches to graduates of the institution, thus helping to preserve amateur athletics.[28] When Harvard President A. Lawrence Lowell opposed paying the football coach more than the $8,000 full professors were receiving, a meeting was called between the three chairmen of the athletic committees at Harvard, Yale, and Princeton. The three, not considering any antitrust implications, agreed to limit football salary budgets to no more than $22,500 beginning in 1926, much less than Yale's $39,000 and more than Harvard's $18,500 in 1924. More to the point, the head coaching salaries for Harvard and Yale were not to exceed $10,000 in 1925, $9,000 in 1926, and $8,000 after 1927, with no bonuses from the alumni.[29] Because of a long-term contract for Princeton's coach, Bill Roper, Princeton was exempt from the agreement until a new contract was written. This kind of salary reform did not help the Big Three to remain as the leaders of football in America, but it presaged the slow decline of eastern football in the 1930s and 1940s. There was plenty of criticism of the professional coach in college sport, even those of the restricted coaches at the elite Big Three. Wrote one critic: "The incubus of commercialized athletics can not be shaken off until we throw out of our educational system all of the extravagantly paid professional coaches." Writing in *Science,* E. G. Makin complained in 1922 that "for a fraction of a year of work we pay a football coach three or four times as much as an able and experienced professor in any other department will receive."[30]

As the cries for reform grew in the early 1920s, Wesleyan University's Edgar Fauver suggested that a large foundation, such as the Rockefeller Foundation or the Carnegie Foundation for the Advancement of Teaching, do a thorough study to assess the status of amateurism and professionalism in intercollegiate athletics. He wanted facts, not sentiment, on which future college athletics could be conducted.[31] He looked forward to a well-researched reform document that would lead colleges to major changes. Actually, the Carnegie Foundation Executive Committee had brought up the idea of a national study in 1921, but the Carnegie Board only suggested possible "action in the future."[32] In 1925, the Carnegie Foundation asked a staff member, Howard Savage, to write a preliminary report on college athletics before being sent to England to look especially at the Oxford and Cambridge athletic programs. However, pursuing the model of Oxford and Cambridge amateur athletics was not intriguing to American universities, which had rejected the Oxbridge model of student-run amateur sports more than a half century before. For instance, John Bascom, a professor at Williams College in 1859, criticized the Amherst team that beat Williams in the first college baseball game, because Amherst "had taken the game from the regime of sport and carried it into the region of exact and laborious discipline."[33] College sport continued to get more workmanlike than sportsmanlike after that.

In January 1926, the Carnegie Foundation for the Advancement of Teaching agreed to finance a study of college athletics, less than two months after Harold "Red" Grange signed the most lucrative contract ever given to a college athlete to play professional sports. Grange, immediately after playing his last football game for the University of Illinois, as the most visible player in America for the previous three years, agreed to a contract with an agent, Charles "Cash and Carry" Pyle. Grange's agent had made arrangements with a professional football team, the Chicago Bears, to split the gate receipts with Grange. The team would go on an extended tour, using the celebrity of Grange as the Bears played teams from the Midwest and East and eventually in the South and West. Grange felt confident that his amateur football playing at Illinois would lead to at least $100,000 after he turned pro.[34] For an athlete to make more money playing than professional college coaches received for having directed the athletes was unheard of at the time. The condemnation of "amateur" Grange going professional was likely the most highly criticized action in intercollegiate history. However, the hypocrisy of a professional coach criticizing a professional athlete was evidently not foremost on the mind of Grange's college coach, Bob Zuppke, who berated Grange at the annual football banquet concluding the season.[35] Yet the amateur ethic and the condemnation of professionalism and commercialism were so strong among the reform minded, that action was deemed necessary.[36] Others in the Big Ten backed Zuppke, and in early December 1925 the Big Ten voted to ban any professional player from coaching or officiating in the conference. So, too, did the Missouri Valley Conference and the Southern Conference.[37] Later that month, the American Football Coaches Association (AFCA), consisting mostly of professional college coaches, banned from membership any person engaged in any professional football capacity while prohibiting AFCA members from selecting all-star or all-American football teams, reasoning that more all-Americans, such as Grange, might turn professional. Opposition to the pros was not new, for at the original meeting in 1921, the professional college coaches resolved that "professional football is detrimental to the best interest of American football and American youth."[38] The NCAA took a stance in 1925 following Grange's professional debut by recommending that members of the AFCA should not employ anyone who has ever been "connected in any capacity with professional football."[39] It may only have been a coincidence that the Carnegie Foundation took up the reform cudgel directly after the Grange signing, but it was not coincidence that the Foundation knew what its results would be before the three-year study began. Amateurism would be the goal through the exposure of professionalism and commercialism.

The Carnegie Foundation for the Advancement of Teaching was headed by Henry S. Pritchett, former president of the Massachusetts Institute of Technology and an educational elitist who condemned colleges for allowing nonintellectual activities to garner the interests of college students. Pritchett had been head of the Carnegie Foundation when it carried out its famous study by Abraham Flexner to help reform medical education in 1910. Asked numerous times to conduct a study of college athletics, first in 1916, Pritchett and the Carnegie Foundation finally agreed in early 1926. Yet Pritchett quite well knew what the study would find and what it would report well before it was conducted. In his annual Carnegie Report for 1923, he wrote: "Athletics, in large measure professional in its methods and organization, fills a larger place in the eyes of students and even of the public than any other one interest." To Pritchett, "the paid coach, the professional organization of the college athletics, the demoralization of students by participation in the use of extravagant sums of money, constitute a reproach of American colleges and to those who govern them."[40] When the study, headed by Howard Savage, was just underway, Pritchett proclaimed: "Hitherto, athletics has absorbed the college; it is time for the college to absorb athletics."[41]

It was not surprising, then, that when the study was released on October 24, 1929, as the U.S. stock market collapsed, Pritchett's ringing preface would dominate: "The paid coach, the gate receipts, the special training tables, the costly sweaters and extensive journeys in special Pullman cars, the recruiting from the high school, the demoralizing publicity showered on the players, the devotion of an undue proportion of time to training, the devices for putting a desirable athlete, but a weak scholar, across the hurdles of the examinations—these ought to stop."[42]

The study team, led by Howard J. Savage, visited more than a hundred U.S. and Canadian collegiate institutions, including seventy-two private and forty public colleges (and ten secondary schools), after it was found that questionnaires sent to colleges were considered untrustworthy. Yet they trusted the interviews that raised questions about recruiting by institutions and alumni, part-time employment and subsidies for athletes, provision for professional tutoring of athletes, the degree of faculty or alumni control of athletics, the salaries and hiring practices of coaches, and athletic slush funds. Those institutions that were honest in their answers were lampooned in the final document, while those that either lied or concealed data were let off generally unscathed.

The 350-page document, *American College Athletics,* attacked current practices, condemning, more than anything, rampant commercialism found in college athletics. It criticized recruiting and subsidization, the hiring of professional coaches, the abandonment of amateurism, and the lack of student involvement in decision making. Calling for more student involvement, it criticized the NCAA for specifically eliminating any student participation in the organization. "From a point of view of education," the report noted, "the most regrettable aspect of the control of athletics in the United States to-day is the meagerness of the responsibility that is entrusted to the undergraduate."[43] Students, who alone had initiated intercollegiate athletics, the report lamented, were now nearly totally eliminated from leadership roles. Students were left to compete for the glory and the commercial interests of their institutions.

One lengthy chapter was devoted to the coaches. It agreed in part with the English don who said, "[T]he paid coach is at the bottom of all difficulties in American college athletics." However, the authors of the report believed an emphasis on being the best required professionals to do the coaching. "Doubtless," the authors stated, "at an ideal university, professional coaching would find no place," but they noted, "it would be indeed a courageous college that abolished the paid coach."[44] The data were revealing, for coaches at both small and large colleges were paid more than the full professors. Surprisingly, coaches at small colleges were paid more relative to full professor salaries than were coaches at the larger schools, though the disparity was only slight. The highest-paid football coach of small colleges ($8,000) was paid $2,000 more than the highest-paid professor. The average small-college coach made $4,163. At the large colleges, the highest-paid coach ($14,000) was also paid $2,000 more than the highest-paid professor, while the average coach made $6,926.[45] Thus at both small and large colleges, the head coaches were considered more valuable from a salary standpoint than full professors. The law of supply and demand, the report noted, favored the football coach.

Though the professional coach may have exacerbated the problems in need of reform, the major question of amateurism in all its forms would have existed with or without the professional coach. Recruiting and subsidization of athletes was far more important to the Carnegie Report researchers than questions surrounding the professional coaches. The payment of professionals to coach had more or less been rationalized by the Carnegie investigators, but not the payment of athletes for participation—a major evil. They found that nearly all institutions subsidized athletes in one form or another. Of the twenty-eight institutions reported inaccurately to have no subsidization, six big-time schools were included: Chicago, Cornell, Illinois, the U.S. Military Academy, Virginia, and Yale. Of those, only Virginia might have been clean.[46] The Carnegie Report showed the various kinds of subsidization, including outright athletic "scholarships," loans to athletes with dubious repayments, jobs for athletes within and outside the institutions, alumni gifts, training tables as subsidies, free tutors, complimentary tickets, and cash grants.[47] The report concluded naively: "The man who is most likely to succeed in uprooting the evils of recruiting and subsidizing is the college president."[48] It hadn't worked in the first half century, and it was not likely to be successful in the foreseeable future.

The Carnegie Report on *American College Athletics,* for all its condemnations of commercialized and professionalized sports, for all its numerous recommendations for reform, and for all its biased faults would remain the reform document most referred to throughout the twentieth century and into the next. Nevertheless, the Carnegie Report did little to change the direction taken by intercollegiate athletics. While a few institutions were influenced to get out of big-time athletics, most major institutions continued to promote athletics by recruiting the best athletes, paying highly for professional coaching, trying to fill giant stadiums and arenas, and reaping whatever prestige they could garner from winning athletic teams. Yet reformers would make attempts to change the direction of intercollegiate athletics following many of the revelations found in this key intercollegiate reform document.

8

Individual Presidential Reform
Gates, Hutchins, and Bowman

Though college presidents for eight decades had generally been unsuccessful in effecting reform that would reduce commercialism and professionalism in intercollegiate sport, some uncommon presidents attempted to do so at their own institutions. After all, with the prestige of the Carnegie Foundation for the Advancement of Teaching advocating presidential direction in reform, it was not illogical for several brave presidents to do so, including Thomas S. Gates at the University of Pennsylvania, Robert Maynard Hutchins at the University of Chicago, and John Bowman at the University of Pittsburgh. While the 1929 Carnegie Report gave some hope to the few reformers, critics among the colleges who violated amateur ideals attempted to discredit the report. Because the Carnegie Report named individual colleges for their misdeeds, a number of those associated with colleges, including presidents, athletic officials, alumni, faculty, and students, protested the results.

The Carnegie investigators had "no intention to be fair and accurate," stated Ralph Aigler, a law professor and chair of the University of Michigan Board of Athletic Control. He was angered that a Carnegie investigator, Harold Bentley, had secretly removed letters from Coach Fielding H. Yost's files, and when asked to return them, the head of the Carnegie investigation, Howard Savage, only returned photostatic copies of the originals.[1] Norman Taber, head of the Brown Athletic Council, reacted, stating the report is "in part false and in toto . . . misleading." Penn State's Hugo Bezdek, president of the National Football Coaches Association, warned that the Carnegie Report "should not be taken too seriously." This was evidently what many athletic leaders thought about the report. The Associated Press queried faculty advisors, athletic directors, and publicity directors in the South about a year after the report's release and found little impact on rabid southern fans, even as the Great Depression was having its negative effect on the commercial side of sport. The *New York Times* headlined the AP findings "Carnegie Report Called Fruitless."[2] Reformers, by their very nature, were fighting the status quo and, in this case, not winning.

College presidents were divided on the importance of the Carnegie Report, with a number of university heads rejecting the findings at their own institutions, although often acknowledging the problems existing in other colleges. Yale had come through the investigation unscathed, surprisingly, and its president, only shortly after the report was released, gave a talk in which he joked that he would be happy to swap the purity credited to Yale by the report "for a couple of good running backs or a pair of great ends."[3] Many of the other presidents indicated that they would strive to take greater control of athletics, generally reducing the role of alumni, and place them under university control. A few even accomplished this. The most visible of the reformers who quickly made significant reforms was Thomas S. Gates, the new president of the University of Pennsylvania.

Thomas Gates, a lawyer, partner with the banking firm J. P. Morgan, and longtime member of the Penn Board of Trustees, was elected president of the University of Pennsylvania only months after the Carnegie Report was released and during a period at Penn in which athletics were in turmoil. Gates had, a few years earlier, been on a committee of the Penn trustees to consider the relationship of intercollegiate athletics to intramurals and physical education.[4] Now, with the backing of the trustees, he was secure in his position to achieve reform. Not only had the trustees elected one of their own, but he agreed to the presidency with no salary; he was beholden to no one, unusual for any college president. Almost as soon as he took office, he formed a small committee to recommend athletic policy changes. This committee of former Penn athletes visited a number of universities, including California, Stanford, and Southern California on the West Coast and Notre Dame, Michigan, and Wisconsin in the Midwest, to see how they controlled athletics.[5] At the same time, the alumni of the University of Pennsylvania formed a committee on athletics. This group, surprisingly, also wanted to reform Penn athletics. Football, the alumni group charged, had become a "contest between professional coaches and their systems," and the game threatened "to be a racket" for the financial advantage of the coaches.[6] Together, the two groups sought reform at Penn, in line with President Gates's belief that athletics would not "interfere with the prosecution of normal student life and the enjoyment that comes from wise and proper participation in sports of all kinds."[7]

Once he had heard from the committees of alumni, Gates proceeded to create a policy statement, releasing it in early 1931, about a half year after assuming the presidency. The Gates Plan was born. He emphasized that the new policy would favor the well-being of the students rather than the interests of the coaches. Furthermore, participation in sports would be made available to a greater number of students—a policy of athletics for all. In order to accomplish his reform, he abolished the controlling athletic committee, formed of alumni, students, and faculty, and created a new Department for Health, Physical Education, and Athletics under faculty control and responsible to the president. Coaches would be hired as faculty members and housed in Physical Education and paid salaries similar to those who taught philosophy or physics, unlike the previous football coach, who had a three-year salary of $40,500, more than what many college presidents were paid.[8] Gates said that if he could not find a coach for a professor's salary, he would then raise the salaries of the entire faculty, "which after all," he noted, "would not be the worst thing in the world."[9]

Specifically, Gates's reform efforts included eliminating athletic dorms and the free training table for athletes, abolishing spring football practice and early pre-season fall practice, doing away with "rest" trips for athletes at resorts, controlling financial assistance to athletes by the university scholarship committee, and competing against natural rivals. Students, he said, would be seated at the center of the stadium, and students would be part of an advisory board consisting of faculty and alumni. Football, he emphasized, would not be given special treatment and concessions, and the entire athletic budget would be brought under general university control.[10]

For Pennsylvania and especially a number of eastern institutions, this was considered a radical reform. Alumni since the late 1800s had often controlled the hiring of coaches and the budgets of athletic teams. When Dr. E. Leroy Mercer became the dean of the Department of Health, Physical Education, and Athletics at Penn, moving from Swarthmore College to take charge of the new program, he indicated why this reform was so difficult and hinted why action by other colleges would be arduous: "The East may find itself more behind in faculty control of athletics because of the greater tradition that must be overcome. Powerful and interested alumni bodies that are accustomed to the old ideas are always difficult to root. Naturally Pennsylvania finds it difficult to change its entire policy. That is one reason why President Gates had to take such drastic action."[11] Nevertheless, President Gates accomplished the reform at Pennsylvania in record time.

Satisfied that his new reform would be successful at Penn, Gates moved to push for reform at the national level. As a member of the Association of American Colleges, Gates became a national leader for reform of college athletics. The Association of American Colleges (AAC) was founded in 1915, reforming higher education by attempting to save liberal arts colleges.[12] In a way, it was similar to the founding of the National Collegiate Athletic Association (NCAA) as a reform organization to save college football. Neither group had any legislative or administrative power to enact change, but the AAC, like the NCAA, could be a moral leader for change. When the AAC created the Commission on College Athletics, Gates became its chairman. Not long after the Gates Plan was put into effect at the University of Pennsylvania, Gates presented a list of what he and the Commission on College Athletics considered essential points of athletic reform. There was to be no subsidizing, recruiting, or proselytizing athletes, with scholarship aid distributed impartially to all students based upon need; elimination of training tables and athletic dorms; coaches of faculty caliber given academic rank and pay; creation of an "athletics for all" climate in which physical education, athletics, and health services were under an academic head; a shortened football season with no preseason practice; trustees and presidents responsible for athletics and physical education, not the alumni; participation of natural rivals who have similar physical and mental powers and like ideals; and greater player control of their own athletic destiny, where athletics would cease to be drudgery.[13]

That the leadership of Gates and the AAC plan made little progress nationally can be attributed not only to the lack of power of any national organization to enact reform legislation, especially that emanating from liberal arts colleges, but also to no consensus on the need for reform. Neither the AAC nor the NCAA had legislative or enforcement authority. For example, unless forced by an agency with power, what college would eliminate the powers of the pro coach and return the game to the captain? What institution would take the lead in returning the game to the players? Probably only one that announced that winning was not important, and American colleges had made a choice of winning over other goals more than a half century before. Professional coaches had proved to be far more successful in turning out winners than had amateur coaches or captains. Indeed, recruited players with financial inducements were important in turning out winning teams and raising the prestige of both large and small institutions. In addition, turning athletics over to faculty control had been suspect since the 1880s, when faculties at institutions such as Harvard and Princeton put restrictions on athletics that not only students and alumni protested, but even presidents and governing boards began either putting limitations on faculty control or overruling faculty decisions.[14]

Two years after the AAC adopted the Gates Commission recommendations, the Pennsylvania president reported, inaccurately, "a growing resistance to the commercialization of athletics, and institutions who still find it to their interest to persist in it must look to a loss of prestige in the college world."[15] Like many presidents before and since, Gates was wrong in his assessment of college athletics and the presidential role in reform. Not only was his assessment wrong relative to most colleges in big-time sports, but even his own AAC soon voted down a resolution to appoint a commission to make "a comprehensive survey of the athletic situation" concerning subsidization of athletes, drinking at contests, and other "deplorable" phases of athletics.[16] The resolution rejection may have been influenced by an AAC report that alumni giving to colleges had increased in 1935 for the first time since the 1920s, and presidents did not want to negatively influence alumni giving by doing another investigation of the evils of athletics. "The only drawback to having a strong alumni body and interested wealthy alumni," stated the general manager of the University of Pennsylvania office of giving, "was in some instances alumni interference in college administration and college affairs."[17] He might have emphasized specifically interference in the administration of athletics.

The year 1936 was the last time the president-led AAC made a concerted effort to reform college athletics. It was also the last time that President Gates would take a leading role in athletic reform. The Gates Plan, however, would remain the guiding policy at the University of Pennsylvania until Harold Stassen took over leadership of the university in 1948. The young, ex-governor of Minnesota moved Penn into the big time with his policy of "Victory with Honor" while encouraging football powers, such as Notre Dame, to schedule games with Penn. With Stassen, the Gates Plan succumbed to outside forces and with it the death of Gates's reform ideas at the University of Pennsylvania.

Another 1930s reform effort was introduced to the Midwest by a leading institutional president, Robert Maynard Hutchins of the University of Chicago. Hutchins was the son of a college president and the youngest dean of a law school, Yale's, before becoming president of the University of Chicago in 1929. Chicago was already undergoing an educational reform to raise its academic standards before Hutchins ascended to the presidency. But Chicago had one of the greatest names in collegiate football history as its coach and athletic director, Amos Alonzo Stagg. Stagg had been football coach at Chicago for more than thirty-five years when Hutchins arrived. He was a power figure at Chicago, but his teams that had won a number of Big Ten championships had declined since capturing the championship in 1924, in part due to improved academic standards. Stagg was removed as coach in 1933 when he turned seventy years of age, but the team continued losing. From 1925 through 1938, Chicago lost fifty-four games to Big Ten teams and won only eleven times, less than one each year. Hutchins may have been plotting his reform by abolition, but he was slow to do so. In 1938, Hutchins penned his famous "Gate Receipts and Glory," published in the *Saturday Evening Post,* in which he stated that "young people who are more interested in their bodies than their minds, should not go to college" and certainly not to the University of Chicago. Besides, he did not believe that football was important to his institution's welfare, contrary to the thinking of most presidents. Let the less intellectual universities have their football, he stated, for "if football continues to move to the poorer colleges, the good ones may be saved."[18] The next year, 1939, however, brought down football at the University of Chicago.

The reform by abolition was due more to Chicago's disastrous season than to Hutchins. Chicago began the season by losing to a small liberal arts college in Wisconsin, Beloit. It was crushed 61–0 by Harvard and then lost its only three Big Ten games, 46–0 to Illinois, 61–0 to Ohio State, and 85–0 to Michigan. Unable to compete successfully in the Big Ten, Chicago could have chosen to leave the conference and compete with other schools closer to its ability level. However, playing schools with lesser academic reputations, such as Wabash, Butler, or Carroll College, would diminish Chicago's status as a premier university, according to Hutchins. "We do not like to be classed with Monmouth and Illinois Wesleyan," he stated to the Board of Trustees.[19] The only way out, Hutchins believed, was to drop football entirely. To this end, he campaigned vigorously among the members of the Board of Trustees during the fall of 1939 and even persuaded the influential Harold Swift, head of Swift and Company meatpacking in Chicago and head of Chicago's Board of Trustees for years. Swift was probably Chicago's greatest supporter of athletics, being a principal recruiter for the football team in the 1920s and 1930s and known for his "Swift's Premium Hams" recruits. As a trustee, Swift had once used his position by writing an earlier president to push for retaining the academic eligibility of the failing team captain.[20] Though the meatpacker had organized train trips to away games through the years, he decided not to take an active hand as the president of the Board of Trustees when President Hutchins moved toward persuading alumni and the Board of Trustees to eliminate football at Chicago and remove itself as a football member of the most prestigious conference, the Big Ten. Hutchins's argument was that Chicago would have to openly subsidize athletes and discontinue amateur sports or ban intercollegiate football. Knowing that there might be some strongly discontented and moneyed alumni, Hutchins wrote to his Board: "Since we cannot hope to win against our present competition and since we cannot profitably change our competition, only two courses are open to us: to subsidize players or to discontinue intercollegiate football. We cannot" he stated emphatically, "subsidize players or encourage our alumni to do so without . . . losing our self-respect."[21] The Board agreed with Hutchins and voted to ban the game in December at the close of the 1939 season.

Unlike President Gates at Pennsylvania, President Hutchins could not have carried out his reform at Chicago without first mollifying his governing board. Of principal importance was working with John Nuveen Jr., who was a successful stock broker, member of the Board of Trustees, and chair of the alumni council. Nuveen was convinced that banning football would not create a financial crisis at

Chicago—and it did not. Strategically releasing to the press a series of well-timed university gifts of about $8 million to the university around Christmastime, Nuveen was able to somewhat mute the criticism of the ban of football, and a major fund-raising campaign, though it came up short of expectations, was begun for the university. Trustee Swift, who only voted in a second vote to make the decision of the governing board unanimous, remarked: "Football as practiced in some of the Big Ten institutions has done much to undermine character and learning, which in my judgement it is the university's responsibility to foster."[22] A cheerleading trustee member had joined the reformers.

The University of Chicago had done what no other big-time athletic school had done since the football crisis of 1905–6: banned football for something other than financial reasons. It set the precedent for other institutions to follow, but none followed. Chicago and Hutchins became icons not for athletic reform, but more for athletic eccentricity and intellectual elitism. It was not that Hutchins and Chicago were more honest about big-time college athletics than were other presidents and institutions, for if Hutchins would have been more true to his principles it would not have taken ten years to make his move to remove football from Chicago's agenda. He had, like other Chicago presidents before him, gone to the football games and the football banquets. He had made appropriate comments about the greatness of Amos Alonzo Stagg and Chicago football. When the embarrassment of losing to traditional rival Michigan, 85–0, brought alumni and trustees to consider abandoning football, Hutchins was shrewd enough and articulate enough to bring the trustees to vote for the abandonment of football. To Hutchins, the university was for intellectual vitality, not athletic or other prowess. Chicago, he came to believe, did not need football gate receipts and glory. It needed intellectual vigor. By banning football, Chicago did not reform the game or change the nature of intercollegiate sport, except on the Chicago campus. Hutchins made no concerted effort, unlike President Gates at Pennsylvania earlier that decade or Chancellor Henry MacCracken of New York University had in the 1905–6 football crisis, to bring the Chicago "plan" to other institutions. However, he helped move the University of Chicago to a level of intellectual inquiry that few other institutions of higher education could match—and this was certainly true on the undergraduate level. Hutchins, more than anything else, was out of tune with higher education since World War I, for in the period following the war American college life, growing far more rapidly than the population, was dominated by its social life, including athletics and the prominence of football, not academic vigor.[23]

A third important reform effort in the 1930s, though generally forgotten, was made by the head of the University of Pittsburgh. Chancellor John Bowman was claimed to be the highest-paid college president, $35,000, when he challenged a most successful football program under the famed John Bain "Jock" Sutherland. Bowman had taught English at Columbia, was for a short time secretary of the Carnegie Foundation for the Advancement of Teaching in the early 1900s, and became president of the University of Iowa before leaving to become director of the American College of Surgeons. From there, he was elected in 1921 head of the University of Pittsburgh, an institution described by Upton Sinclair as "the only high school in the country that gives a [college] degree."[24] At the time, Glenn "Pop" Warner was the coach at Pitt, winning several consensus national championships before being hired away by Stanford University. Sutherland, who had played on several championship teams under Warner, succeeded Warner in 1924 and proceeded to produce four unbeaten teams and an overall 111–20–12 record in fifteen seasons at Pitt. Bowman was not opposed to winning football games, but he thought that Pitt was doing it in the wrong way, that was in a professional rather than amateur manner.

At about the same time that alumni and the athletic department were pushing successfully to construct a new stadium, costing more than $2 million, Chancellor Bowman had another dream: constructing the tallest academic building on any university campus in the world in a city that needed an academic icon. While the stadium was going up, Bowman was in the process of raising about $10 million for his project, a forty-two-story "Cathedral of Learning" that would eventually contain 600,000 square feet of space. Unlike many stadiums built in the 1920s, the one at Pittsburgh was not completely paid for by either contributions or gate receipts, and it eventually became a drag on finances at the university. To attempt to fill the nearly 70,000-seat stadium, which had few large crowds despite great records, Pitt scheduled contests with a number of the best football teams. To win and draw crowds, Pitt needed a number of quality players, who could not be attracted unless it was financially worth their while. The pay for Pitt football players probably exceeded most other colleges at the time. Francis Wallace, a journalist in the tradition of the muckrakers of the Progressive Era, chronicled the subsidization at Pitt from Sutherland's first year in 1924 to 1936. At first, players were paid monthly based upon their worth—up to $100 per month plus tuition and books. In the late 1920s, the payments were standardized at $50 per month, increasing to $65 per month for several years. During the depths of the Great Depression, the monthly payments were reduced to $40, but the subsidies were significant, and a number of players got married, catching the fancy of sportswriters as the "married men's team."[25] Following the undefeated 1936 campaign, Sutherland took his team to Pasadena, California, for the Rose Bowl and a 21–0 victory over the

University of Washington. This was great publicity for the University of Pittsburgh, but Sutherland's payment out of his own pocket to the players after the victory and other issues irritated the athletic director, who resigned shortly thereafter in a power struggle with Sutherland.[26]

With a new athletic director, Jimmy Hagan, Pitt changed its policy of player payment, this time requiring that the athlete work for his wages. This did not seem to greatly affect the players because the team was again undefeated in the 1937 season. With another Rose Bowl invitation, the players made demands upon the university before they would agree to participate. If the Congress of Industrial Organizations union could strike successfully during the Depression, the players figured they could do the same. They demanded that every member of the team be taken to Pasadena, not just those expected to play; that pocket money be increased to $200 per player; and that they receive a two-week vacation. They would not make the trip to the Rose Bowl unless the demands were met. In a 17–16 vote, the players voted not to go West. Internal turmoil in Pitt athletics, with players protesting, with the football coach and athletic director at odds, and with the Middle States Association questioning the accreditation of Pittsburgh, in part because of its athletic program, Chancellor Bowman finally decided to take action.[27]

The reform, named Code Bowman, was devised by the chancellor and adopted by the Board of Trustees, but not without a strong reaction from athletes and the alumni. Its two major planks were the elimination of athletic scholarships and the addition of academic requirements to remain athletically eligible. Bowman also irritated the Alumni Association's Athletic Council that ruled athletics and replaced it with the university-controlled Faculty Committee on Athletic Policy. With fewer recruits to fill the Pitt football team, and with a number of players declared ineligible because of academic deficits, the long-term prospect, if not the immediate result, was for inferior teams and losing records. The 1938 season began with a strike by the sophomore football players, who were required to work more than the juniors and seniors to pay for their tuition. The strong Pittsburgh letterman's club charged the university officials with "dishonesty and fraud."[28] The Alumni Association formed a committee to investigate athletics at Pitt, and its findings showed that the administration had failed to anticipate the effects Code Bowman would have on Pitt's athletics. At the season's end, Bowman spoke at the College Physical Education Association conference at the time the NCAA was meeting. In a talk called "Athletics in Student Life," and with Coach Jock Sutherland in the audience, Bowman called it "a sin to go to college to play a sport."[29] The chancellor was not about to dispense with his Code Bowman, and Jock Sutherland soon resigned, claiming that coaching at Pitt was "intolerable."

Students began a protest of Sutherland's resignation, but only about five hundred of them joined the strike that interrupted a number of classes in Bowman's Cathedral of Learning.[30] The Committee of the Trustees was formed to investigate the Bowman administration, later reporting that the resignation of Sutherland "was a distinct loss," the university lacked an adequate library and laboratories, and its public relations had deteriorated under Bowman. However, the committee recognized that Bowman had indeed raised $20 million for Pitt and enrollment had risen from 5,000 to 12,600.[31] Bowman stayed while the football coach left, but not without a lot of soul searching.

Chancellor Bowman was distraught over the whole athletic situation at Pitt with the unfavorable publicity, bad student attitudes, and terrible alumni relations, and he was ready to resign only days after he accepted Sutherland's resignation. Yet it was more than athletics and the backlash of accepting Sutherland's resignation that troubled him. Bowman had recently fired a popular historian, presumably because he was favorable to Franklin Roosevelt's New Deal, opposed by many of the rich men on the Board of Trustees. He had, only a few years before, required a loyalty oath from every student at Pitt. Bowman also opposed faculty tenure, something that nearly all the best universities across the country granted faculty members. Because of his opposition to tenure, the American Association of University Professors placed the University of Pittsburgh on a blacklist. In addition, the Pittsburgh library was so inadequate that the national scholastic Phi Beta Kappa honorary fraternity would not allow a chapter to exist on campus.[32]

Chancellor Bowman wanted to react strongly to the committee of the Board of Trustees, but he was advised by those closest to him as well as the president of the Carnegie Foundation for the Advancement of Teaching, Walter A. Jessup, to accept the recommended changes rather than to fight the Board. Jessup wisely told Bowman that "every college president he knew who started a fight with his board got into a mess."[33] Bowman did react rather strongly, but much less so than he might have done without advice. He had enough support from the trustees to continue in his role of leading the University of Pittsburgh. Code Bowman continued, and with the predicted results of the alumni and students. As the historian of the University of Pittsburgh has stated: "Attendance dropped off at Pitt games, gate receipts paid less of the interest on the stadium debt, and a drive was launched to persuade alumni investors to turn back their bonds as gifts."[34] Specifically, the football team became what Penn State had experienced a decade before when it gave up athletic scholarships: moribund. Pitt now could beat few big-time teams and began scheduling lower-ranked teams to try to be somewhat competitive. Pitt had a losing season in 1940, the first since 1912, and eight more years passed before it had a winning season. Pitt lost twenty-four straight games to Big Ten opponents following the resignation of Jock Sutherland and did not recover athletically from Code Bowman for three more decades.

Of the three presidential reformer plans, the Gates Plan and Code Bowman were unsuccessful in the long run because they were dropped by the University of Pennsylvania and the University of Pittsburgh, respectively, when they returned to big-time play in a highly professionalized and commercialized manner. In the short run, both the Gates Plan and Code Bowman turned out losers on the athletic field. Only the Hutchins ban was successful in the long run, for there were no scandals and no professionalization and commercialization of football at Chicago for the next seven decades, though Chicago did bring back intercollegiate football three decades after dropping it. Of the big-time universities, Hutchins's Chicago stands alone. Presidential reform by individual institutions, as shown by these three instances and a number of other attempts, has not proved effective in most cases. Individual reform, as opposed to collective reform, has proved to be nearly impossible. Collective reform by groups of colleges and universities has shown to be more successful, though the plan of the Southern Conference in the 1930s proved to be a disaster.

9

Presidential Conference Reform
The 1930s Graham Plan Failure

The three president-initiated institutional reforms could be considered failures, for none of the three had a lasting impact on reform at the regional or national level. President Frank Graham of the University of North Carolina, however, had plans to reform the Southern Conference, and later to take his reforms nationally, at the time university leaders Thomas S. Gates, Robert Maynard Hutchins, and John Bowman were carrying out their reform plans at Pennsylvania, Chicago, and Pittsburgh. One would not have expected a reform movement to arise in the South, where athletics were perhaps more important for the image of southern colleges than anywhere, but President Graham was an unusual individual. A North Carolinian by birth, Graham loved sports, especially baseball, but his lack of stature and strength limited his abilities, unlike his brother Archie, who played professional baseball. He was a leader in other ways: president of his class at the University of North Carolina, on the debate team, editor of the student newspaper, president of the athletic association, and even head cheerleader for athletics. Graham became a professor of history at North Carolina before being elected president in 1930. Unusual for a southerner in expressing his political liberalism, he favored the right to unionize, reduction of hours in the work week, workers' compensation laws, child labor laws, improved race relations, federal aid to education, and academic freedom.[1] He also wanted to reform athletics.

The year Graham was elected president of North Carolina, a famous educational reformer, Abraham Flexner, published an important book on the reform of higher education, *Universities: American, English, German.* Flexner's most influential work came two decades earlier, when he was asked by Henry Pritchett of the Carnegie Foundation for the Advancement of Teaching to conduct a study aimed at reforming medical schooling in North America. This 1910 Carnegie Report, unlike its unsuccessful athletic reform effort in 1929, was almost surely the catalyst for a major change in medical education across North America. When Flexner spoke on any educational issue, professionals listened. In 1930, when his book on universities of three major countries was published, *Universities: American, English, German,* it raised the ire of many who favored the status quo and energized those who supported reform to make American colleges more intellectually invigorating. Flexner was on the side of the educational elite, such as Robert Maynard Hutchins of the University of Chicago.[2] Flexner was highly critical of any institution that offered such courses as copyediting in journalism, clothing decoration in home economics, advertising layouts in business, poultry raising in agriculture, or gymnastics and dancing in physical education. Fluff courses, he might have called them.[3]

Right at that time, Flexner had been asked to create an institution to provide for advanced study for new and outstanding PhDs, who would be in contact with senior intellectuals, a proposition made possible with a $5 million grant by Louis Bamberger and his sister Caroline Bamberger Fuld. The result was the Institute for Advanced Study in Princeton, New Jersey, located adjacent to what Flexner believed was the best university in America: Princeton.[4] Flexner wanted a haven for scholars and scientists, and the Institute for Advanced Study provided support for postdoctoral fellows and senior scholars to do independent research and writing. Unlike colleges and universities in America, Flexner would have his intellectual center unencumbered by the distractions of a host of undergraduate extracurricular activities, including athletics. In his book, Flexner criticized American universities for many things, including athletics. He especially condemned the compensation of athletic coaches because "it pays better to be an athletic coach than to be a university professor" and complained that no university in America "has the courage to place athletics where everyone perfectly well knows they belong."[5] He gave a talk at the National Association of State Universities (NASU) soon after Graham took over as head of the University of North Carolina, and Graham was influenced by both Flexner and the Carnegie Report on *American College Athletics* that had been released the previous year. Graham, like the authors of the Carnegie Report, particularly believed that recruiting and subsidizing athletes were the greatest problems facing athletics and that presidents should lead in solving athletic problems.[6]

The NASU had been formed at the end of the nineteenth century to give greater visibility and prestige to state universities, but it was, early on, a kind of club of university presidents to debate problems common to them, not too dissimilar from the debating society for faculty representatives at the National Collegiate Athletic Association (NCAA).[7] The NASU decided after Flexner's talk to debate the place of athletics. By 1934, President Graham became chair of the Committee on Group Life of Students, where he could influence presidential concern for the place of athletics in the university. In 1935, using the strength of the Carnegie Report and the influence of Abraham Flexner as well as understanding the athletic policies of the Big Ten Conference and the Big Three of the Ivy institutions, Graham presented his committee's reform agenda to the NASU. The eleven-point athletic reform platform included the ending of aid to athletes based solely on their athletic ability, ineligibility of freshmen and athletes on scholastic probation, a ban on recruiting by the athletic staff, payment of coaches only by college authorities, certification of athletic budgets, and no postseason contests. Following Graham's presentation, the NASU asked members of each conference to discuss and approve the athletic standards.[8]

Before President Graham took his plan to the Southern Conference, opposition to Graham and his reform plan arose, particularly among students and alumni. The University of North Carolina Athletic Council, composed of alumni, students, and faculty, unanimously passed a resolution against the Graham Plan, for it prohibited alumni from providing financial aid to athletes as it had been doing for years.[9] North Carolina students, by more than 80 percent, favored alumni subsidization of athletes, and more than two-thirds favored athletes getting preferential treatment in scholarships.[10] The president of a North Carolina cotton mill believed that the prohibition of aid to athletes would damage the University of North Carolina. "Carolina will be unable to compete with any of the teams that would bring from the public widespread interest and bring to the University an athletic reputation," the cotton entrepreneur wrote Graham, "which is a tremendous force in our national life."[11] A friend told Graham outright that if his policy resulted in Carolina having a "third and fourth rate football team, when its competitors, such as Georgia and Tennessee, have first rate teams, the alumni are going to rise up in their wrath."[12] When a number of negative reactions to the Graham Plan reached the president's office, Graham asked Howard J. Savage, the principal author of the 1929 Carnegie Report, to write him a letter supporting the action. Graham had concluded that not all the presidents of the NASU, some in the Southern Conference, would back the new NASU regulations. "College presidents," Graham complained, "for this reason and that reason do not want to stand back of the proposed regulations." Savage replied that the proposed regulations "cut too deeply into entrenched practices to be adopted," but the fight should still be made. In addition, the reformer Savage noted in the negative that the Carnegie Foundation had decided to discontinue athletic studies.[13] Graham nevertheless plowed forth, though he recognized, even before taking his reform plan to the Southern Conference, that it had "produced an organized movement among our alumni to resist these regulations."[14]

President Graham moved quickly to take the reform package to his Southern Conference brethren. He had discussed his plan with his Board of Trustees, but apparently he had not received a confirmation by vote. Still, he had the support of his faculty and the NASU. In addition, the leaders of the NCAA were campaigning for a code for controlling the subsidizing and recruiting of athletes. That fall, the secretary of the NCAA, Frank Nicolson, sent a letter to all NCAA presidents asking them to join the movement to reduce the objectionable features of intercollegiate athletics, especially football.[15] Knowing there was a groundswell of support for change, and cognizant of opposition, Graham presented the athletic reform package to the Southern Conference, of which North Carolina was a member. The Southern Conference had its origins in the Southern Intercollegiate Athletic Association, an early conference formed in 1894. Larger southern schools withdrew and formed the Southern Conference in 1921, with a group of the strongest withdrawing in 1932 to form the football powerhouse Southeastern Conference. In spite of the withdrawals, the Southern Conference was left with formidable schools, including North Carolina, North Carolina State, Clemson, Duke, Maryland, South Carolina, Virginia, the Virginia Military Institute, Virginia Polytechnic Institute, and Washington and Lee. Graham made his initial presentation to the presidents of the conference institutions in late 1935, though those who opposed the reforms did not attend. President W. P. Few of Duke, one of the opponents, cautioned to "go slow on the Graham Plan proposal of December 12, 1935" for he thought other important conferences, such as the Big Ten, Pacific Coast, and Big 6 in the Midwest, should adopt the reforms, not just one southern conference.[16]

President Graham, however, was on a reform crusade, and at one point when he felt under attack he told his friend Josephus Daniels, U.S. Ambassador to Mexico, that "I am not going to yield one inch." He wanted overwhelming support, but the Graham Plan was accepted by the conference in early 1936 only by a close vote, 6–4, with Clemson, Duke, South Carolina, and the Virginia Military Institute opposed.[17] This was obviously not a clear conference mandate for reform, yet the early 1936 vote of presidents called for the measures to begin that fall. For the Southern Conference reforms to be successful, it was particularly unfortunate that the neighboring Southeastern Conference (SEC), which included Alabama, Auburn, Florida, Georgia, Georgia Tech, Kentucky, Louisiana State, Mississippi, Mississippi State, Sewanee, Tennessee, Tulane, and Vanderbilt, had just voted overwhelmingly to allow financial aid to athletes not to exceed expenses. Significantly, this was the first conference to openly allow financial aid for athletic prowess. Ironically, the SEC believed that its action was an important reform in that aid to athletes would now be open rather than sub rosa payments.[18] However, to many, the objection to paying athletes was probably the single most important issue in the reform, and the SEC had just legalized it. With only a slight majority of university presidents favoring the Southern Conference decision and with the SEC favoring open athletic scholarships, it was going to be difficult for the Southern Conference to accomplish its intended reform.

One might have anticipated some opposition to President Graham and the implementation of the Graham Plan in the Southern Conference. Several years before, when North Carolina's football coach, Chuck Collins, had completed another losing season, there were calls by the alumni to pay for a recognized coach, such as a chief rival, Duke, had in Wallace Wade. The idea of hiring someone like Coach Wade, who had a reported huge contract of $25,000 during the depths of the Great Depression, was anathema to President Graham. "We are not going to consider," stated Graham in 1933 after Duke beat North Carolina, "having any of the big-time football coaches here," just as a newspaper claimed a Tar Heel fan group might begin a campaign for Graham's ouster.[19] The alumni had other reasons to oppose the Graham Plan, for Graham had earlier announced that athletes would not be given preferential treatment in granting scholarships at North Carolina, though Graham said that he would not stand for "discrimination against athletes any more than we intend to stand for any discrimination in favor of athletes."[20] Alums across the state were not so sure.

Most criticism of the Southern Conference Graham Plan was aimed at its author, and most of the criticism came from the alumni, especially at the University of North Carolina. "This is the hottest wire that I ever got my hands on," confided

Graham to a supporter, the president of Yale, James R. Angell.[21] And it surely was. Alumni chapters throughout North Carolina condemned the Graham Plan. The High Point alumni group questioned the right of Graham to "commit the University to such a policy without consulting the trustees, alumni, and student body." A Wilmington alumni association sent a resolution to the Board of Trustees and all presidents of Southern Conference institutions. "The Graham Plan," the document read, "will definitely undermine the quality of the university athletic teams by encouraging athletes to go elsewhere." The Montgomery County Alumni Association resolved that if the Graham Plan were adopted "we shall withdraw all our support from the University until such injustice is corrected."[22] Apparently only one North Carolina alumni group supported Graham's reform measures.

President Graham got the message, though he did not accept the criticism of many or the advice of Ambassador Josephus Daniels, who counseled: "Sometimes you have to bow to the storm for a little while."[23] Graham did little bowing. President Angell of Yale read the new regulations and told Graham that the "proposed regulations are remarkably complete, and if you can secure the conscientious execution of such regulations, you will have accomplished an extraordinary piece of house cleaning." The Yale president, however, followed with a telling statement: "There is no such irrational group to be dealt with in our academic life as the athletic brethren."[24] There were other supporters of Graham, but they were in the vocal minority. A member of his Board of Trustees wrote to the president, giving him support and indicating, as it turned out, wrongly, "You will win out in the long run. . . . God save us from the Alumni."[25] Another trustee backed Graham, noting that the trustees had been partly responsible for the growth of semiprofessional athletics, and if athletics weren't cleaned up, the trustees should act to do so. "Intercollegiate football today," the lawyer-trustee Charles Tillett wrote, "is a great big goiter on the neck of higher education."[26] President Graham must have been buoyed by one of his faculty members, an English professor at North Carolina, John Booker, who pleaded with the president not to resign. "You are the main hope of this University and of liberalism in this state," he wrote.[27] The professor was likely referring not only to Graham's stand on athletics, but also to his positions on academic freedom, rights of workers to organize and bargain collectively and for farmers to organize cooperatives, and for standing up for a leftist and former student who backed a strike against the textile industry in the recent past. The president must have believed that if he could lead these liberal causes in the conservative state of North Carolina, he could be successful in reforming athletics. He was wrong.

Death of the Graham Plan came almost immediately upon its birth, but not the resignation of President Graham.[28] When the fall of 1936 arrived, few colleges in his own Southern Conference strictly followed the Graham Plan. Six new members had been added to the Southern Conference, The Citadel, Davidson, Furman, Richmond, Wake Forest, and William and Mary, making it a sixteen-member conference. Within two months of the implementation of the Graham Plan, Forest Fletcher, president of the Southern Conference from Washington and Lee, a former track Olympian, and head of the physical education department, proposed the abolishment of the policy because, as he stated, all members were "violating the spirit of the Graham Plan." The University of Virginia challenged Fletcher's statement, for Virginia officials did not believe they were violating the new rules, through they recognized that the Graham ideals had not been fulfilled by a number of schools. Virginia, in a huff, resigned from the conference, claiming there were no uniformity of rule interpretations and no method of enforcement within the conference. The resignation of the leading academic institution within the Southern Conference shocked the conference leaders, who then almost immediately abolished the Graham Plan by allowing aid to athletes if it were not "primarily" for athletic ability. Thus, the important antisubsidization plan was dead. At the same time, the Southern Conference wanted to retain some of its purity and voted 11-4 not to allow full subsidization as the Southeastern Conference had recently done. Virginia, ironically, then voted to cease denying outside financial aid to athletes to make for more "honesty in athletics."[29] President Graham had experienced defeat, but the Board of Trustees took no action to replace him.

Less than two years after the Graham Plan was implemented, the Southern Conference rescinded its rule against athletic scholarships as long as they were funded and managed by off-campus contributors, allowing the alumni, once again, to be the principal support for athletes' aid.[30] Nevertheless, this policy allowed what grant money the university had to be used for funding high-scholarship students, rather than principally for athletes. In 1938, several Carolina alums received a charter from the state of North Carolina to create a tax-exempt and independent foundation, the Educational Foundation, to raise money for funding athletes.[31] President Graham conceded he had failed in the larger contest. "We had a bitter fight in North Carolina," the president stated, "and there was practically unanimous opposition" to his plan from the alumni, student body, public, and press.[32] The crusader Graham stated at the end of the fight that his proposals were intended to "actually carry out what we profess to carry out."[33] He opposed the hypocrisy of the payment of amateur athletes.

While the Graham Plan was almost an immediate failure because there was divided sentiment in the South regarding financial aid to athletes, it stands out as a beacon of athletic reform efforts in the 1930s. It attempted to do what a few individual presidents had attempted in the period following the Carnegie Report on *American College Athletics* in 1929 and what no other conference was willing to take up in that decade. The reform discussions, which had been taking place in the faculty-controlled NCAA for three decades, were tried in one conference at a time when unofficial financial aid to athletes, especially in football, was growing throughout the nation. By the end of the decade, and just before U.S. entry into World War II, the NCAA decided to move toward restrictions on both financial aid and recruiting. What occurred next in reform was the creation of a national "Sanity Code," created under the National Collegiate Athletic Association, the first attempt by the NCAA to legislate athletic reform. When the "Sanity Code" was passed shortly after World War II, Frank Porter Graham was still president of the University of North Carolina, though he had never again attempted to reform college athletics.

10

The NCAA and the Sanity Code
A National Reform Gone Wrong

The Sanity Code following World War II was to college athletic reform what President Woodrow Wilson's "War to End All Wars" was to world peace following World War I. Neither worked. As the naïveté of the leaders of the National Collegiate Athletic Association (NCAA) led to the belief that all would be well with the passage of the Sanity Code in 1948, Wilson's idealism fed the idea that fighting a war would end future conflicts. It wasn't the first time that Wilson had been the idealist, for he once believed, when he was president of Princeton University, that if the presidents of the Big Three—Harvard, Yale, and Princeton—reformed athletics, all other institutions would follow.[1] In a similar way, the leaders of the NCAA, many from the Big Ten Conference, were convinced that the NCAA's first national legislation would bring purity to intercollegiate athletics across the nation. Unfortunately for successful reform, passing legislation did not mean that it would be followed or that those who did not conform to the legislation would be disciplined. One thing, however, may have been learned: Reform would not likely ever be successful on a large scale unless it was conducted on a national basis. Yet as the Graham Plan of the 1930s had not led to national reform, neither would the NCAA's first attempt to do away with its longtime policy of Home Rule be a success in the 1940s. Unfortunately for reform, one president's comments had more than a small amount of truth: "This Sanity Code," he stated, "will make liars of us all."[2]

From the creation of the NCAA in 1905 until World War II, the NCAA had never legislated on a national level, except for rules of the various sports, leaving reform legislation to individual institutions and conferences. The NCAA constitution of 1906 calling for Home Rule and the passage of the nine fundamental principles in 1922, including the freshman rule and absolute faculty control, prevented the NCAA from both legislation and enforcement. However, on the heels of the Carnegie Report of 1929, several failed reform efforts in the 1930s, and the growth of outright financial grants to athletes, stronger calls were heard for national reform through the NCAA. The principal driving force for reform was to create a level playing field, especially dealing with those who gave athletic scholarships and those who did not. As in the past, the question of the lack of academic integrity was not nearly as important as whether some institutions had athletic advantages over others. At nearly every NCAA convention in the 1930s, major concerns over the recruitment and payment of athletes were raised. In 1934, with the Great Depression in its fifth year, only a few NCAA members, such as Prof. B. F. Oakes of the University of Montana, favored granting "legitimate athletic scholarships."[3] Most were strongly opposed. The president of the NCAA and Big Ten commissioner, Maj. John L. Griffith, was one of those. He noted that university presidents believed recruiting and subsidizing athletes was the greatest problem in intercollegiate sports. Nevertheless, Griffith opposed giving a national body "police powers," for, he said, the NCAA "cannot make men good in athletics by legislation." Speaking for many in the NCAA, Griffith repeated what others had often said, that the NCAA "has never assumed the responsibility of trying to be a governing body. We believe," Griffith emphasized, "in states' rights."[4] The NCAA was not ready then to abandon Home Rule for reform at the national level, though it did pass a nonenforceable code recommended by its Committee on Recruiting and Subsidizing.[5]

When the Southeastern Conference (SEC) openly allowed full athletic scholarships in 1935, the members of the NCAA who opposed athletic scholarships were upset over a change in the balance of power, especially in football, and they were becoming less enamored of states' rights and the southern use of it. At the NCAA convention in 1938, questions had been raised about the inequality of recruiting and payment of athletes, particularly as southern institutions began to recruit athletes from the North by offering full athletic grants in aid. There was a call heard by the NCAA Executive Committee to do something by the next conference. At the 1939 NCAA convention, Lynn St. John of Ohio State gave a report for institutions representing the Big Ten. He spoke of the number of athletes being recruited and paid to attend southern institutions that were openly giving athletic scholarships. He noted the movement within the Big Ten to participate only with institutions that did not sanction financial aid to athletes, for, he said, intercollegiate athletics may not be able to continue, using President Abraham Lincoln's words eight decades before, "half slave and half free." Importantly, he suggested that the NCAA "can no longer function with satisfactory results in the role of a purely educational body."[6] This echoed what Michigan's faculty representative said at the previous NCAA conference: "We can't have intercollegiate athletics," said Ralph Aigler, "half on a professional basis and half on an amateur basis."[7] The vice president of Ohio State University, Justin L. Morrill, pointed out the transgressions of "certain southern institutions" as setting back intercollegiate athletics in a similar way to "gambling or prostitution" being detrimental to the larger society.[8]

At the same time, the president of the NCAA, W. B. Owens of Stanford University, asked the NCAA delegates to "translate its discussion into action." The Executive Committee of the NCAA, he said, had devoted the year to considering whether the NCAA should become a governing body, for which, he said, there was little sentiment. However, Owens believed that a definite code of sound institutional practices should be incorporated into the NCAA constitution, with termination of membership the punishment for nonadherence to the code. Owens concluded his lengthy talk by stating that reform through "isolated action by individual institutions or conferences will not adequately meet the problem."[9] Yet with more than three decades of Home Rule, it was understandable that many NCAA officials would not want to abandon the practice. The president of a small college, Thurston J. Davies of Colorado College, warned of the danger of the NCAA becoming a regulatory agency with enforcement powers, probably reflecting a number of other institutions' thinking about keeping the traditional Home Rule. On the other hand, the NCAA representative from the University of Texas claimed it was time for the NCAA to have a "more aggressive attitude toward the administration of intercollegiate athletics."[10] Reflecting this attitude, the 1939 NCAA convention, for the first time, passed a constitutional amendment providing a section on financial aid. It stipulated that all aid to athletes would be based on financial need, athletic participation could not be a condition of aid, and aid must be channeled to the athlete only through a regular university agency, not by alumni or an outside group.[11] "We can and should subscribe to the code," a skeptical engineering faculty member from the University of Colorado wrote to his president, "even though it is a great deal like a Mother Hubbard in that it covers everything and touches nothing."[12] The cupboard had food for reformist thought, but that thought could not be enforced.

The NCAA decided to go halfway toward becoming a regulatory agency. The NCAA now had an athletic code included in its constitution, but enforcement of recruiting and subsidizing athletes was left to individual institutions. In particular, presidents of colleges and universities would have to enforce the code. This was a proposition that past practice would indicate would be unsuccessful. Presidents had generally been athletic cheerleaders and not athletic reformers and certainly not leaders who would antagonize the alumni, who were providing most of the money for financially sponsoring athletes. The next year, the constitution included a section on how an institution might be terminated for athletic indiscretions: a two-thirds vote by convention delegates.[13] There was a major problem, however, and that was who would investigate the accused violators, because the NCAA had almost no budget to carry out any activity. In the last few years of the 1930s, the NCAA had about $10,000 in the bank. The NCAA basketball tournament, begun in 1939, brought in the most money, but it was only a few thousand dollars each year, certainly not enough to pay for a body of investigators. When the 1940 convention voted to authorize the Executive Committee to "investigate alleged violations," it was agreed that an educational foundation, such as the Carnegie Foundation for the Advancement of Teaching, was needed to finance such a venture.[14] The NCAA, without the financing to do so, was nevertheless finally getting close to becoming a regulatory agency at the national level.

Before Home Rule was completely abandoned in the area of recruiting and sub- sidization, the attack on Pearl Harbor, on December 7, 1941, brought the United States formally into World War II in both Asia and Europe. For the next four years, there was more concern whether intercollegiate sports would continue effectively than whether a movement toward athletic reform would be maintained. Still, only three weeks after Japan's attack on Pearl Harbor, NCAA officials felt the necessity of amending the constitution by adding several pages of informational explana- tions relative to financial aid to athletes.[15] With students being drafted or leaving voluntarily for the military service, there was little talk of athletic subsidization, as institutions were struggling, financially and in numbers of available athletes, to maintain some type of intercollegiate program at most institutions of higher education. The colleges or universities that had the most viable athletic programs during World War II were those that had specific military-sponsored training, such as the Navy V-5 or V-12 programs and the Army Specialized Training Program.[16]

One major eligibility action taken during the war by most institutions and conferences was to do away with possibly the most important and nearly universal reform of the twentieth century: freshman ineligibility.[17] To keep many programs viable, seventeen- and eighteen-year-olds were immediately given varsity status by institutions of higher education.[18]

World War II caused a delay in athletic reform, but the need for future reform, particularly recruiting and subsidization, was not far from the surface of discussion. When college presidents were asked in the fall of 1941, just prior to the Pearl Harbor attack, slightly more than 50 percent of a small number of responders believed that the NCAA should be given legislative and enforcement powers. As the war came to an end in the summer of 1945, presidents were again polled. This time the presidents responded in large numbers, with a large majority affirming the NCAA constitutional mandates regarding recruiting and subsidization, though only a few suggested strong enforcement by the NCAA.[19] At every NCAA convention during the conflict, the question of reform came up. In early 1944, the NCAA Resolutions Committee presented its view by stating that the NCAA must "prepare for the period following the war, when new problems must be faced," and it was seconded by NCAA President Philip Badger of New York University, who claimed that the NCAA must "weed out extravagant practices which crept in during the past two decades.[20] Dean A. W. Hobbs, who, as faculty representative from the University of North Carolina, was as cynical as anyone about big-time college sports, was on target when he said, "[R]ecruiting, subsidization, athletic scholarships, and the like are sure to be just as prevalent as ever" following the war. Speaking about a half year before the conclusion of the war, when the Communist Soviet Union rather than Nazi Germany would become the U.S. enemy in Europe, he told his peers at an NCAA convention: "We are not in danger of communism but of commercialism" of big-time sport.[21] Hobbs and a number of others were concerned about how the 1944 GI Bill of Rights and its financial support for a college education for veterans would impact the commercialization and professionalism of college sport. Could veterans enjoy the benefits of GI Bill tuition payments of up to $500 yearly and a monthly stipend and still be able to get jobs given to other athletes? Would veterans be able to transfer from their previous institution to another with impunity? Would veterans migrate from previous high-tuition schools to lower-tuition schools? Could veterans play as freshmen if the freshman rule were reinstated? Would the recruitment of veterans unbalance the competitive level playing field?[22] All these potential problems, recalling the post–World War I growth of commercialism and professionalism, were discussed before victory was achieved in Europe and finally in Asia.

When the war was concluded, first in Europe by the collapse of the Nazi regime and three months later by the fall of Japan following the two atomic bomb raids on the island in August 1945, there were those who wanted almost immediately to take on the question of national controls of recruiting and subsidization. A standing Constitution Committee, at the end of the war, had been formed to do just that, consisting of Clarence Houston of Tufts, Karl Leib of the University of Iowa, and Ogden Miller of Yale, all of whom were reformists at heart.[23] Because of an increasing workload, the NCAA Executive Committee asked for and received for the first time an office for the NCAA, a full-time executive assistant to the president, and secretarial assistance for the secretary-treasurer.[24] This could be afforded with an increase in NCAA dues and the knowledge that one of its nine national tournaments, basketball, was bringing in substantial money, while the rest of the tournaments were barely breaking even. The NCAA then set up a committee of five to survey the regulations of the various conferences to determine whether Article III of the constitution, the one setting recruiting and subsidization parameters, was being implemented across America.[25]

Less than a year after the surrender of Japan concluded World War II, the NCAA leadership supported a call by some members for a "Conference of Conferences" for the summer of 1946. Meeting in Chicago, twenty conferences discussed the familiar problems of athletic recruiting and subsidization. The two-day Conference of Conferences was chaired by NCAA President Karl Leib, a lawyer, Big Ten professor of business at the University of Iowa, and former athlete at Stanford. The recommendations that came out of the conference were basically to forbid athletic scholarships and prohibit athletic recruiting off campus. Even the SEC, with its full scholarships policy, offered little opposition to the ban on scholarships, but the southern leaders may have hoped that by the time the full NCAA convention took up the matter, modifications could be made to the athletic scholarship policy, possibly continuing aid from the alumni outside of the NCAA policy.[26] Six months later, the full NCAA met to vote on the various draft proposals, then called the Purity Code. The Purity Code, consisting of six Principles for the Conduct of Intercollegiate Athletics, included a statement on (1) amateurism; (2) institutional control of athletics; (3) admitting athletes on the same basis as other students; (4) no recruiting off campus; (5) financial aid, limited to tuition and incidental fees, based on need, awarded only by an agency approved by the institution, and employment allowed commensurate with the service rendered; and (6) competition with only those who uphold the principles. Each of the six principles was passed unanimously, except for the regulation of off-campus recruiting. The Big Ten and Pacific Coast Conference had already placed restrictions on recruiting off campus, but nearly one-third of the members opposed the limitations on recruiting.[27] President Karl Leib was delighted with the vote and soon after made the bold statement: "Once the Principles become part of the constitution it will be a case of 'conform or get out.'"[28] He wasn't quite right.

A year was required to place the principles in the NCAA constitution, a year of discussion and recrimination. Almost as soon as the 1947 convention was over, the athletic director and football coach at the University of Michigan, Fritz Crisler, broadcast his perception of a divided NCAA: southerners who favored recruiting and subsidies were at odds with the Big Ten, Pacific Coast Conference, and the Ivy League, who favored "amateur" athletics. "I can foresee the possibility of a group of schools," Crisler said, "seceding from the N.C.A.A."[29] Crisler was aware of the feelings of southern members, for soon the Southeastern, Southwestern, and Missouri Valley Conferences met to discuss their concerns with the Purity Code, soon to be named the Sanity Code, making it less pejorative.[30] Giving the southern group more prestige was President John J. Tigert of the University of Florida, who presided over the SEC. The meeting was perceived by some as a southern boycott of NCAA policies, but James H. Stewart, executive secretary of the Southwestern Conference, stated: "This was definitely not an indignation meeting against the NCAA."[31] Nevertheless, there was definitely an attitude of defiance by some within conferences from the South, probably the strongest being the SEC. "The N.C.A.A. doesn't want the schools to pay the room and board of athletes," the secretary of the SEC said. "We in the S.E.C. think we should pay them." The president of Louisiana State University believed strongly that LSU should abide only by the SEC rules and regulations and not those of the NCAA. Kentucky's president, H. L. Donovan, assured his SEC colleagues that Kentucky would "not secede from the conference," but could leave the NCAA. The vice chancellor of Vanderbilt conceded there was "considerable writhing in some quarters" of the SEC. "The Southeastern Conference," the president of the University of Alabama wrote to the head of Tulane, "must either conform to whatever code may ultimately be adopted by the NCAA or face ostracism at the hands of all other conferences in the country. . . . We cannot afford to fail to conform."[32] Obviously not everyone was in agreement.

Going into the historic 1948 NCAA convention, which was to make probably the most important decision the NCAA had made to that point, the *New York Times* headlined: "College 'Purity Code' in Athletics Certain to Fail, Experts Believe."[33] Undeterred by naysayers, the president of the NCAA, Karl Leib, a strong believer in reform, wrote each member, noting how regional conferences had previously helped solve problems and created a level playing field for sectional athletics. "Now," Leib emphasized, "comes the time when there is a need for a national 'conference.'"[34] At this momentous meeting, Leib and the NCAA Council had set up an agenda to accomplish what it desired: a national organization with both legislative and enforcement powers that it had never had before. Meeting with the American Football Coaches Association and the College Physical Education Association, as the NCAA had been doing for a number of years, Leib first asked the president of the American Football Coaches Association, E. E. Wieman of the University of Maine, to speak. Though having coached for a quarter century, Wieman was in some ways an idealist, because, among other things, he opposed, like a number of reformers, the rapid growth of the commercialized season-ending bowl games run by those outside of college control.[35]

More important, Leib then called upon the president of the American Council on Education, George F. Zook, to talk about reform in education and reform in intercollegiate athletics. The American Council on Education (ACE) had been formed during World War I as an umbrella association for numerous higher education organizations to work with the federal government in its wartime activities. The ACE, unlike the NCAA when it was founded in 1905, created a full-time paid administrator and established a central office in Washington, DC, where it could have a major influence on educational policy.[36] George Zook had become president of the ACE in 1934, and during World War II he was involved in the creation of the GI Bill of Rights for war veteran college education, a law that opened up college education to a far greater number of individuals than had gone to college previously. When Zook made his early 1948 presentation to the NCAA, a constituent member of the ACE, college enrollments had expanded to overflowing, and the growth of commercialization and professionalism among college athletes had never been higher, even in the 1920s. Zook placed the NCAA reform effort in historical perspective, noting that most educational associations, such as those for engineering, medicine, law, or liberal arts, had often passed "pious resolutions" of reform that were often discarded when members went home to their institutions. From this standpoint, the NCAA was similar to other educational groups that set standards by well-intended delegates but returned "home under the naïve assumption that having set up a fine piece of machinery, it will work automatically." This, Zook said, was what the NCAA did in 1939 with its first constitutional reform policy relative to recruiting and subsidizing athletes. He reported what a college coach said to a Washington, DC, newspaperman: "Many will vote for the code but are figuring out ways to beat it." Reform legislation in the form of the Sanity Code, Zook told the delegates, will only be successful if it makes the NCAA a regulatory body and enforces its standards. It would turn the NCAA from "a discussion body into a regulatory body."[37]

There was little dissention before the vote to place the Sanity Code into the constitution and make the NCAA into an enforcement agency, but the language of the Sanity Code certainly contributed to the hypocrisy of the NCAA as an amateur organization. For the first time and in a nearly unanimous vote, the NCAA was given the power to enforce an amateur code, but it allowed payment of athletes, through tuition and incidental fees, in direct violation of the concept of amateurism. Only one representative, J. E. Knapp of little Texas College of Mines and Metallurgy (now University of Texas at El Paso), noted the hypocrisy of the "Principles of Amateurism," which stated, "any college athlete who takes or is promised pay in *any* form for participation in athletics does not meet this definition of an amateur."[38] The hypocrisy of amateurism in college sport clearly went back to the nineteenth century, but now it was included in the constitution governing NCAA action. Voting unanimously to support the "Principle of Amateurism" and then allowing some payment to players was a little like voting to oppose drunkenness but allowing some intoxication. Continuing to use the concept of amateurism by the NCAA when college sports were certainly not amateur was similar to the NCAA demand upon television networks to include an athletic-educational statement in their highly professionalized and commercialized football TV contracts of the 1960s. The statement was that the networks needed to add to the dignity of NCAA football by "representing college football as an integral part of the educational program."[39] Neither being amateur nor being an *integral* part of the educational program was true to the way intercollegiate sport was practiced by big-time athletics in America.

The problem of amateurism, one could argue, was not that players were paid but that it was an outdated and nonegalitarian concept, despite being nearly universally accepted. Historically, no society had ever had a concept of amateurism in sport, certainly not the ancient Greeks, until it was invented by the upper-class British in the nineteenth century.[40] It was merely a way for the elite British sport participants to separate themselves from those considered below them socially. In more egalitarian America, that was less acceptable, but the amateur concept appeared to be more fitting for collegians, to make them appear to be above what was considered crass commercialism and professionalism found in professional sports, such as baseball.[41] There were, however, more pragmatic reasons. Amateurism and athletes being an *integral* part of education also allowed the colleges to be treated differently than the professionals by being exempt from federal and state taxes.[42] Claiming amateurism also exempted colleges from paying workers' compensation to injured athletes in the twentieth century as well as benefiting from tax-free booster donations to athletic programs. To define collegiate sports

as being amateur when nearly all aspects of intercollegiate athletics were professional in nature was, indeed, hypocritical in the 1940s as it had been in the late
1800s. Branch Rickey, of professional baseball's Brooklyn Dodgers, speaking at the
Sanity Code conference, defended pro baseball against allegations of encroachment
for signing "amateur" collegians to pro contracts and made a poignant comment
about the hypocrisy of the colleges. Universities that induce boys to enter the
university through financial favors, Rickey said, "are as much professionals . . .
as if we had them on our payrolls."[43] Under the Sanity Code, then, the players
could be recruited and paid, though not much; the coaches were professionals
and highly paid; the arenas and stadiums were generally larger and better than
the professional facilities; and the competition was of such a high quality by the
mid-twentieth century that the best of the amateur college football players were
capable of beating the champion team of the National Football League.[44]

Even if the Sanity Code put some controls on the expanding professionalism in
college sport, it could only succeed if the violators were banished from the NCAA.
Despite Karl Leib's pronouncement that the NCAA had "made great progress toward forming a great National Conference," it was not true.[45] Through the first
year of the Sanity Code, there were few complaints of violations, as the Compliance Committee was being set up to investigate any wrongdoers. Still a number
of southern schools were especially opposed to the new constitutional provisions,
though resistance certainly was not confined to the South. Pointedly, the three
major southern conferences—the Southern, Southeastern, and Southwest Conferences—gathered in May 1949 to discuss whether the Sanity Code served the needs
of southern schools. The conclusion was that it did not, that financial aid should
be increased to include not only tuition and fees but also room, board, books,
and laundry expenses. The three conferences even discussed withdrawal from the
NCAA, considering if any one conference could do so and compete successfully.[46]

That summer, the University of Virginia became the first institution to announce
secession from the NCAA if the Sanity Code were not amended. The NCAA Compliance Committee, with a meager budget of $5,000, had already warned of taking
action against twenty violators and nineteen potential violators of the Sanity Code.
President Colgate Darden Jr. of Virginia, with his governing board opposing the
Sanity Code, announced that Virginia would withdraw from the NCAA if the financial aid allowed by the NCAA were not changed. Darden wanted athletes to be paid
enough to allow them sufficient time both to participate and to study. Holding a
job to pay for college expenses as well as participating in athletics, Darden believed,
would mean "sacrificing his academic career." Virginia had high academic standards
that it would uphold with athletic scholarships, Darden maintained, and, besides,

its "honor code was more important than the NCAA's Sanity Code."[47] Virginia had been giving out athletic scholarships since it withdrew from the Southern Conference in 1936 following passage of the Graham Plan. As an independent, Virginia's moribund football team improved but was not one of the truly big-time schools when Darden announced Virginia's rejection of the Sanity Code. While the Virginia governing board wanted to amend the Sanity Code rather than withdraw from the NCAA, Athletic Director Norton Pritchett wanted to wait until institutions broke away regionally and then join the one closest to Virginia's views.[48]

Prior to the 1950 NCAA convention, the Compliance Committee announced that seven institutions that had not changed their ways to conform to the Sanity Code would be brought before the NCAA for a vote for banishment from the organization. The "sinful seven" was a strange group of five southern and two northern schools, with only the University of Maryland being a football power. The other four southern schools were Virginia, The Citadel, Virginia Military Institute, and Virginia Polytechnic Institute. Only two northern schools were included, Villanova and Boston College, two Catholic universities. After six hours of debate, the vote to disenfranchise the seven schools was taken. President Karl Leib, who had invented the name "Sanity Code," reported the vote of 111 to expel and 93 not to expel. Leib, who should have known better, declared, "The motion is carried for expulsion." Leib, the lawyer, knew that a vote to remove a member institution required a two-thirds vote. Loud cries of "No, No," rang through the hall, and after a moment Leib corrected himself, and from that moment on the Sanity Code, though still on the books, was dead.[49] The defeat of the Sanity Code, according to Walter Byers, who had just begun his tenure as head of the NCAA in the early 1950s, was, he later recalled, one of the three or four most important decisions in the history of college sports.[50] Writer Tim Cohane, writing at the time, noted that the Sanity Code "died aborning, of hypocrisy," for it was reluctant to call an athletic scholarship an athletic scholarship and insisted on requiring either employment, to the academic detriment of the athlete, or under-the-table payments to pay for the cost of an education.[51] The president of the University of North Carolina, Gordon Gray, agreed. Every institution had to make one of two decisions: admit that they were in noncompliance and withdraw from the NCAA or be hypocritical and remain.[52]

The tying together of amateurism and hypocrisy had a long tradition in America. The Sanity Code had carried that tradition, begun in the nineteenth century, into the mid-twentieth century. The borrowed British amateur, noblesse-oblige attitude toward sport did not fit into a more egalitarian American society. Though the Americans had used the borrowed term *amateur* from the British, because it made intercollegiate sport more socially acceptable, they had developed a professional model. The upper-class amateur ideal of participation for the joy of competition and for no other motive was destined to be a failure in a society whose ideology of freedom of opportunity provided for all to seek excellence through effort and ability. Amateurism did not fit well into that ideological model. As a result, a meritocratic approach developed in intercollegiate athletics, one based upon exertion and talent. Achieved status in athletics was the American way rather than the ascribed status as seen in England's elitist universities and their amateur athletics. The English system of amateurism that Caspar Whitney had craved around the turn of the century, elitist and separatist, never gained a foothold in American college athletics. The highly competitive spirit resulted, with merit dominating status by birth. The amateur ideal never reached fruition. Rather, a professional spirit blossomed. Only the term *amateur* remained, perverted and hypocritically applied. The history of amateurism in American college sport, then, was one of playacting, using the name *amateur* because it was considered a positive term that middle- and upper-class institutions were expected to use, but the result was a highly professional model emphasizing excellence and winning. The mid-twentieth-century Sanity Code had not come to terms either with amateurism or the level playing field. Searching for the level playing field continued for the recruitment and payment of players, but the concept of amateurism had long before lost most of its meaning, and it would continue to deteriorate for most institutions. One notable exception may have been in the creation of the Ivy League.

11

Ivy League Presidential Reform

Presidential reform had not succeeded in individual colleges in the 1930s, nor had the presidential reform Graham Plan met with success at the conference level. The national reform Sanity Code, undermined by a number of presidents specifically in the South, had died shortly after World War II. One league, however, with presidents in the lead, gave pause to skeptics, who felt that presidents could not or would not move in the direction of athletic reform. The Ivy League was, like the Big Ten a half century before, created by presidential reform leaders in higher education. The group of eastern institutions that had given the nation big-time commercialized and professionalized athletics in the latter half of the nineteenth and in the early twentieth centuries moved in the opposition direction, somewhat akin to sinners seeking salvation from earlier errant lives. The schools that gave higher education intense recruiting of precollege athletes, allowed payment to skilled athletes to attend college, hired the first professional coaches, and built the first stadiums to hold commercialized and professionalized contests decided to change somewhat the directions they had taken sport for the first century.

The Ivy League, in some form, had existed in the late nineteenth century and through the early years of the twentieth century.[1] One may recall Brown University calling an 1898 conference reform meeting of faculty, alumni, and students. Those invited were the same institutions that formed the Ivy League in 1945: Brown, Columbia, Cornell, Dartmouth, Harvard, Pennsylvania, Princeton, and Yale. In 1898, Yale, the dominant "jock" school in America, declined to participate because it was reluctant to reform anything, while prior to the 1945 formation of the Ivy League, Brown, the weakest institution, was nearly left out. By the mid-twentieth century, most American colleges and universities were part of some conference. Even the Ivy League institutions were in conferences in many sports, but the most important, football, lacked conference affiliation. In the early years, the Big Three of Harvard, Yale, and Princeton—and always in that order and with Princeton a distant third—felt they were superior to all the other eastern institutions and remained independent of them if for no other reason than to maintain their position. When the Big Three met at Theodore Roosevelt's White House Conference in the fall of 1905, they felt that they could reform football by themselves. They overestimated their own importance. In 1906, however, the Big Three made an agreement to prohibit both freshmen and graduate students from athletic competition in the major sports while limiting participation to three varsity years.[2] Princeton faculty member Henry B. Fine, one of many who believed in the Big Three's athletic divinity, said, "[T]he example of these three universities would soon lead to the general adoption."[3]

The Big Three continued to remain aloof and above the others in their region and in 1916 expanded their eligibility agreement of the previous decade. Besides limiting graduate and freshman participation, the new agreement precluded any pecuniary rewards, such as room and board, and no financial support to play summer baseball. In addition, students not in good academic standing, or who had lost class standing because of poor scholarship, were ineligible.[4] Seven years later, the presidents of the Big Three met to supplement the 1916 Triple Agreement. This time, transfer students were the point of reform. The three schools agreed that transfer students who had previously played either freshman or varsity athletics could not play that sport in the Big Three institutions.[5] Combining these agreements to level the playing field with the 1925 Big Three agreement to limit football coaching salaries, the leaders of what would eventually become the Ivy League had put significant reforms in place.

It did not take long, however, for the agreements to be broken, as a controversy over scheduling football games between Harvard and Princeton caused a break in athletic relations in 1926. Harvard always considered Princeton a distant third in their elite triad, and it decided, after a rather bitter football game in 1926, to schedule Princeton when it wanted to, rather than on an annual basis. Instead, Harvard would grant Yale its "most-favored" status and continue to play its annual Yale contest as the traditional last game of the season. Naturally, Princeton took this as a bad-will gesture, and after it was announced that Harvard would play Michigan the following year rather than Princeton, the third member of the Big Three severed relations with Harvard. President James Angell of Yale, in a private letter to his counterpart at Princeton, John Hibben, called Harvard's action "a blunder of the first magnitude and as inconsiderate as it is stupid."[6] Because the break lasted for eight years, there was little chance for any additional reform effort to be led by the Big Three. Besides, the leadership of big-time athletics by the late 1920s was already passing to the large state universities and a few private institutions outside of the East. The Big Three was no longer the most influential group in college athletics. Possibly the best they could accomplish would be to heal their own wounds caused by the separation within the Big Three, withdraw from big-time sports, and isolate themselves in a conference away from those who would further professionalize and commercialize their athletic programs.

Proposals for an Ivy League were eventually forthcoming as they had been in the past. Shortly after World War I, the chairman of the University of Pennsylvania's Council on Athletics had proposed a seven-member football league among the present Ivy League eight, leaving out Brown.[7] This did not gain much attention, for the Big Three ignored the proposal. By the 1930s, conditions had changed following the reuniting of Harvard and Princeton, and then a group of Ivy school newspaper editors had a surprising impact. Initiated by the editor of the *Daily Princetonian,* the editors of Columbia, Cornell, Dartmouth, Harvard, Penn, and Yale school newspapers published simultaneously an editorial favoring the creation of an Ivy League for football. The seven student newspapers did a month-long cooperative investigation into crafting a league, concluding that "the Ivy League exists already in the minds of a good many of those connected with football." The student editors called for a uniform time to begin preseason practice, constructing scouting agreements, postseason game regulations, rules of eligibility, reporting of athletes' financial records, and standard guarantees for visiting teams.[8] All of these proposed rules were for the sake of leveling the competitive playing field.

The Ivy editors' proposal led to a great deal of discussion but was premature. Within two weeks of the student-led proposition, the athletic directors of the seven schools met at the Georgia plantation of Cornell's athletic director, Jim Lynah. While the athletic directors recognized that each institution was in a seven-institution basketball and baseball league, it took only one institution, such as Yale, to obstruct such a scheme. Yale's athletic director, Malcolm Farmer, thought an Ivy League requiring five or six games each year would disrupt traditional games with other institutions. Besides, he thought, the standards of the seven schools were not compatible with regard to admission requirements and rules for eligibility. An important issue, in addition, was that some of the schools would have to play half of their games away from home, something that the Big Three had always rejected.[9] By early 1937, the Ivy leaders had rebuffed the conference idea, claiming the difficulty of round-robin scheduling.[10] The situation of students asking for a conference and being rejected showed clearly the change that had taken place over the previous half century. If students in the 1880s had decided to have a conference for competition in rowing, baseball, track and field, or football, undoubtedly it would have been formed. Now there was hardly any student protest against those who had come to control athletics—governing boards, presidents, athletic directors, faculty, and alumni—when they rejected a desire by students to form a collective regional league. Now students who suggested a reform conference were being rejected by those who had taken control from the students over the previous fifty years—the irony of it all.

Only days after the Ivy proposal was abandoned, a group of eastern college presidents gathered with Howard Savage, secretary of the Carnegie Foundation for the Advancement of Teaching and lead author of the 1929 Carnegie Foundation study of athletics. All eight future members of the Ivy League were at the meeting, plus Amherst, Lehigh, New York University, Wesleyan, and Williams. Though the Carnegie Foundation had rejected a request by the National Association of State Universities to again study college athletics in early January, Savage indicated that the Carnegie Foundation would be amenable to appointing a Board of Review for interinstitutional auditing of athletic eligibility of privately endowed eastern colleges.[11] Ostensibly, the Carnegie Foundation's prestige could help more eastern schools to accept the eligibility rules of the recent Big Three Triple Agreement. James Conant, president of Harvard, believed that only an outside group, such as the Carnegie Foundation, could get the private colleges to come together, for he could see from Harvard's "own internal problems and my alumni relations" that even Harvard would not be successful without an outside Board of Review.[12] From the very beginning, there were "concealed hostilities" among the presidents, according to President Harold Dodds of Princeton. "A willingness to risk something for success . . . I fear," wrote Dodds to Conant, "is lacking in the majority of institutions."[13]

After several months of negotiating to create a Board of Review with a kind of czar, Lewis Douglas, as its head and a panel of investigators at his disposal, it was not clear that everyone was on board, as institutional freedom would be lost. Douglas was a graduate of Amherst College, a World War I veteran, and member of the U.S. House of Representatives before becoming President Franklin Roosevelt's director of budget in 1933. Shortly after resigning as director of budget, President Conant asked Douglas to be assistant president at Harvard. Douglas declined and became vice president of American Cyanamid.[14] While employed at the chemical company, Conant asked Douglas if he would be willing to serve as a reform head of the athletic Board of Review. However, the plan, like other presidential reform efforts, was never consummated.

Yale, with its remarkable athletic successes in the past, was most reluctant to give up its autonomy to a large group of institutions. From this standpoint, Yale was consistent for more than a half century. Nearly a year after the first discussions of an athletic Board of Review, the longtime president of Dartmouth, Ernest Hopkins, conceded that the idea of an outside group monitoring athletics "would not be successful if Yale did not participate." Hopkins questioned Yale's use of its scholarships for athletes, a traditional practice by the athletic power, and he did not believe Yale would ever cooperate with or without a Board of Review. "I find myself in the paradoxical situation," Hopkins noted, "of one moment thinking that the plan would be a failure without Yale's participation in it and the next of feeling myself under the conviction that the plan could not possibly be worked to full effectiveness with Yale in it."[15] Soon, Conant, head of the Board of Review committee, lost interest in its pursuit, stating that "if Yale is not interested, then the scheme is out the window."[16] An Ivy League interinstitutional athletic Board of Review and a potential Ivy League were for the moment dead, even though following the 1938 season the sports editors of the Ivy League schools, who favored an Ivy League, voted Cornell as the first Ivy League champion in football.[17]

The Big Three, however, was not dead or dying, for in October 1939, another Big Three presidential agreement was signed, with a desire for other institutions to follow the rules. It included previous statements to level the playing field and added new reforms, including the promise not to pay for recruiting expenses of athletes and not to recruit in preparatory schools, something that had been going on since the 1800s.[18] The Big Three soon rejected Cornell's push for an Ivy League, or at least Cornell's entry into the Big Three. Yale squelched the proposal because allowing Cornell in would open the door to others, and besides, as new Yale President Charles Seymour stated privately, the Big Three agreement is "personal and informal."[19] As America entered World War II, what the Big Three presidents evidently wanted was for other institutions to accept the Big Three rules without having them join with the Big Three to produce a football conference. Discussions took place during the war among the Big Three, including at times the other future five of the Ivy League, deliberating over the future of athletics following the war and whether they should jointly prevent a return to big-time football. The Big Three presidents were cautious of any league that might again place their schools in the top tier of football-playing institutions once the war was concluded. De-emphasis was the order of business and a major reason why the U.S. Military Academy and the U.S. Naval Academy, dominating eastern football, were rejected from discussions over a future league. By war's end, the Big Three were ready to support a set of principles with the lesser five for the conduct of football.[20]

Three months after the surrender of Japan ended the war, the eight Ivy League presidents signed the 1945 "Ivy Group President's Agreement," requiring that football players "shall be truly representative of the student body and not composed of a group of special recruited and trained athletes." The new Ivy League stood for amateur athletics, requiring financial aid coming only from personal or family resources or scholarships awarded through regular academic channels.[21] Yet the Ivy League was not quite a league in generally accepted terms. There was no required number of games to be played by members and no round-robin schedule requiring a school to play against other members of the league on a regular basis. What the Big Three had intended to do with the "Ivy Group President's Agreement" was not to bring about reform nationally as leaders in higher education might do, but, as one historian has stated, "to escape from it."[22] The Ivy League, in the public mind since the mid-1930s, was coming closer to reality, but it was not quite there yet. The Sanity Code had reached the Ivies before it reached the National Collegiate Athletic Association (NCAA), at least on paper. One outsider noted: "There are plenty of people all over the United States who think that subsidization goes on in the Ivy League to about the same extent as in other sections, but it is done with more finesse."[23] Wrote an anonymous source:

> Said Dr. Dodds of Princeton, "Our football team is pure."
> Said Yale's Dr. Griswold, "Why so is ours, I'm sure."
> Then both called Dr. Conant, and much to their delight,

They found that Harvard's players were also lily white. . . .
Uncertainty is ended, the evil days are past,
Glory be! I've lived to see the Big Three pure at last.[24]

If the Big Three of the Ivies were not pure as the poem factitiously suggests, and they weren't, the newcomer, University of Pennsylvania, was less so. In 1948, a former governor of Minnesota, Harold E. Stassen, was elected president of the University of Pennsylvania, shortly after he had lost the Republican presidential nomination to New York's Thomas E. Dewey. He inherited an institution that had been telecasting its football games for the past eight years, nearly as long as commercial television had existed in America.[25] The University of Pennsylvania had been supporting its football team with a number of scholarships, including those given by members of the Pennsylvania State Senate. Most members of its football team had senatorial scholarships or tuition wavers plus stipends, stretching the limits of allowable aid of the NCAA's 1948 Sanity Code.[26] In other words, Pennsylvania was big time, and when Stassen came to Pennsylvania he brought a Big Ten mentality with him from his native Minnesota. "Victory with honor," Stassen intoned. The scheduling of the dominant American football school, Notre Dame, and the hiring of an ex-National Football Leaguer, Fran Murray, as his athletic director clearly showed the direction he wanted to take Pennsylvania. For a short time, Penn had the most lucrative football television contract, only challenged by Notre Dame. As a comparison, the undefeated University of Oklahoma under Coach Bud Wilkinson received $3,000 to telecast all its home games in 1950, while Penn's contract with the American Broadcasting Corporation called for up to $175,000. The next year, Penn was offered a three-year $850,000 contract, with games scheduled with California, both military academies, and Notre Dame. Both the telecasting and scheduling of Notre Dame's outstanding football team galled the other Ivy schools, as well as other members of the NCAA, who were at that time instigating a ban on college football telecasting, for fear that it would destroy gate attendance.[27] Penn was caught in a tight squeeze by two factors. One was the Ivy schools who did not want to play against a team that could challenge Notre Dame while having a TV plan that threatened the other schools' stadium attendance income. The other factor came from members of the NCAA who voted overwhelmingly in 1951 to restrict telecasting of football games because it would hurt gate receipts, the chief revenue producer for most college athletic programs. For Penn, Stassen's go-it-alone program threatened its standing in the Ivy League and instigated a boycott in scheduling by both the Ivy League and outsiders. No matter what, Penn was forced to drop its independent TV plan. However, on a more important note,

Penn had to make a decision either to deemphasize football and remain in the Ivy League, thus gaining the prestige that Harvard, Yale, and Princeton brought to it, or to leave the Ivy institutions and continue big time. Penn eventually gave up its desire to remain big time and to telecast its home games so that it could continue the relationship with the other Ivy League institutions. Penn, pressured by Ivy League institutions, even lost its undergraduate major in physical education, thought by others to be an easy way to keep its football players eligible.[28]

Once Stassen and Penn came more in line with Ivy ideals, an arrangement for a real Ivy League in football took place, but only after a series of scandals in 1951, on the heels of the failure of the Sanity Code, placed intercollegiate athletics in as bad light as had the football crisis of 1905–6. A cheating scandal involving thirty-three players throwing games or shaving points among seven big-time college basketball teams, including Adolph Rupp's Kentucky, Nat Holman's City College of New York, and Clair Bee's Long Island University, was the most disturbing. The same year, a cheating scandal at the U.S. Military Academy caused the expulsion of nearly the entire Army football team under Earl "Red" Blaike. William and Mary had both corrupt basketball and football programs that engaged in the forging of grades and the granting of credits for courses not taken, eventually leading to mass resignations of the coaches, president, alumni director, and a number of faculty. Then there was the racial incident of an Oklahoma A & M player deliberately slugging and breaking the jaw of Johnny Bright, a great African American football player on the Drake University team.[29] With all the negatives going on, it was only logical that Penn would wish to stay with the downsizing of athletics among Ivy League institutions.

When the Ivy League presidents met in December 1951, not only was America in the midst of fighting the Communists in the Korean War, but American universities were also at the lowest point in athletic integrity since the creation of the NCAA in 1905. The Ivy League agreement of 1945 was near collapse, with the Big Three threatening to withdraw from the group unless tighter rules of amateurism were accepted by the others. The threat was likely the push needed to amend the 1945 presidential agreement of the eight schools and create a real Ivy League. The product of the presidential intervention was the Ivy Group Agreement of 1952.[30] A stronger de-emphasis resulted with the tightening of eligibility, recruiting, and subsidization standards, including a ban on subsidies to athletes by alums or others not closely related to the athletes' families. Probably more important symbolically was a ban on postseason or bowl games, a later date for starting fall practice, and the elimination of spring football practice.

While the Ivy presidents voted unanimously to oppose participation in bowl games, there was division over banning spring football practice. As it turned out, Stassen's vote was the swing vote to ban spring practice. Though Stassen and his coach favored the extra practice time for their football team, he drew a concession from those institutions who favored banning spring practice—they would vote for every Ivy school to play Penn at least every five years, ending the boycott that had been exacerbated by Stassen's desire not to abide by the TV restrictions imposed by the NCAA.[31] For one of the few times in history, the presidents held firm against athletic authorities when they upheld the no-spring-practice decision, even though the Ivy League coaches petitioned the presidents favoring a three-week spring practice schedule.[32] Symbolically, the Ivy presidents taking action to restrict football was far more important than the hypocrisy shown by the same leaders in not applying the same action to other sports, such as rowing, which not only continued to have spring practice but fall and winter as well. Two years after the vote to abolish spring practice, President Harold Dodds of Princeton conceded: "The abolition of spring practice was a gesture and not a fundamental attack on over-emphasis as conducted in most of our institutions, but I have to concede that it turned out to be a significant gesture."[33] He was right. Symbols, such as a flag, religious icon, stadium, or even spring practice have always been important in human activity.

The creation of the Ivy League had only minimal importance in reforming intercollegiate athletics, for by the time the Ivy League had been truly implemented, the rest of the nation had passed it by, athletically if not educationally. The Ivy League became a byword for athletic inferiority at the same time it was upheld as a model of athletic-academic integrity. Both became accepted myths, which generally contained some truth. Ivy League schools could no longer compete on a national level in football, but they won national team and individual championships in a number of other sports. Academically, most of the Ivy League institutions winked at the proposition that athletes "shall be truly representative of the student body and not composed of a group of special[ly] recruited and trained athletes" as the Ivy presidents demanded in 1945. Despite the rhetoric of brainy Ivy League athletes, and there were many, as late as the turn of the century, Ivy League schools were shown, in a finely tuned study by a retired Princeton president, to admit athletes who were academically inferior to their nonathlete peers, and they performed academically below them as well.[34] To raise the academic standards of athletes, the Ivy League developed the Academic Index in the 1990s, using standardized test scores and high school grade point averages to attempt to prevent Ivy schools from recruiting and harboring separate athlete populations.[35]

While the reformed Ivy League became a model for several conferences, the Ivy reforms were of a limited nature.[36] A. Bartlett Giamatti, president of Yale, stated in the 1980s that the Ivy League was "drifting away" from its principles.[37] It was true. The Ivy League began with a major reform intact, one adopted in the early 1900s: freshman ineligibility. Nevertheless, the Ivies yielded shortly after the NCAA began allowing freshman to compete on varsity teams in the late 1960s. First, the Ivy League approved freshman eligibility in all sports except baseball, basketball, football, ice hockey, lacrosse, rowing, and soccer in 1971; then allowed it in lacrosse, rowing, and soccer in 1974; hockey in 1975; basketball in 1977; and finally football in 1991. The Ivy League banned postseason football games when it was formed, but by 1990 approved the Epson Ivy Bowl all-star football game in Yokohama, Japan. It has allowed postseason play in other sports. The Ivies increased the number of football games to ten in 1977, further commercializing the most important sport for the Ivies as in many other institutions, and in 1991 allowed spring football practice once more. The Ivy institutions continued the tradition of firing coaches after losing seasons, indicating the importance of winning rather than the educational goals of athletics. The firing of Joe Yukica at Dartmouth in 1985 is a good example; he had coached three Ivy League championship teams and then suffered a losing season. The Ivy schools fought vainly to preserve their NCAA Division I-A status in football, but other NCAA institutions created a Division I-AA for the lesser-competitive schools in 1981, and the Ivy League then moved into a lower status. The Ivy League eventually signed contracts for game-of-the-week contests with both television and radio networks, indicating that commercialism was vitally alive in the reform conference. In addition, the Ivy schools moved in the direction of the corporate naming of athletic buildings and other commercial activities. The creation of the Ivy League was marked as a major reform in college athletics, but it has not lived up to standards that it set in 1945 and 1952 when it was created. The fact that the Ivy League presidents allowed Columbia to drop its academic standards for football players in the 1980s so that it might end its record losing streak speaks to the ineffectiveness of presidents to truly reform intercollegiate athletics, even at the most prestigious educational institutions in America.[38]

Nevertheless, when one compares the Ivy League with other major conferences that have had or desired to have big-time aspirations, the elite eastern league generally held to a higher standard than have many others. During the 1940s and 1950s, when the Ivy League was being formed, the crisis of ethics then was much more pronounced in other leagues and institutions than it was in Ivy League schools. The scandals of the early 1950s and the reactions to them by the American Council of Education and other agencies showed the way to another major reform effort.

12

Scandals and the ACE Reform Effort in the 1950s

Not since the football crisis of 1905–6 had the nation experienced the need for intercollegiate athletic reform as it did during and after the scandalous year of 1951. Whereas the earlier crisis in football had been based upon brutality and questionable ethics under the existing football rules, the early 1950s crisis was the result of gambling and the fixing of basketball games, academic cheating, and racially inspired brutality. In the post–World War II era, basketball had come to join football in its level of public popularity, becoming the second most commercially viable intercollegiate sport. It is not surprising, then, that the spirit of professionalism and commercialism in basketball would create problems similar to those found connected to football since the late 1800s. While football continued to be a focal point of reformers, basketball became the victim of the worst gambling scandal in collegiate history: the point-shaving scandal of 1951.

Until after World War II, there was little pressure to reform any other college sports than football, a perennial target, and baseball, because of the summer-baseball-for-pay problems that had never been solved. Basketball, however, became colleges' second-leading sport behind football by the 1930s, as it was a fast-growing sport for both men and women since its invention in 1891 by Canadian James Naismith at the YMCA Training School in Springfield, Massachusetts. It was definitely the most important sport for women in colleges by the early 1900s, but it was not a commercial entity, for the women leaders of college sport were diametrically opposed to making any sport commercial or professional in the model of men's sport.[1] For men, however, it became the winter competitive sport, with arenas being built by the 1920s to accommodate the growing number of spectators. Early during the Great Depression of the 1930s, basketball was given greater national visibility when Madison Square Garden in New York City sponsored intersectional games. The idea for Madison Square Garden double- and tripleheader basketball games originated with Ned Irish, a young reporter with the New York *World-Telegram*, who, in 1931 during the depths of the Depression, helped the unemployed in New York City by sponsoring benefit basketball games in the Garden. Irish soon saw the commercial possibilities of Garden basketball games pitting some of the best New York teams against those from across the country. By 1934, a doubleheader of St. Johns against Westminster and New York University versus Notre Dame drew more than 16,000 fans. That winter, despite the Depression, about 100,000 fans saw eight doubleheaders featuring such teams as Pittsburgh, Purdue, Duquesne, and Kentucky. Probably the greatest showcase for basketball at the Garden was Stanford versus Long Island University in 1936, in which Stanford's Hank Luisetti, the most prominent one-hand shooter, helped stop Long Island's forty-three-game winning streak. By 1938, Madison Square Garden hosted the first college national championship, the National Invitational Championship, when Temple beat Colorado and its all-American football player, Byron "Whizzer" White, for the title.[2]

While Madison Square Garden provided the national window for basketball's popularity, the Catskill Mountains north of New York City gave collegiate players an opportunity to hone their skills during the summer while coming in contact with the gambling fraternity at the many resorts. Skilled collegiate players, similar to summer baseball players, could enjoy making money at summer resorts while playing their favorite game. Eventually, several hundred Catskill hotels fielded teams in what was called the "Jewish Alps," with as many as five hundred college varsity players from all over the country. Playing several games a week, players such as Bob Cousy, Alex Groza, George Mikan, and John Bach split $150 or so a game. The summer players could make even more when they colluded with gamblers on the outcome of the game or in "split-line" gambling, in which points could be shaved to stay within the point spread for the game.[3] The Catskills provided the training ground for a number of players who shaved points for the gambling fraternity during the 1940s and early 1950s. It is not surprising that a number of the teams caught in the gambling scandal of 1951 were from New York City, or that many of the players involved had played summer basketball in the Catskills.

Six decades before the basketball scandal of 1951, Yale's Walter Camp warned: "A man who begins by selling his skill to a college may someday find himself selling an individual act in a particular contest—selling races, selling games."[4] By the end of World War II, Camp's warning became reality as betting on college basketball and the payment of players were known facts. In 1945, the New York City District Attorney's office, tapping a phone of a suspected thief, discovered a basketball fixing plan by five members of the Brooklyn College basketball team. A leader of the five, Larry Pearlstein, was a World War II veteran who joined the Brooklyn College basketball team under Coach Morris Raskin in 1944, though he was not admitted to the college and attended no classes. He played for a year in this state while the Committee on Athletics did nothing. The Brooklyn College president, Harry D. Gideonse, claimed ignorance of athletics when he publicly stated: "Neither the president of the college, nor any of its deans, were in any way involved in the administration of intercollegiate athletics."[5] Surely Gideonse and Brooklyn College administrators were either naive or incompetent, or they were more likely hypocritical. Colleges across the nation were warned of the possibility of gamblers taking control of the outcome of contests. The National Collegiate Athletic Association (NCAA) in 1944 set up a Committee on Gambling to look specifically at betting on the outcome of basketball and football games.[6] Justin Morrill, new president of the University of Minnesota, warned the members of the NCAA that players were "an easy prey to the easy-money approaches of unscrupulous gamblers" and that "a devastating betting scandal hovers like a black Harpy over the big-time intercollegiate athletic scene."[7] The Eastern College Athletic Conference and other conferences discussed gambling concerns, including tip sheets, point spreads, and betting odds, particularly on basketball games, well before the point-shaving scandal broke in early 1951.[8]

A new kind of betting on games developed by the 1940s, one that replaced betting odds such as found in horse racing, 4 to 1 odds on Whirlaway in the Kentucky Derby, or in basketball, 2 to 1 odds that Duke would beat North Carolina. Rather, teams would be rated and an estimate would be made by how many points the favored team would win. Thus Kentucky might be favored by 6 points over Long Island University. Those who bet on Kentucky would have to have Kentucky beat LIU by 7 points to win their bets. People would thus bet on the point spread. If gamblers paid off Kentucky players to keep their margin of victory to 6 points or less, both gamblers and Kentucky would win, and the players would be paid off for staying under the spread. Players would presumably not feel as guilty because they won, having not thrown the game, even though they had rigged the outcome to benefit themselves and the gamblers. New York City and Madison Square Garden may have been the center of the point-shaving scandal, but players outside New York were affected, probably in areas other than Kentucky, Ohio, and Illinois, where players eventually admitted to point shaving.

The 1951 scandal was a number of years in the making. Two years before the betting scandal was exposed, an attempted $1,000 bribery of a George Washington University captain from Brooklyn to lose by more than the spread in a Madison Square Garden game with Manhattan College was unsuccessful when the captain reported the bribe to New York District Attorney Frank Hogan. Four men were arrested and sentenced to prison.[9] Frank Hogan would play the most prominent role two years later when the major scandal broke. The following year, the National Invitational Tournament (NIT) included five teams that would be featured prominently in future point shaving, three from New York: City College of New York, Long Island University, and St. Johns University. The two outsider miscreants were Kentucky and Bradley. Shortly before the NIT began, an all-American, Paul Unruh, from the number one ranked team, Bradley in Peoria, Illinois, was offered a bribe to shave points in the tournament that was then more important than the NCAA championship. Unruh was given the opportunity to "make some easy money": $100 if Bradley won by six points and $500 if his team won by two points in any of the NIT games. Unruh rejected the offer but told nobody during the tournament when Bradley beat Syracuse 78–66 and St. Johns 83–72, before losing in the finals to CCNY 69–61. A month later, the bribe attempt was revealed by Unruh and reported in the *New York Times,* buried on page 41.[10] Few appeared overly alarmed about previous bribes and attempted bribes.

Soon, the major gambling scandal in collegiate history exploded. Early the next year, five men were arrested for trying to fix a 1951 Manhattan-De Paul game in Madison Square Garden. One of the bribers, Hank Poppe, a former Manhattan player, bemoaned his arrest: "Why did they have to catch us . . . when so many other guys are doing it? This has been going on for years."[11] A month later, the real shock occurred to basketball and the nation. City College of New York, the winner of both the 1950 NIT and the NCAA tournaments, had three of its star players, Ed Roman, Al Roth, and Ed Warner, arrested for taking money to fix games. Roman and Roth, likely, had been recruited by gamblers the previous summer when they played for the same resort hotel in Catskills.[12] Two days later, the top player in America, Sherman White of Long Island University, and two other LIU players admitted shaving points. Soon New York University players were under indictment. But it was not only in New York City, as players from the strong University of Toledo, formerly number one ranked Bradley, and the great University of Kentucky team were arrested for fixing games.

Adolph Rupp, coach of the University of Kentucky, responded to the point-shaving scandal coming out of New York City and Madison Square Garden, telling reporters that the fixers "could not touch his players with a ten-foot pole." Rupp, the most successful basketball coach in America following World War II and no stranger to taking Kentucky to Madison Square Garden, played in the opening game of the National Invitational Tournament of 1949. His team had won more than 90 percent of its games since the war but had been much less successful against the point spread. One of the reasons was that two all-Americans, Alex Groza and Ralph Beard, and another player, Dale Barnstable, had been shaving points.[13] In the NIT game against Loyola of Chicago, Kentucky was favored by 10 points and lost by 11. Later it was revealed that the three players were paid $500 by the gamblers. Losing the NIT championship did not prevent Kentucky from winning the NCAA championship a few weeks later, making it two straight NCAA national championships. Kentucky won again in 1951, shortly after the scandal erupted involving the New York City teams and before Kentucky was exposed. Cheating in middle America surprised many Americans, more than the shaving of points in New York. By early 1952, Judge Saul Streit in New York found the three Kentucky basketball players guilty of shaving points. He penned a sixty-three-page report condemning the University of Kentucky and its professionalized and commercialized program in which Adolph Rupp not only gave cash bonuses to players following games but also had a close relationship with a big-time bookmaker. The entire Kentucky program, Streit said, was a "disintegrating influence of money-mad athletics" that was the "acme of commercialism and over-emphasis."[14] Judge Streit let Kentucky and the world know what he believed was in need of reform: "I found undeniable evidence of covert subsidization of players, ruthless exploitation of athletes, cribbing on examinations, illegal recruiting, a reckless disregard for the players' physical welfare, matriculation of unqualified students, demoralization of the athletes by the coach, the alumni, and the townspeople."[15]

The 1951 gambling crisis at Kentucky and in a number of basketball programs called for reform, but the revelations coming that same summer from the U.S. Military Academy and its football team were probably a bigger shock. A massive cheating scandal was exposed, involving nearly the entire football team and coach Earl "Red" Blaik, who had national championship teams in 1944 and 1945 and a 57–3–4 record from 1944 to 1950. Blaik, by far the most powerful individual at West Point, obtained privileges beyond the ordinary for his football players: getting out of guard duty, being excused from chapel service, obtaining special seating assignments without going through proper military channels, and creating a special tutoring program to maintain athletic eligibility. He tolerated his players breaking the honor code at the Military Academy. Cadets knew they would be expelled from West Point if they were caught cheating or knew of others cheating and did not report it. Beginning with a few football players who obtained the exams for courses such as mathematics, physics, and English, by 1950 it grew to include nearly every member of the football team. A total of eighty-three cadets admitted their guilt, with nearly the entire team dismissed from the Academy.[16]

The West Point scandal shocked the nation in the midst of the Cold War and the shooting war in Korea. Comments about the moral strength of the nation's youth and the values of athletics were everywhere. Many came from congressmen and senators, who voted on appropriations for the military academies. Stated Harry F. Byrd, senator from Virginia: "The moral fiber of the nation is deteriorating." Senator J. William Fulbright of Arkansas felt that intercollegiate athletics had "become so perverted that it's a corrupting influence on all the youngsters in the big universities." Senator William Benton of Connecticut declared that football was a "cancer which eats at the vitals of academic integrity."[17] Yet those who had cheated in America were generally given second chances, a traditional national virtue according to many. A number of the ousted football players readily found athletic homes and available scholarships offered by other institutions of higher learning, including Colorado College, the University of Houston, Kansas State University, the University of Kansas, and Villanova University. Interestingly, Joseph P. Kennedy, father of future President John F. Kennedy, offered a free education to any of the dismissed West Point cadets to the University of Notre Dame, if they qualified. However, they could not participate in football. Twelve of the cadets accepted the offer.[18] Because many of the West Point football players were weak students who were given preferential treatment by the Military Academy, some reformers raised a larger issue. Should universities continue big-time athletics at the risk of weakened academic standards? For most of those who had power to change the system, the answer was "yes."

Yet "yes" was not the answer at a less visible school than West Point. At William and Mary College, which had its own scandal break in 1951, the school chose to reform rather than remain at the scandalous big-time level. It took, however, the resignation of the president, the football and basketball coaches, a dean, the director of admissions, several faculty members, and the head of the alumni association to undo what the Board of Trustees had imposed upon little William and Mary. The scandal at America's second oldest institution of higher education typified what was considered wrong with college athletics in post–World War II America. The quest for victory and institutional prestige overwhelmed the sense of morality on many college campuses. College presidents and especially governing boards lacked the moral fortitude to effectively lead their institutions. William and Mary was a clear example supporting the view that governing boards—the policy makers—hold the ultimate power in the control of intercollegiate athletics, not the presidents. The presidency of William and Mary's John Pomfret may be symbolic of the many institutional leaders who have historically lacked both the power and the courage to make athletics an integral part of the educational aspect of higher education. The scandal opened when the dean of William and Mary, Nelson Marshall, wrote President Pomfret: "The present administration of our intercollegiate athletic program is dishonest, unethical and seriously lacking in responsibility to the academic standards of William and Mary."[19]

John Pomfret became president in the midst of World War II, when William and Mary considered closing the school for lack of male enrollment, but was saved when an Army and a Navy program were brought to the institution. When the war was over, the governing board made it clear that it wanted a virile athletic program when it mandated that it expected "to *win* more contests than we lose."[20] Translated into administrative policy, this meant that the football coach would be paid more than any professor in an effort to turn out winning teams. It also meant that a double standard would be created for athletes who entered William and Mary with minimal academic qualifications but would receive nearly all of the college's scholastic financial aid. In order to compete in football against the likes of Michigan State and Oklahoma, academic standards were not only low, but the football coach (who was also athletic director and head of the physical education department) also began altering high school transcripts, college transcripts, and granting grades for courses not taken by athletes, which included not only football players but basketball players as well.[21] When an injured football player reported that his football scholarship was to be taken away by Coach Ruben McCray, he also indicated to a faculty member that athletes were accepting unauthorized money and receiving credit for courses not taken. The scandal was ready to break.

The task of investigating the rumors of wrongdoing was assigned to Dean of Students J. Wilfred Lambert, whose findings were then given to the dean of William and Mary College, Nelson Marshall. He in turn reported the findings in April 1951 to President Pomfret. When Pomfret dragged his feet rather than acting decisively, Marshall offered his resignation. Pomfret refused the resignation and, to gain time, asked Marshall to investigate more fully. In the meantime, Pomfret made good on a promise of several years to recommend to the governing board that Coach McCray be advanced to full professor.[22] Then the hypocritical Pomfret asked for the resignation of Coach McCray as well as that of the basketball coach, Barney Wilson, who was also involved in grade changing to keep players eligible. The governing board, which previously had set the stage of the scandal by its written policy of winning more games than were lost, chose only to blame President Pomfret for the scandal, now public knowledge. The board, however, not the president, was most responsible for the big-time athletic program gone wrong. It was nearly impossible for a student body of about seven hundred and fifty males to maintain a high-quality big-time program without going astray. The time was ripe for little William and Mary to carry out its own reform program, regardless of what other institutions were doing.

For once, the faculty of an institution took a strong hand in reforming athletics, in direct opposition to the governing board. With the absence of a president following President Pomfret's resignation, the faculty attempted to make its case for deemphasizing athletics with the governing board, but the board locked the faculty out of its hearing on athletics. The faculty responded in near unanimity with a manifesto demanding that there be faculty control of athletics, a necessity under the Southern Conference constitution. The faculty printed 20,000 copies of its manifesto and sent it to all William and Mary alumni, students, and the national press. The manifesto called the governing board's athletic policies "insidious influences," sapping the academic standards of the college. The angry faculty stated that "the principle of faculty control has not hitherto been practiced [and] it must be practiced in the future."[23] The governing board detested the faculty uprising and soon elected a new president, a naval officer, Admiral Alvin Duke Chandler, without any faculty involvement.

Athletics might have remained completely under governing board control had not the William and Mary alumni become involved. Evidently, the alumni had been embarrassed enough and sided with the faculty rather than the governing board. Alumni gifts for athletics dropped precipitously after the scandal and forced a de-emphasis on the big-time program.[24] Changing the ambitious big-time program at William and Mary was not easy to accomplish, but it made a statement about the importance of governing boards. Governing boards must be considered as an important component of the athletic equation. As governing boards set athletic policy either by direct action or by default through inaction, they are and have been critical units in the development of intercollegiate athletics. While historically bringing athletic programs in line with concepts of academic integrity has generally been considered the task of faculty and presidents, it was nearly impossible unless the governing boards were willing participants.

If the 1951 scandals of point shaving in basketball, the academic cheating at West Point, and the toxic situation at William and Mary highlighted the year of despair for reform, an individual act by Oklahoma A & M against a black player from Drake University showed the need for racial reform in athletics and in America. The process of desegregating sport in America was in its initial stages in the early 1950s. Colleges in the southern states were segregated both academically and athletically. Even in the less segregationist North, there were few African Americans who attended college or who participated in intercollegiate athletics. Only four years before the Oklahoma A & M-Drake University racial incident, Jackie Robinson had desegregated major league baseball by playing for the Brooklyn Dodgers. Less important professional football had desegregated the year before. Professional basketball's time would arrive in 1950, the year Althea Gibson was allowed to compete at Forest Hills in the U.S. tennis championships. There had been African Americans playing college football in the North since the late 1800s, but that was rare. Yale did not have a black football player until after World War II, and Princeton's first African American did not compete until the mid-1960s, nearly as late as most southern schools.[25] Drake University in Des Moines, Iowa, however, had probably the outstanding player in America, Johnny Bright, an African American quarterback and total leader in rushing and passing in the nation for several years.[26] Drake was a member of the Missouri Valley Conference that had voted in 1947 to end racial discrimination in all conference schools by 1950. At the time, four years before the *Brown v. Board of Education* Supreme Court case, only conference members Tulsa and Oklahoma A & M were segregated.[27] When Oklahoma A & M played Drake in 1951, there were rumors of betting pools on when the Aggies would injure and remove Bright from the game. On the game's first play, Bright handed off the ball, and when far removed from the action and from the officials' eyes, the A & M defensive tackle went directly toward Bright and hit him with a forearm blow with so much force that the attacker's feet were well off the ground at impact. Bright's jaw was broken, and despite this he threw a 60-yard touchdown pass on the next play. Soon Drake got possession of the ball again, and the same tackle once again hit him on his blind side well away from the play. This time Bright was taken from the field. Pictures of the assault were taken for the *Des Moines Register and Tribune* and republished nationally in *Life Magazine.*[28] The fact that Drake broke relations with Oklahoma A & M and withdrew from the Missouri Valley Conference did not help to immediately reform athletics racially, but the incident showed that this was an area in need of reform.

With all the negative events, it would have been logical for the NCAA to take action to show America that it was serious about providing solutions for reforming college athletics. However, the NCAA had only the year before failed to enforce the Sanity Code, and what little power it possessed had been wasted on the failed effort to restrict the perceived sins of recruiting and payment of athletes. On the other hand, the scandals of 1951 would provide the prestigious American Council on Education (ACE) with its best opportunity for athletic reform. The ACE was controlled by college presidents, and it was logical in its collective mind that college presidents should lead the athletic reform effort.[29] Most presidents, with short memories for athletic reform history, could at least look to the presidents of elite eastern institutions who formed the Ivy League only a few years before. Those with a sense of history could ask if presidents had ever been truly effective in reforming college athletics, even in forming the Ivy League. Yet the presidential leadership of the ACE knew that its favored reform measures contained in the defeated Sanity Code would likely be in the historical wastebasket unless it took action at this critical time. In the fall of 1951, the ACE announced a reform committee of presidents to right the wrongs of college athletics. The fact that presidents had often been on the wrong side of reform did not deter presidents from choosing their own to initiate the reform. Eleven presidents were chosen from across the nation, mostly from big-time universities, including Mississippi, Notre Dame, Nebraska, and Yale.[30]

Unfortunately for the creditability of reform, the group chose as its chairman John Hannah, a major athletic promoter who later was found to have condoned cheating while he was president of Michigan State College.[31] However, to Hannah's credit, he helped build the Michigan Agriculture College into Michigan State University, in part by using winning athletics to promote the institution, even being invited to replace the University of Chicago in the Big Ten in 1948. Like many other college presidents before and after, he acted as an athletic cheerleader by allowing fine athletes who were unacceptable students into his institution of higher education. Before becoming president at Michigan State, Hannah was the administrator of a fund for athletic scholarships at a time when the Big Ten and other colleges in the Midwest had outlawed the grants. A Michigan State NCAA faculty representative, Harold Tukey, later revealed that the administration knew of grade fixing, slush funds, and drug use at Michigan State but overlooked them. Because most of the evils were not uncovered during Hannah's administration, the result was that the graduation rate for football and basketball players went down while the prestige of the university went up as it excelled in the big-time sports.[32]

As chairman of the ACE committee, President Hannah led a series of meetings with other college presidents from major conferences: Big 7, Big Ten, Ivy, Pacific Coast, Southeast, Southwest, Southern, and two midmajor conferences, Mid-America and Mountain States. Notre Dame was the independent representative. President Hannah commented after the opening sessions of the ACE reform committee: "Subsidization has been necessary to produce winning teams and satisfy the demands of the alumni. We must eliminate those factors which give undue emphasis to winning."[33] It sounded good, but there is no evidence that he meant it. Less than two months after the first ACE committee meeting, the group of eleven presidents came to a unanimous decision on what should be reformed, and the recommendations were presented to the NCAA by the time of its convention in early January 1952. The ACE recommended making "intercollegiate athletics not as an end in themselves, but as a valuable part of a well-rounded program of higher education." To accomplish this, the committee proposed nearly two-dozen policy changes, including athletic admission standards to be the same as for other students; no freshman eligibility; a normal progress rule leading to recognized degrees; athletic grants not conditional on athletic participation and limited to tuition, room, board, books, and fees; elimination of bowl and postseason games; elimination of free substitution or platoon football; clearly defined sport seasons;

coaches with faculty status and salaries in line with other faculty; and athletics controlled under university administration.[34]

As the ACE had no directive power, its reform measures could only be carried out by others. The most logical was the NCAA, but its Sanity Code had recently failed, and the NCAA was not in a good position to make another attempt. Besides, most presidents, who appointed the majority of NCAA faculty representatives and were thus in position to demand reform, were not in favor of any reform that would upset their governing boards or the alumni. Reform might even put their presidential positions at risk. However, college accrediting organizations, all of which were members of the ACE, were suggested as the agencies that could insist upon reform in order to maintain accreditation. The ACE could ask each of the five accrediting organizations—Middle States Association, New England Association, North Central Association, Northwest Association, and Southern Association—to direct individual colleges to accept the ACE recommendations or lose their accreditation.[35] Accreditation, though, was a contentious issue since the beginning of the accrediting associations in the late 1800s, and accreditation of athletics was even more so, for accrediting organizations came into being to raise academic standards, not athletic standards. College presidents were constantly questioning accrediting organizations when it was their institutions that were in the spotlight. According to historian Hugh Hawkins, "professional accrediting programs . . . aroused militant opposition." He noted that by 1950, presidents "applauded attacks on some accreditor's intrusiveness."[36] When the suggestion was made that accrediting organizations, such as the powerful North Central Association, should take it upon themselves to reform college athletics, big-time universities rebelled. Some leaders surely remembered what happened about a decade before when accrediting agencies felt it was their duty to concern themselves with "coaches salaries and stipends for athletes."[37] Following the scandals of 1951, presidents did not want the accrediting agencies determining whether coaches would be paid salaries similar to those of other faculty members; whether financial aid should be limited to tuition, room, board, books, and fees; or whether freshmen should be eligible for athletic participation.

One 1952 incident involved the North Central Association (NCA) and rankled leaders of the Big 7, including the University of Missouri. The North Central Association charged Missouri with violating NCA guidelines by subsidizing athletes, something generally accepted in many institutions and conferences across America, including the Big 7.[38] The Big 7 took up the NCA concern and indicated that not only were all conference members observing the same rules, but they also were in accord with the NCAA and the ACE. The NCA responded by asking whether "intercollegiate athletics, as conducted, . . . contribute clearly and directly to the stated educational purposes of the institution?"[39] The NCA had little support from the Big 7, the ACE, the American Association of University Professors, or the NCAA, all of which believed that athletic ability might be of some consideration in the awarding of university financial grants, just as were scholastic achievement, financial need, and good character.[40] At the NCAA convention, at which President Hannah presented his ACE committee report, President Fred Hovde of Purdue was asked to speak about the place of intercollegiate athletics. He praised the reform efforts of the ACE, but he opposed asking accrediting associations to enforce its reform measures, since it would be wrong to punish the academic side of education for the sins of the athletic side. There should be athletic penalties, Hovde said, not academic penalties.[41]

In the end, neither the NCA nor other accrediting associations carried out threats of loss of accreditation for offering athletic scholarships, and universities continued to generally do what they had been doing previously. The NCAA, while voting overwhelmingly to support the general principles of the ACE recommendations, carried out few of the specifics in the next few years. The NCAA, however, had two accomplishments following the scandals of 1951. First, despite some strong opposition, it changed the constitution to allow itself to vote on "any subjects of general concern" and pass them with a simple majority instead of the previous two-thirds majority.[42] This would allow reform legislation to be more easily passed in the future. Second, the NCAA decided to take strong action against the University of Kentucky after the Southeastern Conference voted to suspend Kentucky from conference basketball for one year after the point-shaving scandal and other improprieties. The NCAA banned all intercollegiate competition with Kentucky for one year by boycotting the school. This was an aggressive NCAA stand, especially since its own Sanity Code had failed to be upheld only a couple of years before. Walter Byers was at his first NCAA conference as full-time executive director when Kentucky was punished in what has sometimes been called the first NCAA death penalty. It wasn't officially a death penalty, for the Enforcement Committee of the NCAA called for a boycott of Kentucky, and fortunately for the NCAA, Kentucky's president, Ab Kirwan, did not challenge the decision. Kentucky did not play basketball the next year, though Kentucky's basketball team practiced and had several sellouts for its intrasquad games during the 1952–53 season. Much later, Walter Byers conceded that the NCAA penalty wiped out the failure of the Sanity Code and gave legitimacy to the NCAA's first successful effort to enforce its policy.[43] The NCAA had punished Kentucky, but true reform did not occur after the scandals of 1951. Problems of reform worsened as academic standards for athletes entering college dropped in big-time athletics in the 1950s.

13

Lowly Standards
Chaos in the Sports Yards

The scandals of 1951 led to no long-term, meaningful reform in college athletics. This was not unexpected, for past history would indicate that governing boards, presidents, alumni, and students, though not faculty, preferred the professionalized and commercialized model that had developed over the previous century. That model for men's sport dated back to the first intercollegiate contest, a crew meet between Harvard and Yale sponsored by a new railroad passing through the vacationlands of New Hampshire. In 1852, there were no eligibility standards and students were in nearly complete control of their sports. A hundred years later, there were recruiting and eligibility standards at the institutional and conference level, and the sports that colleges sponsored had passed from the hands of students to alumni, presidents, and governing boards, with a nod to college faculties.

The reform that had taken place was created principally to attempt to ensure competitive equality, a level playing field, among the various institutions and conferences. Little had been done to ensure that recruited athletes would fit the academic profile of the rest of the student body as they entered college or during their college years. In other words, the governing boards and institutional presidents, from the elite Ivy League schools to state universities to private institutions large and small, generally accepted athletes who were inferior academically for the benefits they might provide the individual institutions on the playing fields. The athletic payback was generally the prestige a good football or men's basketball team might provide, but it could also be the perceived need for the virile, manly element athletes brought to colleges, often considered effete through the first half of the twentieth century.

By then, colleges stood for much more than the traditional classical education that had existed for most of the nineteenth century. The pursuit of academic excellence never entirely disappeared, but attending a university increasingly became important for social contacts instead of intellectual growth. Social status, not knowledge, became a twentieth-century trait of higher education, with social activities, fraternities, and athletics dominating student interests.[1] Two prominent educational leaders, both intellectuals, who most opposed the direction higher education was taking were Abraham Flexner of the Carnegie Foundation for the Advancement of Teaching, who fought the "service station" mentality of many institutions of higher education, and Robert M. Hutchins, the president of the University of Chicago, who was greatly pleased when the trustees of Chicago voted to abolish football just prior to World War II. They were, though, definitely in the minority, and the desire by university leaders to allow big-time athletics to continue their professional and commercial growth prevented meaningful reform in the decades following World War II.

By the early 1950s, there was a greater need for legislating athletic standards on the national level, even though the first attempt, the Sanity Code of 1948, was not complied with by many institutions and was never enforced. The growth of air travel, making interregional travel less burdensome, and the development of national networks, first in radio and then, more important, in television, created national audiences for the important sports, specifically football and the emerging basketball.[2] The recruiting of athletes on a national level and the increase in interregional contests brought about the need for recruiting and financial aid to be on an equitable basis. This could not be done if some conferences allowed athletic grants-in-aid to fully pay for an athlete's college expenses, such as took place in the Southeastern and Southwestern Conferences, while others, including the Big Ten Conference, opposed athletic scholarships. In short, a kind of civil war occurred, with most southern schools favoring athletic scholarships not tied to either academic skills or financial need and many northern schools advocating athletes meeting academic and scholarship standards similar to other members of the student body. The southern schools were not only more realistic but also less hypocritical, as many northern schools, including the academically elite Ivy League institutions,[3] often winked at academic standards when they admitted needed athletes.

The period following the defeat of the Sanity Code was one caught between attempting to retain some semblance of amateurism on the one hand and the payment of athletes at a subsistence level on the other. No national standard for the payment of athletes was reached until 1956, when, to the dismay of a number of reformers, the NCAA agreed to allow "full rides," or athletic scholarships that would pay for tuition, room, board, fees, books, and "laundry" money, what the NCAA said were "commonly accepted educational expenses," and thus still considered amateur.[4] What most officials did not understand, or wished to ignore, was that by creating expensive athletic scholarships, alumni who would often be asked to pay for the grants would come to expect even greater control over the athletic programs than they already had. Or as Fritz Crisler, Michigan's football coach, indicated: "A lot of good programs are going to mortgage their integrity by raising money from alumni to pay for grants-in-aid, not only in football but also the other sports."[5] Yet, conferences would not have to accept the new national norms if they chose to be more "amateur" than others. The Big Ten was divided between those favoring full athletic scholarships without regard to academics and others who wanted no scholarships, except to students who met scholarly requirements. The Big Ten had opposed the conferences in the South that granted full athletic scholarships in the 1930s and 1940s, if for no other reason than it tended to draw superior athletes to the South and away from Big Ten institutions. But because the Big Ten was run by representatives of the institutions' faculties (and on important issues by the presidents), there was a strong opposition to awarding scholarships based solely upon athletic ability. In 1956, when the NCAA voted to allow full scholarships, the Big Ten was debating whether it should offer financial aid based upon high scholarship and financial need or whether athletic scholarships should be available based upon athletic prowess. The Big Ten presidents, in a 6–4 vote, accepted a need-based athletic scholarship program, which pleased neither those presidents who opposed any athletic scholarships nor others who favored scholarships based upon athletic ability.[6]

The division of thought was best revealed by two presidents, Justin L. Morrill of Minnesota and Virgil M. Hancher of Iowa, his neighbor to the south. President Morrill, a transplant from Ohio State University, opposed even a need-based plan if it was open to all athletes with a high school diploma. He believed any aid to athletes not based on scholarship would further erode the academic standing of athletes and would identify athletes with full scholarships, setting them apart, putting them in an athletic ghetto and away from all other students. The integrity of the athletic program would be further eroded. In addition, the cost of full scholarships would create financial problems and contribute to what he considered "the highly debatable principle . . . of using gate receipts as a means to finance" the scholarships. He said need-based scholarships were unworkable, as they turned out to be, and would lead logically to full support of athletes and "the paid player basis."[7]

Iowa's Virgil Hancher, on the other hand, favored full scholarships based upon athletic talent. Hancher, a farm boy from Iowa as well as a Rhodes Scholar at Oxford University, wrote a brilliant letter to fellow Big Ten presidents arguing for full athletic scholarships based upon talent. It was ironic that a man from Oxford, where financial aid to athletes was unthinkable, would promote athletic scholarships, but his reasoning was as different as Oxford athletics were from the American-born system of intercollegiate athletics. Though he knew of no universities "where learning and culture are more at home" than Oxford and Cambridge, the Oxbridge experience would not be duplicated in America, for the British-marked distinction between the gentleman amateur and the professional in sport did not exist in America.[8] Maintaining a standard of amateurism and need-based aid, he wrote, should not be the first consideration; searching for talent was the American way in athletics and in the larger society. In America, Hancher stated, "the fascination with athletics on the part of parents, alumni, and sponsors" can best be met with honesty and integrity by providing "above-board provision for room, board, tuition, books . . . and incidental expenses." He wanted to make "the rules so fair and equitable, so clear and understandable that an unintentional violation of them is almost impossible." He explained why a need-based program would result in "unfairness and inequities . . . hypocrisy and evasion." Since he believed that athletic scholarships based on talent would ultimately be the future, he saw "no reason for subjecting ourselves to the intervening agony."[9] Both Hancher and Morrill lost their cases initially, but Hancher's view eventually won out, for after several years the Big Ten institutions found that they could not effectively compete with the Alabamas, Nebraskas, and Oklahomas that were giving full scholarships based upon athletic talent. Thus the Big Ten remained in the big time of intercollegiate athletics by joining those to the South and West, when the presidents soon accepted the level playing field of full grants-in-aid to athletes.

While the Big Ten was attempting to reform its athletic scholarship program, the Pacific Coast Conference, with high ideals and low practices, was in the throes of a scandal that would break up the conference and influence NCAA policies. The Pacific Coast Conference (PCC), in one form or another, had been in existence since 1915.[10] Several times before World War II, the conference broke up over questions of eligibility. Shortly after the war, the commissioner of the PCC reported eight pages of violations by a number of the institutions, with the University of Washington threatened with expulsion if it did not open its records to the conference and the University of Oregon barred if it did not fire its football coach for recruitment and athlete payment violations.[11] The situation in the league got worse by the mid-1950s with the revelation of illegal payments to numerous athletes from slush funds run by alumni groups. The PCC was led by Commissioner Victor O. Schmidt, a lawyer and a true advocate of amateurism. He experienced the conflict between professionalized and commercialized college sport and amateurism in his conference, once stating that "we are trying to perform an impossibility: to operate a professional program on an amateur basis."[12]

The secret slush funds, which were certainly not unique to Pacific Coast Conference institutions, became known to the public in 1956 when Commissioner Victor Schmidt released his report of the four major offenders, the universities of

Southern California, UCLA, California, and Washington.[13] When exposed, the private institution, Southern California, considered unilateral withdrawal from the conference but reconsidered when the lucrative Rose Bowl football game and the advertising value of 60 million TV viewers and a similar number of radio listeners would be lost. "There is no way to purchase the type of institutional publicity which SC receives," a Southern Cal report noted, "by Rose Bowl participation."[14] It could also have concluded that Southern Cal would not likely have won a Rose Bowl bid if it had not illegally supported forty-four athletes with a slush fund known as the Southern California Educational Foundation.

The University of California, Los Angeles was threatened with ouster from the PCC, for it had another slush fund. More important, however, UCLA was part of the University of California system dominated by UC-Berkeley, and UCLA competed with Berkeley for student enrollment, academic prestige, and athletic victories. There were those in the Los Angeles area who wanted UCLA to break away from the University of California system and move ahead on its own. The strain between the two California institutions was at a breaking point when an outstanding athlete, Ronnie Knox, transferred from Berkeley to UCLA. Knox, the star passer from Los Angeles, arrived as a freshman on the UC-Berkeley campus with promises of a monthly stipend, hundreds of dollars from selling football tickets, free family travel back and forth to Los Angeles, a $400 per month job for his interfering stepfather, and a position on the California football staff for his high school coach, all made possible by the Southern Seas Club, a booster group for UC-Berkeley.[15] Following a fruitless year at Berkeley, Knox transferred to California's grown-up little sibling, UCLA, causing turmoil between the two schools. Often injured, Knox played only sparingly, left school, and joined the Canadian Football League when the Pacific Coast Conference pinned a fine on UCLA and penalized the football players who were receiving financial favors from a UCLA slush fund with the loss of one year of eligibility. Knox remarked: "I found college football [was like] pro football—only the salaries were much smaller."[16]

With most of the Pacific Coast Conference schools having alumni-driven slush funds for athletes and with rampant recriminations within the conference, it was only a matter of time before the group broke up. In 1957, the conference fired its "too pure" conference commissioner, Vic Schmidt, for doing what the conference presidents had asked him to do: clean up college sport on the West Coast.[17] Certainly, Chancellor Raymond Allen of UCLA was not unhappy that Schmidt was dismissed, for Allen had blocked the PCC's investigation of the UCLA athletic department prior to the commissioner fining UCLA for its violations, suspending athletes, and preventing UCLA from participating in the Rose Bowl game for three years. Soon the dissolved conference was re-created as the PAC-8, with nearly all of the former institutions brought into the new league.[18]

Not all scandalous behavior was made public; probably most was hidden, including the case of the University of Tennessee and its illegal slush fund. Revealed slush funds were a major concern for reformers. Some, like the Pacific Coast Conference, became headline news. Others were known only by insiders, including presidents such as Cloide Brehm of the University of Tennessee, where possibly the most egregious case was that found in the 1950s. Tennessee was one of the featured big-time colleges in football, and its coach and later athletic director was a godlike figure, General Robert Neyland. Neyland became head football coach at Tennessee in 1926 following his career at the U.S. Military Academy, where he starred as an end on the football team, was the Academy heavyweight boxing champion, and was offered a major league baseball contract. At the close of the 1930s, his Tennessee team won thirty-three straight games and the national championship in 1939, when it held its opponent scoreless. Following decorated military action in World War II, Neyland returned to Tennessee, where his 1951 team was undefeated and again national champions. The general retired in 1952 with 173 wins and only 32 losses, the best record ever for a coach with twenty years of tenure.[19] By the time he became athletic director, he was revered enough to have a stadium named after him, but he followed *his* rules, not those of the University of Tennessee, the Southeastern Conference, or the NCAA.

When he became athletic director, and likely well before, Neyland had an illegal athletic slush fund, which President Cloide Brehm knew existed but feared doing anything about. Just like many presidents before and after, Brehm was not naive about what was going on in the administration of athletics, yet he feared for his own position if any wrongdoing was discovered. In Brehm's tenth year as president, he called a meeting of trusted advisors, including Andy Holt, who would follow him as president. All of the important administrators knew about the illegal fund held by Neyland, but as President Brehm told them, as revealed in a lengthy meeting transcript: "I am not so sure that you can get rid of [Neyland's] 'slush fund.'"[20] Brehm noted that Tennessee had been illegally funding the "bought" football team with a "'pay-off' man since 1924," and it was not easy to change the system since important members of the Board of Trustees wanted a winning football team, and if the Board found out that Brehm was about to "wade in" on illegal football practices, "they may cut my throat." Brehm conceded that Board members Bill Pettway, Judge McAllester, and Mr. Cox were in Neyland's pocket and wanted to ensure a winning team. The president was looking out not only for his own future but also to the welfare of the University of Tennessee, and he knew that if the Southern Association Accrediting Agency found out about the slush fund, the accrediting group could take away the university's accreditation. What to do? One vice president warned: "You cannot help this with surgery—to deemphasize football; the public will not let you; the Board will not let you."[21] After several hours of discussion, no solutions were proposed, and Bob Neyland continued to use his slush fund as he had in the past. Presidents, such as Cloide Brehm, have not been unusual in their approach to intercollegiate athletics. Generally they have known what problems and illegal activities existed but were not prone to combat them or were powerless to do so. Presidents, as had been revealed since the 1800s, were almost never the solution to problems of athletic reform.

While the Tennessee affair was successfully covered up by university officials, the fiasco on the West Coast and other less-publicized actions helped the NCAA to strengthen its rules enforcement arm. As Vic Schmidt was forced out as commissioner of the Pacific Coast League and other conference commissioners feared an early exit from their positions if they enforced conference athletic regulations too closely, there was a feeling that the NCAA should carry out the enforcement on a national level. Some believed that only by using the threat of removing the financial rewards from football telecasting and the national basketball tournament from individual institutions could enforcement reform be accomplished. Specifically, the new NCAA game-of-the-week television contract for football and the Final Four in basketball became the financial weapon of enforcement. By the mid-1950s, the college basketball tournament was bringing in more money to the NCAA than receipts from football telecasting and membership dues combined, the next largest incomes for the NCAA.[22] While football telecast and Final Four money was mostly distributed to the participants, the cost of administrating the NCAA was almost entirely paid for by those two mediums, particularly the basketball championship. The Final Four basketball money would allow for the hiring of enforcement officers, beginning with the first one in the mid-1950s, Arthur Bergstrom, the former athletic director from Bradley University, the institution that had suffered from the point-shaving scandal of 1951. With enforcement, schools could be punished by withholding both football telecasts and entry into the basketball play-offs. By the 1960s, enforcement had generally been transferred from conferences to the NCAA enforcement machinery.

Enforcement was only one of the problems facing the NCAA; setting academic eligibility standards for freshmen athletes and continuing academic progress were other major ones. For most of the twentieth century, conferences, not the NCAA, prohibited freshmen from participation. The exception was wartime, when the number of male athletes was limited, and freshmen were allowed to play during World War I, World War II, and the Korean War. While waiting for athletes to become eligible in their sophomore year, coaches were most concerned that the athletes remain academically eligible. But those concerned about athletics wanted a level playing field with their competitors, and there were calls for entrance and eligibility requirements for athletes not only in conferences but across the country as well. A level playing field could not be attained, however, if the general standard for institutions to accept athletes who were academically representative of their student bodies was not observed. As a Big Ten document pointed out: "The special devices available for entrance seem not to be missed where an athlete is concerned."[23]

Because of the lack of standards, individuals began to speak out for setting minimal academic requirements to participate in athletics. Probably the first, in 1959, to make the case before the NCAA for national academic requirements was Rixford Snyder of Stanford University, historian, director of admissions, and faculty representative to the Pacific Coast Conference. Snyder told the convention delegates the best predictors for academic success in college were, first, high school grades and, second, scores on standardized test such as the Scholastic Aptitude Test. When the two were weighed together, the prediction of scholarly attainment was greater. With the Cold War between the Soviet Union and the United States becoming hotter, Snyder told the delegates: "The age of rockets and of satellites will not accept the free ride for an athlete of limited academic potential while the physicist with only moderate physical prowess goes unaided financially." The Soviet Union putting the first artificial satellite into earth orbit two years earlier led Snyder and some others into believing that college athletes should be capable of doing college-level academic work.[24] National standards would soon be demanded.

By the early 1960s, there were no national standards, but the Atlantic Coast Conference, organized in 1953, became the first major conference to require minimum academic standards for awarding athletic scholarships.[25] The ACC minimum was a 750 SAT score, adopted in 1960, and raised to 800 four years later.[26] The ACC knew that the minimum standard would be a recruiting and competing detriment to ACC members when playing outside the conference but believed that some minimum standard was needed.[27] In response to the lack of any national academic standards, the NCAA set up a committee in 1962, led by ACC Commissioner James Weaver, to determine a formula for "predicting academic success for those who are given grants-in-aid." After deliberations with officials of the Scholastic Aptitude Test and the American College Testing Program, the NCAA debated and passed a minimal academic standard for freshmen to receive athletic scholarships of a predicted 1.600 grade point average (about a D+/C– average) based upon standardized test scores and high school grade point averages. To continue with the athletic scholarship, an individual needed to maintain a minimum 1.600 grade point average.[28] The NCAA had finally achieved a minimal academic standard, but not without a great deal of soul searching and rancor.

There was opposition to the 1.600 rule from the beginning, but the impact upon race and lower economic status of athletes was not at first the dominant arguments used against it. Surprisingly, the Ivy League and other more elite academic institutions fought the 1.600 rule from the start. President Robert Goheen of Princeton expressed the Ivy resistance because they favored institutional autonomy and the principle of Home Rule. The Ivies believed that the faculty of individual colleges, not the NCAA, should determine eligibility. The Ivy League also believed that the 1.600 rule worked "most severely against students in institutions which have the highest admissions and academic standards." The reasoning was that, competing against high-achieving students, Ivy League athletes might well be below the 1.6 GPA after their freshman year, though they were potentially good students. This was seconded by a southern school, Duke, with Ivy academic aspirations. Duke, in a study on the impact of the 1.600 rule, revealed that fifteen of fifty-three sophomore football and basketball players would be ineligible, and a professor of economics, Robert Dickens, reported: The 1.600 rule "is patently designed to penalize the quality [university] that requires its student-athletes to take a normal program in competition with high quality students. It does not happen in the low quality school . . . with special courses tailored to his needs."[29] The Ivy League leaders also felt that "late bloomers," "slum-school" students, and "disadvantaged" students would be hurt by the new NCAA rule.[30] The Ivy League never adopted the 1.600 rule, though it never withdrew from the NCAA because of its opposition.

More important to the eventual demise of the 1.600 rule was that it came at a time of the civil rights movement, affirmative action, and turmoil from the war in Vietnam. For African Americans, it was a time of breaking down legalized and de facto segregation in American society, and the rule came to symbolize for college sport the racist nature of America.[31] Soon after the rule's passage, the charge of racism was made to challenge the rule and eventually became the principal argument in its defeat after its tumultuous seven years of existence. The argument against the use of standardized scores to determine eligibility for athletic scholarships was that African Americans scored lower on the tests because the scholarly assessments were culturally biased against them. This was shown to be true. Yet when the Atlantic Coast Conference inaugurated its "racially biased" SAT score standard, there were no blacks in the racially segregated ACC. Thus, the ACC standard and the NCAA rule were hardly created to prevent blacks from receiving athletic money to attend college and participate in athletics as was sometimes charged.[32] The number of blacks in northern institutions was also small, but growing. For example, the year after the 1.600 rule was passed, Texas Western, in El Paso, with five black starters beat the segregated University of Kentucky team for the national championship in basketball. By the late 1960s and early 1970s, southern institutions were recruiting blacks and attempting to meet the requirements of the Civil Rights Act of 1964. The American Civil Liberties Union (ACLU) had challenged southern schools to desegregate their athletic programs and comply with Title VI of the Civil Rights Act, which prohibited discrimination on the basis of race, color, and national origins in programs that received federal financial assistance. The ACLU noted in 1966 that there were no blacks among the 113 Louisiana State football players and none at the University of Georgia, while Georgia Tech refused to recruit a great black football prospect who lived only ten miles away.[33]

With the open admissions policies spreading across America around 1970 and with Educational Opportunity Programs (EOP) for underprivileged students growing, there was a movement to remove academic barriers to those entering college. The NCAA 1.600 rule ran counter to growing opportunities for minorities, especially African Americans. The Eastern Collegiate Athletic Conference, a large athletic conference of about two hundred members that was created originally in the late 1930s to procure quality sport officials, debated the 1.600 rule in 1970, recognizing that for many eastern colleges and their open admissions and EOP policies, the 1.600 rule was in conflict.[34] Robert Tierney of Queens College, which had open admissions, told his NCAA colleagues in 1971 that "many colleges today find themselves in a position where this particular rule is not relevant," and that because of "sociological changes taking place throughout the country, they find they cannot conform" to the 1.600 rule.[35] Nevertheless, the NCAA members voted no to abolishing the 1.600 rule. The next year, it was again debated, with Edwin Cady, a longtime faculty representative, quoting his president: "There is not any possible way in which a man can be ineligible to compete in athletics in Indiana University because he is poor and black and government-aided."[36] That year, 1972, the NCAA had just allowed freshmen to participate in varsity athletics in basketball and football, while most other sports had been granted freshman eligibility four years previously. John Larsen of the University of Southern California commented that with freshmen eligible for the two most important sports in college, it was "more urgent than ever that we have some measure of the prospective student-athlete's ability to succeed at the university level." Larsen was temporarily successful, as the vote to abolish the 1.600 rule lost again, this time 186–125.[37]

Opposition to the eligibility rule would not die. Robert Tierney of Queens College summarized the major arguments against the 1.600 rule, noting that it discriminated against special students (principally inner-city blacks), it violated institutional autonomy (the old Home Rule), and the SAT and ACT tests were of questionable validity. He predicted a lawsuit might overturn the 1.600 rule if the NCAA did not soon do so.[38] Nevertheless, when a motion to abolish the 1.600 rule came up again in 1973, Alan Chapman of Rice University, a longtime champion of the rule, believed it would be "a serious mistake for this Association to remove any academic standards at all; and when one couples that with the present freshman eligibility rule, the opportunities for the abuse of the young man grow enormously."[39] Before a vote was taken, Robert Behrman of City College of New York summed up the opposition and asked for a clean break with the rule, for it was "a source of confusion, embarrassment, frustration and hostility for ever-increasing numbers of member institutions." In a close vote, 204–187, Behrman won.[40] Walter Byers, executive director of the NCAA, lost. He later recalled: "Losing the 1.600 rule was one of the most painful experiences in the 22 years I had then served as executive director. It was a terrible day for college athletics."[41] The result was that not only were freshman eligible to compete in all sports, including football and basketball, but there were no minimal academic standards once the individual was admitted to college. The only requirement for varsity competition was a high school 2.0 grade point average in any high school curriculum.[42] The future could look to chaos in the sports yard as increased money was funneled into intercollegiate athletics with the growth in gate receipts, football bowls, the ever-more-popular basketball tourney, and lucrative television contracts. The drive to recruit the best athletes, with or without academic credentials, increased accordingly, and with it, of course, the call for intercollegiate athletic reform.

14

The Hanford Report, Rejected Reform, and Proposition 48

In the same month the National Collegiate Athletic Association (NCAA) convention decided to remove all national academic requirements for athletes to participate as freshmen and throughout their college years, the January 1973 peace agreement was reached, theoretically ending the Vietnam War. The war had brought social and economic turmoil, a conflict that began in 1959 and soon involved U.S. troop support and recognized combat troops beginning in 1965. Along with social unrest, a tremendous period of inflation resulted in America, and with it came the rising costs of running intercollegiate athletic programs. Inflation was the major reason why freshmen were allowed to compete in most sports beginning in 1968 and four years later in football and basketball. Further cost reductions in expenditures for athletics were expected from the NCAA decision to award athletic scholarships for only one year, when previously the intent was for four years.[1] Of course, the one-year athletic scholarship was much more than a financial decision. It was brought about to threaten with the loss of scholarships those athletes who were not obedient to coaches. At the time, there were numerous protests by African American athletes, especially in the North, for social justice as well as protests from all athletes as part of the rampant opposition to the Vietnam War.[2] Another cost-cutting measure was not considered: the elimination of free substitution (platooning) in football. A limit on special teams for offense and defense would eliminate the need for many of the expensive athletic scholarships and other expenses and would require fewer coaches.[3] Nevertheless, financial stability was threatened during the Vietnam War, and university academic standards were being jeopardized by open enrollments, allowing anyone who graduated from high school to attend many colleges. The combination of deficits caused by inflation with the passage and costly mandates of Title IX of the Educational Act of 1972, providing women with equal opportunities in athletics and other areas, did not create the best conditions for reforming intercollegiate athletics from an academic standpoint. Yet that is exactly what George Hanford, the vice president of the College Board and the organization administering the SAT exams, was asked to do.

Shortly after the 1973 NCAA convention, when, according to Executive Director Walter Byers, "supposedly responsible educators had voted for sports expediency,"[4] George Hanford was in a discussion with Alden Dunham of the Carnegie Foundation for the Advancement of Teaching, the organization that financed and conducted the 1929 classic study on *American College Athletics*. Hanford agreed with Dunham that a "sorry state of intercollegiate athletics" existed, and a second Carnegie Report should be produced. With modest grants of $15,000 and $58,000 from the Ford Foundation and the Carnegie Foundation, a team of about twenty individuals produced a lengthy document in six months, *An Inquiry into the Need for and Feasibility of a National Study of Intercollegiate Athletics.*[5] Unlike the 1929 Carnegie Report, the 1974 study was, as Hanford later stated, "an analytical treatise, not an exposé,"[6] and it was only intended as a preliminary to a full-fledged study, such as that of *American College Athletics* nearly a half century earlier. Hanford held back on the polemics of the earlier document and used guarded words to portray the nature of intercollegiate athletics in the 1970s, for he didn't think it made sense "to offend the educational establishment with which I was associated."[7] What he found in this inquiry was that the problems existing in the 1929 Carnegie study and the 1952 American Council on Education report were similar to those in 1974—activities such as recruiting, subsidies, campus care of athletes, commercialism, and competitive excesses.[8] In concluding his report, Hanford did not appear to have great faith that university presidents could or would effectively reform college athletics and raised a specific question for further study: "Do college presidents have the power, individually or in concert, to correct the ills associated with intercollegiate athletics?" He had more or less answered the question earlier in the report by noting "that the majority of presidents of big-time sports institutions tend to avoid paying direct attention to athletics."[9] If the report had any future effect, it might have been in two of Hanford's highlighted areas that would soon gain more attention: the plight of blacks and the status of women in intercollegiate athletics. He suggested that courts and federal and state legislation might have a greater impact upon reform than did actions of the NCAA.[10]

While the Hanford Report gained praise from reformers, it was not well received by the NCAA or others in the athletic establishment, including college presidents. One big-time university president told Hanford: "Amateurs shouldn't get involved in things they don't know anything about."[11] Amateur or not, Hanford suggested that accreditation of athletics by the six regional accreditation associations would prove to be of value, though they had previously "abdicated responsibility for sound standards of conduct in intercollegiate athletics" and were not likely to take up efforts as they had attempted and failed to do in the 1950s.[12] Hanford requested a $1.8 million grant for an extensive follow-up study to find solutions to the questions he raised, but the Carnegie Foundation trustees were little interested and offered only a match of up to $200,000 if the American Council on Education (ACE) would put up a match. The ACE, however, which was run by college presidents, "wanted to let sleeping dogs lie," according to Hanford, and declined a further study.[13] As a result, the orange-colored Hanford Report was generally discarded or possibly shelved, waiting for a historian to look at it during the next reform period.

From the 1970s into the 1980s, there was a period of increased interest in college sport with rapidly growing football television contracts and income from "March Madness," the national men's basketball tournament. At the same time, the lack of eligibility standards and no freshman rule contributed to painful eligibility transgressions. "The tyranny of the lowest common denominator would control," observed Walter Byers, following his retirement as the NCAA executive director.[14]

And indeed it did. The lack of academic standards led to some of the most egregious disregard of academics in the history of the NCAA.

Academic travesties were rampant. Dexter Manley, an eventual all-pro defensive end with the Washington Redskins in the National Football League, was recruited to play football at Oklahoma State University in the mid-1970s, though he could read only at the second grade elementary school level and scored so low on his ACT test for college, a 6, that it hardly registered.[15] Yet his football linebacking skills, regular attendance in class, and advising by the athletic department helped him to complete his athletic eligibility, if not an academic degree, at Oklahoma State. His illiteracy, at that time, did not make any kind of case for academic reform in athletics, for Manley was able to keep secret his illiteracy until he was well along in his professional football career, often carrying a *Wall Street Journal* and pretending to be reading it while seated in the locker room. Only by his revelation to the nation when testifying at a 1989 U.S. Senate hearing on "Eliminating Illiteracy" in America was his story told. There he told the senators that he learned to read and spell at age twenty-five by attending the Washington Lab School with tutoring help from Sarah Hines, who helped Manley raise his reading score from the second grade level to the high school level in less than a year.[16]

The case of Kevin Ross, however, did have an almost immediate impact. Ross was functionally illiterate when in 1978 he entered Creighton University in Omaha, Nebraska, to play basketball. He had scored a 9 out of a possible 36 on his ACT examination while the Creighton student body averaged 23. Taking courses such as marksmanship and the theory of basketball at Creighton, with the athletic department hiring a secretary to do his homework, and receiving help from some professors who asked that Ross merely fill in his name on tests already filled out, Ross was able to remain eligible to participate athletically. Upon completion of his eligibility, and with no degree, Creighton paid for him to enter the Chicago Westside Preparatory School, where he sat with second and third graders and eventually jumped eleven grade levels in reading in about a year. Photos of Kevin Ross sitting with grade school children and a lawsuit by Ross against Creighton University brought great publicity to his academic plight and shame upon an institution of the NCAA for complete lack of academic integrity. Though Ross did not win his case of academic negligence and breach of contract for Creighton's failure to educate him, Ross settled out of court for $30,000.[17] However, far more important to academic reform efforts, the Ross case was held up as a red flag to the failure of the NCAA to have any academic eligibility requirements.

In a similar way, the Chris Washburn situation at North Carolina State University by the mid-1980s revealed the unsavory practices of recruiting and admitting insufficiently educated individuals to big-time universities. As Chris Washburn entered his high school freshman class, he received a letter from Coach Dean Smith of the University of North Carolina indicating that the Tar Heels were interested in him and his basketball abilities. By his sophomore year, Coach Jim Valvano of North Carolina State University wrote Washburn: "Chris . . . if you come to State you will be an All-American and a first round choice" in the National Basketball Association. Heady things for a high school underclassman. After 278 letters, postcards, and mailgrams from Valvano and North Carolina State, including 77 to Washburn's mother, Chris Washburn, the 6-foot 11-inch, 250-pound center, with a lowly 470 SAT score (200 verbal and 270 math), decided on North Carolina State.[18] Allowing academically inept athletes into North Carolina State was almost a given when it was shown that the coaches acted as "a separate admissions committee" and were "admitting some athletes even *before* they took their SATs."[19] At North Carolina State, Washburn was kept alive academically by admiring professors and changing of grades, if the charge by the head of the physical education department was true that grades had been changed so that Washburn could remain eligible. He remained eligible for several years before being drafted high by the National Basketball Association. By then, a muckraking volume by Pete Golenbock, *Personal Fouls,* was published, helping to lead to the eventual resignation of Coach Valvano and Chancellor Bruce Poulton, who had been charged with a cover-up of the grade changes.[20] In the 1980s, Golenbock was not particularly overstating the situation when he charged that in big-time college athletics many players end up with "no education, no degree, no skills, no money, no pro career, and no hope."[21] In Washburn's case, it was only no education and no degree.

No particular athlete attracted attention at the University of Georgia in the early 1980s, but embarrassment about the lack of an attempt to educate a number of athletes made national news and the need for reform apparent. The situation involved the whistle-blowing of a remedial English teacher, Jan Kemp, who revealed widespread academic fraud at the university, which reached into the upper echelons of the university administration. Kemp was fired by the University of Georgia following the whistle-blowing after she refused to ask professors to change grades and complained that the vice president for Academic Affairs, Virginia Trotter, promoted nine failing football players from Developmental Studies into the regular curriculum so that they could continue to participate in athletics. Kemp sued the university for firing her without just cause, and the jury agreed with her. The jury heard a tape recording of the head of Georgia's remedial studies, called Developmental Studies, in which he admitted "that these kids would not be here if it were not for their utility to the institution. They are used as a kind of raw material" for athletics.[22] Judge Horace Ward stated that the University of Georgia was guilty of "reckless or callous indifference to the federally protected rights of" Kemp, and she was originally awarded more than $2.5 million before the amount was reduced by the judge. There was irony in that Judge Ward had once been denied admission to the University of Georgia law school because he was black, while a generation later he presided over a trial involving the university in which many of the players involved in the academic fraud were African Americans.[23] A year after the Kemp trial, twenty-three football and basketball players at Georgia were "academic casualties," and President Fred Davison, who had headed the College Football Association, had resigned as leader of the University of Georgia.[24]

The Manley, Ross, Washburn, and Kemp cases were symptomatic of the lack of academic standards in athletics. The fact that most of the individuals involved were African Americans added a new element to academics and athletics. Blacks, for a variety of reasons, were underperformers in academics if not in athletics. Any reform efforts should have taken into account the increase in African American participation in big-time athletics in the decade of the civil rights movement. Desegregation resulted in the mass entry of black athletes in northern colleges, but especially in the South from the 1960s on. That the members of the NCAA paid little attention to the question of blacks and academics eventually led to the failure of the next academic reform effort of the NCAA by the 1980s. Yet the lack of vision was somewhat understandable, for the institutions of the NCAA were attempting to find a balance between the need for all athletes to meet minimal academic standards while at the same time using football and men's basketball to promote the institutions and bring in revenue needed to run the big-time athletic programs.

Even without the highly publicized Manley, Ross, Washburn, and Kemp cases, there was cause and momentum to reverse the NCAA's failure to require any kind of academic standards. A number of educators and athletic officials were concerned, but one group unexpectedly took a leading role in setting a minimum standard: the newly organized College Football Association. The College Football Association, nearly forgotten a generation later, came into existence in the mid-1970s as a result of big-time football-playing schools wanting a bigger slice of the TV money gained by telecasting their games. The rapidly increasing TV revenue came from the NCAA-created game-of-the-week monopoly telecasts that had begun in the early 1950s. TV money grew exponentially and became the object of various interests within the NCAA that had little to do with big-time football. There were a number of "Robin Hoods" who wanted to appropriate the TV money from the institutions that were being telecast. Robin Hood, the twelfth-century robber who stole from the rich to give to the poor, was made manifest in one individual, Stephen Horn, president of "poor" California State University, Long Beach and envious of the rich schools. Unlike the "March Madness" money coming to the NCAA from the national basketball tournament that was used to pay the expenses of the tournament and nearly completely financed the activities of the NCAA, only a small amount of the football telecast monopoly went to the NCAA, while most went to the competing schools. Early on, when there were suggestions that the football TV money be divided more evenly among all NCAA schools, Theodore Hesburgh, the Notre Dame president who would eventually cohead the Knight Commission on athletic reform in the 1990s, criticized the share-the-wealth plan as being part of the "socialistic tendency" in the country.[25] Yet there was concern among the football powers that the NCAA had increasingly siphoned off football TV revenue to non-big-time football projects, such as fighting the Amateur Athletic Union for control of amateur athletics in America or building a new NCAA headquarters near Kansas City. In 1975, President Horn, at a rare special convention of the NCAA to discuss a variety of methods for cutting athletic costs, called for reducing football scholarships from ninety-five to sixty-five, eliminating some of the "raw meat for practice."[26] Only the month before, he had asked all NCAA presidents to create a new scheme for distributing football telecast income. Under his plan, the money would be divided among Division II and III institutions as well as big-time Division I. Alarmed, the Big Ten presidents called a special meeting with Big Ten Commissioner Wayne Duke, who afterward indicated that Horn's plan might lead to the "breakup of the NCAA organization."[27] Concern spread throughout the major institutions of the NCAA.

The result was the creation of the College Football Association (CFA), when, following Horn's letter to university presidents, commissioners of seven big-time conferences—the Atlantic Coast, Big 8, Big Ten, Pacific 8, Southeastern, Southwest, and Western Athletic Conferences—met to discuss Horn's "Robin Hood" plan. Television, not athletic reform, was the key to the creation of the CFA.[28] Had the Big Ten and the PAC-8 (soon to be the PAC-10) joined the CFA, there would likely have been a movement by members of the CFA to withdraw from the NCAA, creating another competing national organization. However, both the Big Ten and PAC-8 had good reasons to remain outside the CFA—a major one being that these two conferences had a contract to participate in the most lucrative season-ending bowl game, the Rose Bowl. But, as University of Michigan President Robben Fleming stated, speaking for the Big Ten presidents, the "principal concern is one of overemphasis upon football," fearing that the CFA wanted "to eliminate any restraints placed" on football and possibly withdraw from the NCAA.[29] Without the Big Ten and PAC-8, the other major football conferences and independents, Notre Dame and

Penn State, agreed not to separate from the NCAA but rather to "become a forum through which the major football programs might refine and sponsor points of view consistent with their needs."[30] By the end of 1976, the CFA was formed, and with it came the pressure to reorganize Division I of the NCAA by eliminating the smaller Division I schools, including all of the Ivy League institutions.[31] Almost as an afterthought, the CFA decided to put forth reform efforts to create greater academic integrity in the recruiting process and promote academic progress for athletes once they were in college.

Soon after the CFA was founded, Fred Davison, president of the University of Georgia, was elected chairman of the CFA board, giving it some respectability as an academically run athletic organization. Although history and the Jan Kemp case would show that Davison was more interested in victories for the Georgia Bulldog football team than in how many of the players would graduate, Davison asked Joe Paterno, Penn State football coach, and his CFA Committee on Academics and Research if the organization could help schools "return to some realistic prediction of success" of its athletes with the "re-establishment of a SAT floor of the 1.6 rule or some other as yet untried procedure." Davison noted that something was needed "to remove from the coaches the burden of choosing between scholars and athletes which is being brought about by a system of one-year grants."[32] By 1978, five years before the important Proposition 48 was passed by the NCAA, the CFA had created its reform recommendations for the NCAA, using football jargon and calling it the Triple Option. Though Paterno believed that freshmen should not be eligible to play varsity sports, his committee came up with the Triple Option for freshman eligibility. The recommendation to the NCAA was passed by the CFA over the objection of many other football coaches. It proposed setting an academic standard for incoming freshman athletes that would have to be met by one of three criteria: a 2.25 high school grade point average, a 750 on the SAT test, or a 17 on the ACT test—the Triple Option. Tom Osborne, the highly successful football coach at the University of Nebraska, observed that "it seemed to be very important to the faculty people present that this rule be passed in order to enhance the 'respectability' of the CFA."[33] Whether the CFA did this for political expediency or not, it was a reform effort, though the NCAA did not then adopt the Triple Option.

By the early 1980s, the CFA Committee on Academics made another bold proposal: For athletes to be eligible, they would have to have had fifteen core (academic) courses in high school, rather than the eleven the NCAA would soon mandate. The fifteen courses in high school would include four English, including composition; three math; three social sciences; and two natural sciences, including one lab; along with a minimum score of 15 on the ACT test or its equivalent on the SAT. That proposal, however, was too demanding for most coaches and athletic directors and did not pass the CFA.[34]

The efforts of the CFA for academic reform soon became lost in the CFA's desire to control television money, its main purpose of being. The CFA financially backed a lawsuit of the universities of Oklahoma and Georgia in the early 1980s, testing whether the NCAA television plan was a monopoly and should be broken up under the Sherman Antitrust Act of 1890. Notre Dame and Penn State of the CFA were the first to financially support the lawsuit, and the Southeastern Conference was the largest financial backer in attacking the NCAA TV policy. When the case finally reached the U.S. Supreme Court in 1984, a 7–2 decision resulted, the first time the Supreme Court had ruled amateur sport to be in violation of antitrust laws. The justices ruled that the NCAA TV plan was a purely commercial venture in which the universities participated solely for the pursuit of profits.[35]

With the CFA's energy directed to breaking up the NCAA TV monopoly, the locus of academic reform of the early 1980s moved to the auspices of the American Council on Education (ACE), a president-run university umbrella organization that had been attempting to reform college athletics since the close of World War II. The ACE's Presidents' Ad Hoc Committee on Athletic Reform presented its position as Proposition 48 to the NCAA conference in 1983, a conference attended by about a hundred institutional presidents. Proposition 48 looked suspiciously like the CFA's proposals of the late 1970s, but like previous academic standards it paid little attention to the problems associated with athletes from low-income and minority families. A mathematician and opponent of Proposition 48 spoke out at the convention: "I threw the SAT scores into the analysis," stated Luna Mishoe, a mathematician and president of the historically black Delaware State College, "and I tell you that the SAT is a restraint which penalizes low-economic students and is an unnecessary restraint pertaining to whether or not a student can do college work."[36]

A major criticism of the ACE committee was that it had no representation from historically black colleges, which opposed the cutoff scores as being racially biased.[37] Edmund P. Joyce, vice president in charge of athletics at Notre Dame, tried to convince convention delegates that "we must guard against using the test-score argument as an excuse to prevent a much-needed reform from being initiated." Because the NCAA had defeated numerous proposed academic eligibility standards since the 1973 defeat of the 1.600 rule, it was not surprising that the new rules, in addition to the old 2.0 high school grade point average, would require only eleven core high school courses and a meager 700 SAT combined score in math and English out of 1,600 points. To be sure, it was at the low end of mediocrity for success in college. As a comparison, the heavily debated Proposition 48 requirements were less stringent than the CFA's Triple Option proposal of the 1970s. When Proposition 48 passed as a considerably less vigorous standard than the 1.600 GPA dropped in 1973, it became the new minimal standard, delayed until the 1986–87 school year for high school students to better meet its requirements.[38]

Because of minority and low-income criticism of Proposition 48, the NCAA added a partial qualifier to its freshman eligibility. An athlete who met either the 2.0 high school grade point average or 700 in the SAT test was eligible for an athletic scholarship but could not practice or play for the team during the first year.[39] If the individual school ruled that the partial qualifier had made satisfactory progress during the first year, then the athlete was eligible for varsity competition. Thus, the athletic department, with its counseling program and knowledge of easy courses, often played the eligibility game, and the athlete took courses that might or might not lead toward graduation requirements. Louisiana State University chancellor and head of the ACE Committee on Academic Standards, James H. Wharton, was either naive or disingenuous when he said, "We no longer will have students majoring in eligibility."[40]

Proposition 48 was put into effect and would last longer than a decade, with amendments made to make it more palatable to academics as well as to those involved in athletics before it was challenged in the courts. It never satisfied true academic reformers because its minimal standards were far too low. It remained a discriminatory target of proponents of minorities and products of low-income families for its entire existence.[41] It was the lightening rod of academic reform for athletics, and it was an important piece of legislation that involved numerous presidents. It never was a good solution for poorly prepared athletes entering college or for improving graduation rates for athletes. Because of the lack of meaningful reform and continued problems facing intercollegiate athletics, presidents became more involved in the control of NCAA legislation through the Presidents Commission, and within a few years of its passage another outside commission, the Knight Commission, was created in an attempt to drive intercollegiate athletic reform. While academic reform was continually in the headlines, two specific groups became the center of reform during the civil rights movement and the women's movement of the 1960s and 1970s: African Americans and women.

15

Title IX and Governmental Reform in Women's Athletics

Historically, reform generally originated within the National Collegiate Athletic Association (NCAA), conferences, or individual institutions, but possibly the greatest reform in college athletics arose from federal legislation: Title IX of the Educational Amendments Act of 1972. With civil disorder resulting from the Vietnam War, civil rights turmoil, and the women's movement, the U.S. Congress passed legislation that would have a major influence on gender equity, especially as it related to girls' and women's participation in sport. The push for gender equity, found in Title IX, arose not in athletics but in the hiring practice at the University of Maryland, where in 1969 a woman, Bernice Sandler, asked a department member why she was not even considered for the full-time faculty position, a faculty on which she had been teaching part-time. A faculty member told Sandler, "You come on too strong for a woman."[1] Sex discrimination soon dominated Sandler's thoughts, and that one incident led directly to the passage three years later of Title IX.

Shocked into looking at the history of discrimination, Sandler noted that Title VII of the Civil Rights Act of 1964 prohibited discrimination in employment based on race, color, religion, national origin, and *sex* but said nothing about discrimination in education. Title VI of the same act prohibited discrimination in any program receiving federal financial assistance "on the grounds of race, color, or national origin," but it left out sex. Sandler found out that the Fourteenth Amendment to the U.S. Constitution assured individuals of "equal protection of the laws" by states, yet no Supreme Court case of discrimination against women in education had ever been decided favorably toward women. Furthermore, she discovered that the executive order prohibiting federal contractors from discriminating in employment based on "race, color, religion, and national origin" had been expanded by President Lyndon Johnson to include discrimination based on sex. Eureka! Sandler made the connection between universities, federal contracts, and sex discrimination. Since most universities, including the University of Maryland, received federal contracts, she could help eliminate future sex discrimination at Maryland and elsewhere. With the help of the Women's Equity Action League, she began a national campaign to end discrimination in education, culminating in the passage of Title IX.

When Title IX was under consideration by Congress, there was, at first, little said about gender equity in sport; rather, it was gender equity in education. The American Council on Education, the college president-led group that since World War II had been attempting to reform intercollegiate athletics, was basically silent on the merits of Title IX. At the first congressional hearing on education and employment of women, headed by Representative Edith Green of Oregon, an American Council on Education (ACE) representative told the subcommittee that "there is no sex discrimination in higher education, and even if it did exist, it wasn't a problem."[2] The ACE was silent on Title IX and its stance on gender equity in education and silent on gender equity in sport. The predominantly male college and university presidents were seemingly as uninvolved in the passage of Title IX as was the nation. Little was reported in the press upon its passage, and it generally remained out of sight until questions arose about the negative impact equity for women in sport might have upon men's athletic budgets.

Until the 1960s, few universities offered women's intercollegiate athletics, for most women physical educators for well over a half century had opposed competitive sports for women similar to those conducted for men. When Vassar College had started the first Field Day in 1895, a kind of intramural track meet, there was little thought of competing against other women's colleges in the area, though male-only Harvard and Yale had been rivals for a number of years.[3] Yet, even then, the women of Vassar compared their times and heights to those of the men at Yale: 16 seconds in the 100-yard dash as opposed to 10 seconds for the Yale men and 3 feet 10 inches in the high jump relative to 5 feet 10 inches for the men.[4] Eight decades later, the comparison to men's athletics is what brought women greater equality once Title IX had been passed. By then, women's competitive intercollegiate sport had been established, and not only were most of the sports the same as the men's, but by the force of federal legislation and the courts, the move to equity in the important areas of sport was demanded and enforced.

For about the first century of college women's sport, there was little need to control unethical, commercial, or professional aspects of the sport involvement. Nearly all the activity was controlled by women physical educators, who considered sport to be an integral part of education, not public exhibitions. This was unlike the men's athletics in which students organized the first generation or more of intercollegiate athletics with little or no thought to educational goals. The women physical educators insisted that sport be part of an educational model, strictly under women's control.[5] The male model was a commercial one from the very first intercollegiate contest, a commercially sponsored crew meet between Harvard and Yale on Lake Winnipesaukee in New Hampshire. Women physical educators, nearly all members of the faculty, unlike most male coaches, were emphatic in their desire to keep women's sport under their control and away from the men's commercial-professional model. From the 1870s, when sport was first introduced to college women, to the 1970s, women wielded power and control in college women's sport. Or as sport historian Joan Hult has noted, "[W]ithin the sacred walls of the school gymnasium the women physical educators reigned supreme."[6] The supremacy, until the women's movement in the 1960s, was highly anticompetitive, with no intercollegiate athletics for most colleges.[7]

The century-long tradition of control cannot be overemphasized. It may be the most important point in attempting to understand how women's athletics developed in the twentieth century and how women physical educators remained in power and control until Title IX was implemented in the 1970s. Even in the late 1950s, as Mary Yost of Ohio State University noted, most women's physical education had a number of "dirty words" relative to athletic competition. Three of them were *intercollegiate* (*extramural* or *sports days* were acceptable), *coach* (*teacher* was much preferred), and *varsity* (*outgrowth of intramurals* was allowed).[8] In the early 1960s, when competition was growing slowly for women, Phebe Scott, a leader who favored increased competition stated, "Whether we like it or not, we have educated a whole generation of women to believe that somehow there was something slightly evil or immoral in competition for the highly skilled girl."[9] Until the 1970s, there were few concerns by women leaders about athletic scholarships, high school grade point averages, eligibility of freshmen, transfer students, or graduation rates, for the model was educational until the passage of Title IX. The irony, of course, is that with Title IX the women's model of athletics with women physical educators in control quickly vanished, while skilled women athletes, who had been restrained for a century by those same women physical educators, were given opportunities that had not generally existed before.[10] A nearly 180-degree change had occurred in the cliché, "the good of those who play." In the 1920s "the good of those who play" excluded skilled women athletes for two generations, but since the 1960s the statement has emphasized skilled women athletes.

Two major forces changed the direction of women's sport in the 1960s: the women's movement and America's Cold War with the Soviet Union. In the midst of the Cold War, there was a palpable national need to defeat the Soviets in many areas of life, including sports. A special NCAA report in 1962, only months after the Communists began erecting a wall between the Communist countries in Eastern Europe and those of democratic Western Europe, concluded: "Competitive sports have become a vital factor in international relationships and the 'cold war propaganda.'"[11] It was clear that America had lost leadership in Olympic sports, having lost decisively to the Soviets in both the 1956 and 1960 Olympics, with the Soviet women winning twenty-eight medals to the American women's twelve in 1960.[12] Improving women's performance in international competition, especially the Olympics, was not as dramatic but may have been as crucial to America's Cold War image as was the success of President John F. Kennedy in forcing the Soviet Union to dismantle its missiles being constructed in Cuba and aimed at the United States in 1962.

The NCAA saw the need to get involved in raising the level of college women's athletics well before the Association for Intercollegiate Athletics for Women became operational in 1972 at the time of Title IX. A decade before Title IX, the NCAA helped sponsor the educational Institute for Women's and Girls' Sports in cooperation with the U. S. Olympic Development Committee and the Division of Girls' and Women's Sport (DGWS), part of the American Association for Health, Physical Education, and Recreation.[13] In the early 1960s, only a few years after the Soviets appeared to be leading America in scientific developments, such as orbiting the first artificial space satellite and then sending the first astronaut, Yuri Gagarin, into outer space, the United States needed to produce more Olympic winners, and the colleges (except for some Negro colleges) were contributing almost no women Olympians who could compete at the highest levels. At the same time, nearly all male Olympians were participants in intercollegiate athletics. The NCAA also had a self-serving reason to be involved with women's sport development because it was in a generations-old power struggle with the leading amateur athletic organization, the Amateur Athletic Union (AAU), over the control of amateur athletics.[14] If the NCAA was to retain a power position in its longtime fight with the AAU, it was natural to want to be involved on the women's side of athletics.[15]

As competition in women's athletics was rising in the late 1950s and early 1960s, along with the women's movement, college women physical educators organized the Commission on Intercollegiate Athletics for Women (CIAW) in 1966 to govern national championships. The CIAW was organized, in part, as a foil to any NCAA attempt to bring women into the NCAA. The year before the formation of the CIAW, the NCAA's Long Range Planning Committee was discussing the "need for encouraging opportunity for young women to compete in intercollegiate athletics."[16] Thus both women physical educators and the NCAA were discussing women's intercollegiate athletics, but from entirely different perspectives. The women physical educators were responding to the women's movement's desire for greater physical expression and equality of opportunity while fighting to retain women's control of women's sport. The men were far more interested in controlling amateur sport, trying to wrest control of amateur sport from the AAU, and college women's athletics were part of the equation. The die was cast for a fight over control of highly competitive women's college sport *before* either the Association for Intercollegiate Athletics for Women (AIAW) came into existence or Title IX was passed in 1972. But the legality of Title IX forced action on the issue of equity between men's and women's programs rather quickly.[17]

Title IX of the Education Amendments of 1972 was only thirty-seven words long, but its impact for the reform of women's athletics was eventually profound: "No person in the United States shall, on the basis of sex, be excluded from participation in, be denied the benefits of, or be subjected to discrimination under any educational program or activities receiving federal financial assistance."[18]

There was no discussion that this act would fundamentally reform college sport and women's place in it. In fact, few paid much attention when Title IX was passed, and the all-male NCAA became alarmed only when the law was applied directly to intercollegiate sport and threatened the financial viability of men's sport during the inflationary 1970s. The president of the NCAA, John Fuzak, cried foul, but only after the Department of Health, Education, and Welfare (DHEW) regulations threatened men's sports. The DHEW, Fuzak said, was using an "illegal quota system for determining equality of opportunity." His memorandum to all NCAA members said that "the increasing intrusion of the Federal government into the educational process is repugnant to basic concepts of an institution's freedom to pursue its own education goals."[19] Opposition to Title IX, however, came at the exact time the NCAA was campaigning hard for federal government intrusion to prohibit professional football from televising its games on Friday nights and all day on Saturday, in an effort to preserve its recruiting and financial base. When Title IX was passed, only about 1 percent of the average university athletic budget was expended on women's sports, and the average women's athletic expenditure of institutions of higher learning was about $1 per student.[20] Soon, financing of women's sport rose rapidly when compared to men's sport.

The impact of Title IX on equity for women, ironically, was that the male norm was used as the measure against which to judge equality. The result was that the women's educational model was lost to the male commercial-professional model.[21] That change occurred rapidly in financial aid to women athletes, when in 1972 a tennis player for Florida's Mary Mount College, Kathy Kemper, was denied entry into a collegiate tennis tournament because she had an athletic scholarship. She, her coach, Fern "Peachy" Kellmeyer, and others challenged the antischolarship policy of the AIAW, because denying athletic scholarships to women in an institution of higher education in which men were receiving scholarships violated the equal protection clause of the Fourteenth Amendment. In short, the AIAW was discriminating against its own athletes by denying scholarships.[22] Only months after the challenge to scholarships, the AIAW abandoned its philosophical stance in a pragmatic attempt to save control over women's sport by voting to allow athletic scholarships. Not all women sport advocates favored caving in to athletic scholarships. As two leaders wrote, by voting to allow "talent" scholarships, they were "stooping to do the expedient thing."[23] June Galloway of the University of North Carolina was another. "I believe that not only scholarships are at stake here," she wrote a member of the AIAW Executive Council, "but the entire programs for women in sports."[24] A male supporter of the AIAW, Harold Falls, agreed: "If grants-in-aid are allowed, the educational aspects of the program will no longer exist."[25] He was on target. The Kellmeyer court case and a federal law brought about radical reform in women's athletics, leading directly to far greater participation for women, though at the same time it was destroying the women's educational model.

The Kellmeyer court case broke the bedrock policy of the AIAW and began the movement for equality based upon the male model, a commercially constructed one.[26] Once the AIAW was forced to give athletic scholarships on an equal basis as men, other planks in the education model eroded, including a move toward the male model of recruiting, transfer regulations, negotiations for commercial broadcasts rather than public broadcasting of events, commercial subsidies for AIAW championships, commercial sponsors for all-American teams and all-star contests, and alcohol advertising for events. It also eventually led to the end of the sex-separatist policy in women's athletics and the loss of women physical educators' position of influence in college sport. The women's educational model had been sacrificed by the women leaders in an unsuccessful attempt to prevent their loss of power over the control of women's sport. Eventually, the women leaders of the AIAW lost their leadership in women's athletics as its member institutions left to join the NCAA and its far-better-funded national championships, but that took a decade of strife.

Once Title IX regulations were put in place by the mid-1970s and the Kellmeyer court case moved the AIAW model toward the male model, there was an almost unavoidable clash between the NCAA and the AIAW over the control of women's athletics. To be equal under Title IX, the male model was used as a reference. If women did not receive equal scholarships, coaching, practice and game facilities, equipment, and funding relative to men, lawsuits were almost inevitably based upon not only Title IX but also the Fourteenth Amendment to the U.S. Constitution equal protection clause and equal rights amendments of state constitutions.[27] Title IX, however, not the equal protection clause of the Fourteenth Amendment, kept women's sport in the public eye and constantly present in the minds of members of the NCAA. As soon as the proposed Title IX regulations were sent out for comment, the NCAA opposed the Department of Health, Education, and Welfare interpretations of the law and began a frontal attack in the legislative and executive branches of the federal government. The NCAA backed Senator John Tower's unsuccessful amendment to Title IX, which if enacted would have exempted revenue-producing sports, such as football and basketball, from the regulations, thus limiting perceived damage to men's athletics.[28]

As the efforts to water down the Title IX regulations were failing, the NCAA moved to see if it, rather than the AIAW, should control college women's sports. The NCAA began a concerted effort to portray itself as the only organization that was strong enough to provide equal opportunities for women athletes. As early as the fall of 1974, the NCAA Council began an examination of possibilities of providing national championships for women.[29] When, the following year, the NCAA Council proposed a resolution for possibly conducting "pilot programs for women's national championships," the ire of women in the AIAW was raised higher than it had before.[30] Yet the NCAA Council and legal counsel warned that if the NCAA did not provide championships and athletic scholarships, it would be in violation of the equal protection clause of the Fourteenth Amendment to the U.S. Constitution.[31] A massive telephone campaign by members of the AIAW to NCAA convention delegates put a damper on the Council's resolution for pilot programs. For a short time, the AIAW was able to keep its identity: conducting championships and allowing women to remain in power positions in women's sport.

For the remainder of the 1970s, the AIAW and NCAA made feigned attempts to resolve governance issues so that there might be one organization, but it was clear that the NCAA believed it was the one organization qualified to conduct college athletics. A legal opinion from its counsel in 1975 stated that the NCAA "would be ill-advised to rely upon a 'separate but equal' approach to the administration or operation of programs designed to benefit both males and females."[32] However, as the NCAA was jousting with the AIAW over such issues as combining into one organization or creating common eligibility rules, the National Association of Intercollegiate Athletics, an organization of lesser influential men's college athletics, decided in 1978 to provide championships for women.[33] Compounding defections from the AIAW was the worst inflation in America since the 1920s. Double-digit inflation and compliance to the demands of Title IX placed intercollegiate athletics at all division levels in jeopardy. Obviously, one solution to expanding costs was for individual institutions to form one administrative unit for athletics rather than for each sex. Sex-separate athletic departments and the sex-separate AIAW could not withstand the force of Title IX and equal protection of the Fourteenth

Amendment. When the NCAA in 1980 decided to offer championships in Division II and III, the AIAW was doomed, unless the NCAA could be convinced to not implement its championships or a court ruling could save the women's organization.[34] Not only did the NCAA not rescind its Division II and III championships for women in 1981, but it also voted, in a close vote, to begin championships in the big-time Division I.[35]

Moving from what had once been an educational model of the AIAW to the commercial model of the NCAA could be considered reactionary, not reform. However, for women athletes, there is little question that they would be better served athletically with the financial backing of the NCAA. For instance, the AIAW was continuously in financial straights, and from 1974 until its demise it had spent far more each year for its legal counsel, Margot Polivy, than it had for the conduct of national championships.[36] By 1981, the women's model had been effectively lost as the AIAW had gone the commercial route in an effort to survive. As Judith Sweet, women's athletic director at the University of California, San Diego, said, "[S]tudent-athletes may best be served" by creating NCAA championships for women. The disputed vote for women's championships was a reform for athletes but a major defeat for those women who felt betrayed by the loss of what they believed was an educational model for sport in higher education. Title IX, which had been hailed by many for requiring equity in girls' and women's sport, had been cruel to those who clung to an educational model of sport. All that remained was an antitrust lawsuit by the AIAW against the NCAA, one that did not convince the U.S. district judge and a circuit court that the NCAA had used its monopoly to destroy the AIAW.[37] The lawsuit had devoured all the AIAW assets, and the organization lay prostrate with a number of unpaid debts. The educational model and a sex-separatist philosophy were buried with the financial debts.

The reform organization, which was the AIAW, could have had its educational model adopted generally in higher education, but there was no powerful group, other than women in physical education and sport, that supported it. Division III of the NCAA might have gone along with many of the AIAW policies, as, for instance, both opposed athletic scholarships. The power, however, lay with the major athletic powers found in Division I. Within those institutions, there were likely no governing boards, no athletic departments, no alumni groups, no student organizations, and few presidents who would allow an educational model to come into existence, since that model was lifeless among most of the leading institutions of higher education for the entire twentieth century. Only groups of faculty would have been sympathetic toward an educational model, and they had long before been effectively eliminated from the power equation in athletics. The sex-separatist, educational model of intercollegiate athletics had a short shelf life and became a footnote in athletic reform.

While the AIAW died a painful death for many who favored an educational model for athletics run by women, the dynamics of federal Title IX legislation continued its reformation of women's athletics in educational institutions nationally. Title IX did not produce what President W. Robert Parks of Iowa State University believed it would, "the law of equality of millstones," which presumably meant that everyone would drown equally.[38] Rather, it was the driving force reforming college athletics and causing the greatest growth in the number of competitive athletes in American history. Federal legislation had created an athletic reform that would likely have taken decades to achieve had it not passed. It was not easy to get athletic departments, run by males for generations, to treat emerging women's athletics with anything approaching equity. The logic of their argument was, of course, that it had taken decades for men's athletics to reach the stage of general prosperity, and it was unfair for women's athletics to immediately demand an equal division of scholarships, facilities, travel accommodations, equipment, and coaching salaries. The administration of President Ronald Reagan and the U.S. Supreme Court agreed in the 1980s. The same year that the AIAW lost its court case with the NCAA, the U.S. Supreme Court reversed the interpretation of Title IX so that only those programs receiving direct federal aid needed to be mindful of the law. Thus, if the athletic department of the University of Virginia or Stanford received no federal funding, they could legally discriminate against women athletes. Four years later, however, the Civil Rights Restoration Act of 1988 was passed by Congress over the veto of President Reagan, and it specifically applied Title IX to athletic programs.[39]

From that point on, the Title IX reform could progress as rapidly as individual institutions complied with the law and the courts could make decisions, generally in favor of upholding equity rights provided by law. Following a 1979 compliance interpretation of the Office for Civil Rights, an institution could meet the requirements of Title IX in one of three ways: (1) by providing athletic opportunities proportionate to student enrollment, (2) by demonstrating continual expansion of athletic opportunities to the underrepresented sex, and (3) by full accommodation of the interests and abilities of the underrepresented sex.[40] There were numerous court cases testing whether one of the three prongs of compliance was met. Possibly the most important was the 1992 Brown case, in which it was found that Brown University discriminated against women by not supporting female athletes at a level at which male athletes were sustained.

Cohen v. Brown University resulted after the Brown University Athletic Department, for financial reasons, dropped two men's teams, golf and water polo, and two women's teams, volleyball and gymnastics. Outsider lawyers came in to force a court case, claiming that while women made up 51 percent of the Brown student body, they represented only 39 percent of Brown's athletes, thus the sports lacked proportionality.[41] Even though Brown University had fifteen women's sports, far more than most universities, it had not added any new women's team since 1982 and thus lacked continuous expansion of women's opportunities. Because it dropped two women's sports, it failed the test of providing for interest and ability of women students. Though Brown showed clearly that there was far greater interest among men than women in participation, the judge ruled that the lack of interest was a result of women's place in society, historically, socially, and politically. The Court of Appeals agreed, and the U.S. Supreme Court allowed the decision to stand. The impact of the Brown case has been that since 1991, no NCAA Division I school has dropped a women's team, though many men's sports have been eliminated or relegated to intramural-club status. The benefit to women's sports in colleges has been positive, for the Brown case has been used, as the U.S. Court of Appeals for the Ninth Circuit has stated, "to encourage women to participate in sports."[42] In this case, passing social legislation through the courts was successful.

In a short period of time, the greatest reform in American intercollegiate athletics had taken place, essentially without major positive action by the NCAA, its faculty representatives, conferences, or individual institutions. Rather, it was the force of federal government legislation and litigation in the court system that brought about reform. Once the action of the federal government had been taken, eventually the male-dominated NCAA and presidents of universities brought about the integration of women's athletics into the cultural mainstream. This was done with increased financing by institutions in providing greater equity in such areas as scholarships, coaching, facilities, and equipment. At no other time was there a period in American history that experienced such rapid growth in intercollegiate competition. The reform that impacted women's athletics was in some ways similar to the reform in integrating African Americans into intercollegiate athletics. In both cases, the federal government and the courts, not individual institutions, conferences, or the NCAA, precipitated the reform. As the reform for women came with the events of the women's movement and Title IX, greater opportunities for African Americans followed on the heels of the *Brown v. Board of Education* decision in 1954 and the Civil Rights Act of 1964.

16

African Americans, Freshman Eligibility, and Forced Reform

If the women's educational model was losing its impact during the Association for Intercollegiate Athletics for Women's (AIAW's) decade-long control of women's sport, there was no comparable model for the participation of African Americans, men or women. While most collegiate African American athletes were in the historically black colleges for the period until the 1970s, their model had been the same traditional commercial-professional model of the dominant "white" institutions of higher learning. By the 1970s, there was a major effort to recruit talented black male athletes by the major northern and southern powers in both basketball and football. Not only was there no educational model for African Americans, there was a general lack of educational preparation among the masses of black athletes. African Americans were generally recruited from low-economic urban settings in the 1970s and 1980s when the National Collegiate Athletic Association (NCAA) and individual institutions had few or no academic standards. This was combined with a dominant image of ill-prepared, white male athletes in colleges since the time of the famous cartoonist Thomas Nast's 1879 cartoon depicting an athlete with an oversize body and small brain and the anemic scholar with an oversize head and fragile body, with the caption "Education: Is There No Middle Course?"[1] This was a white caricature, but by the 1970s the color had darkened.

The influx of academically deficient blacks into the traditional athletic power institutions a century after Nast provided unprecedented grist for reform. The increased number of African Americans in the most visible college sports between the dropping of the 1.600 rule in 1973 and the implementation of Proposition 48 in 1986 led to a crisis of academic integrity in universities across America. The plummeting academic standards for athletes was combined with "open admissions" to anyone with a high school diploma and the national educational strategy designed to encourage at-risk student enrollment. Added to the desire to admit minority and low-income students to the university was the desire by scores of cheerleading presidents to allow "special admits" to participate on the major athletic teams. Many of those athletes were African Americans who could not get into school under the traditional academic guidelines, including meeting minimal SAT or ACT test scores. According to Richard Lapchick, director of the Center for the Study of Sport in Society, more than one-fifth of football players and male basketball players in Division I-A were special presidential admits, while only 3 percent of all students were special admits who could not meet ordinary academic standards. As well, more than 50 percent of basketball players were African Americans and nearly 40 percent of football players were blacks. Special provisions were made by presidents to stock their teams with athletic talent—black talent—and to continue to reap the profits from the expanded television revenues of the 1970s and 1980s.[2] Thus it was not unexpected that the University of Georgia under President Fred Davison would experience a scandal of large proportions when he and the university admitted unqualified athletes, primarily blacks, who could contribute to the prestige of the university by bringing victory on the playing field but who would not graduate even with illegal and unethical help through the athletic counseling program.[3]

African American men had been participating in college athletics for more than a century, but the influx in the 1970s and 1980s was unprecedented. Two of the first black athletes in the period after the American Civil War were Moses Fleetwood Walker and William H. Lewis. Walker played baseball at Oberlin and the University of Michigan before becoming the first African American major leaguer. Lewis played football at Amherst and became an all-American center at Harvard, later becoming assistant attorney general under President William H. Taft, then the highest governmental position ever attained by an African American.[4] One of the greatest athletes during the World War I era was Paul Robeson, whose father had been a slave. Robeson scored highest on a statewide examination for a scholarship to Rutgers. While at Rutgers, he became an all-American football player; won twelve letters in football, basketball, baseball, and track and field; led his class academically; and was elected to Phi Beta Kappa his junior year before becoming a world-renowned singer and actor.[5] Yet few universities, such as Rutgers, had more than one black player on a team until after World War II, and there were none on teams in the South until the decade after the *Brown v. Board of Education* Supreme Court desegregation decision in 1954.[6] A year after the famous Brown decision, Governor Marvin Griffin of Georgia attempted to prevent Georgia Tech from playing Pittsburgh, which had a black starter, in the New Orleans Sugar Bowl. Griffin trumpeted, "The South stands at Armageddon. The battle is joined." Griffin continued, "There is no more difference in compromising the integrity of race on the playing field than in doing so in the classrooms. One break in the dike and the relentless seas will rush in and destroy us."[7] The game, nevertheless, went on. Georgia won on a disputed interference call against the defensive back, Bobby Grier, the African American whose presence created the furor over race.

The reform of accepting black men, unlike black women, into college sports came rapidly.[8] That entry had been prompted less by NCAA legislation than by federal laws and judicial decision, important actions that moved society toward greater social and legal equity.[9] A major breakthrough in college athletic desegregation occurred a decade after the *Brown v. Board of Education* decision and only two years after the passage of the Civil Rights Act of 1964. The all-black starting five of Texas Western College defeated the all-white University of Kentucky basketball team in the NCAA championship.[10] By then, every university in the Atlantic Coast Conference (ACC) and Southeastern Conference (SEC) had African American undergraduates, and the first black Heisman Trophy winner had been chosen, Ernie Davis of Syracuse University in 1961. Teams across the nation by the 1970s were being dominated by African Americans in the most important sports, and by 1972 every varsity basketball program in the ACC and the SEC had desegregated.[11] The entry of blacks into American college athletics was a reform that had been created not by NCAA legislation but, like Title IX, by federal laws and judicial decisions that had helped change society in bringing about greater social and legal equity, certainly in the realm of sport participation. In another decade, college football would see the beginning of ten consecutive black Heisman Trophy winners.[12] In less than a generation of national reform, African Americans went from only slight visibility on most college campuses to dominant sport figures.

Yet there was a darker side to the major integration of college athletics in the 1970s and 1980s, and it was related to grade inflation in colleges. In those years, there were essentially no national academic standards in college athletics, and at the same time university grade inflation, which had begun in the 1960s, grew at an unprecedented rate and continued for more than a decade.[13] The breakdown of academic standards in higher education came when the civil rights movement and the Vietnam War made their impact on American society. Many believed that if African Americans were to have equal rights in America, certainly they should be given the opportunity to attend college, similar to the right to have a high school education. The trend of open admissions and affirmative action in the 1970s combined with the action by university officials, especially professors, to move students toward graduation by passing rebellious students of the Vietnam era resulted in marked grade inflation. Grade inflation was the most pronounced in history. For instance, Dartmouth students averaged a 2.2 GPA in 1958 and 3.06 in 1976; University of North Carolina was 2.39 in 1967 and 2.72 in 1975; University of Minnesota was 2.33

in 1964 and 2.90 in 1973; and University of Washington was 2.31 in 1964 and 2.91 in 1974. Other institutions had similar grade inflation, and the estimated average GPA rose about 0.35 point from 1967 to 1974, a dramatic increase.[14]

The great increase in the number of African American male athletes in American universities was occurring while academic standards dropped precipitously. At the same time, the NCAA abandoned its more than a half century of promoting freshman ineligibility. Beginning in 1968, the NCAA, for financial reasons, began allowing freshmen to play in all sports except football and basketball, and then in 1972 it allowed freshman eligibility in the two most commercialized sports. The next year, the NCAA abolished its only important eligibility standard that had been in existence for a decade: the 1.600 GPA rule. With discarded academic standards and the lure of unprecedented, TV-driven salaries for athletes in professional basketball and football, the big-time universities became way stations for athletes who were not interested in a college education but who saw the opportunity for professional athletics through "minor-league" colleges as a way out of poverty or to riches. Blacks were particularly attracted to football and basketball, the two most visible male sports in colleges and two of the three highest-paying professional sports, along with baseball.

The entrance statistics for blacks under established academic standards were appallingly low, as were the college graduation rates for African Americans. A study by the NCAA showed that black athletes with scholarships who entered college in 1977 were dreadfully unprepared for academic study. The lower quartile of black male athletes averaged only 560 on the 1,600-point SAT exams, with a median score of 650, while the lower quartile of white athletes averaged 820, with a median score of 940. High school grade point averages also showed a similar disparity of 2.39 for African Americans males and 2.90 for white males. Female scholarship athletes showed a similar, though higher, difference compared to their male cohort. Black female athletes in the lower quartile average 598 on the SAT, with a median of 710, and an average 2.62 high school GPA, while white female athletes in the lower quartile averaged 830 on the SAT exam, with a 960 median score, and an average 3.20 high school GPA.[15] Though these statistics were not known at the time of the passage of Proposition 48, it was no secret that blacks scored significantly below whites in standard evaluations of academic preparedness. The highly successful football coach at Nebraska, Tom Osborne, supported higher standards while recognizing that "minority students will usually score substantially lower than non-minority students" and estimating that one of every three in the Big 8 Conference would not qualify under the 700 SAT rule.[16] It was obvious to most, but not all, that a reform in raising test standards for athletic participation should be carried out by the NCAA.

Rather than returning to freshman ineligibility, which had been a major reform for most of the twentieth century, most individuals believed that a combination of the high school grade point average and standardized test scores would be a major solution to the lack of academic standards existing since the defeat of the 1.600 grade point average of the early 1970s. But the standardized test scores were an anathema to many black leaders. Nevertheless, during the summer of 1982, without major concern for the impact upon African American athletes, President William Friday of the University of North Carolina, President Derek Bok of Harvard University, and Jack Peltason, head of the American Council of Education (ACE), joined forces to lobby the NCAA to reform the academic requirements for freshman athletes entering college.[17] Soon, the Ad Hoc Committee on Intercollegiate Athletics of the American Council of Education, without any involvement of historic black institution presidents, created a proposal known as Proposition 48 for the 1983 NCAA convention. Ignoring African American participation in determining standards of eligibility was a strategic mistake by the president-controlled ACE and by the NCAA. While steps had been taken in the previous generation to integrate more blacks into NCAA proceedings, too little progress had been made since 1954, when the African American athletic director at Central State College of Wilberforce, Ohio, appeared before the NCAA and asked unsuccessfully for NCAA members not to discriminate and thus allow Negro colleges to gain berths in NCAA championships and to have representation on NCAA committees.[18]

When Proposition 48 came before the NCAA convention through Donald Shields, president of Southern Methodist University and a member of the ACE Ad Hoc Committee, it was immediately attacked by historically black colleges, first by Joseph B. Johnson, president of Grambling State University. Johnson represented the National Association for Equal Opportunity in Higher Education, an organization founded in 1969 for presidents of historically black colleges and universities. Division I, II, and III of the NCAA had no representation from the 114 predominantly black institutions in the formation of Proposition 48, Johnson stated, showing the ACE and NCAA lack of sensitivity to questions impacting black athletes. Johnson condemned the proposal, for it "discriminates against student-athletes from low-income and minority-group families by introducing arbitrary SAT and ACT cutoff scores as academic criteria for eligibility."[19] Edward B. Fort, chancellor of another traditionally black university, North Carolina A & T, said that Proposition 48 had "unfortunately become a black-and-white issue," one in which the aptitude test

(SAT and ACT) had been repeatedly "challenged by empirical evidence of numerous studies" discriminating against "the working and middle classes, black and white."[20] The first Caucasian to address the black-white issue was Joe Paterno, a prominent football coach for thirty-three years at Penn State University. Arguing for the passage of Proposition 48, Paterno said that blacks would take the challenge to meet the requirements of Proposition 48 and would not be eliminated from big-time college sports as some had suggested. But, he said, universities "have had a race problem. We have raped a generation-and-a-half of young black athletes. We have taken kids and sold them on bouncing a ball and running with the football. . . . We cannot afford to do that to another generation. We cannot afford to have kids come into our institutions and not be prepared to take advantage of what the great education institutions in this country can do for them."[21]

After several hours of debate, Proposition 48, the first important academic reform since the 1.600 rule, was passed and scheduled to take effect in 1986. Implementation was delayed three years to allow high school athletes an opportunity to meet Proposition 48's relatively low academic requirements for athletic participation—a 2.0 high school grade point average in eleven core courses and a 700 score on the SAT exam or 15 on the ACT.[22] (It should be pointed out that proposed legislation by the Atlantic Coast Conference to reinstitute the higher academic 1.600 GPA rule, defeated in 1973, was withdrawn upon passage of Proposition 48.[23] Under the old 1.600 rule, a person who scored a 700 on the SAT would have to have a 3.0 high school GPA to predict a 1.600 in college.)

Passage of Proposition 48 only intensified the efforts of those opposed to the racially and economically biased standardized tests into challenging the new NCAA initial eligibility rules. Immediately after the NCAA convention and the passage of Prop 48, the American Council on Education and the NCAA were embarrassed by the reaction of the African American community. Two studies were quickly created to evaluate academic performance of freshman athletic scholarship recipients.[24] The study groups made sure that race was factored into the results. Two of the findings showed that blacks, indeed, had greater differences compared to whites in standard test scores than in high school grade point averages, just as blacks had pointed out before Prop 48 was passed. For example, 75 percent of blacks earned ACT composite scores below the cutoff for athletic eligibility, while only 25 percent of whites scored below the cutoff.[25] It was also shown that more than 50 percent of African American football and basketball players entered college with preferential presidential admits, while less than a quarter were given to whites. In addition, the research indicated that nearly three-quarters of black male athletes who actually graduated from college would not have qualified for participation under Prop 48.[26] Their research suggested three alternatives to Prop 48: dropping the standardized test scores, permitting eligibility with either the 2.0 GPA or standardized test results, or using an index score based upon both the GPA and tests. Nevertheless, the NCAA chose not to change its formula that was shown to be prejudicial against African Americans.[27]

Passed in 1983, Prop 48 was not put into effect until 1986. In the intervening three years, had it been in effect, 92 percent of the ineligible basketball players and 84 percent of ineligible football players would have been black.[28] President of the College Board, which produced the SAT test, and a friend of the presidents who ran the American Council on Education, George Hanford, proclaimed, inaccurately, that Prop 48 and the SAT test were not biased against blacks.[29] Only a few African American leaders favored setting standards for eligibility using standardized test scores. One of them was Harry Edwards of the University of California. Edwards, who once led an unsuccessful black boycott of the 1968 Mexico City Olympic Games, believed that Prop 48 standards "are arbitrary and so *low* as to constitute virtually no standards at all."[30] But he was in the minority. So was Arthur Ashe, the first black winner of the men's Wimbledon tennis tournament. Ashe commented that Prop 48 standards were set in the NCAA cloakrooms at a level "quote, even black athletes could pass, unquote." Blacks, Ashe said, "should have complained that the number wasn't higher," not that it was too high for blacks.[31]

Once Prop 48 was initiated, the percentage of failures remained unduly high for African Americans, with nearly nine of ten Prop 48 casualties being black. Ursula Walsh, NCAA director of research, conceded the bias against blacks: "We know that standardized test scores are correlated with socioeconomic status," a euphemism for African Americans.[32] To the NCAA, its representatives, and institutional presidents, the desire to raise academic standards and improve the image of institutions was far more important than was the issue of racial equality. Even James Frank, the first African American president of the NCAA, the head of Lincoln University in Missouri, and a member of the American Council on Education, agreed that Prop 48 was needed to change the image of athletics in institutions of higher education.[33] Freshman eligibility under Prop 48, with slight but controversial changes, would remain until after the turn of the century.

Proposition 48 had raised the issue of what kind of balance there should be between academic priorities on the one hand and enhanced opportunities for blacks and other minorities on the other. The development of freshman eligibility standards would be determined by a combination of the values placed on athletic performance in higher education and on the values of higher education itself. If maximizing athletic (and educational) opportunities for blacks and other minorities was most valued, then only minimal academic standards should be set, such as the 2.0 high school grade point average in the period from the 1970s to the mid-1980s. The lack of a meaningful 2.0 academic standard had both created a crisis of academic integrity and upset any kind of level playing field in athletics. Under the 2.0 GPA provision, schools would go to the bottom of the academic barrel to find the best athletes to turn out winners, as evidenced by the entrance of such athletes as Kevin Ross at Creighton University, Chris Washburn at North Carolina State University, and Dexter Manley at Oklahoma State University.[34] However, raising the standard, even to the low criterion of Prop 48, would be detrimental to those whose education had often been thwarted by coming from low socioeconomic backgrounds, such as that of many inner-city African Americans. Referring to Prop 48, Frank Rienzo of Georgetown University commented: "What started out as a question of academic integrity has become an issue of social justice."[35] He was right. Blacks and others would continue to challenge the bias of Prop 48.

The NCAA bowed somewhat to pressure when it included in Prop 48 the term *partial qualifier*. To be a partial qualifier meant that the incoming athlete had achieved either a 2.0 GPA or a 700 SAT/15 ACT score, but not both. In that case, the individual could attend college on an athletic scholarship but not participate during the freshman year. However, the Georgia-Jan Kemp scandal and nationally important court case in 1986, in which a number of African American partial qualifiers had been central to the cheating scandal, placed pressure on the University of Georgia and the Southeastern Conference to close the loophole by eliminating partial qualifiers. Georgia President Davison, who had admitted nonqualifying students to feed the talent pool for Georgia football and men's basketball, banned nonqualifiers from attending Georgia in 1986.[36] Georgia, fearful of being on the wrong end of an unlevel playing field, asked the Southeastern Conference to ban partial qualifiers soon thereafter. The SEC, sensing the same unlevel playing field in recruiting athletes on a national level, then asked the NCAA to do the same in 1989. This was the origin of Prop 42, which banned athletic scholarships to partial qualifiers.

The brouhaha in 1989 created by the passage of Prop 42 had seldom been seen in the history of the NCAA, though the struggle over scholarship limitations of the Sanity Code around 1950 certainly surpassed the controversy over the new legislation. The legislation was passed principally to stop the flow of academically ill-prepared athletes entering college and to restore the original intent of Prop 48 in 1983 by eliminating the partial qualifier. In the first NCAA vote, Prop 42 was defeated 159–151 but was then reconsidered, and by a 163–154 vote the partial qualifier was eliminated.[37] John Thompson, the Georgetown University basketball coach who had won a national championship only a few years before, called the

NCAA a "racist organization" for passing the discriminatory Prop 42. Thompson, like President Joseph Johnson of Grambling State University, who had previously called Prop 48 the "NCAA's apartheid," decided that he would protest individually and walked off the floor before a game with Boston College and did not accompany the team to a game with Providence College[38] Protests by black basketball coaches such as Thompson, the first African American coach to win a national championship, and John Cheney of Temple University were part of what leaders of the NCAA believed threatened the most important sport to the NCAA from a financial standpoint. That sport was basketball and the NCAA "March Madness" basketball championship. The men's basketball tourney brought in more than 90 percent of the NCAA's income, and a protest by black coaches and black players would jeopardize the whole commercial enterprise and thus all of college sport.

NCAA leaders listened to the protesters and soon made an amendment to Prop 42. At the next NCAA meeting, the Presidents Commission backed down from its previous recommendation and decided to support the partial qualifier. Thus athletes could be recruited and receive scholarships based upon financial need, but not paid by the athletic department. To help the coaches in recruiting, the partial qualifiers would not be counted under the limits for the number of football or basketball athletic scholarships awarded.[39] The fear of some was realized: that the big-time institutions that could afford it would continue to stockpile athletes for future years of eligibility by having their universities pay for the attendance of the academically unprepared during their freshman year. By again allowing the partial qualifier, the NCAA was essentially returning to the 2.0 high school grade point average for athletes to be eligible for a scholarship, as failures came primarily from standardized tests. Academic corruption would likely continue as it had in the 1970s when the 1.600 GPA rule was voted out. As ex-NCAA head Walter Byers put it, the academically deficient athlete will get a scholarship, get remedial help, take easy courses and play the eligibility game, and compete as a sophomore.[40] According to Richard Lapchick, director of the Center for the Study of Sport in Society, black athletes "are kept eligible by taking courses unlikely to lead to a degree" and nearly half of African American athletes would leave school in poor academic standing, generally after completing their athletic eligibility.[41]

Academic reform to raise freshman academic standards may have appeared to be led by the NCAA's Presidents Commission, but the real push to raise eligibility standards came from outside individual institutions and the NCAA. The federal government in the early 1990s, led by two reformers, Maryland's Representative Tom McMillen and New York's Representative Edolphus Towns, began hearings, implemented by congressional subcommittee chair Cardiss Collins, on intercollegiate athletics. Collins was an African American from Illinois, and she began the hearings by noting that college athletics were "rapidly getting out of control," as evidenced by athletes such as Kevin Ross of Creighton, who could not read after four years of college.[42] Tom McMillen, however, took the leadership and was pushing hard for colleges to make more reforms, including raising academic standards for athletes. McMillen had been the token elected governmental official on the Knight Foundation Commission on Intercollegiate Athletics formed in 1989, a blue-ribbon group dominated by college presidents. McMillen felt that the Knight Commission had done too little in its recommendations to improve the integrity of intercollegiate sports, and he pushed hard for the federal government to become involved by requiring universities to reform, especially because they had been reluctant to do so for the past generation. McMillen presented a bill called the "Collegiate Athletics Reform Act" in 1991 to go far beyond the Knight Commission's recommendations. Soon after, his book *Out of Bounds* was published, in which he discussed Prop 48 and its amendments. He stated inaccurately, however, that the freshman eligibility rules are "neither antiblack nor antipoor." McMillen, a former star at the University of Maryland, a solid pro basketball player, and a Rhodes Scholar, believed "it is absurd for schools to lavish money on athletes who are not ready for college when the same funds could be channeled to scholarships for minority applicants who have demonstrated their capability of handling college work."[43] In addition, he wanted the federal government involved to force a rise in academic standards.

The push by legislators, such as McMillen in the House of Representatives and Bill Bradley in the Senate, caused the NCAA to move more aggressively on academic reform. Dick Schultz, NCAA executive director, had warned NCAA delegates at the end of the 1980s of the threat of greater federal intervention if the NCAA did not move actively toward reform in such areas as publishing graduation rates of athletes by race, sex, and sport. Francis Rienzo of Georgetown believed that federal government intervention would "probably be one of the most serious mistakes this convention would have made in its history." With the federal threat, the NCAA passed by a 323–3 vote a mandate to publish graduation rates. Stated one: "We either take this action for ourselves or we shall have it done for us" by the federal government.[44] Representative McMillen had other reform measures in mind, and through congressional hearings he kept pressuring the NCAA to make changes, which it had been traditionally reluctant to do. When McMillen announced his omnibus bill, called the "Collegiate Athletics Reform Act" in 1991, the NCAA took special notice. In it were provisions mandating more equitable distribution of NCAA revenues, which principally went to the successful teams in the NCAA tourney; requiring constitutional due process procedures by the NCAA when it punished wrongdoers; and restructuring of the NCAA governance, giving control to the presidents. Included in the congressional testimony was a letter from the president of the American Council on Education (ACE), Robert H. Atwell, who represented the president-controlled ACE in opposing "federal involvement in intercollegiate athletic affairs."[45]

As part of the testimony, the American Association of University Professors (AAUP) presented a report that spoke to the African American issue. The AAUP called for college admission standards for athletes to be the same as for the general student body, something that presidents, by their use of presidential admits, would not approve. The AAUP took a stand against athletics being used in affirmative action programs for blacks. "Athletic programs" the AAUP stated, "never should be considered as a major way of supporting students [read African Americans] from disadvantaged backgrounds in institutions of higher learning." To prevent the loss of academic integrity caused by the admittance of inadequately prepared students, the AAUP called upon the faculty to monitor athletic admissions, academic progress of those admitted, courses of study of athletes, and graduation rates.[46] However, faculty, who generally had been dismissed from athletic policy or reform for most of the previous half century, appeared to have little influence in the marketplace of ideas for athletic reform.

Presidents, not faculty, continued to press for increased academic standards to the original Proposition 48, but not without challenge. Proposition 16 in 1992 became the newest amendment to Prop 48, and it was to eventually become effective in 1996. The amendments to Prop 48 were to raise the number of core high school courses from eleven to thirteen and, to appease blacks and those who knew the bias of standardized tests, to include a sliding schedule to eliminate the previous SAT/ACT cutoff scores. Thus, the indexing would allow a lower SAT/ACT score to be balanced with a higher high school grade point average to achieve athletic eligibility.[47] Yet there was also a cutoff to the sliding scale that was slightly below the previous 700 SAT score. Shortly after Prop 16 was passed and before it took effect, Congresswoman Cardiss Collins of Illinois challenged the NCAA over what she considered a new racist policy of the NCAA. She was chairwoman of the Congressional Subcommittee on Commerce, Consumer Protection, and Competitiveness, and she asked NCAA President Joseph Crowley if he knew that the head of the NCAA group studying standardized testing, Jack McArdle, a professor of psychology at the University of Virginia, was a member of a group called Beyondism. McArdle and several of his colleagues, who were influenced by the eugenics-based Beyondism group, were on the NCAA Data Analysis Working Group that was supporting the racially biased Propositions 48, 42, and 16. The believers of Beyondism suggested that a better race of people could be produced through genetic manipulation, what some people equated with the 1930s Nazi racist policy of Adolph Hitler. The Data Analysis Working Group test analysis may have said more about the Data Analysis Working Group than about athlete's academic performance. Cardiss Collins charged that the group of psychologists in the NCAA Data Analysis Working Group was "particularly offensive" to African Americans, and it lacked academic, racial, and ethnic diversity. Thus, their influence on Proposition 48 and its amendments was likely racially biased from the beginning, and any eligibility changes should not be implemented until a thorough investigation of the Data Analysis Working Group was conducted.[48] This indictment gave pause to the NCAA leadership, but not more than the action of the Black Coaches Association.

The Black Coaches Association, formed in 1988, became even more vehement in its opposition to the new Prop 16 than it had been before.[49] Black coaches pointed out that the racist group of psychologists who created the guidelines for Prop 16 occurred at the same time that the NCAA had cut the number of scholarships for basketball from fifteen to thirteen and the NCAA had negotiated a new $1 billion TV contract for its basketball tournament, dominated by black athletes.[50] The group of black coaches believed that what the NCAA claimed was an attempt to cut expenses, while revenues were expanding, was a racist move to cut the number scholarships for African Americans. After all, African Americans dominated basketball teams and were a major reason for the increased popularity of the money-making Final Four. The black coaches threatened to disrupt the basketball season and especially the "March Madness" basketball tourney. This placed the NCAA in a most difficult position, for the NCAA was almost completely dependent for its financial existence on proceeds of the tourney. When a move to restore one of the two basketball scholarships was voted down, the Black Coaches Association (BCA) voted to prepare a boycott of basketball and threatened a possible boycott by black players. The leaders of the NCAA, officials of all Division I conferences, and government officials, including the Congressional Black Caucus, discussed the impact of a boycott. With help from the office of President George H. W. Bush, the BCA agreed to call off the boycott when the NCAA agreed to place an emphasis on greater opportunities for African Americans and other minorities in all aspects of NCAA governance. The effective date of implementing Prop 16 was put off by a year despite opposition from both the Knight Commission and the NCAA's Presidents Commission.[51]

Opposition to Prop 16 did not die, and almost as soon as it was implemented in 1996, a class action court case, *Cureton v. NCAA,* was brought against the NCAA.

Black athletes claimed that the standardized test scores had an "unjustified disparate impact" against African Americans, a violation of the Civil Rights Act of 1964.[52] After Judge Ronald Buckwalter stated that standardized test scores were "not justified by any legitimate educational necessity," the NCAA decided to change its attack against inadequately prepared athletes by allowing any score on the SAT/ACT tests, even a zero, to be combined with the high school grade point average to determine freshman eligibility. No matter that Buckwalter's judgment was overruled by the U.S. Court of Appeals, the NCAA decided that more cases would arise if it did not eliminate the racial bias of standardized tests.[53] At the time, another discrimination case against the NCAA, *Pryor v. NCAA,* was about to be decided. This case involved a woman soccer player who claimed that Proposition 16 and its standardized test were "purposeful discrimination" and "intentional discrimination" and that the NCAA considered race as one of its reasons for adopting Proposition 16."[54] While the court eventually found for the NCAA, litigation was weighing heavily upon the NCAA and its member institutions. With pressure from the courts, the NCAA decided to again modify Prop 48.

The Prop 16 sliding scale for standardized test scores was extended in 2003 so that a zero score in a test (400 SAT, 37 ACT) would still allow an individual to participate in college sport if the high school grade point average was high enough. To improve the possibility that such an athlete might have a better chance to graduate from college, the number of core high school courses necessary for participation was raised to fourteen. By 2008, the number of core courses was raised to sixteen, what many quality colleges in the early 1900s were requiring for entrance into college.[55] After a century, the NCAA followed suit.

Reform for blacks in college sport, as with racial justice in the larger America, had come at a great cost, with most of the reform generated by threats of federal legislation and judicial decisions. What the NCAA had accomplished in helping to raise both black and white graduation rates since Prop 48 was passed (and rates did rise for both blacks and whites) had a tremendous cost in the antagonism of African Americans and those who favored racial justice. It cost the NCAA millions of dollars in research and enforcement as well as litigation costs. While the controversy over standardized tests may have subsided in the early twenty-first century, institutions of the NCAA continued to use the cutoff of a 2.0 high school GPA as the basic measure for eligibility for freshmen in college sport, which was, except for the sixteen high school core courses required, still below the requirements of the old 1.600 rule. With the rapid grade inflation in the public schools, it was relatively easy to achieve a 3.0 GPA and combine it with the recalibrated and abysmally low 620 SAT or 52 ACT score to achieve eligibility. How much easier it might have been to continue the traditional policy of freshman ineligibility, eliminated in 1972 by the NCAA, to see if freshman, black and white, could do quality college work leading toward a degree during the freshman year before participating in varsity athletics. A return to freshman ineligibility might have been the grandest reform for African Americans and for all collegians, men and women, but it was consistently rejected by the presidents who were in control of the NCAA. As it was, most of the reform for African Americans in college sport, as with women's sports, came not from the institutions and the NCAA but from legislative pressure and judicial decisions.

17

Presidential Control, Minor Reform, and the Knight Commission

While major reform came from outside the universities in the form of federal legislation and judicial decisions, big-time college presidents wanted a greater say in how athletics were run. College presidents, since the beginning of the National Collegiate Athletic Association (NCAA), had a great deal of power to control the direction taken by intercollegiate athletics if they desired to do so. After all, it was a college chancellor, Henry M. MacCracken, who called the meeting that set in motion the creation of a reform organization, the NCAA, at the conclusion of the 1905 football season of despair. During the twentieth century, most college presidents appointed faculty representatives to the NCAA, a position that could effectively dictate how those individuals would vote. College presidents could, and a number actually did, attend NCAA meetings. It is not as if the Carnegie Foundation for the Advancement of Teaching or the American Council on Education needed to emphasize that presidents should be in control of intercollegiate athletics, for they had always been in a position to direct athletics if they had chosen collectively to do so. However, there were constituencies in each university that were part of the power equation in athletics, including members of the governing board, alumni, and the athletic department. While most presidents were more often athletic cheerleaders than reformers, those who were favorable toward reform had many individuals or groups who put large roadblocks in the way of positive change in the integration of athletics with education. By the early 1980s, conditions had worsened to the point where presidents decided to wrest control of the NCAA away from faculty representatives and athletic directors, both of whom presidents had appointed but previously didn't control or didn't want to control for reform purposes.

The move toward greater presidential control was not new in the 1980s. When the Sanity Code passed shortly after World War II, there was a suggestion to create a Presidents Committee within the NCAA. President Hugh Tiner of Pepperdine College in Los Angeles recommended to the NCAA that a "committee of college presidents" be formed to serve in an advisory capacity and be "urged to make recommendations to the N.C.A.A. from time to time." President Tiner wanted the Association of American Colleges, not the American Council on Education, to appoint such a committee.[1] The Association of American Colleges (AAC) had been formed just before America's entry into World War I, in an attempt to promote liberal education for undergraduates in the smaller colleges. In its own way, the AAC was a reform agency. Even in the early twentieth century, membership in the AAC, serving as a kind of accrediting agency, required that freshmen admitted to its colleges have fourteen high school units. Advocating high standards in colleges, the AAC was a logical locus for reforming academic requirements for athletes, but because the AAC lacked as members most of the dominant big-time athletic institutions, it would not have the power to enact change. Nothing came of Tiner's recommendations or those of Senator William Fulbright, who had recently been president of the University of Arkansas. Fulbright, a triple-threat halfback at the University of Arkansas in the 1920s, a varsity tennis player, and an all-star lacrosse player at Oxford during his Rhodes Scholar years, spoke out in 1951 for college administrators to take control and "not depend on athletic conferences and the coaches" to control big-time athletics. Fulbright believed that big-time football was a "phony," for it pretended to be amateur while it was in fact professional.[2] Neither Tiner nor Fulbright was effective in bringing about presidential control and reforming athletics, and one might note that at the time the NCAA could not even enforce its own reform Sanity Code.

In the 1970s, there were only two college presidents on the governing NCAA Council, but with the backing of the Pacific-8 Conference, there was an effort to dramatically increase presidential power in the NCAA. Of the sixteen members of the NCAA Council, the proposed plan would dictate that half would be institutional presidents. While there was no lengthy discussion (as there had been at the same convention before the members defeated a motion to allow only need-based scholarships to replace full athletic scholarships), Ed Steitz of Springfield College and member of the NCAA Executive Board spoke for the majority who opposed the transfer of power to presidents. Steitz was wary of presidents who would sit in a controlling position but would lack sufficient knowledge of athletics. He did not believe that "the title of chief executive officer automatically carries with it an expertise on athletic matters." He may, though, have feared placing presidents on the Council, such as Stephen Horn of California State University, Long Beach, who had been regularly attending NCAA meetings and rankling members, especially officers, with what some believed were pompous and misguided opinions. A number of NCAA representatives did not soon forget Horn's "Robin Hood" attempts to take money from the rich to pay the poor that helped create the College Football Association a couple of years before. The 1977 proposition to seat more presidents on the Council was voted down by faculty representatives, and the idea awaited a new decade.[3]

Presidents of big-time intercollegiate institutions had more than their share of athletic troubles in the post-Watergate, Richard Nixon period of the 1970s and into the early 1980s. It was a time of increased cynicism in America and its institutions, and it was no less true in intercollegiate athletics and the NCAA. Presidents of numerous institutions of higher education saw their athletic programs punished by the NCAA or their conferences, and it appeared that they often had little control over what was happening in their own athletic departments. Examples of programs out of control, mostly in football, existed in all sections of the country.[4] In the expanded PAC-10 Conference, sanctions against Arizona State, Oregon, Oregon State, UCLA, and the University of Southern California made them all ineligible for the Rose Bowl of 1980. USC may have been the worst of the lot, for it had admitted 330 scholastically deficient men and women athletes in the 1970s, most of whom were football players. This was condoned by President John Hubbard, who directed his admissions office "to keep hands off" their admittance policies. Many of these athletes at USC, and elsewhere, were being given credit for courses not attended or even registered, so that they could remain athletically eligible.[5] At the Big Ten's University of Illinois, a junior college quarterback, Dave Wilson, transferred from Fullerton Junior College, where he had played in parts of three seasons, and was ruled ineligible by the Big Ten Conference because he lacked sufficient credits. Illinois, under President Stanley Ikenberry, went to court to allow him to continue playing, but Illinois's actions eventually brought about a three-year probation and a ban on postseason play.[6] Ikenberry, the pragmatist, was playing the role of cheerleader for Illinois football and the state of Illinois, not the role of reformer.

In the Atlantic Coast Conference, Clemson became the nation's number one ranked football team in 1981, even while it was under investigation by the NCAA for multiple recruiting violations. President Bill Atchley may have been head of the institution, but the athletic program was to a great extent run by a booster club, IPTAY (I pay $30 a year), which was illegally recruiting athletes with gifts of autos, TVs, clothing, and cash. Atchley, a reformer only after his institution was penalized by depriving his football team of TV money, postseason play, and twenty athletic scholarships, was eventually fired (forced resignation[7]) after he attempted to replace his athletic director, Bill McLellan, and bring athletics under greater institutional control. He admitted, "I felt I had to deal with Iptay. You treat them as an important complement to the university. To some degree, there is pressure from them, and you tend to give in." By then, President Atchley was some kind of national hero for standing up to athletic forces (and losing), and he had advocated a "coordinated national effort" to clean up intercollegiate athletics. He favored a system of national accreditation of athletic programs, a requirement of academic progress of athletes, certification of athletic recruiting representatives, and punishment for coaches who violated the rules. Above all, Atchley believed that the presidents needed to gain control of athletics at their universities.[8] Atchley, a former athletic scholarship student at the University of Missouri, Rolla, was among a number of presidents who were demanding collective action to place presidents in a more commanding position within the NCAA.

In addition to football, basketball was increasingly involved in scandals in the 1970s and early 1980s. Probably the most disturbing was the point-shaving scandal at Boston College. Reminiscent of the 1951 and 1961 betting scandals, the point-shaving during the 1978–79 basketball season at Boston College and the ten-year sentence of Rick Kuhn in 1982 for his part in the scheme led to additional support for greater presidential involvement in athletics.[9] This was the most severe penalty ever given to a college player, what the judge believed might deter future player corruption. It didn't. Three years after Kuhn's prison sentence, Tulane University experienced another point-shaving scheme in which three players were involved, and Tulane President Eamon Kelly asked his governing board to drop basketball.[10] At the University of San Francisco, President John Lo Schiavo had earlier dropped basketball for the improper payment of athletes by an alumnus.[11] Generally, individual presidents were embarrassed to lead institutions in which athletics violated ethical and legal standards. Collectively, presidents were coming closer to acting in concert to clean up the national athletic mess.

The movement for greater presidential influence was delayed until the 1980s, when the lamentable lack of academic standards for athletes was most visible and the number of scandals appeared to reach an apex. The impetus for presidential involvement came from the president-run American Council on Education (ACE), in which the group could act collectively and presidents would be less likely to be negatively singled out for promoting some type of reform. Derek Bok, Harvard president and head of the ACE, led a drive to change the power structure within the NCAA. Beginning in 1981, an ad hoc group of university presidents under the ACE recommended tightening academic standards for athletes and creating a board of presidents within the NCAA. According to Bok, "If some institutions choose to ignore admissions standards for athletes and are indifferent to whether their athletes ever graduate, other colleges will find it hard to compete with them on the playing field." What to do? Create collective rules, under presidential leadership, intended to level the playing field and maintain reasonable academic standards with enforcement by the NCAA.[12] The Harvard president campaigned vigorously for a board of presidents within the NCAA to have authority over academic standards, financial integrity, and the reputation of member institutions. Under such a plan, the presidents' decisions would stand unless a two-thirds majority of the NCAA representatives overruled their decisions. In other words, presidents would have control of the NCAA under the ACE recommendations, not merely provide advice as the NCAA leaders desired.

When the ACE recommendations were brought to the NCAA convention in 1984 in the form of Proposition 35, they were shot down by the NCAA membership. This, despite the backing of four president-backed organizations: the American Association of State Colleges and Universities, the National Association of State Universities and Land Grant Colleges, the Association of American Universities, and the National Association for Equal Opportunity in Higher Education.[13] The ACE proposal, according to the representatives, went too far toward presidential control of the NCAA, changing traditional one-institution–one-vote governance through faculty representatives to a representative form of governance led by presidents. The proposed Board of Presidents would have consisted of forty-four members (including a required three women), twenty-two representing the big-time institutions, whose decisions could be overturned only by a two-thirds vote at a future convention. Strong opposition came from the faculty representatives, athletic directors, and some presidents for a variety of reasons, but none was more important than the feeling that presidents did "not trust their athletic directors and faculty representatives," whom they appointed in the first place. James Wharton, head of Louisiana State University and a member of the ACE ad hoc committee, stated emphatically that the ACE proposal was "a slap in the face to the athletic directors and faculty representatives."[14] Well short of a two-thirds majority vote, it did not even receive a simple majority. However, in a few years a similar proposal would pass.

What the NCAA convention did pass was the creation of a forty-four-member Presidents Commission in an attempt to keep presidents involved but limited in power. Rather than a presidential legislative body under the ACE's Board of Presidents plan, the Presidents Commission could only make recommendations to the old NCAA Council, dominated by athletic directors and faculty representatives. The creation of the Presidents Commission, with heavy Division I football interests represented, might have satisfied a number of presidents who could use the faculty representative-run NCAA as a scapegoat for any criticism of the lack of meaningful reform. Presidents, according to University of Wisconsin Chancellor Donna Shalala, were "scaredy cats" when it came to making hard decisions relative to athletics as well as all activities in higher education.[15] This was likely true, in that presidents had been pulled in many directions by a variety of forces, including governing boards, alumni, and faculty.

Nevertheless, the new Presidents Commission had the power to call special conventions, and it did so in 1985. It was the first president-initiated national conference since Chancellor Henry MacCracken of New York University called a meeting at the end of the disastrous 1905 football season, leading to the creation of the NCAA. The Presidents Commission presented eight proposals, all requiring a roll-call vote so that institutions could not hide behind the anonymity of a voice or hand vote. Each of the eight proposals was passed with overwhelming numbers, allowing the presidents to claim a major victory for reform. The reform measures included mandatory institutional self-studies of athletics every five years; institutional control, with the athletic budget brought under the president's control and an external audit of the budget; penalties for coach and athlete violations; affidavits from coaches relative to proper financial aid and amateur status; and discipline of institutions with secondary and major penalties, including the "death penalty" or cessation of a particular sport for a year.[16] The "death penalty," while not particularly controversial when it passed with a 427–6 vote, was imposed upon Southern Methodist University two years later (and not again for more than a generation). At the time, some considered these eight measures to be major reforms, but none would change the basic environment of big-time college athletics. One action suggested but not taken, which would become troublesome to the NCAA, was lack of a statement to honor due process when accusing and punishing violators.[17]

With a very modest reform package, the Presidents Commission soon moved to see if it could reform athletics financially by cutting costs. At the annual convention in 1987, the presidents backed a cost-cutting measure by reducing the number of annual football scholarships from thirty to twenty-five and the total number in basketball from fifteen to thirteen. These two reforms were not enough for the Presidents Commission, so a second special convention was called in an effort to save money. Many of the president-backed measures, however, were defeated. In fact, the measure cutting the number of basketball scholarships had been in effect only five months before the number was raised again to fifteen, following the protest of basketball coaches, among others. The proposal to cut the total number of football scholarships from ninety-five to ninety and shaving the number of minor sport scholarships were defeated.[18] The restoration of the fifteen basketball scholarships was specifically important financially to the NCAA, several individuals believed. Vic Bubas, a former highly successful big-time basketball coach at Duke University, argued that he did not want to hurt the sport that provided most of the "revenue that we need in the NCAA."[19] It might be good to cut costs some place, but not in big-time basketball, for the NCAA basketball tournament financed nearly the entire cost of running the NCAA. For the most part, the important issues of cost containment were not effectively addressed, such as the possibility of eliminating all athletic scholarships or allowing only need-based aid, curtailing recruiting costs, redistributing bowl game receipts or television revenues, or drastically reducing the number of coaches or limiting their inflated salaries. The Presidents Commission only had a minor role in reforming in the financial arena, but the presidents would continue to be involved in all aspects of reform.

Violations did not diminish following greater involvement of presidents with the Presidents Commission. President Ira Michael Heyman of the University of California, Berkeley, spoke at the 1987 special convention, condemning universities for condoning "one abuse after another," including bribing of high school students, altering transcripts, admitting functional illiterates, allowing athletes to take meaningless courses, and physically and emotionally abusing athletes. He criticized "presidents who turn a blind eye to all of this."[20] Pointedly, President Heyman had himself sent out the agenda for reform for the meeting, noting that to be successful there was a need for presidents, trustees, alumni, conference officials, athletic directors, coaches, and students to be involved. Ironically, he did not mention the faculty, and when questioned about this at the convention, his quick wit covered his glaring mistake when he replied, "[I]t is just a typical oversight of a college president."[21] It was far more than that, because the faculty had been excluded for most of the twentieth century from meaningful reform efforts. Heyman was not the exception; his "oversight" was the rule, and it more than likely was intentional.

Some of the most nationally visible abuses continued, including those at the University of Florida, when it was charged with 107 NCAA violations, including extra payments to athletes, jobs for athletes' relatives, payment for work not performed, and illegal scouting of opponents, all leading to the resignation of the football coach, Charley Pell, in 1984.[22] At President Fred Davison's University of Georgia, a 1986 trial took place in which English tutor Jan Kemp sued the university for her unjust firing. Kemp had refused her superior's order to persuade other professors to change the grades of five athletes and had protested promoting nine failing football players so that they could participate in a bowl game. Davison, who had been president of the College Football Association while claiming that college athletics needed to be reformed, admitted at the trial that Georgia could not "disarm unilaterally" and remain athletically competitive.[23] Thus it needed the athletes, who were academically ill-suited for college, to participate on its foot-ball and basketball teams. The trial embarrassed President Davison, who resigned within a month of the verdict against Georgia in which Kemp was given an initial judgment of more than $2.5 million. It was humiliating to leaders of higher edu-cation and the NCAA's Presidents Commission as well. However, nothing was more upsetting than the repeated violations of Southern Methodist University in the 1970s and 1980s, scandals that reached up to the SMU president's and the Texas governor's offices.

The scandal that led to the "death penalty" was not new to SMU. A half century before, not long after SMU was founded, it was in danger of becoming a women's college as its male enrollment decreased and the percentage of women increased dramatically. Two SMU trustees decided that the masculine image could be best developed with a winning football team. Led by a trustee and Dallas judge, Joseph Cockrell, a group of local businessmen raised an $80,000 slush fund for securing skilled football players.[24] The SMU trustees also hired themselves a fund-raiser president, Hiram Boaz, a Methodist bishop. Upon assuming the presidency, Boaz said that it was time "to lay some emphasis on securing a winning football team."[25] Soon, a Southwest Conference investigation revealed athletic corruption of trustees and administration involving illegal payments, wages paid for work not performed, reinstatement by administrators of failed athletes, and grade changes to maintain eligibility.[26] That was in the 1920s, only a few years before the Carnegie Report was released showing the high degree of professionalism and commercialism in college sport. It all sounded familiar five decades later.

In 1987, three years after the NCAA Presidents Commission was created, South-ern Methodist was given the second NCAA "death penalty"; that is, if the NCAA demand for a boycott of Kentucky basketball following the basketball point-shaving scandal of 1951 is considered the first. SMU football had been highly success-ful, with a 41-5-1 record from 1981 to 1984 and starring running backs such as Eric Dickerson and Craig James, but doing it illegally under the illicit recruiting practices of coaches Ron Meyer and Bobby Collins. The president of SMU, L. Don-ald Shields, was involved in the cover-up of the scandal along with the former governor of Texas and leader of the SMU board of trustees, Bill Clements, and the athletic director, Bob Hitch. High school athletes were given signing bonuses and paid thousands of dollars each year while at SMU, provided automobiles, and allowed to sell football tickets for far more than their face value.[27] While the NCAA investigation was going on, Clements again ran for governor and was reelected. Clements was intimately involved in the payment of players with the SMU athletic boosters. The fact that SMU had the most major violations of NCAA rules since 1958 and its second within five years led to a year-long ban of football competition, a two-year ban of bowl games and TV revenue, loss of three assistant coaches for two years, loss of fifty-five scholarships over four years, and its players allowed to transfer with no penalty to their eligibility. It ruined football at SMU for far longer than the one-year ban, for in the next two decades, SMU had only one winning football season. The whole episode did little to uphold the SMU motto: "The truth shall set you free." There was little truth or freedom. Walter Byers, who began his NCAA leadership role with the Kentucky "death penalty" and ended it with the SMU case, noted the change in the NCAA over that three-and-a-half-decade period. It changed, Byers said, "from simple rules and personally responsible officials to convoluted, cyclopedia regulations with high-priced legal firms defending college violators against a limited NCAA enforcement system."[28] The rules that the NCAA had crafted in order to create a level playing field had failed, even under the action of the presidents. The deviant individual institutions, with some mendacious presidents such as Davison and Shields, desired to illegally tilt the playing field to their advantage.

One should have been suspect when the Knight Foundation's Creed C. Black announced in 1989 that a Knight Foundation Commission on Intercollegiate Athletics, with presidential leadership, would be formed "to propose a reform agenda for intercollegiate athletics."[29] Suspect because many of the presidents had been the problem, not the solution. Creed Black and the Knight Foundation believed that athletics "had reached proportions threatening the very integrity of higher education," and a group principally made up of college presidents should make recommendations to effect change. Chosen to lead the $2 million Knight Commission were two former big-time college presidents, Theodore M. Hesburgh of the University of Notre Dame and William C. Friday of the University of North Carolina. There were twelve other college or former college presidents included in the Knight Commission, which also included four chief executive officers of corporations and one member each from an alumni association, a governing board, the NCAA, the United States Olympic Committee, television, and the U.S. House of Representatives. Significantly, there were no faculty members represented.[30] It was not surprising that the group dominated by presidents should conclude that "university presidents are the key to successful reform, . . . the linchpins of the reform movement."[31] That the Knight Commission made this proclamation in light of the fact that presidents had made efforts in this direction but had few accomplishments since the 1880s did not deter the efforts of the more than 90 percent male group. Diplomatically, the Knight Commission stated that Proposition 48 had "served intercollegiate athletics well," just after noting that for athletes there was "dreadful anecdotal evidence of academic progress," and only one-third of men's basketball players and less than 40 percent of football players graduated.[32] The universities and athletes were not well served.

The president emeritus of Notre Dame, cleverly came up with the Knight Commission's One-Plus-Three model for the solution to athletic problems.[33] One, there must be presidential control of intercollegiate athletics, with the backing of the governing board, directed toward three: (1) academic integrity, (2) financial integrity, and (3) independent certification. One of the problems of presidential control was that governing boards generally set university policy, not presidents. The Knight Commission did not recommend how governing boards should create athletic policy with academic integrity and concluded that if governing boards do not wish to reform "we do not know how reform can be accomplished."[34] The Knight Commission might have had a more equitable 13:1 ratio of presidents to governing board members, but it chose not to. Without the backing of governing boards, there would not likely be a high degree of academic integrity. Governing boards, as the Knight Commission knew, were part of the problem. Governing boards had allowed the policy of presidential "special admits," a device to allow university heads to admit inferior students who were athletically superior. Academic integrity was violated for the benefit of athletic success. Something on the order of 20 percent of all football and men's basketball players entered Division I universities as presidential special admits, all with governing board approval. Without a governing board policy stating that athletes would be academically representative of the rest of the student body, and unenforced by presidents, one could not expect academic reform. There probably was not one big-time institution in which either football or basketball athletes were close to the academic average of the rest of the student body.[35] It should be noted that the Knight Commission did not recommend the reform of freshman ineligibility to better ensure that athletes could meet the academic standards of college work before participating in athletics. It only praised Proposition 48, the low standard and racially biased reform, indicating that "Proposition 48 has served intercollegiate athletics well."[36] The Knight Commission's presidents had fallen short on the question of academic integrity.

Besides academic integrity, the Knight Commission added financial integrity, emphasizing the reduction of athletic costs.[37] Yet financing athletics was mostly an individual college responsibility, and if institutions such as the University of North Carolina (cochair Friday's institution) wanted to compete with the University of Notre Dame (cochair Hesburgh's institution) in terms of athletic facilities, athletic scholarships, and coach's salaries, North Carolina would have to spend at least as much as Notre Dame, and more if it wanted to be better than Notre Dame. There was no recommended solution to the current "arms race" to outspend the competitors. Thus, stadium enlargement to the 100,000 range and the million-dollar coaching salaries would not be kept under control by individual presidents. There was no discussion of need-based athletic scholarships as had been discussed in the 1950s. The Knight Commission made no proposal to distribute television money more evenly among participating institutions, a topic that had been taken up in the 1970s. There were no proposals for limiting the runaway coaching salaries in the important sports. The Knight Commission did, however, recommend (with no success) banning shoe and equipment contracts with individual coaches.[38]

The Knight Commission reworked the old idea of certification of the individual athletic programs by an outside agency. It, however, did not promote the idea of certification coming from accrediting agencies, as had been suggested in the early 1950s. Certification would incorporate academic issues of athletes, such as admissions records, academic progress of athletes, and graduation rates. Specifically, it recommended comparing athletes' academic records with those of the rest of the student body.[39] Nevertheless, the Knight Commission did not indicate recommended actions to be taken if an institution failed certification. For instance, if athletes on a specific team consistently failed to graduate, would that team be punished by cutting the number of scholarships or be prohibited from participating in television revenues or the NCAA tournaments?

What is significant about the Knight Commission Report is what was left out of the report, probably because consensus could not be achieved. There was no discussion of what to do about the rapid increase of commercialism in college sport, the movement away from amateurism toward professionalism, cutting time demands on athletes for practice and contests, the possibility of limiting the number of contests and the length of seasons or off-season practice, the control of television during all days of the week, the impact of extraordinary salaries of coaches and administrators, the limiting of presidential admits of academically ill-prepared athletes, the creation of courses of study principally to keep athletes eligible and of professors who were known to coddle athletes with high grades, the lack of any discussion of integrating faculty into reforms needed in athletics, and what penalties should be laid upon individuals and institutions who broke the rules. In short, there was nothing new in the Knight Commission Report that was not discussed over the years, but because of its high visibility it was used in the following years to get the NCAA and others to discuss problems that were known to exist for decades. To this end, the Knight Commission Report had succeeded in being visible.

The Knight Commission had spent about $2 million, but the report had little lasting impact on athletic reform, as evidenced by the reorganization of a second Knight Commission a decade later because the athletic situation had further deteriorated. Wrote a pessimistic Walter Byers shortly before the Knight Commission Report was released: "The reform proposals by the Presidents Commission and those that are supposedly going to come from the Knight Commission are miniature in form and really won't change much of anything."[40] He was correct. The Knight Commission Report, which was discussed continually for the next two decades, made the leaders of college athletics feel better about athletics and academic integrity, yet it failed to bring about important reforms either academically or financially. What it did do was to show that presidents, when they controlled a commission on reform, were woefully inadequate in helping to reform intercollegiate athletics. This, however, would not stop presidents from gaining complete control of the NCAA.

18

NCAA Reorganization, the Board of Presidents' Reform, and the APR

University presidents had not been the major leaders of reform after the creation of the National Collegiate Athletic Association (NCAA) in 1905, but by the end of the century they demanded more power within the NCAA. The presidents, though they had just been successful in pushing for minor reforms, were not satisfied with being advisors under the NCAA's Presidents Commission created in 1984. With incidents on nearly every campus of athletes breaking rules or committing serious violations of the law and institutions regularly violating NCAA recruiting and eligibility rules, presidents continually had to apologize or make excuses for their athletic programs. The University of Georgia eligibility fiasco and the Southern Methodist University "death penalty" were merely the most visible of the problems of integrity facing college athletics in the 1980s and 1990s. A major push for presidential change came from the president-dominated Knight Commission on Intercollegiate Athletics and its 1991 report, *Keeping Faith with the Student-Athlete: A New Model for Intercollegiate Athletics*. The report, written under the chairmanship of William Friday and Theodore Hesburgh, former presidents of the University of North Carolina and the University of Notre Dame, respectively, stated that "university presidents are the key to successful reform. They must be in charge . . . in the decision-making councils of the NCAA."[1]

Presidents, despite having their own Presidents Commission in the NCAA and appointing nearly all of the representatives to the NCAA, felt the need to be raised from having what they considered mere advisory powers to full powers in forming national athletic policy. In other words, the presidents would not trust their own faculty and administrative appointees to carry out their wishes for the direction that intercollegiate athletics were taking on the national level. The perceived need to show complete presidential control demonstrated the dominance that athletic leaders, athletic directors, coaches, and president-appointed faculty representatives had garnered over university policy during the twentieth century. If the direction of athletics had strayed so far from the desires of presidents, it was questionable if a change from an NCAA Presidents Commission to a Presidents Board could change the direction of intercollegiate athletics. The first decade of reform under a new Presidents Board might be telling.

In the mid-1990s, when university presidents secured complete control of the NCAA, there were likely few institutional leaders who would have agreed with Harvard President Charles W. Eliot's statement nearly a century before that presidents "certainly cannot reform football," the most important sport, or other lesser college sports.[2] Yet from the beginning of the NCAA in 1905 until the end of the century, Eliot was correct. Presidents, instrumental in the forming of the NCAA, did little over the years to reform athletics. Presidents, who were asked by the Carnegie Foundation for the Advancement of Teaching to reform athletics in 1929, were unimportant in bringing athletics under an educational model rather than continue in a commercial-professional mode. Individual presidents, such as Thomas Gates of the University of Pennsylvania, John Bowman of the University of Pittsburgh, Robert Hutchins of the University of Chicago, or Frank Graham of the University of North Carolina, showed great effort but little progress toward reform in the decade following the Carnegie Report. The president-led American Council on Education reforms, prompted by the post–World War II scandals of 1951, were not successful. Only the president-created Ivy League could be considered a partial success, and when it occurred none of the institutions were among the dominating athletic-elite schools they had once been. Was the lack of effectiveness of presidents due to their lack of power over athletics during the twentieth century, or were the presidents unwilling to use their power to change athletics to conform to the educational goals of higher education?

In the early 1990s, E. Gordon Gee, the president of the University of Colorado just before taking the presidency of Ohio State University, wrote about football the day that Colorado was playing in the Orange Bowl. "Football has become a business with enormous commercial opportunity," Gee stated, "even at the expense of academic standards and expectations."[3] While he later helped reform Vanderbilt University's athletic program by collapsing the athletic department and bringing athletics under the educational wing of the university, it was not likely that he would have much impact calming the rampant commercialism at Colorado or his soon-to-be institution, Ohio State, one of the top universities in America in expenditures for intercollegiate athletics. Gee asked, "Can we afford to satisfy commercial interests if, so doing, we lose our academic souls?"[4] Presidents, such as Gee, could speak in generalities about commercialism and losing academic souls, but when it came to the institutions they headed, most would do very little to assuage their "souls" by calming commercialism. Yet that is exactly what presidents said they would do in the 1990s, and especially after they took over control of the NCAA by 1997. How ironic it was that the last major football bowl site to allow corporate sponsorship to name the bowl was the Rose Bowl, in 1998, when it signed with AT&T.[5] There was no united opposition by Ohio State and the heads of the other Big Ten football institutions or those of the PAC-10 participating annually in the oldest and most prestigious bowl event in America to restrain the commercialism.

Even before the presidential NCAA "coup," some presidents believed that the slight reform of the early 1990s indicated that reforms would continue and athletics would be cleaned up under educational leadership. One of these was Hunter Rawlings III, the head of the University of Iowa. Returning from the 1991 reform NCAA convention where president-initiated legislation passed overwhelmingly, Rawlings naively noted, "Contrary to the presidents' own expectations, our control of the NCAA was relatively simple to assert and, once established, nearly absolute. . . . Narrow athletic interests," Rawlings emphasized, "are powerless in the face of presidential will and consensus."[6] The president of Wake Forest University and member of the Knight Commission, Thomas K. Hearn Jr., agreed with Rawlings. "There is reason now for those who have been concerned about the capacity of the N.C.A.A. to change its direction to be reassured."[7] Walter Byers, the retired NCAA executive director, was more accurate when, after that 1991 convention, he challenged the idea that the strong presidential influence in the "reform" meeting was the most important action in the previous generation. They "won't change much of anything," Byers stated.[8] At about the same time, a muckraking author, Don Yaeger, who was highly critical of intercollegiate athletics, told a congressional subcommittee on intercollegiate sports that each president was "desirous of winning, and it was as important to him to be in that national championship game as it was to the coach." It was naive to believe, Yeager underscored, that lasting reform would come from presidents.[9]

After a decade of the NCAA Presidents Commission making recommendations for reform, the NCAA decided to reorganize, giving the presidents full control. The presidents sensed the need to be in control as big money came with conference realignments and conference TV contracts a few years after the Supreme Court nullified the NCAA football TV monopoly. Conference realignments in all of the major conferences except the PAC-10 in the early 1990s resulted principally from attempts to increase football revenues. As an example, independent Penn State was invited into the Big Ten to gain entry into the eastern TV market. At the same time, all of the conferences were abandoning the College Football Association's lucrative TV contract to create separate conference TV deals that were even larger. For instance, when the Big 8 expanded to the Big 12, it signed a $100 million dollar contract with ABC and Liberty networks to telecast its football games. President Rex Lee of Brigham Young University noted the importance of TV monies: "People would be lying if they told you it wasn't about making money and getting on TV."[10] Presidents often spoke of the need for them to keep control to contain the noneducational aspect of college sport from expanding, but what they were doing was expanding the commercial aspect, especially in football and men's basketball.

So when the movement began in earnest to turn toward full presidential control in 1994, it was part of a larger restructuring of the NCAA that came into being three years later. Division I, though not Divisions II and III, moved away from a democratic form, with each institution having a vote on all issues, to a representative system of governance in which conferences, not institutions, determined the representatives. Faculty representatives, under whom the NCAA had been run for much of the previous ninety years, were addendums in the power equation. In charge was a new Board of Directors, first proposed in 1984 as a Board of Presidents and shot down by the membership for a less threatening Presidents Commission. The newly created Division I presidential Board of Directors was dominated by the major football-playing institutions in Division I-A, while the lesser football-playing Division I-AA institutions and the non-football-playing Division I-AAA universities received a less significant role. To placate Division II and III, a provision was written into the NCAA constitution that the current Division I revenue distribution allocations to II and III would remain (except for any future Division I football playoff revenue, which was reserved for the football powers). The presidents of the so-called Equity conferences—the big-time football ACC, Big East, Big Ten, Big 12, PAC-10, SEC, Western Athletic Conference, and Conference USA—would dominate the proceedings.[11] A Division I Management Council, subservient to the Board of Directors, was to be a practical group made up principally of athletic administrators and faculty representatives appointed by the conferences.[12] Because the big-time conference commissioners and athletic directors were increasingly selected from the law profession, the Management Council would be composed of those who would have a tendency to be concerned with legal issues and contracts more than with educational issues and the impact on athletes' education.[13]

At the time of the restructuring, President James Loughran of St. Peter's College in New Jersey fairly well summed up the situation for restructuring. Because of "cheating, greed, financial extravagance, anti-academic courses, hypocrisy," restructuring was demanded, Loughran said. "Big-time college sports are caught between irreconcilable objectives," he believed. "Amateurism and academic integrity, on the one hand, prominence and profit on the other. But in the tug of war, it seems amateurism and academic integrity don't have a chance."[14] This was not new, but like replays of controversial plays on TV, the public and especially campus leaders were constantly being inundated with bad news. The presidents would continue tinkering with reform efforts, particularly with trying to find ways to promote higher standards for scholarship athletes.

Yet, four years after full presidential control, the Knight Commission felt the need to once again reconstitute itself with essentially the same group that advocated reform a decade before. With retired presidents Theodore M. Hesburgh and William C. Friday still in charge, the Knight Commission found that the problems of big-time college sports "have grown rather than diminished" under presidential leadership. "Academic transgressions, a financial arms race, and commercialism" were apparent more than ever, with "ugly disciplinary incidents, outrageous academic fraud, dismal graduation rates, and uncontrolled expenditures."[15] This was a condemnation of college sport that even the censorious Carnegie Report of 1929 was hard-pressed to match. The condemnation was especially pointed at academic failures in athletics. The report noted, "Big-time athletics departments seem to operate with little interest in scholastic matters beyond the narrow issues of individual eligibility," and this was particularly evident in the two principal profit-making sports: football and men's basketball. "Too many athletic directors and conference commissioners," the report emphasized, "serve principally as money managers" who are there with the athletes "to provide bread and circuses but otherwise unconnected to the institution that supports them."[16] The report did not mention that the presidents appointed the athletic directors and conference commissioners.

The Knight Commission of 2001 did recognize, finally, that presidents were not the singular agents for reform, and it must have been difficult for the president-dominated Knight Commission to make this confession. "Time has demonstrated," the Knight Commission admitted, "that the NCAA, even under presidential control, cannot independently do what needs to be done."[17] Presidents, it reasoned, would need the help of governing boards and faculty, two units that were never brought strongly into the reform equation. Showing that the Knight Commission had lost faith in the NCAA presidents' Board of Directors, the commission called for an independent Coalition of Presidents, independent of the NCAA and conferences, to be a watchdog for the NCAA, bringing reform to the forefront. The independent Coalition of Presidents could then prod the elected university presidents to pass reform legislation, which would bring college athletics back into the fold of higher education.

The Knight Commission came up with few new ideas, but it was more an irritant to get university leaders to take serious reform measures rather than "tinkering," as in the past. It called for a mountain of reforms, including mainstreaming athletes into the academic institution; raising graduation rates with severe penalties for low graduation rates; raising the one-year athletic scholarships to four or five years; reducing the practice and playing schedules; controlling when games would be telecast; reducing expenditures for football scholarships, coaches' salaries, and coaches' outside income; redistributing television money by not having it based principally upon winning; eliminating corporate logos; banning legalized gambling on college sports; restricting athlete recruiting; considering need-based athletic scholarships; and even reinstituting freshman ineligibility.[18]

One Knight Commission suggestion unique to most, though not a new idea, was the possibility of receiving an antitrust exemption from the U.S. Congress to allow reform to occur.[19] Two important reforms of the commercialization of college sports could be achieved only through antitrust-exempt legislation: control of television by the NCAA and a halt to the escalating coaching salaries. The NCAA had lost its control of football telecasts in 1984 when the U.S. Supreme Court declared that the NCAA had restrained trade in violation of the Sherman Antitrust Act of 1890 and did so solely for the pursuit of profits by fixing prices and artificially limiting the production of football telecasts.[20] Less than a decade later, the NCAA, in a financial move, decided to restrict the salary and tenure of a third assistant basketball coach. When the restricted earnings issue was taken to court as a class-action suit, it, too, was found to be in violation of antitrust legislation, and the triple-damage antitrust violation cost the NCAA and its member institutions more than $50 million.[21] Reducing coaching salaries, to something comparable to professors' salaries or even to presidents' salaries, could only be done by individual institutions. Major reform by a single university had never been successful, unless it was to drop out of competition, such as occurred in football at the University of Chicago under President Robert Hutchins.

The U.S. Supreme Court's NCAA telecasting decision of 1984 and the restricted-earnings final judicial decision in 1999 certainly put the NCAA on alert that collusions to restrain trade for reform or other actions should first take into consideration federal antitrust laws. This was especially true when actions were taken to increase profits of intercollegiate athletics and away from any educational objectives that might have existed. U.S. Supreme Court Justice Byron White in a 1984 minority opinion noted a number of collusions by the NCAA to control intercollegiate athletics: circumscribing the number of coaches hired, preventing professional athletes from competing, restricting the number of athletic scholarships, establishing minimum academic standards needed for participation, regulating the recruiting process, restricting practice and game schedules, and limiting the size of squads.[22]

All of these instances had antitrust implications, especially after the 1975 Goldfarb case, in which the U.S. Supreme Court stated that educational institutions would not be exempt from antitrust action, and the 1984 Oklahoma case, breaking up the NCAA football TV contract.[23] Later issues with antitrust implications were questions of revenue sharing of the annual basketball tournament and football bowl system, doing away with four or five years of athletic scholarships, limiting the size of athletic scholarships, prohibiting athletes from signing with agents for professional teams, prohibiting athletes from using their images for commercial purposes, barring athletes from holding jobs, and forbidding athletes from breaking their letters of intent but allowing coaches to break their contracts.

The NCAA has never received an antitrust exemption similar to that professional baseball has enjoyed since 1922 and professional football, basketball, baseball, and hockey received in the telecasting of their games since the passage of the Sports Broadcasting Act of 1961.[24] Though Walter Byers, retired from his position as NCAA executive director, was not an advocate of antitrust exemptions, he became a strong critic of the NCAA and its weak reform measures.[25] He said that the NCAA had left its amateur roots long before, even though amateurism continued to be used by the NCAA for its own purposes. "Collegiate amateurism is not a moral issue," Byers stated. "It is an economic camouflage for monopoly practice."[26] Whether this was true or not, specific reforms demanded antitrust exemption as the Knight Commission suggested in 2001.

With the push from the Knight Commission, the Board of Presidents continued to press for raising the minimal standards for freshman eligibility and for increasing the graduation rates. Yet it was no surprise that the presidential reform of the late 1990s and early twenty-first century would be built around legal more than educational concerns. Institutions of the NCAA had been burned by legislative and judicial decisions in the previous two decades, including judgments relative to women's equity under Title IX and racial equality demanded by the Civil Rights Act of 1964. In addition, the NCAA lost its monopolistic football TV policy in 1984 because of its unconstitutionality, and it lost the ability to limit coaching salaries in 1999 in another antitrust case lost by the NCAA. The Board of Presidents felt the need to tread lightly when trying to reform minimal standards for academic eligibility. That the Board of Presidents took no major steps in changing policy was not surprising to Jon Ericson, a Drake University faculty member and one who led a group of more radical faculty in what became known as the Drake Group at the end of the twentieth century. Testifying before the Knight Commission on Intercollegiate Athletics in 2000, Ericson criticized the presidents, who "will do little, if anything, to end the corruption" in intercollegiate athletics. "Presidents," Ericson said, "will give you words, their favorite of which is concern" over the conduct of college sports. They are, he told the Knight Commission, "not hired to clean up college sports. They are hired, among other things, to protect big-time college sports."[27] Obviously, the Board of Presidents did not outwardly agree with Ericson. Reform, the presidents agreed, would go forth.

A half decade after becoming all-powerful within the NCAA and after the Knight Commission charged that the condition of intercollegiate athletics had deteriorated even more than before, the Board of Presidents appeared ready to pass reform legislation. The Board of Presidents rejected the Knight Commission's recommendation of forming an outside group to create reform measures. William "Brit" Kirwan was president of Ohio State University and chair of the NCAA Board of Presidents in the early twenty-first century. Kirwan was the son of a former University of Kentucky football coach and president. Kirwan, himself, had gone to college on a football scholarship. As a former athlete and mathematics scholar, Kirwan was in a good position to lead a reform movement. As leader of the Board of Presidents, Kirwan stated, "It is clear to us that the Board is the appropriate body to drive the reform efforts" not an outside group such as the Knight Commission suggested.[28] How difficult that would be was never more apparent than when Kirwan, at almost the same time and during a speech at the Pro Football Hall of Fame in Canton, illegally recruited a star quarterback to attend Ohio State.[29]

Though it was an inauspicious start in the twenty-first century for Kirwan and the Board of Presidents, the NCAA was in position to create real reform if the presidents had the will to do more than speak about integrity in intercollegiate athletics, an issue plaguing the organization from its beginning a century before. The NCAA had relocated its offices a few years before to Indianapolis, the "amateur sports capital of the world." This would add to the image of the NCAA as an amateur organization, supporting amateur athletics, even when most of its actions were commercial and professional. Needing more than image, the NCAA would require action to meet its purpose "to maintain intercollegiate athletics as an integral part of the educational program and the athlete as an integral part of the student body."[30] With the abysmally low graduation rates, especially in the most commercial sports, the NCAA set out to attempt to improve the academic image by improving graduating rates.[31] Cedric Dempsey, the chief executive officer of the NCAA, asked if presidents had "the will to act," noting that academic standards and performances were the number one priority for the NCAA.[32]

After studying the low graduation rates for athletes and possible reform measures, the NCAA passed what it considered "a landmark academic reform package." Passed in 2004, the NCAA created a measure intended to increase graduation rates, called the Academic Progress Rate (APR). New NCAA President Myles Brand called it "the most far-reaching effort of its kind in the history of the NCAA." More than setting the minimal standard for entrance into college for freshman participation, which remained an especially low standard of a 2.0 high school grade point average, the APR was created to track progress through college. An institution's team was graded negatively if an athlete left the institution or failed academically. The legislation called for a student to meet 40 percent of graduation requirements by the end of the sophomore year, 60 percent at the conclusion of the junior year, and 80 percent after the fourth year. For the first time, the NCAA demanded that institutional teams be accountable for student academic progress, for if a team did not meet certain standards there would be the possibility of losing scholarships, having limitations on recruiting, making teams ineligible for postseason competition, and restricting membership in the NCAA.[33] In other words, eligibility standards applied not only to the athlete, the traditional method, but to the institution, with sanctions for poor team academic performance.

The problem with the APR was that the institutions' athletic programs felt pressured into ensuring that academic progress would be met, not to promote the athlete's education but to help guarantee the institution's needs for athletes to remain eligible. Pressure would surely be placed upon the athlete to enter certain curricula and specific majors, in which the athletes could make progress toward a degree, even if that degree was less meaningful to the athlete than to the institution. As Linda Bensel-Meyers, a professor of English at the University of Denver, stated at the time of its passage: The APR "will ask institutions to corrupt their own academic mission to prevent the loss of scholarships and the loss of millions of dollars in postseason revenue."[34] Bensel-Meyers probably knew that for a generation the NCAA philosophical statement for Division I, big-time sports promoted commercialism and not education in that each institution was to "finance its athletics program in so far as possible from revenues generated by the program itself."[35] Winning programs, regardless of educational outcomes, produce more revenue for athletics than losing ones, and athletes' education could become victims of institutional goals.

The APR was intended to raise academic standards to help ensure graduation rates that were no longer embarrassing to institutions, but the unintended consequence was for institutions to provide curricula designed to meet the needs of the APR and for athletes to choose, or be persuaded to move into, less demanding majors. The name given to this phenomenon was "clustering," or as an academic honors football player, Steven Cline of Kansas State University, noted following pressure to major in a program in which he felt shortchanged, "I majored in football." Clustering in certain majors was not a new phenomenon, but the intensification of clustering could be seen across the country, fostered by the APR. In Division I-A (what became known as the Football Bowl Subdivision), more than four of every five schools had one team with at least 25 percent of its juniors and seniors entered in the same major. At Stanford, probably the football team with the highest academic standards among the big-time institutions, seven of seventeen juniors and seniors were majoring in sociology. At the University of Southern California, 58 percent of its football team members were in sociology, while 48 percent of Boise State University football players were in communications. At Texas-El Paso, 100 percent of its men's basketball team majored in multidisciplinary studies. Georgia Tech was found to have 63 percent of its basketball team, 83 percent of its baseball team, and 82 percent of its football team majoring in management.[36] At the University of Michigan, an interesting change occurred in the academic curricula of football players. In the 1990s, Sports Management was the academic dumping ground for the Michigan football team, but the department decided to tighten the program requirements. The result was that by the early twenty-first century, nearly the entire team moved to major in general studies. As Michigan is generally considered one of the great universities in America, a non-football-playing Michigan student stated sarcastically, "We'll take care of the classwork, and they'll take care of the football."[37]

When the penalties were announced by the NCAA for poor performance on the APR, it was not particularly surprising that few of the big-time names were on the list. After several years of APR data, two that were severely punished were little-recognized Delaware State and Portland State. The more prosperous athletic departments had long before created athletic counseling programs to help keep their athletes eligible. Spending millions of dollars on academic counseling for athletes, they could easily afford to give one-on-one counseling to help pick curricula and courses and provide tutors for test preparation and the writing of academic papers for those athletes who either could not do acceptable academic work or who chose not to apply themselves. As for Delaware State and Portland State, they chose to drop their wrestling programs, with abysmal APR scores, to prevent losing Division I status for their four straight years of substandard APR scores. Dropping men's sports to provide for institutional needs to remain in the upper division of the NCAA was another unintended consequence of the APR program.[38] One might question if dropping a low APR-scoring women's sport could be accomplished legally to save the university from dropping out of Division I. Court cases dealing with Title IX would emphatically indicate no.

In the first few years of the APR program, it was not clear what its long-term effect would be on raising academic standards and bringing athletics closer to an academic emphasis in institutions of higher learning. The first half decade of the APR resulted in a general rise of APR scores, as the retention rate for athletes staying in school and graduating rose slightly. For men, the average APR scores remained low for basketball, football, baseball, and wrestling. For women, the problem area was women's basketball, the most important sport for women for well over a century.[39] The fact that the least prominent institutions among Division I-A were found lacking in APR scores was somewhat similar to African Americans traditionally scoring lower on SAT and ACT tests. The institutions with the higher economic status, as in athletic income, have generally done better on APR scores, just as economically privileged individuals generally score higher on standardized tests. There was some feeling that if an institution could not financially provide for an effective academic support staff for athletes, then it might logically drop out of big-time athletics and move to a lower level of competition. Stated Myles Brand, NCAA president: "If you're going to participate in high-level intercollegiate athletics, you have to provide for academic opportunities for the students. And that's not inexpensive."[40] One possible result of the APR was that lesser athletic institutions might leave Division I, something that the big-time athletic leaders would probably support.

Critics of big-time college sports demanded greater reform than that presented by the presidents in the NCAA, including the APR reforms. Even the president-dominated Knight Commission felt that presidents would be unsuccessful in meaningful athletic reform unless faculty would become involved in the effort to achieve academic integrity in higher education. When the Knight Commission pushed for presidents to make a greater effort to reform college athletics at the beginning of the twenty-first century, its report, *A Call to Action,* admitted that "time has demonstrated that the NCAA even under presidential control, cannot independently do what needs to be done."[41] Yet even the faculty in the form of Faculty Athletic Representatives (FAR), generally appointed by each institution's president, felt estrangement from any influence on athletic policy. One FAR member, David Bernstein of Long Beach State University, admitted at an NCAA meeting that he now felt "personal alienation" from the NCAA, where, he said, "my presence is not needed." Art Cooper, the North Carolina State University FAR and a member of the NCAA Management Council, agreed, responding that faculty representatives "feel disenfranchised."[42] Most big-time FARs, with no real power in the NCAA, at least had some perks given to them by athletic departments, such as free football and basketball tickets, flights to away games, and involvement and recognition within athletics, including social events and banquets.[43] Other faculty members were almost entirely out of the loop relative to athletics, even as they were involved in helping to protect the academic integrity of the institution. Faculties, who in the late nineteenth and early twentieth centuries had a major influence over the integrity of intercollegiate athletics through athletic committees, had long since been stripped of any power they once held. If there were still athletic committees, they had essentially no power to influence policy—that was generally held by the athletic departments, presidents, and sometimes governing boards in important issues.

Nevertheless, some important individuals were calling for a renewed effort by faculties. Among them were retired presidents Derek Bok of Harvard University and James Duderstadt of the University of Michigan—names that meant something to educators, if not to athletic leaders. Derek Bok wrote an important volume in the early twenty-first century, *Universities in the Marketplace: The Commercialization of Higher Education.* In it, he traced the growth of commercialism in higher education, noting that commercialism first existed in intercollegiate athletics. Now, he said, it had become endemic throughout higher education. For Bok, the need to control commercialism and to preserve academic integrity was important. However, Bok said that "the hoped-for reforms did not materialize" in athletics under presidential control. "Presidents," he noted, "unilaterally can not reform college athletics." Faculty, not presidents, he insisted "have the greatest stake in preserving proper academic standards and principles."[44] Like Bok, James Duderstadt eventually came to the conclusion that presidents could not significantly reform athletics. "I have become increasingly skeptical," wrote Duderstadt following several years of the NCAA APR regulations, "that university presidents are capable of taking the lead in the reform of college athletics." Presidents, he believed, were often "tilting with windmills" when it came to athletics, and "few contemporary university presidents have the capacity, the will, or the appetite to lead a true reform movement in college sports." Duderstadt concluded that faculty—tenured faculty—must get involved in the preservation of university academic integrity.[45] Even the NCAA's own 2006 "Presidential Task Force on the Future of Division I Athletics" concluded that faculty should "again be significantly involved in the monitoring of academic performance" of the athletes.[46] Yet despite studies that indicated that faculty members were no longer interested in athletics, there were individual faculty members and groups who, if given the opportunity, would attempt to bring college athletics into higher education in a meaningful way.

19

Faculty Reform Efforts
CARE, the Drake Group, and COIA

University faculties for well over a century have generally been reticent to call for athletic reform, with some notable exceptions. Harvard and Princeton faculties in the 1880s decided they must do something to slow the dominance of intercollegiate athletics that was negatively influencing the education of their undergraduates. A Harvard athletic committee commented: "The necessity of regulation implies the existence of abuse."[1] At that time, professionalizing the coaching staff, subsidizing athletes, playing contests all days of the week and sometimes against professional teams, conducting extended travel, and devoting too much time to athletics were reasons enough for faculty action. A generation later in the early twentieth century, Frederick Jackson Turner, the frontier historian at the University of Wisconsin, led his faculty in a fight against the evils of intercollegiate athletics. Speaking to a Wisconsin alumni gathering, Turner said that football "has become a business, carried on too often by professionals, supported by levies on the public, bringing in vast gate receipts, demoralizing student ethics, and confusing the ideals of sport, manliness, and decency."[2] He wanted to ban football and athletics at Wisconsin and among the other Big Ten institutions, but following the turmoil in 1905 and 1906, the faculty voted unanimously in 1907 not to "contemplate the abolition of intercollegiate athletics at the University of Wisconsin."[3]

Faculties, by the early years of the twentieth century, were generally powerless to impact the growth of athletics in major ways, as whatever power they previously had enjoyed was generally taken over by presidents, graduate managers of athletics (athletic directors), governing boards, and alumni. Thorstein Veblen, the eccentric sociologist and economist noted with a bite of sarcasm that university "faculties have become deliberative bodies charged with the power to talk . . . [and their] subservience [to the presidents] . . . may safely be counted on."[4] Nevertheless, there were instances in the twentieth century in which faculty members fought what they considered the perversion of higher education by intercollegiate athletics. A notable example occurred at William and Mary College in the early 1950s, when the faculty protested to its president, governing board, alumni, and the nation about the academic corruption of its football and basketball programs. So blatant was the corruption that a number of faculty members resigned, and the college moved from big-time sports to something they considered less corrupting: academics.[5] Only a few other faculties, however, would consider such action.

In the 1950s, the Ohio State University football team was placed on probation and banned from participation in the Rose Bowl after Coach Woody Hayes was found guilty of providing extra pay to his players. The Ohio State faculty set up a committee to investigate the athletic program, and under a new president, Novice G. Fawcett, athletics were placed under the control of the faculty. A resolution was passed opposing the commercialized bowl games to which the Buckeyes were often invited. The first real test came following a 50–20 victory over archrival Michigan and the Big Ten championship in the fall of 1961. The Athletic Council voted 6–4 to accept a bid to play against UCLA in the Rose Bowl, but the Faculty Council, in a close 28–25 vote, rejected the Rose Bowl offer.[6] In this case, the president and governing board did not intervene and overturn the faculty decision. Several thousand students protested with signs damning the faculty, burning President Fawcett in effigy (for not overruling the faculty), and marching on the state capitol. Meanwhile, the alumni association, faculty council, and president were bombarded by angry Buckeye fans with phone calls, telegrams, and letters.[7]

Coach Woody Hayes stated, "I don't agree with those 28 'No' votes, but I respect the integrity of the men who cast them, if not their intelligence." One of the faculty members who voted no was Bruce Bennett, who said that "playing in a commercial venture had no educational value."[8] The University of Minnesota faculty, unlike Ohio State's, voted 108–23 to accept the bid to represent the Big Ten in the "granddaddy" of all the bowls. One should note that never again did the Ohio State faculty deny Ohio State's participation in the Rose or any other bowl game, and the Faculty Council soon voted 36–20 to accept the next bowl bid.[9]

Bowl games, like participation in the big-time basketball tournament, were too important to athletics and to the university to have faculty deny their participation for academic reasons. The Ohio State incident had occurred at the height of the Cold War, after the United States appeared to have fallen behind the Soviet Union in education and technology. The Soviets had placed the first man in space, and the Soviet Union had antagonized the West by erecting the wall between Communist East Germany and democratic West Germany. Big-time athletics would continue to be big time during and following the Cold War. Those faculties, such as Ohio State's, might for a time advocate academics first and athletics second, but they had only minimal effect on intercollegiate athletic reform. That condition would remain well into the future.

For the most part, university faculties had little say about the direction taken by intercollegiate athletics, even though most faculty senates had a committee on athletics, a committee with some prestige but almost no power. From time to time, individual faculty groups would protest athletics when some athletic official or team embarrassed the university, such as the scandal at Southern Methodist University in the 1970s. There was, though, no united effort on the part of faculties on a regional or national level to help reform athletics to bring them more in line with the educational goals of higher education.

It was not likely that a faculty or an individual faculty member might make a difference in reforming athletics; however, some faculty members continued their efforts to promote academic integrity in intercollegiate athletics. Allen Sack of the University of New Haven was one who certainly made a spectacular start in the early 1980s. As a football player on a national championship football team at Notre Dame in 1966, Sack had a good view of big-time athletics under a power coach, Ara Parseghian. Drafted to play in the National Football League but knowing that he was probably not good enough to compete at that level, he chose an academic life, completing a PhD in sociology at Penn State during the turbulent Vietnam era. With a political stance on social issues far to the left of center, he began an academic career looking at the place of sport in society, particularly

interested in the "million-dollar slaves" in professional sport and the exploitation of athletes in big-time institutions of higher learning.[10] Sack saw the need
for an organization, unlike the National Collegiate Athletic Association (NCAA),
that would advocate for the rights of college athletes and not the needs of the
institutions. After setting up an athlete advocacy group on his New Haven campus,
he moved to a national level with what eventually became known in 1981 as the
Center for Athletes' Rights and Education (CARE).

The Center for Athletes' Rights and Education was sponsored by a New York
City–based Sports for the People project and was funded by a grant from the U.S.
Department of Education with support from the National Football League Players Association and the National Conference of Black Lawyers. In the summer of
1981, Sack and CARE came to the attention of athletic officials with CARE's Bill of
Rights for athletes. Among the rights anticipated were multiyear athletic scholarships; tuition-free courses up to graduation, regardless of athletic eligibility
being completed; letters of intent outlining educational and financial obligations
of the institution; and legal assistance and due process for athletes. Two of the
more controversial provisions were CARE's right for athletes to form unions and
to bargain collectively and the right to share television revenue.[11] Sack reasoned
that the multimillion-dollar TV contracts being negotiated by both the NCAA and
the College Football Association took no financial account of the players, whom
fans tuned in to watch. A percentage of money from the TV contracts (15 percent),
CARE said later, should go to a trust fund for athletes who needed funding to
graduate from college.[12] The unionization of college players, whom Sack believed
were much more like professionals than amateurs, was as appropriate for the par-
tially paid collegians as for the fully paid professionals.[13] The thought of unions
and bargaining collectively raised the ire of athletic officials, leaders of the NCAA,
and specifically government officials when President Ronald Reagan's antiunion
administration was elected that fall. Opposition by the Reagan administration
was probably more than the new organization could handle. To NCAA Executive
Director Walter Byers, the Sack proposals were "an immediate red alert," and for
good reason, as the NCAA's Washington, DC, law firm warned NCAA leaders not to
be complacent.[14] Funding was soon withdrawn by the Department of Education,
and within a short time CARE became past tense. Founder Sack, with resignation,
commented that CARE took "its place in the graveyard of failed attempts at collegiate athletic reform."[15]

While CARE went the way of many reform efforts, Allen Sack did not go away.
When in the 1990s a discontented professor from Drake University organized a
group of athletic-reform professors from across the nation, Sack was among them.

Jon Ericson, Drake University provost and professor of rhetoric and communications, began a fight against athletic improprieties in the early 1990s. Drake University, Ericson believed, had too many "eligibility majors." Ericson wanted to expose the complicity of the faculty and administrators at his institution, which he said were 99 percent of the problem. At that time, Ericson wrote a report, "While the Faculty Sleep," asking that the courses taken by athletes should be published. Thus professors and their easy "jock" courses would be identified and embarrassed and corrective action would be taken.[16] By the end of the 1990s, Ericson, not long after the University of Minnesota athletic department was exposed for hiring tutors who would write term papers and complete take-home exams for athletes,[17] decided to call a conference on athletics: "Corruption in College Sports: The Way Out."

The 1999 gathering at Drake University consisted mostly of tenured faculty, such as Allen Sack, who along with others had become disaffected with the commercialized-professionalized sports programs that were destroying the academic integrity of many big-time athletic schools. Among the alienated faculty members present included Andrew Zimbalist, an economist who had just published *Unpaid Professionals: Commercialism and Conflict in Big-Time College Sports,* and Murray Sperber, an English and American studies professor who was about to publish his vitriolic diatribe against college sport, *Beer and Circus: How Big-Time College Sports Is Crippling Undergraduate Education.* Ellen Staurowsky was there, coauthor with Sack of *College Athletes for Hire: The Evolution and Legacy of the NCAA's Amateur Myth,* published the year before. So, too, was William Dowling, a literature professor at Rutgers University, who two years before helped organize a coalition at Rutgers, called the Rutgers 1000, in a failed attempt to get Rutgers to leave the Big East Conference for some lower level of competition. Dowling would later write his account of the Rutgers reform efforts in *Confessions of a Spoilsport: My Life and Hard Times Fighting Sports Corruption at an Old Eastern University.* There were others, including Dale Brown, the ex-Louisiana State University basketball coach, who was disaffected with college athletics; Larry Gerlach, a University of Utah NCAA faculty representative, who had failed at earlier reform efforts within the NCAA; and Rich Purple, a faculty observer of the scandal at the University of Minnesota. Also present were Creed Black, president of the Knight Foundation, and Lou Harris, the pollster whom Black had used to set up the need for a major reform effort that the Knight Foundation funded. There were others, all of whom had their own agendas for reform.

The Drake Group had as many troubles focusing on what reforms should be advocated as it did with its name. At that first meeting, it was decided to use the name National Association for College Athletic Reform, but its acronym, NAFCAR, sounded too much like stock car racing, so it soon reverted to the more functional and clearly identifiable Drake Group. Of the forty or so present, there was no consensus, no shared vision on what college sport should be or could be. Sack called the first meeting a "modern-day Tower of Babel."[18] Yet there was some basic agreement that counseling for athletes should be removed from the athletic department and placed under university counseling and that scholarships should be taken away from teams whose athletes failed academically. The proposal by Jon Ericson that would require universities to make public the academic majors, courses taken, course GPAs, instructors, and advisors did not make the cut, nor did the proposal for freshman ineligibility[19] Larry Gerlach, who worked inside the NCAA as a leading faculty representative for a number of years, was skeptical of any success the Drake Group might have in the future. At the conclusion of the first meeting, Gerlach said, "Faculty representatives and faculties themselves need to have substantially more power and authority," but he doubted that they would be given influence.[20] Historically, this had not been granted, nor had faculty demanded a leadership role.

The Drake Group continued to meet, draw up reform proposals, and then provoke rather than attempt to work with the NCAA. While this is what more radical groups tend to do, the picketing of the 2004 NCAA Final Four basketball tournament did not endear the group to the leaders of athletics, nor was it intended to. Not long afterward, President Myles Brand of the NCAA called the Drake Group "self-appointed radical reformers and incorrigible cynics . . . consisting of a small number of faculty members with an eye for publicity."[21] Brand's harsh words for these faculty members came at the time the NCAA was beginning its new reform Academic Progress Rate (APR) measures. An executive board member of the Drake Group, Michael Malec, responded to Brand, stating that the new APR requirements will allow university athletes to "continue to search for the path of least resistance to remain eligible."[22] As the football players at the University of Michigan switched from majoring in sports management to general studies showed, this was true.

The published Drake Group reform measures appeared to be much less radical than the individuals who made up the mostly faculty organization. Foremost, the Drake Group wanted academic transparency for athletes by publishing their majors, advisors, courses and instructors, grade point averages, and grade changes by those instructors. In addition, they asked for multiyear athletic scholarships (or its more favored need-based scholarships), freshman ineligibility, a requirement of a 2.0 GPA each semester to participate, and athletic counseling to be part of the university counseling system.[23] In the long run, the Drake Group might have a number of its reform measures become policy, but because of the strident nature of its reform efforts by its members and the lack of institutional support, the Drake Group appears to have a tenuous existence and may be lost in the reform efforts of the twenty-first century.

Less strident, but with many of the same reform goals, a new organization came into being in 2002: the Coalition on Intercollegiate Athletics (COIA). This important reform agency was a coalition of big-time university faculty senates that desired to work with faculty, presidents, governing boards, and the NCAA to promote "academics first." The idea for COIA began at the University of Oregon when James W. Earl, a professor of medieval literature and president of the university senate, became outraged that the Oregon athletic department planned a $90 million expansion of its football stadium at a time the state legislature was making cuts in the university budget. He decided that the University of Oregon faculty senate should endorse an "academics first" resolution and then present this to the university senates of the PAC-10 Conference for their endorsement.[24] This was accomplished in rather quick order, and the PAC-10 asked its traditional playing partner in the Rose Bowl, the Big Ten, to see if Big Ten faculties could become involved in athletic reform.

Taking the Earl-initiated faculty-senate-reform movement in the PAC-10 to the national level was Robert Eno, an Indiana University professor with an unrelated interest in East Asia languages and cultures with an emphasis on the Chinese Confucius School of pre-Christ times. Eno, like James Earl, was head of his faculty senate and an activist on his campus. The Big Ten was better fitted to carry out faculty senate actions than was any other conference in America, for it had established a traditional interuniversity Committee on Institutional Cooperation (CIC) in 1958. The CIC was created to discuss mutual educational problems among the Big Ten institutions (plus the old Big Ten University of Chicago) after a vice president of the Carnegie Foundation contributed seed money for a collective action. The Carnegie Foundation's James Perkins had asked the Big Ten presidents, "Why," after meeting twice a year for the previous two decades, "do you Big Ten presidents only talk football when you get together?" The Big Ten leaders told him that many educational problems were taken up by the CIC, even though the newspapers reported only the popular athletic issues. The Carnegie Foundation then gave over a quarter million dollars to help fund the CIC. Once the CIC was formed, a number of mutual cooperative actions were taken, including the Big Ten online library, connecting some of the largest libraries in America.[25] With this type of cooperation, it was easier for Big Ten faculty senates to come together to discuss athletic reform. At a fall 2001 CIC meeting of faculty senate leaders, the theme of athletic reform was taken up and an ad hoc athletic committee was created.[26]

Working with the PAC-10, Bob Eno and the Big Ten moved toward national reform by inviting faculty senates from the universities in the six conferences of the Bowl Championship Series to join the Coalition on Intercollegiate Athletics in late 2002.[27] Not surprising, Bob Eno and James Earl became cochairs of COIA. Soon a charter for COIA was drawn up. The scope of reform included raising eligibility and admission standards; improving the welfare of athletes relative to scholarship policies; raising advising, gender, and race issues; restricting the length of playing seasons; controlling training time and engaging the athlete into college life; slowing the "arms race" in building state-of-the-art facilities; checking the rampant commercialism that was in conflict with academic missions; and, importantly, sharing athletic governance, to include faculty, athletic administrators, governing boards, and presidents.[28]

Unlike the Drake Group, COIA immediately decided to engage any group interested in the reform of college athletics, including the NCAA and the Knight Foundation. Within the first year of existence, COIA joined with NCAA President Myles Brand, the Association of Governing Boards, and the American Association of University Professors for an AAUP-sponsored conference in Indianapolis, Indiana, home of the NCAA.[29] COIA kept hammering away for significant reforms that presidents, governing boards, and faculty must make in order to bring greater sanity to college sport. In 2005, COIA presented its principles and best practices for attaining academic integrity in college sports.[30] It called to admit only athletes who fit the profile of the rest of the student body to get a verbal "yes" from presidents, but the continuance of presidential admits[31] would suggest pointed hypocrisy by the very people who had the power to reform athletics. COIA was not content to suggest reforms specifically on the academic side of athletics; it also made suggestions over the whole range of reform measures, including coaching salaries, diversity in hiring, national championships, fiscal responsibility, commercialism, and presidential leadership.[32]

COIA was active at the same time that Myles Brand, the new NCAA president, organized a Presidential Task Force on the future of intercollegiate athletics, composed of fifty institutional chiefs. The Presidential Task Force, after a year and a half of deliberation, produced a report, "The Second-Century Imperatives: Presidential Leadership—Institutional Accountability."[33] There was little new in the report, but it resurrected the old idea of Home Rule, in which presidents on the local level could bring about reform, especially in the area of financial reform to end the escalating costs of building athletic facilities. Many of the Presidential Task Force ideas for integrating athletes into the mainstream of university life and preventing the exploitation of athletes came from COIA, the Drake Group, and the Knight Commission on Intercollegiate Athletics.

It was relatively easy for the Presidential Task Force to make numerous reform recommendations, but it was extremely difficult, without major faculty involvement, to carry them out. "There must be presidential leadership," the task force presidents emphasized, "that begins at the campus level, and there must be institutional accountability for the conduct of the enterprise."[34] Presidents being primarily cheerleaders at the local level would not likely end their practices of allowing fine athletes who were inferior in academics into their institutions. Nor would they be prone to slow down the construction of grandiose athletic facilities on most university campuses, structures loved by alumni and local communities. The Presidential Task Force took time to lecture faculties, whom the presidents said need to "play a productive role . . . and not merely accept pre-existing biases" about athletics.[35] The presidents on the task force went out of their way to point out the weaknesses of faculty participation and missed a major opportunity for presidents to unite with faculty groups to reform athletics. It was not surprising that the presidents favored president-appointed Faculty Athletic Representatives as the faculty "best equipped . . . to monitor the successful integration of athletics and academics."[36] COIA and others, however, believed that engagement of the larger faculty, not appointees by presidents, was needed if lasting reforms were to be achieved. As Nathan Tublitz, a leader of COIA, would tell the NCAA in early 2007: "Athletic reform will not succeed until the NCAA and college officials partner with faculty."[37] He had logic, though much less significant historical precedent, behind his suggestion.

The NCAA would tolerate COIA and even state that COIA was a model "for faculty engagement," but the risk that faculty might push reform to fully integrate athletics and academics was a threat to presidential control and what presidents "knew" was best for institutions of higher learning. A case in point was the recommendation from both the Drake Group and COIA that transparency of athletes' courses and majors, the faculty who teach the courses, and the grades they give was threatening to the presidents and to athletics. Myles Brand opposed academic transparency, stating in a piece aimed at university faculty that transparency was "nothing more than an attempt to embarrass colleagues unjustly" for their courses and grading policies. The NCAA leader said that, early on, COIA's "recommendations failed to reflect a good working knowledge of the current rules and practices in intercollegiate athletics."[38] Brand was willing to listen to faculty groups, but implementing their ideas to attain greater academic integrity was another matter. Reform in athletics was almost never fast moving, just as reform in general society is almost always slow, unless there is a major cataclysmic event such as a war or rebellion. The only major war or rebellion in intercollegiate history was the 1905–6 conflict over football and the creation of the NCAA. There was no such major conflict a century later.

COIA, however, continued to try to make a difference. In 2007, a COIA white paper was produced: "Framing the Future: Reforming Intercollegiate Athletics." Faculty, it emphasized, needed to monitor athletes' courses and enrollment in majors—and back it up with published data. Athletes should not be allowed to participate if their grade point averages were under 2.0. There should be no academic programs or majors that are predominately filled with athletes. Athletic scholarships should be awarded for up to five years, not the current one-year awards. Athletic advising should be integrated into university advising. Athletic budgets should be transparent. Above all, freshmen and transfer athletes should have the same academic profile as nonathletes. To ensure that the academic integrity of the institution is not breached, faculty should continually monitor the entire athletic program.[39]

While individual faculty members, such as Allen Sack, unorganized faculty, including the Drake Group, or more formally organized faculty, such as COIA, were working for reform, possibly a more important group of elected officials was making reform noise. The U.S. Congress was conducting hearings on intercollegiate sport that concerned the NCAA and big-time universities more than COIA or faculty groups. For example, when an athletic-recruiting sex scandal occurred at the University of Colorado, a House of Representatives hearing was carried out in 2004. Colleges knew they had many friends in Congress who would look out for the welfare of institutions of higher education, such as Representative Tom Osborne, former University of Nebraska football coach. Osborne reflected what many in Congress tended to support. "It's very important that Congress *not* try to get involved in N.C.A.A. legislation," Osborne stated, "It would be like having the Washington Redskins come in here and write tax policy."[40] Two years later, William Thomas, the powerful chair of the House Ways and Means Committee, made inquiries of the NCAA over whether intercollegiate athletics were educational and therefore possibly subject to taxation. In response to a series of question by Thomas, President Myles Brand of the NCAA composed a twenty-five-page letter with an appendix nearly twice as long to tell Congress that all the activities the NCAA engaged in were both educational and nontaxable.[41] To counter Brand, a staunch reformer in the mold of the Drake Group and former professor at Northwestern University, Frank Splitt, stated, "Congress is the best, and perhaps last, hope for college-sport reform."[42] The likelihood that federal laws, or even lawsuits, may be more effective in reforming athletics than the influence of COIA or the

Drake Group remained. Others believed the NCAA, with the help of governing boards and faculties, could be effective in the reform movement. Some even believed that a return to the freshman ineligibility rule would eliminate a major source of the academic integrity issues of big-time sport.

20

The Freshman Rule
A Nearly Forgotten Reform

For much of the twentieth century, a nearly universal rule existed in American intercollegiate sport for men: the freshman ineligibility rule. However, when the first intercollegiate football game (a soccer-like match) took place between Princeton and Rutgers in 1869, the question of freshman eligibility was not discussed, but it might well have been; ten of the twenty-five starting players on the winning Rutgers team were freshmen. On the one hand, senior William Leggett, the captain of the Rutgers team, was the outstanding scholar and athlete of his class by winning prizes in Latin, mathematics, and declamations; was president of his class and editor of the student newspaper; and was head of the baseball club and captain and stroke of the crew.[1] He was well respected by the faculty. On the other hand, three of the Rutgers freshmen were failing their algebra course. None of the freshmen had ever taken a Scholastic Aptitude Test or American College Testing exam, and there were no precollegiate grade point averages. Yet three of the Rutgers men might have been declared ineligible, which could have resulted in a reversal of the 6-4 Rutgers victory. Apparently no one questioned the eligibility of the three freshmen. There was no pressure by faculty or others in the early years of college sport following the American Civil War to prevent freshmen participation. This, however, was about to change.

President Charles W. Eliot, who was inaugurated as the leader of Harvard less than a month before the Rutgers-Princeton game, became the most visible supporter of limiting freshmen athletic eligibility by the 1880s. In the next decade, Eliot conducted his own study of the relationship of Harvard football players to academic progress. In a two-year study, he found that freshmen football players during the season received more failing grades than the total of those who received *A*s and *B*s. Eliot also found that football players received almost ten times more *D*s than *A*s. He concluded his 1898 study by stating that football caused an "interference with their studies at the worst possible time."[2] For the next century, freshman eligibility for varsity competition was the most debated eligibility rule among American colleges.

The story of freshman eligibility symbolizes the ambiguity over the reasons why eligibility rules were passed, especially the conflict between educational and athletic values. A clear theme emerges: Freshman eligibility rules have been influenced by three primary forces:

First, the desire to create *competitive equity* among institutions,
Second, the need to achieve *financial solvency* in athletic programs, and
Third, the concern for maintaining institutional and athlete *academic integrity*.

For the first century of freshman eligibility legislation, the dominating interest of the rule makers was to legislate for competitive athletic equity—the *level playing field*—not for maintaining athletic integrity. Athletic interests have nearly always come well before academic considerations.

From the first eligibility rule created in 1855 between Harvard and Yale, competitive equity was the major reason for most eligibility rules. In that year, Yale bitterly opposed Harvard bringing back one of its graduates to be coxswain in a victorious Harvard crew. Yale wanted a "level body of water" on which to row. Harvard agreed to Yale's desire, and the concept of competitive equity in American college sport was launched. Later interinstitutional agreements, including those dealing with freshmen, were most often based upon attempts to create the "level field of play" rather than protecting the institution or the athlete from educationally unwise policies.

The practice of bringing in ill-educated athletes or those unconcerned with academics in order to produce victories was common. This freshman situation, though, was similar to the practice in colleges of enrolling athletes in graduate programs or professional schools, such as law and medicine, as a pretext for additional athletic participation. The question of barring freshmen from participation came even before banning graduate school students from competition. Walter Camp, the "father" of American football, proposed in 1893 barring every first-year man from sport participation in an effort to reduce the intense recruiting of subfreshmen.[3] Most others who favored some restriction on freshman eligibility wanted to restrict the procurement of athletes to prevent the competitive advantage gained by one college over another.

To be successful, restrictions on freshman eligibility required interinstitutional agreements. These were not easy to forge among institutions that for generations, if not centuries, had been independent of one another. Harvard, for instance, would not restrict freshman eligibility unless other colleges cooperated. The Harvard Athletic Committee in 1899 passed a one-year residency rule before a student could compete in varsity athletics, but it was conditional upon its major competitors agreeing to the same rule. Since its opponents, particularly Yale, chose not to, the early attempt at banning freshmen's participation went for naught.[4] If any conference were to ban varsity athletic participation by freshmen, the Big Ten would have been a logical choice. When the conference started in 1895, it set a precedent for the entire nation with its decision to have faculty control over athletics. Freshman eligibility, however, was not a major concern for the Big Ten during its first years. When the 1905–6 football crisis broke nationally, the Big Ten and some others took action. The Big Ten voted for no varsity competition until students had one year of residency.[5]

The decision of the eastern Big Three was somewhat more difficult because of their fierce devotion to institutional autonomy. Nevertheless, Harvard, Yale, and Princeton did forge an agreement not to place freshmen on varsity teams, but only after the football crisis of 1905–6 nearly brought the abolition of football at Harvard. Recalcitrant Yale, with undergraduate student control of athletics, was nearly forced to agree with a ban on freshmen. As one of Yale's alumni advisors stated, "Yale will get a savage black eye in the papers and from the public if Harvard adopts it and we do not at the same time, and," attorney Samuel Elder noted, "it will be all the worse if Princeton and some other colleges unite with Harvard."[6] Most other colleges, especially smaller ones, still refused to pass restrictive legislation for freshmen.

A number of small colleges did not follow the lead of the eastern elites or the Big Ten. The reluctance of the smaller colleges to give up freshman eligibility had much to do with financial solvency in athletics and the need of smaller schools to compete with larger ones. Athletic support for teams came largely from gate receipts by the early twentieth century. Competing with larger schools and receiving a share of the gate receipts or a guarantee for participating at the site of the large schools were crucial for many smaller schools to balance their budgets. In order to compete with any chance of success, the smaller institutions often felt that they needed to use freshmen.[7]

Though the question of academic integrity was not foremost in the minds of the policy makers, it was nevertheless in evidence. For example, the president of

Dartmouth, William Tucker, wrote to a longtime member of his Board of Trustees to see if the alumni or the faculty had the right to pass freshman eligibility legislation. The Dartmouth alumni had wrested athletic control from the faculty in the 1890s. In the early 1900s, the Dartmouth faculty had a motion pending to bar freshmen from varsity competition. Tucker wanted to know if the alumni had control of "eligibility so far as determined by scholarship" or whether the faculty did.[8] In this case, as has often happened in the history of intercollegiate athletics, the alumni won the battle for control over academic concerns of athletes, an indication of athletic control emanating from outside the educational apparatus of the institution. Dartmouth adopted the freshman rule only after Harvard suggested to Dartmouth in 1909 that if it wanted to continue participation with Harvard in football, it would only be fair for Dartmouth to not play freshmen.[9] Dartmouth, a midsize college, had felt the pressure to conform to the large-college desire to ban freshmen. Nevertheless, most small colleges in New England, including Middlebury, Wesleyan, and Williams, continued to allow freshmen to compete as America was about to enter World War I.[10]

By World War I, a number of conferences had banned freshman competition in varsity athletics, though some allowed frosh to play if their male enrollments were only a few hundred.[11] Fearful that colleges might abandon this restriction because of the war and allow freshmen to play, NCAA President Palmer Pierce asked colleges not to lower "eligibility standards because of present conditions."[12] Among others, Knute Rockne, the Notre Dame football coach, agreed. The reason for the freshman rule was to prevent "the practice of proselytizing, soliciting among high school graduates for particular colleges," according to Rockne, "and having on college teams men who might be strong football players but not genuine college students."[13]

Not everyone agreed with Rockne. The president of Stanford University, Ray Lyman Wilbur, favored freshman eligibility. He thought that there should be no distinction between freshmen and other students, for athletics benefited all students.[14] Stanford's chief rival, the University of California, favored freshman ineligibility, and athletic relations had been severed over this question. The alumni of both schools wanted to resume their football rivalry far more than they wanted to discuss the merits of freshman eligibility. As the president of the Stanford Alumni Association stated in the midst of the controversy, all the Stanford alumni wanted was to have "contests with California on a fair and equitable basis."[15] The University of California had used the large-college argument with its smaller rival Stanford. California's desire to bar freshmen, they believed, would more likely assure that athletes were academically representative of the general student body. President Benjamin Wheeler of California said that allowing freshmen to participate on the varsity not only hindered the athlete's adjustment to college life, but it was more likely that players would be brought in "for a brief period and then disappear."[16] Wheeler obviously could not see in the future that this was what happened for a number of male basketball players by the end of the twentieth century and into the twenty-first century. Eventually, the California-Stanford standoff was resolved when both universities became members of the Pacific Coast Intercollegiate Athletic Conference, which disallowed freshman varsity competition.

Similar scenarios were played out across America.[17] The result was that most major college conferences accepted freshman ineligibility in varsity athletics as a cornerstone of conference regulations. The 1929 Carnegie Foundation for the Advancement of Teaching's *American College Athletics* denounced commercialized and professionalized college athletics; however, it emphasized the salutary effects of the freshman rule. "The practically universal rule which prohibits freshmen playing on varsity teams," the Carnegie Report noted, "has proved beneficial in protecting the newcomer from the distractions incident to intercollegiate competition." But the Carnegie Report went one step farther and advocated the abolishment of all freshman teams because they, too, were a distraction to the purposes of higher education.[18]

Shortly after the publication of the Carnegie Report, there was at least one call for a national rule to ban freshmen from varsity competition.[19] With the dominant belief in Home Rule, there was little chance for national legislation to succeed in the early 1930s. However, the NCAA passed eligibility rules to govern NCAA-sponsored championship competitions, with the intent to limit NCAA championship play to those with only three years of competition. Thus, it was the equivalent to freshman ineligibility for national championships, though conferences and individual institutions could do as they wished the rest of the year.[20] Upon America's entry into World War II, solidarity on the freshman rule broke down both in conferences and among individual institutions. By midwar, the NCAA returned to four years of competition in championship events.[21]

With the conclusion of World War II, the NCAA returned to three years of competition in 1947, and most conferences chose to return to prewar freshman ineligibility rules. Yet in just a few years, the Korean War brought the NCAA to waive its rule regarding championships and prompted conferences once again to permit freshmen to participate in varsity athletics.[22] The Ivy League and the Southwest Conference were notable exceptions.[23] When the second wartime emergency in a decade was resolved, most major conferences again resumed the policy of prohibiting varsity competition for freshmen.[24] One exception was the large, seventeen-member Southern Conference, which decided to allow freshmen to play.

That decision was one in which the smaller colleges outvoted the larger institutions. It had the direct effect of pressuring the largest schools to withdraw from the Southern Conference. Such was the force of the freshman rule in creating the Atlantic Coast Conference in 1953.[25]

Barring freshmen from varsity competition was obviously an emotional issue, and it continued to be so for the next generation. With the rash of scandals hitting college athletics in the early 1950s, including the major basketball point-shaving exposé of 1951, pressure mounted to reform big-time sports. Soon the American Council on Education (ACE) formed its Special Committee on Athletic Policy. Early in 1952, the ACE Special Committee on Athletic Policy recommended banning freshman varsity competition as one of several reform measures.[26] This recommendation was in line with what the major conferences decided the next year at the conclusion of the Korean War.

Freshman ineligibility remained until the end of the 1960s, when extreme inflation resulted from involvement in the Vietnam War and deep financial pressures among athletic departments brought about NCAA legislation to allow freshman eligibility on all varsity teams except football and basketball.[27] (How ironic that a freshman soccer player could participate in a varsity soccer game on Friday night, but the same player could not kick field goals the next day on the football field.) Despite the conclusion of A. M. Coleman, commissioner of the Southeastern Conference, that allowing freshmen to play varsity sports "does not necessarily decrease the cost of participation," most felt that ending the need for freshman teams was a financial advantage.[28] In 1968, the NCAA legislation, passed by the narrow margin of 163–160, was the beginning of the end of about six decades in which freshman ineligibility for varsity competition was the norm. Four years later, the two most important commercialized sports, football and basketball, were allowed to use freshmen on varsity squads.[29]

The question of varsity competition for freshmen has not gone away since the NCAA passed legislation in the late 1960s and early 1970s. Indeed, limitations on freshman participation have remained a continual topic when reform measures have been discussed. When all athletes were declared eligible as freshmen beginning in 1972 and the NCAA voted out the 1.600 grade point average for eligibility the next year, a new nadir in academic standards for college athletics was reached. Massive grade inflation throughout the nation during the turmoil of the Vietnam War contributed to problems created by allowing freshmen to participate immediately, sometimes before they ever entered the classroom. So, too, did the movement for open enrollments in universities, where anyone could enter specific institutions with no restrictions other than a high school diploma. Added to that was the civil rights movement, which led to the desegregation of southern sports by the 1970s and the influx of many academically unprepared African American athletes into northern schools at the same time. If there was a time in which the freshman rule might have been appropriate for academic reasons, it was then. The NCAA, however, decided to do away with freshman restrictions on athletic participation. Financial expediency had trumped academic integrity, as it had done in a number of other cases in the history of intercollegiate athletics.

Financial expediency in athletics and the need for a "level playing field" among the competing institutions nearly always surpassed any desire for academic integrity throughout the history of the NCAA and well before. This was quite logical, for whether the question was freshman participation, or athletes transferring from one institution to another, or the legalization of paying athletes to attend college with athletic scholarships, competitive equity among the schools and financial expediency were far more important than how academic integrity might be maintained. While allowing freshman to participate was allowed principally to help athletic departments meet financial needs, the desire to make athletics look academically responsible was never lost to those in power.

By the 1980s, conditions in intercollegiate athletics appeared to some to be completely outside educational control, and the education of individual athletes looked as if it were irrelevant to the academic goals of a number of institutions of higher learning. Indeed, the historical development of athletics as an entity financed almost entirely from revenues outside the regular institutional budget indicated that educational outcomes for athletics were not a principal concern over the years. While most eligibility legislation has not been intended for the improved education of the athlete, the freshman rule was at least a partial exception. Thus, from the standpoint of individual athletes, the issue of freshman eligibility may be the most important of all eligibility questions historically.

College presidents, bombarded with unfavorable comments about the sordid nature of college sport in the 1980s, decided they must do something to raise standards of athletic eligibility. Action was aimed not at graduation rates of athletes but at entrance requirements. The Presidents Ad Hoc Committee on Intercollegiate Athletics was created under the auspices of the American Council on Education in an effort to bring a greater degree of academic integrity into college athletics. Rather than recommend the financially costly proposition to again abolish freshman eligibility, the group of presidents proposed a modification known as Proposition 48.[30] One of the ACE Presidents Committee members, Donald Shields of Southern Methodist University, presented the Proposition 48 motion to the 1983 NCAA convention. Shields, whose own institution was soon to be given a football "death penalty" for repeated violations of NCAA rules, noted the inadequate academic standards in intercollegiate athletics. At the same time, he questioned the NCAA's organizational integrity in dealing with the recruitment of freshmen athletes. He claimed that Proposition 48 would set "reasonable, minimum academic qualifications for freshmen eligibility."[31] With the force of nearly a hundred presidents in attendance, Proposition 48 passed easily.[32]

Proposition 48's requirement for a 2.0 high school grade point average in only eleven core courses and attainment of a minimal "junior high school" SAT or ACT score did nothing to ensure that athletes would be admitted and be representative of the college student body. There were few, if any, universities in the NCAA's Division I that accepted a general student body with only eleven high school core courses, 2.0 GPA, and 700 SAT or 15 ACT scores. Academic integrity appeared to be only peripheral to the more important concerns of financial solvency and competitive equity. Shortly after Prop 48 was instituted, John Thompson, Georgetown's successful basketball coach, spoke before the NCAA convention. Thompson personally favored freshman ineligibility, but he did not think that the rule would return soon to the NCAA. "I think we teach education and preach education," Thompson told the group, "but we vote money."[33] Regard for financial solvency, Thompson believed, dominated concern for educational integrity. On the same issue of freshman eligibility, President Hunter Rawlings threatened to unilaterally ban freshman eligibility at his University of Iowa. Yet there was a backlash to his statement by supporters of Iowa athletics, who believed that his action would cripple Iowa's competitive stance within the Big Ten and nationally.[34] Here, then, concerns for competitive equity were raised above those for academic integrity, mirroring the situation since intercollegiate competition began in the nineteenth century.

Proposition 48 was reflective of a natural conflict that continued to exist among those who favored, first of all, an emphasis on academics of first-year athletes and those who were concerned with financing athletics and creating a climate of competitive equity. The conflict continued to be a driving force in creating freshman eligibility legislation. Intercollegiate athletics have not traditionally been considered educational activities by leaders of higher education. Because athletics have been thought to be nonacademic, they have not been incorporated into the curricular offerings of colleges and universities. This is unlike a number of other extracurricular activities in the past. For instance, many activities that were once student run and financed have been brought into the general curriculum. Activities such as oratory and debate, popular writing and journalistic endeavors, and the performance of music, dance, and art have been incorporated into such academic departments as English, journalism, music, dance, and fine arts. Intercollegiate athletics, on the other hand, traditionally have been separated from academics. The dichotomy is reflective of the centuries-old, mind-body separation in Western civilization thought. The result has been a relationship between athletics and academics fraught with tension.

The separation of athletics from what has traditionally been considered educational has been exacerbated by the nature of intercollegiate athletics, which have created high external visibility and the competitive desire to produce winners. Recruiting subfreshmen, and thus creating winning teams, has led to a greater propensity to ignore academic concerns than in most other areas of higher education. Because of this, financial concerns and the need to compete on an equal basis athletically with other institutions have often overshadowed the issue of academic integrity and the academic needs of athletes. Whereas eligibility rules, such as allowing freshmen to participate, are generated from within the athletic hierarchy, rules to support academic integrity generally come from influences outside of those directly running athletic programs.

The question of freshman participation since the passage of Proposition 48 in the 1980s has not gone away. Rather than ban freshman participation again, the NCAA has tinkered with what educational qualifications freshmen should have to participate.[35] Balancing issues of competitive equity, financial solvency, and academic integrity is nearly impossible to attain. For those who believed that college athletes should be students first and athletes second, it was hard to justify students entering college with only eleven core high school courses, when 75 percent of college-bound students had completed fifteen or more core curriculum courses.[36] Yet it took the NCAA more than three decades of legislation to reach that minimal level, when in 2008 it required sixteen core courses rather than the previous fourteen.

Over the years, various groups, leading educators, and athletic officials have called for the freshman rule, but to no avail. The College Football Association in the 1980s wanted to eliminate freshman eligibility, as did the College Board, the organization that produced the SAT test. Leading university presidents, including Ira Michael Heyman of the University of California, Edward T. Foote II of Miami University, Charles B. Reed of the University of Florida, Derek Bok of Harvard University, and James Duderstadt of the University of Michigan, were among those who opposed freshman participation. A number of well-known coaches, too, opposed freshman participation so that college newcomers could first become acclimated to academic studies. These included Tom Osborne of the University of Nebraska, Joe Paterno of Penn State University, George Raveling of the University of Southern California, Dean Smith of the University of North Carolina, and John Thompson of Georgetown University.[37] Yet the Knight Commission was silent on freshman eligibility because consensus could not be reached.[38]

As the NCAA moved into its second century of existence, there was no consensus on either the minimal academic qualifications for athletes to participate as freshmen or even whether freshmen should be eligible during their first year of college.[39] For those who believed that athletes of specific institutions should be academically representative of the entire student body, NCAA requirements hardly sufficed. A minimal 2.0 high school grade point average and the possibility that athletes could score a "zero" on either the SAT or ACT standardized test and still be eligible did not meet the test of academic integrity. Nor did the nearly universal practice of presidential admits, allowing athletes into college who could not meet general academic requirements. The important question of freshman eligibility had not been solved, and the presidents, who were in power since the late twentieth century, needed others than themselves to bring about reform. Whether help for presidents would come from faculty, governing boards, governmental legislation, or court action was unclear. What appeared to be clear was that the public supported big-time athletics and its freshmen athletes, who were increasingly making a competitive impact if not an academic one. Meanwhile, many of the problems that have existed in college sport for the past century and a half, including freshman eligibility, would likely remain until a coalition of reformers, more than just presidents, came to consensus about the place of athletics in higher education.

Afterword

Reform in college athletics has meant different things to different individuals. For instance, freshman eligibility when passed in the late 1960s and early 1970s was considered financial reform by some. To others, it was inane from an academic standpoint, for freshman ineligibility had been a major academic integrity reform when introduced in the early 1900s. Similarly, after the Academic Progress Rate (APR) was instituted by the NCAA in 2003, the APR was hailed by those who produced it as a "watershed" reform, if not the greatest in the history of the NCAA. To others, it had not gone nearly far enough, for the APR when combined with the freshman eligibility standards, combining grade point averages and standardized test scores, could be considered less stringent than the 1.600 Grade Point Average Rule of the 1960s. The presidents who passed the APR either did not consider or ignored the potential result of institutions getting around NCAA standards by creating athletic majors or using college curricula to keep athletes eligible at the expense of higher education's academic goals. Reform was in the eye of the beholder in other ways, so that doing away with athletic scholarships or providing only need-based scholarships to some were major reforms, but to another group, allowing athletic scholarships helped provide for excellence in one aspect of American culture. Thus the rewarding of athletic talent in the form of an athletic scholarship could be justified in a way similar to a scholarship for a violinist or a dancer: recompense for achievement in another kind of physical talent. To some, paying athletes for their achievement was more in line with American values than was payment on the basis of need.[1]

Throughout the history of athletic reform in colleges, the principal raison d'être was that there should be equality of competition, a level playing field, among the various institutions of higher learning. Though there was reform justification for financial reasons and academic integrity at times, they were generally secondary to questions of competitive equity or fairness. If issues surrounding intercollegiate athletics were based upon the need for academic integrity, there would be the need for one rule relative to the entrance of athletes into any college: the athlete must fit the profile of the general student body.[2] History would indicate that having athletes fit the student body academic profile was not important to students, presidents, alumni, governing boards, or the general public. For example,

Yale allowed William Spraker, who had failed another college's entrance examination, to enter the Yale law school without an examination and allowed him to participate in Yale athletics in 1900.[3] A century later, one could see the similarity to the University of Michigan placing its academically inferior football players into General Studies so that they could be kept eligible to participate. Helping Yale beat Harvard was little different than enabling Michigan to beat Ohio State in the next century, and complaints only came from a few professors and athletic reformers. The cheerleaders, including many college presidents, accepted the academic hypocrisy of allowing athletes to represent their institutions without them being representative of the general student body.

Why is reform so difficult, and why do similar situations in need of reform appear to intensify from one generation to the next? Or as educational historian John Thelin has cleverly said with irony: "As the scholarship on college sports gets better, the educational and ethical problems of college sports get worse."[4] Some of the same questions arose whether raised by the faculties of Harvard and Princeton in the 1880s, the Brown Conference at the turn of the century, the Carnegie Foundation's Report in 1929, the American Council on Education's Report in 1952, the Hanford Report in 1974, the Knight Commission on Intercollegiate Athletics in 1991, or at the National Symposium on Athletic Reform of the early twenty-first century.[5] Most of the problems that existed with the first intercollegiate contests at the beginning of the railroad era were still in existence a century and a half later as technology had advanced with such innovations as the automobile, steel-reinforced stadiums, airplanes, plastic helmets, aluminum bats, and radio, television, and other means of instant communications.

Technology changes rapidly, but human nature, if it changes at all, moves at glacial speed. As Homer's *Iliad* showed three millennia ago, humans love to compete and too often do it in unethical ways in order to win. When Diomedes passed Menelaus's chariot in the games provided by Achilles at the time of the Trojan War, he did so by trickery.[6] How similar was this to the time that Glenn "Pop" Warner, coach of the Carlisle Indian football team, instructed his team to hide the ball up the back of a player's jersey on a kickoff return for a touchdown during a game against Harvard in 1903?[7] Or how similar was the Diomedes' victory to Colorado's win over Missouri in a football game when Colorado was given five downs rather than four at the end of the 1990 contest?[8]

Individuals and institutions have not been consistently honest and ethical with their intercollegiate dealings. Otherwise, there would be little need to publish hundreds of pages of rules, as the NCAA has felt compelled to do, after the official game rules were agreed upon. If ethics were uppermost in mind, Colorado would have forfeited to Missouri in 1990, as Cornell, with its undefeated team, did to Dartmouth in 1940 when a similar situation occurred. Warner would not have used an unethical, if not illegal, play to score against Harvard, and Diomedes would not have considered trickery against Menelaus 3,000 years before. Similarly, institutions would not use athletes who were not representative of their student bodies in an effort to win, nor would an educational institution pay a coach forty times the average salary of a full professor or ten times the pay of a college president to lead a football or basketball team. Then, too, if humans were always moral, the ancient Greeks would not have felt compelled to create Zanes, bronze statues of the Greek god Zeus, which lined the entrance of the Olympic stadium as an ethical lesson and a way of dishonoring athletes who had cheated at the Olympics.[9] Would institutions of the NCAA consider similar Zanes, such as placing one in front of Rupp Arena at the University of Kentucky as a warning to future athletes and institutions that might consider bribery or throwing games, as coach Adolph Rupp's teams did around 1950. It likely will not happen, indicating that in some ways the moderns may have less concern for obeying the rules than did the ancient Greeks. To punish an institution or individual with Zanes, or a scarlet A in another setting, is frowned upon in twenty-first century America, though it might be considered as a deterrent in any future reform legislation.

One of the problems of any reform legislation of the past century is that the punishment has generally been so slight that individuals and institutions were willing to chance being caught breaking the rules, for the possible punishment was not a significant deterrent. There was only one major penalty ever enacted, the death penalty, and the institutions within the NCAA either refused to uphold the penalty or would not use the penalty again. In one instance, the "Seven Sinners" who were guilty of Sanity Code violations in 1950 were not removed from the NCAA in a vote by institutional members. In a second case, Southern Methodist University was given a one-year football death penalty by the NCAA, but the NCAA refused to use that penalty again for another generation. Stated the president of the University of Florida, John Lombardi: "SMU taught the committee that the death penalty is too much like the nuclear bomb. . . . The results were so catastrophic that now we'll do anything to avoid dropping another one."[10] It will be instructive to see if the potential death penalties in the early twenty-first century occurring as a result of the NCAA's Academic Progress Rate legislation will be imposed against leading institutions who are financially important in raising money from television, major bowl games, or the all-important NCAA big-time basketball tourney. There are those who believe that only when the institutions of the NCAA decide that the rules of enforcement are strong enough to deter rule breaking will reform legislation be successful.

It is quite possible that Zanes and death penalties may not be the answer. Nevertheless, taking away the opportunity to participate in national tournaments, bowl games, loss of television money, banning of coaches and athletic personnel, and loss of team athletic scholarships are major incentives to act properly, and they have rarely been used by the NCAA. There are also legal questions and antitrust actions that must be considered.[11] The fact that the institutions of the NCAA have never asked for antitrust exemption legislation to reform college athletics is something that may be considered in the future, as it has been considered in the past.[12]

For NCAA reform legislation to be successful in the future, several groups, besides presidents, will need to be brought together. History reveals that presidential reform has generally been unsuccessful, or at least not as successful as it might have been had presidents joined with other parties integral to intercollegiate athletics. The two groups that have nearly always been left out of the reform legislation since the NCAA was formed were faculty (not president-appointed faculty representatives) and governing boards. Organized faculties are the one group that could place academic integrity at the head of athletic reform. Possibly more important than faculties are the members of governing boards, who set university policy. If those who govern universities are left out of reform efforts, whatever reform measures are decided upon are likely to be unsuccessful unless reform rules and the policy of university policy makers are in balance. There are too many instances of governing boards and presidents being on different trains of thought regarding athletics dating back at least to the presidency of John Abercrombie at the University of Alabama. In his resignation statement in 1911, Abercrombie said that the Alabama Board of Trustees "does not believe in the policy of administering the institution through the president and faculty" and has allowed "the playing of men who are failing in their studies, or who are known to be ineligible."[13] When governing boards, such as that at Alabama, have allowed increased professionalization, commercialization, and outright dishonesty in their sports at the expense of academic integrity, generally the president who disagreed did not last long as the administrative head of that institution. Examples in the latter part of the twentieth century come quickly to mind, including William Atchley at Clemson, Paul Hardin at Southern Methodist, and John DiBiaggio at Michigan State. Governing boards must be brought into the discussion. In addition, if universities desire to be more democratic in the operation of intercollegiate athletics, athletes should also have a voice in the decisions affecting them. In the nineteenth century, nearly all athletic committees had as many student members as there were faculty members. Athletes, however, were shut out of most decision-making bodies in the twentieth century, just as faculties have been shoved aside. The major players in future reform agendas would logically be represented by presidents, governing boards, faculty, and athletes.[14]

If those within academia—governing boards, presidents, faculty, and athletes— are unable to reform athletics to meet the standards of academic integrity of institutions of higher education, it is quite likely that the future will see greater involvement in the reform arena of the judicial system and lawmakers. Already, two of the greatest reforms have come almost entirely from outside the institutions of higher education—women's entry and equity in college sport and the integration of African Americans on a national level—both during the activist 1960s and 1970s. Women's rights and civil rights laws and judicial decisions for these two important groups were symbolic of how government agencies might influence the nature of college sport and be involved in reform efforts. Past actions would indicate that if major scandals continue to scar college athletics, forces outside the university will likely address the future problems.

Judicial and legislative action influencing college athletics could come about in a variety of reform areas. These might include issues of workers' compensation for athletes; federal tax laws and tax-exempt status for university athletics (unrelated business income tax); athlete licensing agreements; due process for athletes and athletic personnel; athletes working with sports agents; health and insurance coverage for athletes; accident insurance for athletes; limitations on athlete's work opportunities; limits to coach salaries; distribution of TV money; bowl game monopolies; a big-time football play-off; legalized college athletic gambling; and athlete academic transparency, including those of athletes' majors, courses taken and professors' involvement with athletes, number of independent courses taken, team grade point averages, graduation rates, and athlete advisors. An example of the important issue of transparency involves the possible need for Congress to revisit the Family Educational Rights and Privacy Act (FERPA; Buckley Amendment). To protect student records from becoming public, the Buckley Amendment put restrictions on academic records disclosure. To see if academic corruption in college athletics is being hidden, not transparent, by individual institutions under the 1974 Buckley Amendment, Congress could be asked to amend the act to bring light to institutions that are protecting their athletic interests under cover of the FERPA law.[15]

Many of these reform issues are related to the question of whether college sport is both educational and amateur. Since the concept was developed in the nineteenth century, amateurism has lost nearly all of its meaning, but it remains in bold print in the NCAA constitution. The NCAA proclaims its amateur status whenever it is involved in either legislative or judicial actions. However, nearly all athletic decisions engaged in by institutions, conferences, and the NCAA are professional in nature and not amateur, including the minimal payment of athletes to attend college. It appears that the term *amateur* may have a much shorter shelf life in the NCAA constitution.

There is certainly a strong possibility that athletics within the NCAA and its member institutions will no longer be considered either amateur or educational. A judgment of athletics being neither amateur nor educational would likely come from a future court case, similar to the 1984 football telecasting case, *Oklahoma v. NCAA,* in which the Supreme Court held that the NCAA was a monopolist in violation of the 1890 Sherman Antitrust Act. This was the first time the Supreme Court had ever ruled that "amateur" sport was in violation of antitrust laws. If the Supreme Court were ever to rule that college sport is so commercialized and professionalized that it is no longer considered part of the educational function of institutions of higher learning, the reform measures that the NCAA and the individual institutions have taken over the years will have been considered too little, too late.

Intercollegiate Athletic Reform Timeline

"Speak to the past and it shall teach thee."

August 3, 1852

The first intercollegiate contest in America, a crew meet between Harvard and Yale, is held on Lake Winnipesaukee, New Hampshire. Both the Harvard and Yale crew clubs are student run, like those sports clubs at other colleges in the near future.

July 21, 1855

Harvard beats Yale in crew with a graduate, Joseph Brown, who had been coxswain of the Harvard crew in 1852. In the first eligibility-reform case in American intercollegiate athletics history, Harvard's crew agrees not to use its graduates in future contests.

July 1, 1859

The first intercollegiate baseball game takes place in Pittsfield, Massachusetts, between Amherst College and Williams College. Students determine the rules.

March 25, 1868

The Yale faculty votes to ban away baseball games because they are impacting class recitations for both players and students who attend those games.

November 6, 1869

The first intercollegiate football game (soccer) is contested between Rutgers and Princeton in New Brunswick, New Jersey. Three Rutgers freshmen players are failing an algebra course.

May 22, 1871

The Harvard faculty limits baseball games to Saturdays and holidays.

July 21, 1871

The first important student-run athletic conference, the Rowing Association of American Colleges, is initiated by Harvard students, and it conducts a championship. It soon has to deal with questions of professional coaches, graduate students, and other eligibility issues.

November 23, 1876

The Intercollegiate Football Association is created by students of Columbia, Harvard, Princeton, and Yale. Sixty-two rugby rules are adopted, but no eligibility rules. A championship play-off is scheduled for Thanksgiving Day, the first big-time "national" football championship.

December 1879

A conference for eastern colleges is formed for baseball following a controversy over playing of professionals by Brown and graduate students by Harvard.

April 29, 1881

Princeton becomes the first university to form the faculty Committee on Athletics and Musical Clubs to create common policies, especially for time away from campus.

June 15, 1882

The first action of the Harvard Athletic Committee is to prohibit competition against professionals and to disallow the hiring of coaches without the consent of Athletic Committee member Dudley Sargent.

September 11, 1882

President Charles W. Eliot of Harvard attempts the first interinstitutional effort to control athletics, proposing a ban on baseball teams from playing professional teams and limiting the number of games. It fails.

December 10, 1883

The Harvard Athletic Committee invites faculty of eastern colleges to meet to oppose professionalism, especially professional coaches. The December 28 meeting passed eight resolutions, but they were rejected by most institutions.

February 1884

The student-controlled Intercollegiate Association of Amateur Athletics of America (IC4A), a track organization, votes nearly unanimously to oppose the December faculty resolutions.

December 1886

President James McCosh of Princeton calls for a faculty conference of eastern institutions to reform the abuses of athletics. Yale declines to be involved, and that action kills the conference.

November 4, 1889

A special convention of the Intercollegiate Football Association is held to discuss amateurism and eligibility issues, prior to important football games between Harvard, Princeton, and Yale. An unacceptable result causes Harvard to withdraw from the IFA and leads to its eventual dissolution.

July 2, 1890

The Sherman Antitrust Act is enacted. Its first important use in college athletics is to break up the NCAA football telecasting monopoly in 1984.

December 6, 1890

Amos Alonzo Stagg of the University of Chicago is the first professional coach to be given a professorship and tenure. Later, creating full-time positions for coaches is considered a reform measure.

February 11, 1893

Walter Camp of Yale proposes banning freshmen from participating on varsity teams.

January 11, 1895

Seven institutions in the Midwest—Chicago, Illinois, Lake Forest College (later replaced by Michigan), Minnesota, Northwestern, Purdue, and Wisconsin—form the Intercollegiate Conference of Faculty Representatives (Big Ten) to put athletics under faculty control.

February 18, 1898

The Brown Conference for athletic reform convenes with all the present Ivy League institutions, with the exception of Yale. Faculty, alumni, and student representatives meet, but the faculty representatives control the proceedings. The recommendations are to purge professionalism and commercialism by eliminating recruiting and the paying of athletes, hired coaches, participation by freshmen, students not in good academic standing, part-time students, transferring of students for immediate participation, free training tables, and playing contests on other than college grounds. The recommendations are unacceptable to most of the colleges.

November 1903

Harvard begins permanent college stadium construction when it opens the first steel-reinforced concrete stadium in history. Increased commercialism is the result.

June 1905

A muckraker, Henry Needham, stimulates reform action by his condemnation of college athletics in *McClure's Magazine*. Shortly afterward, President Theodore Roosevelt meets with Needham.

September 21, 1905

Headmaster Endicott Peabody of Groton Preparatory School asks President Theodore Roosevelt to call a meeting of the Big Three—Harvard, Yale, and Princeton—to help bring about more ethical play and eliminate brutality in football.

October 9, 1905

President Theodore Roosevelt holds a White House meeting with representatives of Harvard, Yale, and Princeton, who write a memorandum for promoting sportsmanship and eliminating rough play. This memorandum is given to the media with the intention that other schools will follow the leadership of the Big Three.

November 25, 1905

A Union College player, Harold Moore, dies of a cerebral hemorrhage in a game with New York University, leading to a call for reform or abolition of football by NYU Chancellor Henry MacCracken.

December 8, 1905

Institutions that had recently played against New York University meet in New York City and vote 8–5 not to ban football but to reform it. A larger conference of all football-playing colleges is called for the end of December.

December 28, 1905

A group of sixty-eight institutions, with many of the important colleges refusing to attend, meet in New York City in an attempt to reform college football. This is the beginning of the National Collegiate Athletic Association, then called the Intercollegiate Athletic Association of the United States. Importantly, Harvard meets with this group and helps to reform football.

January 6, 1906

The Big Ten meets in Chicago (and on March 19, 1906, as the Angell Conference) to create reforms for its conference, which eventually include banning Thanksgiving Day games and shortening the season to five games, reducing prices to fifty cents, banning freshman competition, abolishing training tables, and requiring future coaches to be appointed to full-year positions rather than seasonal ones.

March 31, 1906

A joint football rules committee of the new NCAA and the Old Rules Committee agree on reform football rules, including a neutral zone between the teams, requiring six men on the line of scrimmage, moving ten yards in three attempts to maintain ball possession, and the introduction of the forward pass.

December 29, 1906

The first annual meeting of the NCAA is held, and its constitution calls for individual institutions (or conferences), not the NCAA, to "enact and enforce" laws governing intercollegiate athletics. This so-called Home Rule would exist until after World War II.

December 28, 1907

The NCAA committee on summer baseball reports that "playing of baseball in summer for gain is distinctly opposed to the principles of amateurism."

April 19–20, 1910

The football rules committee removes many restrictions on the forward pass, opening up the game and greatly reducing mass plays.

June 11, 1916

Harvard, Yale, and Princeton sign the Triple Agreement on eligibility, specifying that no board and room be provided to athletes without going through the university committee on eligibility.

December 28, 1916

The NCAA constitution includes a definition of amateur as one who participates only for pleasure and the physical, mental, moral, and social benefits gained.

December 28, 1916

Upon the motion of Chicago coach Amos Alonzo Stagg, the NCAA Executive Committee is asked to petition a foundation to survey college and high school athletics "from a moral standpoint."

June 17–18, 1921

The NCAA conducts its first intercollegiate championship when it sponsors a track-and-field meet. All other sports, with the exception of big-time football, would conduct championships in the future. Championships would be questioned by reformers in the coming years.

November 1921

The executive committee of the Carnegie Foundation for the Advancement of Teaching discusses studying the governance and financing of college athletics, but takes no positive action.

December 27, 1921

The American Football Coaches Association is formed by the call of Charles Daly of the U.S. Military Academy, who becomes president. Prominent individuals at the meeting are Glenn "Pop" Warner, Fielding H. Yost, John Heisman, Gil Dobie, Hugo Bezdek, and H. L. Williams. The AFCA immediately condemns pro football. The NCAA approves the organization two days later.

June 1922

Wesleyan University's Edgar Fauver suggests that the Rockefeller or Carnegie Foundation make a thorough study on intercollegiate athletics, including the questions of amateurism and professionalism.

December 28, 1922

The NCAA passes a nine-point code for schools, including a definition of amateurism, freshman rule, eliminating graduate students, maintaining faculty control, and prohibiting professional football players, coaches, and officials from being involved in college sport. The NCAA has no power to enforce the code.

January 9, 1925

Harvard, Yale, and Princeton agree to limit coaching salaries at a time when coaching salaries, especially football, are greatly increasing.

December 5, 1925

The Big Ten votes to ban professional players from coaching or officiating in the conference. This appears to be a reform measure, but it is more likely a reaction to Red Grange turning professional after his last college football game.

January 8, 1926

Following a request by the NCAA, the Carnegie Foundation for the Advancement of Teaching, under the leadership of Howard J. Savage, agrees to make a thorough study of college athletics.

April 1926

The American Association of University Professors attacks the hysteria created by college football and the building of giant stadiums as being menaces to higher education.

November 11, 1926

Harvard and Princeton break athletic relations over the scheduling of football contests and a Harvard *Lampoon* attack upon Princeton. The break remains until 1934.

March 7, 1927

The Carnegie Foundation for the Advancement of Teaching publishes its *Games and Sports in British Schools and Universities.*

October 24, 1929

The most cited report on the status of college sport is published by the Carnegie Foundation for the Advancement of Teaching, *American College Athletics,* which condemns the rampant commercialism and professionalism in college athletics.

November 19, 1930

Abraham Flexner, an authority on universities, head of the Institute for Advance Studies, and author of *Universities: American, English, German,* calls for universities to place athletics in their rightful order "where every one knows they belong."

February 2, 1931

President Thomas S. Gates of the University of Pennsylvania announces a reform of athletics at Penn. It calls for coaches to be part of the faculty and paid accordingly, abolishment of athletic dorms and training tables, financial aid to be placed under university control, elimination of spring practice, creation of an athletic director with less alumni control, and a philosophy of athletics for all.

June 1931

The Carnegie Foundation for the Advancement of Teaching publishes a follow-up report to its 1929 study, indicating that there has been a trend away from commercialism in athletics. This, however, was probably due to the Great Depression affecting gate receipts.

December 27, 1934

The NCAA creates the Eligibility Committee and adopts a code for recruiting and subsidizing as a guide to conferences. The NCAA, however, has no enforcement powers.

October 28, 1935

Frank Nicolson, NCAA secretary, calls for the NCAA to begin national controls over subsidizing and recruiting athletes. He soon makes the proposal to the National Association of State Universities.

November 5, 1935

Influenced by Abraham Flexner and the Carnegie Report, President Frank Graham of the University of North Carolina outlines his plan for athletic reform. He opposes preferential scholarship considerations for athletes, no recruiting by coaches, and financial aid placed under university control.

November 23, 1935

The Graham Plan for athletic reform is adopted by the National Association of State Universities in the hope that institutions across America will accept and enforce them.

December 13, 1935

The Southeastern Conference votes overwhelmingly to openly offer athletic scholarships, not to exceed expenses. The SEC considers its action to be an important athletic reform: open rather than sub rosa payments.

February 8, 1936

The Southern Conference narrowly passes the Graham Plan of athletic reform, 6–4. It calls for no financial aid for athletic prowess, freshman ineligibility, auditing all athletic accounts, and a two-year ban for violators. It lasts only months.

December 2, 1936

Undergraduate newspaper editors of the future Ivy League, an eventual reform league, call for an Ivy League to be formed. Only Brown University is missing from the proposed institutions.

December 30, 1936

Stanford, with Hank Luisetti starring before nearly 18,000 spectators in Madison Square Garden, beats Long Island University 45–31, ending Long Island's forty-three-game winning streak in basketball. This game helps set the stage for the National Invitational Tournament in 1938 and the NCAA tourney the following year. Basketball tournament income allows the NCAA to take a national role in reform and enforcement by the 1950s.

January 11, 1937

Athletic directors of seven Ivy League colleges meet in Savannah, Georgia, to discuss a possible league, suggesting potential rules relative to scholarships, admission requirements, and scholastic regulations. They meet again in 1939.

February 1938

Chancellor John Bowman of the University of Pittsburgh declares Code Bowman, radically reforming athletic aid and alumni interference with athletics—a short-term reform, a long-term failure.

December 21, 1939

President Robert M. Hutchins recommends abolishing football to his University of Chicago Board of Trustees, and the board does so. The action by a Big Ten school is noted but has little effect on athletic reform.

December 30, 1939

The NCAA votes to ban violators of its revised bylaws, including expanded rules on athletes' financial aid and institutional control of athletics, enforced by expulsions, but it lacks the authority to investigate alleged offenders.

Fall 1941

Presidents of NCAA institutions indicate by a slight majority that the NCAA should be given legislative and enforcement powers. If this were done, Home Rule would be compromised and national enforceable reform rules could exist.

June 22, 1944

The GI Bill of Rights becomes law, enabling war veterans to be eligible for college tuition and living expenses. This creates new problems for reformers and athletic eligibility in the post–World War II era.

January 12, 1945

A standing NCAA Constitution Committee is appointed, principally to strengthen recruiting and subsidization provisions.

November 20, 1945

An Ivy Group Committee on Administration of eight eastern universities is formed to set athletic policy. It first meets on December 10, 1945.

January 9, 1946

The NCAA raises dues to provide for an office for the NCAA and more secretarial assistance to carry on additional work created by tournaments and coordinating work of institutions and conferences.

July 23–24, 1946

The NCAA sponsors the Conference of Conferences of twenty conferences to create principles for the conduct of intercollegiate athletics, including the payment of athletes to attend college and the control of recruiting.

January 8, 1947

The NCAA adopts recommendations of five principles from the Conference of Conferences: amateurism, institutional control, academic standards, financial responsibility, and recruiting.

January 10, 1948

The NCAA becomes, for the first time, a regulatory body when it passes the Sanity Code, which calls for athletes to be admitted to college on the same basis as other students. Scholarships for athletes are limited to tuition and fees, and athletic officials may not offer financial aid. Punishment for violators, recommended by the Constitutional Compliance Committee, is the banning of institutions from the NCAA.

July 21, 1949

The University of Virginia Board of Visitors resolves not to conform to the Sanity Code and informs the NCAA.

January 14, 1950

The NCAA lacks a two-thirds vote (111–93) to expel seven violators of the Sanity Code, and the Sanity Code dies with that vote.

January 12–13, 1951

The NCAA changes its constitution by eliminating controls over financial aid to athletes and enforcement powers of the NCAA. Ironically, at the same time the NCAA votes to enforce a national TV contract to limit football telecasts, the first successful national athletic legislation.

February 18, 1951

City College of New York's basketball point-shaving scandal is revealed, beginning a horrific series of scandals in college sport.

August 3, 1951

A cheating scandal at West Point is exposed, culminating in nearly all the football team leaving the Military Academy.

August 12, 1951

The resignation of both football and basketball coaches at William and Mary College reveals part of the athletic-academic scandal at the small school.

October 1, 1951

Walter Byers becomes the first full-time executive director of the NCAA, following four years as executive assistant. His position will be important in the enforcement of NCAA national rules, but he "is in no sense a 'national commissioner.'"

October 21, 1951

An Oklahoma State lineman breaks the jaw of African American Drake star Johnny Bright, causing a major racial incident.

January 10, 1952

The NCAA Council offers a twelve-point reform package to the NCAA convention, including requiring normal academic progress for athletes, meeting minimal entrance requirements, limiting financial grants, practicing only during recognized seasons, limiting the number of games, examining postseason games, and reducing alumni recruiting. Few are accepted.

February 16, 1952

The American Council on Education, after a series of college sport scandals and the creation of a Special Committee on Athletic Policy of eleven presidents in October 1951, releases its recommendations. It calls for administration control of athletics; coaches to have faculty status; faculty control of advisory boards; similar admissions for athletes as other students; athletes making normal progress for a degree; no freshman eligibility; grants to athletes limited to tuition, fees, room, board, and books; grants not conditional on participation in athletics; no financial offers by coaches; no tryouts for subfreshmen; no traveling expenses for prospective athletes; clearly defined sport seasons; and elimination of postseason contests. Few are followed.

April 29, 1952

Saul Streit, judge in the basketball point-shaving scandal, condemns coach Adolph Rupp and the athletic program at Kentucky, suggesting in a 15,000-word report that athletic scholarships, postseason games, athletic recruiting, and freshman eligibility be abolished.

May 7, 1952

A new Ivy Group Agreement for football bans postseason, bowl games, spring practice, and athlete subsidization.

October 14, 1952

The NCAA Council votes a one-year death penalty for the University of Kentucky basketball program for paying players and playing ineligible players. It asks members to boycott playing Kentucky for a year and ban Kentucky from participating in the NCAA basketball tourney during that period.

February 7–9, 1953

A Conference of Conferences is held to solidify plans for investigation and enforcement cooperation between conferences and the NCAA.

June 1953

The North Central Association, an accrediting agency, sets a policy of no subsidization for athletes, academic scholarships determined on the same basis as other students, and athletes maintaining the same academic standards as all students. It fails as a reform.

February 11, 1954

The Ivy Group Agreement reforms the Ivy League by banning freshmen from varsity competition, allowing three years of eligibility, banning athletic scholarships, and requiring academic progress leading to a degree.

May 17, 1954

The unanimous *Brown v. Board of Education* U.S. Supreme Court decision in opposition to "separate but equal" under the equal protection clause of the Fourteenth Amendment paves the way for the civil rights movement and massive entry of African Americans into college sports.

January 20, 1955

An athletic slush fund at the University of Tennessee is discussed by the president and his advisors, who cover it up rather than attempt to correct it.

January 11, 1956

The NCAA allows "full-ride" athletic scholarships on a national level.

April 29, 1956

Arthur Bergstrom is hired as the first enforcement officer of the NCAA.

January 11, 1957

The NCAA officially defines athletic scholarships for the first time to include tuition and fees, room and board, and $15 for incidentals.

January 7, 1959

Stanford's Rixford Snyder makes the case to the NCAA for using high school grades combined with standardized tests to predict athletes' college success.

January 11, 1961

A major reform in one sport is taken by the NCAA when it abolishes the National Collegiate Boxing Championship.

January 11, 1961

The NCAA votes to allow five years to complete four years of participation, thus basically recognizing the practice of redshirting younger players.

April 19, 1964

The NCAA, with the backing of women college sport leaders, limits participation in NCAA championships to undergraduate male students.

April 19, 1964

The NCAA creates a Special Committee on Women's Sports, hoping to define the role of the NCAA in women's sports.

July 2, 1964

The Civil Rights Act of 1964 is passed, forbidding discrimination by government agencies that receive federal aid. This is important in helping African Americans to receive equity in college sports and providing guidelines for the passage of Title IX in 1972.

January 13, 1965

The NCAA passes the 1.600 grade point average for freshmen to receive grants-in-aid and be eligible for athletic participation.

March 19, 1966

In possibly the most culturally important game in college basketball history, Texas Western wins the national championship with all-black starters against Kentucky's all-white team, 72–65.

June 1966

The Commission on Intercollegiate Athletics for Women is created by the Division for Girls and Women's Sports to organize, sponsor, and conduct national championships. It becomes the Association for Intercollegiate Athletics for Women in 1972.

January 11, 1967

The NCAA overwhelmingly passes a motion to take away an athletic scholarship if the athlete "voluntarily renders himself ineligible for intercollegiate competition," generally for quitting or not being cooperative.

October 24, 1967

The NCAA Council appoints a committee to study the feasibility of establishing ways to develop and supervise women's college athletics.

January 10, 1968

The NCAA votes 163–160 for freshman eligibility for all NCAA championships except in football and basketball, reversing decades of reform.

September 1, 1968

The new divisional structure of the NCAA shows 223 institutions in the University Division and 368 in the College Division.

January 1971

NCAA legal counsel advises NCAA leadership to strongly consider providing championships for women.

January 8, 1972

The NCAA allows freshman eligibility for football and basketball championships, in a reverse reform move.

June 23, 1972

The federal Title IX of the Education Amendments Act of 1972 passes Congress, banning gender-based discrimination in federally supported educational programs. This law has probably done more for reform in college athletics than any other, inspiring women to take advantage of sport participation on an equal basis.

July 1, 1972

The Association for Intercollegiate Athletics for Women officially begins as an outgrowth of the Commission on Intercollegiate Athletics for Women. Relative to men's athletics, it is a reform, as it originally favors athletes' concerns in an educational model. It soon moves away from these ideals and, by its demise in 1982, looks very much like the commercial-professional model of the men.

January 13, 1973

The NCAA repeals its predicted 1.600 grade point average for participation, 169–145, and allows a 2.0 high school GPA minimum, essentially requiring no academic requirements to participate in college athletics.

January 13, 1973

The NCAA passes, by a show of hands and no debate, one-year scholarships to replace four-year scholarships, granting coaches greater control over athletes.

January 17, 1973

Kellmeyer, et al. v. NEA, et al., a lawsuit to gain equal rights to athletic scholarships for women, begins. Within months women's athletic scholarships are legalized by the Association for Intercollegiate Athletics for Women, beginning the collapse of an educational model for athletics.

August 7, 1973

A special NCAA convention adopts three divisions—I, II, and III—for its members and are self-determined, except in football, which has special classifications for membership. Football still dominates the NCAA.

March 22, 1974

The American Council on Education publishes George Hanford's report on college athletics, *An Inquiry into the Need for and Feasibility of a National Study of Intercollegiate Athletics*. Hanford makes comparisons to the 1929 Carnegie Foundation report. He notes the need to finance women's sport to meet the 1972 Title IX requirements. He suggests accreditation by regional associations as a help for athletic reform.

May 24, 1974

Senator John Tower introduces an amendment to Title IX to exempt revenue-producing sports for determining Title IX compliance. It is rejected.

August 21, 1974

The Buckley Amendment (Family Educational Rights and Privacy Act) becomes law, protecting students' rights to privacy over educational records. It was used by some institutions to cover up athletes' poor academic records.

October 15, 1975

Seven major conferences and independents gather to discuss reorganizing the NCAA to meet the needs of big-time football. This group forms the College Football Association the following year. It discusses reform, but it is mostly interested in promoting big-time football and increasing TV revenue.

January 13, 1976

Division I of the NCAA defeats a motion by the Pacific-8 Conference to allow athletic scholarships based only upon financial need, 121–102.

January 1977

The Ford Foundation grants the American Council on Education $200,000 to establish a Commission on Athletics. The commission publishes its results on possible athletic reform in the fall 1977 issue of *Educational Record*.

January 13, 1978

The NCAA Division I realigns into 1-A and 1-AA in football.

June 17, 1978

The College Football Association proposes the "Triple Option," 2.25 high school grade point average, 750 on the SAT standardized test, or 17 on the ACT for freshman athletic eligibility. The NCAA does not accept it.

Fall 1978

Kevin Ross, symbolic of academically unprepared athletes, enters Creighton University with only lower grade school language skills and plays basketball for four years with a D average and few credits. Following college, Ross returns to grade school to learn to read.

January 9, 1979

A reform, mostly for financial reasons, to limit financial aid to financial need (except for tuition and mandatory fees) is defeated by the NCAA. Income-producing football and basketball would have been exempted.

December 11, 1979

The U.S. Department of Health, Education, and Welfare issues the final policy interpretation of Title IX, creating a three-prong test to determine if institutions are meeting gender equity requirements.

October 12, 1980

The University of Southern California acknowledges that it admitted 330 scholastically deficient athletes in the 1970s, with the president's blessing, and provided credit for courses not taken by athletes.

January 13, 1981

The NCAA adopts a governance plan that includes women's athletic programs.

May 1, 1981

The University of Illinois is placed on probation by the Big Ten for allowing quarterback Dave Wilson to illegally play during the 1980 season.

Fall 1981

The Center for Athletes' Rights and Education (CARE), led by Allen Sack, creates a bill of rights for athletes, including the right of athletes to form unions and to bargain collectively.

November 1981

The first women's NCAA championships are contested.

Fall 1981

Jan Kemp, of the University of Georgia, protests to her superiors that nine football players are failing and ineligible for the upcoming 1982 Sugar Bowl, but all are allowed to play. The 1986 trial of Kemp's firing is publicized widely.

Summer 1982

William Friday and Derek Bok, presidents of North Carolina and Harvard, join with the American Council on Education to lobby the NCAA to reform academic requirements for freshman eligibility.

January 11, 1983

Proposition 48 is passed by the NCAA, dictating that freshmen to be eligible shall have a minimum 700 SAT or 17 ACT, a high school GPA of 2.00, and eleven core courses. This is claimed to be a reform, though the requirements are lower than the 1.600 rule of the 1960s.

October 1983

The American Council on Education proposes the formation of a forty-four-person Board of Presidents, rather than an advisory Presidents Commission, to control sports within the NCAA by being able to veto legislation.

January 11, 1984

Though the American Council on Education recommends a Board of Presidents, the NCAA creates a weaker, advisory Presidents Commission to help reform college athletics.

June 27, 1984

The U.S. Supreme Court rules in *NCAA v. Board of Regents of the University of Oklahoma,* in a 7–2 decision, to reform college athletics by declaring the NCAA TV policy to be a violation of the Sherman Antitrust Act. It is the first antitrust decision against amateur sports.

August 15, 1984

An NCAA study shows that freshmen awarded athletic scholarships are far below the academic standard for nonathletes.

January 14, 1986

An NCAA drug testing program for championships and bowl games is approved in an effort to make college athletics drug free, but it is another step in taking away freedoms from athletes.

August 1, 1986

Proposition 48, passed in 1983, becomes operational with the class of 1990.

February 25, 1987

The NCAA delivers the death penalty to Southern Methodist University football for a series of violations, mostly payments to athletes.

July 1, 1987

A movement by the NCAA's Presidents Commission fails to reform athletics when the NCAA rejects the proposal to reduce the number of basketball and football scholarships allowed at each school.

October 1, 1987

Richard Schultz succeeds Walter Byers as head of the NCAA.

March 22, 1988

The Civil Rights Restoration Act mandates that all educational institutions receiving federal aid, direct or indirect, are bound by Title IX, overriding the Grove City Case of 1984.

January 12, 1989

The NCAA passes Proposition 42 to tighten eligibility requirements amid opposition from African American leaders. Georgetown coach John Thompson soon walks out of a basketball game to show his displeasure.

September 27, 1989

The Knight Foundation creates the Commission on Intercollegiate Athletics to push for reform in college athletics. The commission has a blue-ribbon group of individuals led by two prominent university ex-presidents, William Friday of the University of North Carolina and Theodore Hesburgh of Notre Dame.

January 1990

The American Association of University Professors publishes "The Role of Faculty in the Governance of College Athletics: A Report of the Special Committee on Athletics" in the January–February 1990 issue of *Academe*.

January–February 1991

The American Association of University Professors publishes an issue titled "Reforming College Sports: How? When? Ever?" in its journal *Academe*.

March 19, 1991

The Commission on Intercollegiate Athletics of the Knight Foundation publishes *Keeping Faith with the Student-Athlete: A New Model for Intercollegiate Athletics* as a major effort to reform college athletics. In some ways it is similar to the Carnegie Report of 1929. It recommends reform under presidential control and emphasizes academic and financial integrity and independent certification of athletic programs. It has little long-term effect according to another Knight Commission report a decade later.

May 30, 1991

Government hearings are held on Rep. Tom McMillen's National College Athletics Accountability Act, calling for greater reform in college athletics.

June 19, 1991

A congressional hearing on intercollegiate athletics by a House subcommittee raises issues of racism in standardized tests used to determine freshman eligibility in college athletics.

October 28, 1991

The Rex Lee Commission Report that makes recommendations for a fairer NCAA enforcement process is released. Eleven recommendations include greater transparency in enforcement operations with open meetings, neutral judges, and preliminary notice of impending investigations. The NCAA implements most recommendations, but does not accept independent hearing officers and open meetings on enforcement.

January 10, 1992

The NCAA's Proposition 16 is passed, 249–72, to provide a sliding scale of high school grade point averages and standardized scores for freshman eligibility. More protests result relative to the culturally biased tests.

May 11, 1993

Richard Schultz, executive director of the NCAA, resigns after it is discovered that he violated NCAA rules while he was athletic director at the University of Virginia.

November 5, 1993

Cedric Dempsey is selected as head of the NCAA to succeed Dick Schultz.

January 11, 1994

When the NCAA votes not to reinstate one additional basketball scholarship to make fourteen, the Black Coaches Association threatens to boycott some or all of the basketball season, jeopardizing the NCAA basketball tourney, the financial lifeblood of the NCAA.

October 20, 1994

The Equity in Athletics Disclosure Act becomes law. It is designed to help in Title IX compliance but has become a major source for tracking athletic department operating expenses and revenues, something generally hidden by athletic departments.

May 29, 1995

Brown University loses an important Title IX discrimination case, setting precedent for universities not to drop women's sports.

January 8, 1996

Division I votes 115–0 to approve a new NCAA structure with a president-dominated Board of Directors and a Management Council. It provides stronger federation, greater presidential authority, but does not simplify governance when it removed institutional voting and a major role of faculty representation.

August 1, 1996

The NCAA's Proposition 16 modifies Proposition 48 to determine Division I freshman eligibility. Thirteen core courses and a sliding scale for high school grade point average and national test scores are required. Later, a class action suit challenges the minimum standardized test scores as racist.

January 13, 1997

The NCAA's new governance structure under presidents' control becomes operational. Unfortunately, "lack of institutional control" violations rise.

June 30, 1997

The College Football Association, which had a reform agenda in the 1970s and 1980s, formally closes its books, following individual institutions and conferences withdrawing from CFA television contracts.

January 8, 1999

The *Cureton v. NCAA* court case begins with African Americans charging that Proposition 16's minimum standardized test scores for freshman eligibility are racist. The case at first favors Cureton and is enough to pressure the NCAA to change Prop. 16.

January 11, 1999

The NCAA Division I Basketball Working Group reports that 70 percent in a basketball survey favor freshman participation. Basketball is by far the most important sport for financing the NCAA, as it produces 92 percent of its income.

March 8, 1999

Judge Buckwalter rules in *Cureton v. NCAA* that the standardized tests for freshman eligibility violate the Civil Rights Act of 1964. It is later overruled, but the NCAA changes the Proposition 16 eligibility rule.

March 9, 1999

Restricted earnings for assistant coaches, a cost-cutting measure passed in 1991, is settled after four years in the courts, with the NCAA owing $54.5 million to coaches as violation of antitrust laws.

July 27, 1999

The NCAA opens its office in Indianapolis, Indiana, "home" of amateur sports, and is important for continuing the "amateur" image of intercollegiate sport.

October 22–23, 1999

The Drake Group Conference, calling for faculties to rid college athletics of corruption, is organized by Jon Ericson, former provost of Drake University. It creates the National Association for College Athletic Reform. It meets regularly, returns to be called the Drake Group, but has little direct impact on athletic reform.

November 18, 1999

The NCAA agrees with CBS TV to a $6 billion, eleven-year contract for its basketball championship. Academic reform in basketball will be more difficult than ever because the tourney generates nearly the entire funding of the NCAA, with its new offices in the home of amateurism, Indianapolis.

January 8, 2000

The NCAA announces that 103 Division I schools have athlete graduation rates of less than 30 percent, with 60 percent of the schools graduating less than 50 percent.

Spring 2000

Nine of the PAC-10 Conference faculty senates pass resolutions to support reform by placing academics first. Initiated by the University of Oregon's James Earl, the idea is later used by Bob Eno of Indiana University to bring a faculty senate movement together nationally under the Coalition on Intercollegiate Athletics (COIA).

January 18, 2001

The National College Players Association is created by Ramogi Huma, former UCLA football player, to promote rights for athletes in football and basketball.

June 26, 2001

The Knight Commission calls for athletic reform by mainstreaming athletes with other students, shortening seasons and play-offs, creating four-year scholarships, redistributing "March Madness" tourney money, and reducing athletic commercialism. It again calls for presidential leadership to bring about reform, something that has not previously worked effectively.

January 14, 2002

The Division I Football Committee is appointed to look at a number of football issues, but a football play-off is not to be discussed by order of presidents.

May 6, 2002

The *Pryor v. NCAA* case states that Proposition 16 discriminates on the basis of race, though the NCAA eventually wins the case on appeal.

January 1, 2003

Myles Brand, former Indiana University president, becomes the first university CEO to head the NCAA.

January 2003

The American Association of University Professors Committee on Athletic Problems publishes "The Faculty Role in the Reform of Intercollegiate Athletics: Principles and Recommended Practices" in *Academe*.

March 2003

The Coalition on Intercollegiate Athletics (COIA), a faculty senate reform group from big-time football schools, adopts a charter looking for shared governance reform in improved academics and student welfare, cost reduction, and lessened commercialism.

August 1, 2003

Proposition 16 is modified and takes effect, demanding fourteen courses, but the sliding standardized test score for eligibility is reduced to zero (SAT 400 or ACT 37) for freshman eligibility, provided the high school grade point average is high enough.

October 9, 2003

NCAA President Myles Brand identifies two major problems: the high cost of athletics and low graduation rates for football and men's basketball players, the two most important sports. These issues, along with a steady shift toward the professional model of athletics, concern him.

Fall 2003

The Steering Committee of the Coalition on Intercollegiate Athletics provides a framework for athletic reform. It consists of a network of faculty leaders from more than fifty Division I-A NCAA schools in six conferences.

November 11, 2003

A National Symposium on Athletics Reform meets in New Orleans to consider athletic reform. NCAA President Myles Brand tries to convince people there are two distinct athletic models: amateur and professional.

February 29, 2004

A Presidential Coalition for Athletics Reform holds its first meeting, facilitated by NCAA President Myles Brand. It was initiated by President Scott Cowen of Tulane to reform the Bowl Championship Series, which he believes is a monopoly dominating a Division I football championship and was formed by forty-eight presidents of non-BCS schools.

April 20, 2004

The NCAA adopts what it considers a landmark reform package to increase academic progress and graduation rates and is known as the Academic Progress Rate, with teams being punished if minimal APRs are not achieved.

September 14, 2004

The NCAA due process hearing by the House of Representatives is held following several NCAA denials of athletic participation. Antitrust exemption is suggested if the NCAA wishes to cap expenditures of coaching salaries and recruiting and other commercial ventures.

January 8, 2005

Myles Brand, NCAA president, reemphasizes that the definition of "amateurism" is one of motivation for participation, not financial considerations.

January 10, 2005

The NCAA Division I Board passes legislation to inflict penalties on teams with low (less than 50 percent) graduation rates with loss of scholarships and postseason competition. The Academic Performance Rate is aimed primarily at three sports: men's basketball, football, and baseball.

January 10, 2005

President Myles Brand of the NCAA moves to create a fifty-member Presidential Task Force to focus on the rapid increase in expenses in Division I athletics.

February 17, 2006

An antitrust suit, *White v. NCAA,* was filed by former athletes challenging the NCAA financial limit for athletic scholarships below the cost of college attendance. The judge sided with the athletes, and on August 4, 2008, the NCAA agreed to create a Former Student-Athlete Fund of $10 million.

October 2006

The NCAA Presidential Task Force on the Future of Division I Intercollegiate Athletics releases its findings. The fifty-member committee of presidents calls for presidential leadership and institutional accountability.

November 13, 2006

NCAA President Myles Brand responds to House of Representatives Ways and Means Chairman William Thomas, justifying the tax exempt status of what Brand considers amateur and educational college athletics.

May 14, 2007

The Knight Commission again urges presidents to support athletic reform.

June 15, 2007

The Coalition on Intercollegiate Athletics (COIA) adopts "Framing the Future: Reforming Intercollegiate Athletics" and its twenty-eight proposals covering academic integrity and quality, student-athlete welfare, campus governance, and fiscal responsibility. It calls for local, conference, and national implementation.

October 15, 2007

A faculty summit on intercollegiate athletics, supported by the Knight Commission, meets in Washington, DC, to discuss reform.

Spring 2008

The NCAA Faculty Athletics Representatives Association surveys its membership, showing that its members feel lack of power over athletics and that the organization is "too white and too male."

August 1, 2008

The NCAA new freshman eligibility rule requires sixteen core high school courses with the previous sliding scale of SAT (ACT) scores and high school grade point average.

May 6, 2009

After five years of Academic Progress Rate results, most men's and women's team show improvement, with men's and women's basketball, football, and baseball being the most challenged sports. The lesser known of the big-time schools, those with less money, have the most difficulty meeting APR requirements.

September 16, 2009

Myles Brand, the first university president to head the NCAA, dies.

October 26, 2009

The Knight Commission on Intercollegiate Athletics releases its *Quantitative and Qualitative Research with Football Bowl Subdivision University Presidents on the Costs and Financing of Intercollegiate Athletics.*

December 30, 2009

The Association Press survey of big-time football programs reveals that football players are up to forty times as likely to get special, presidential admission into college compared to other members of the student body.

February 10, 2010

The *O'Bannon v. NCAA* case contains charges against the NCAA for violations of the Sherman Antitrust Act of 1890 for illegal uses of images in video games. There are major implications for "amateur" college sports.

April 27, 2010

Mark Emmert of the University of Washington was named president of the NCAA, the second university president to lead the NCAA.

Notes

Introduction

1. *Boston Daily Evening Transcript,* August 10, 1852, p. 1; *New York Herald,* August 10, 1852, p. 2.

2. The English at Oxford and Cambridge Universities created intercollegiate athletics when the two institutions participated in a cricket match in 1827 and a crew meet in 1829; Ross, *The Boat Race,* 35.

3. Whiton, "The First Harvard-Yale Regatta (1852)," 286, 289.

4. *New York Herald,* August 10, 1852, p. 2.

5. As quoted in Lewis, "America's First Intercollegiate Sport," 639.

6. *Harvard Advocate,* December 17, 1880, p. 77.

7. "A Reply to the Statement of December 18th by the Committee on the Regulation of Athletic Sports of Harvard University, by the Princeton Advisory Committee and Foot Ball Managers, 24 February 1890," General Athletics, Box 1, Princeton University Archives.

8. Friday and Hesburgh, *Keeping Faith with the Student Athlete,* 11.

9. Ibid., vii.

10. Charles W. Eliot, telegram to Chancellor Henry M. MacCracken, New York University, November 26, 1905, as quoted in *New York Daily Tribune,* November 29, 1905, p. 2. This was in response to MacCracken asking Eliot to head a conference to either reform or abolish football following the death of a Union College player in a game against New York University. Henry M. MacCracken, telegram to Charles W. Eliot, November 25, 1905, Eliot Papers, Box 227, Folder "MacCracken," Harvard University Archives. For fuller accounts of the 1905–6 football crisis, see Smith, *Sports and Freedom,* 191–208; Watterson, *College Football,* 64–98; and Bernstein, *Football,* 67–92.

11. *New York Times,* November 27, 1905, p. 5.

12. Savage et al., *American Colleges Athletics,* 80.

13. American Council on Education, "Report of the Special Committee on Athletic Policy of the American Council on Education," February 16, 1952; *New York Times,* November 25, 1951, in "Athletics," 4/0/3, Box 70, University of Wisconsin-Madison Archives.

14. Hanford, *An Inquiry into the Need for and Feasibility of a National Study of Intercollegiate Athletics,* 28.

15. J. W. Peltason, ACE, to "Colleagues," February 7, 1984, Chancellor's Central File, Box 218, Folder "Athletics 1984–85," University of Nebraska Archives.

16. Friday and Hesburgh, *Keeping Faith with the Student-Athlete,* 25.

17. Friday, Hesburgh, et al., "A Call to Action." Nevertheless, the report stated: "But a determined and focused group of presidents acting together can transform the world of intercollegiate athletics." Wishful thinking, written by a group, principally of ex-college

presents, who had done little to reform athletics when they were in a position to do so as leaders of their institutions.

18. *Insidehighered.com News*, October 16, 2007.

19. *Des Moines Register*, April 21, 1999 and October 23, 1999; *Minneapolis Star Tribune*, October 23, 1999; *Washington Post*, October 23, 1999, D7; *Baltimore Sun*, October 24, 1999, E14; and *Wall Street Journal*, November 12, 1999, W7.

20. Coalition on Intercollegiate Athletics (COIA), "Framing the Future."

21. http://www.businessweek.com/magazine/content/03_45/c3857049 (accessed October 4, 2007).

22. Duderstadt, *Intercollegiate Athletics and the American University*, epilogue.

23. A major exception is that Division III schools do not give out "athletic scholarships." However, they give out many scholarships to athletes, often athletes who could not get into the institutions by meeting usual academic standards. The best analyses of this phenomenon, using a massive amount of statistics, are found in two books: Shulman and Bowen, *The Game of Life*, and Bowen and Levin, *Reclaiming the Game*.

24. Institutions, large and small, accept commercial shoe and clothing contracts when they are available; schedule games that will bring in the largest number of spectators; willingly go on television and at times during the day and during the week that are convenient for commercial purposes, not educational purposes; accept questionable advertising, such as alcohol, when binge drinking is rampant; participate in NCAA-sponsored tournaments at educationally inappropriate times; offer naming rights for arenas and stadiums; expect that athletics will pay a significant portion of the cost of athletics, when almost nowhere else in the educational system are educational entities expected to meet educational expenses; pay their coaches more than their highly educated professors; and nearly universally accept athletes into their institutions who are not academically representative of the student body.

Chapter 1. Student-Controlled Athletics and Early Reform

1. Camp, "College Athletics," 139.

2. *New York Herald*, July 24, 1855, p. 3; George S. Mumford, "Rowing at Harvard," in *The H Book of Harvard Athletics, 1852–1922*, ed. John A. Blanchard (Cambridge, MA: Harvard Varsity Club, 1923), 26.

3. For a list of first competitions, winners, and dates, see Smith, *Sports and Freedom*, 219–20. If chess is considered a sport, then the third intercollegiate sport was chess, as it was contested as part of the College Union Regatta in 1860; *New York Times*, July 25, 1860, p. 3.

4. *New York Clipper*, July 30, 1870, p. 130; *New York Times*, July 23, 1870, p. 5; Hurd, *A History of Yale Athletics*, 14–16; B. W. Crowningshield, "Boating," in *The Harvard Book*, ed. F. O. Vaille and H. A. Clark, vol. 2, 231; Bagg, *Four Years at Yale*, 389–99.

5. G. H. Gould and Robert Grant, Harvard Boat Club, to I. H. Ford, Yale Boat Club, May 17, 1871, as quoted in Blanchard, *The H Book of Harvard Athletics*, 56.

6. *Yale Record*, April 16, 1873, p. 249; *Harvard Magenta*, April 4, 1873, p. 69.

7. *Harvard Advocate*, December 11, 1874, p. 89.

8. Smith, "The Rise of College Baseball," 23–26. Williams used a 2 oz., 7" circumference ball and Amherst had a 2.5 oz., 6" ball. The teams used the New England rules rather than

the rules that became standard of the National Association of Base Ball Players formed in 1858, an outgrowth of New York City baseball.

9. W. D. Sanborn, "Base Ball," in Vaille and Clark, *The Harvard Book,* vol. 2, 286, 324.

10. As quoted in Presbrey and Moffatt, *Athletics at Princeton,* 20, 67.

11. Smith, "The Rise of College Baseball," 23–41.

12. *Harvard Advocate,* December 12, 1879, p. 79; *Worcester Daily Spy,* December 8, 1879, p. 4. A decade later, two-thirds of Harvard's baseball team was composed of students in Harvard professional schools; *Report of the President of Harvard College, 1888–1889,* 12, Harvard University Archives.

13. Smith, *Sports and Freedom,* 67–82.

14. Oriard, *Reading Football,* 62.

15. The Intercollegiate Football Association (IFA) established its Graduate Advisory Committee in 1887 at the recommendation of Yale's Walter Camp and continued until the dissolution of the IFA in 1893. The Graduate Advisory Committee proposed rule changes for the IFA to act upon. Camp served on both the IFA and the Graduate Advisory Committee, thus influencing the IFA toward the desires of Yale for any football rule changes; Nelson, *Anatomy of a Game,* 60–64.

16. *Harvard Crimson,* November 6, 1889; *New York Times,* November 20, 1889, p. 5; *New York Times,* November 27, 1889, p. 5; Edgar Allen Poe, Princeton, to Walter Camp, November 9, 1889, Walter Camp Papers, Box 14, Folder 553, Yale University Archives; Davis, *Football the American Intercollegiate Game,* 87–90. Princeton, however, almost immediately withdrew a starter, E. O. Wagenhurst, who had graduated from Princeton two years earlier, played baseball for money, and returned to Princeton to continue playing for the Princeton football team.

17. McCarty, *All-America,* 3.

18. Newspaper clipping of the conflict, ca. December 1889, Moses Taylor Pyne Scrapbook, Vol. 8, p. 74, Princeton University Archives.

19. *Harvard Crimson,* December 20, 1889.

20. *New York Times,* November 27, 1889, p. 5. Princeton, at the same time, claimed it had evidence that Harvard had "offered pecuniary inducements" to players to enter Harvard to play football. Professor Sloane would, in 1896, be the most important individual in promoting American participation in the first International Olympic Games in Athens, Greece, in 1896.

21. For a fuller account of the development of Harvard's athletic committee, see Smith, *Sports and Freedom,* 127–31.

22. *New York Times,* December 20, 1889, p. 6.

23. "Overseers Athletic Abuses Committee Report," ca. April 1888, HUD 8388.5, Harvard University Archives.

24. Knowlton L. Ames to H. O. Stickney, *Boston Post* clipping, December 20, 1879, "1889 Football Controversy," HUD 10889.2, Harvard University Archives; *Harvard Crimson,* December 20, 1889.

25. "A Harvard Graduate's Proposition to Yale," newspaper reprint of *Yale News,* November 26, 1889, in the "1889 Football Controversy," HUD 10889.2, Harvard University Archives.

26. For a more thorough study of the Dual League, see Smith, "A Failure of Elitism," 201–13.

27. For a discussion of professionalism in college athletics and the failure of amateurism as a reform ideal, see "Amateur College Sport: An Untenable Concept in a Free and Open Society," in Smith, *Sports and Freedom*, 165–74.

Chapter 2. Faculty, Faculty Athletic Committees, and Reform Efforts

1. *Harvard Crimson*, December 20, 1889.

2. For background on in loco parentis, character building, and student responses, see Rudolph, "The Collegiate Way," in his *The American College and University*, 86–109; Veysey, *The Emergence of the American University*, 28–29; Mattingly, *The Classless Profession*, 65–69; Kett, *Rites and Passages*, 51; Handlin and Handlin, *The American College and American Culture*, 11; and Geiger, *To Advance Knowledge*, 3.

3. *The Laws of Yale-College, 1774* (New Haven, CT: Thomas and Samuel Green, 1774), 14.

4. Princeton Faculty Minutes, November 26, 1787, Princeton University Archives.

5. *The Black Book, or Book of Misdemeanors in King's College, New-York, 1771–1775*, 4.

6. David Yancey to David Watson, June 6, 1795, *Virginia Magazine of History* 30 (July 1922): 224–25.

7. Smith, *Sports and Freedom*, 67–69.

8. In the reading of the minutes of the Princeton and Rutgers faculties before and after the 1869 contest, there are no comments on the original football games. If there were negative concerns, they almost surely would have been recorded in the faculty minutes; see Princeton Faculty Minutes, Princeton University Archives, and Rutgers Faculty Minutes, Rutgers University Archives.

9. Graham, *Cricket at the University of Pennsylvania*, 11.

10. Yale Faculty Minutes, March 25, 1868, Yale University Archives.

11. Harvard Faculty Minutes, May 22, 1871; John W. White, W. S. Chaplin, and A. B. Hart, "Athletic Report," June 12, 1888, HUD 8388.3B, Harvard University Archives.

12. Princeton Faculty Minutes, April 29, 1881.

13. Princeton Faculty Minutes, June 2, 1882, and October 13, 1882.

14. Princeton Faculty Minutes, February 13, 1884, and October 17, 1884.

15. Blanchard, *The H Book of Harvard Athletics, 1852–1922*, 182–83; Harvard Faculty Minutes, May 27, 1871, and April 21, 1873, Harvard University Archives.

16. White, "The Constitution, Authority, and Policy of the Committee on the Regulation of Athletic Sports," 209; Sargent, "History of the Administration of Intercollegiate Athletics in the United States," 252.

17. Harvard Athletic Committee Minutes, June 15, 1882, Harvard University Archives.

18. Harvard Athletic Committee Minutes, September 27, 1882, Harvard University Archives.

19. For an analysis of the British elite form of amateurism and why it would not be successful in America and its institutions of higher learning, see Smith, "Amateur College Sport: An Untenable Concept in a Free and Open Society," in his *Sports and Freedom*, 165–74.

20. Harvard Athletic Committee Minutes, December 10, 1883, Harvard University Archives.

21. J. W. White, W. E. Byerly, and D. A. Sargent to James Storrow, crew captain, December 19, 1884, January 10, 1885, and October 8, 1885, Harvard Athletic Committee Minutes, Harvard University Archives.

22. Harvard Athletic Committee Minutes, October 8, 1885, and May 21, 1886; Charles W. Eliot to D. A. Sargent, May 18, 1886, Harvard University Archives.

23. The Harvard faculty voted to ban football in 1885, 1895, 1902, and 1906. Only in 1885 was it successful in prohibiting the game, and then only for one year; "Report of the Joint Committee on the Regulation of Athletic Sports," 648.

24. Harvard Athletic Committee Minutes, November 22, 1883, March 12, 1884, and November 25, 1884, Harvard University Archives.

25. Harvard Athletic Committee Minutes, October 8, 1885, Harvard University Archives.

26. White, "The Constitution, Authority, and Policy of the Committee on the Regulation of Athletic Sports," 214–17.

27. M. H. Morgan, Harvard Faculty, to Athletic Committee, February 20, 1894; James Barr Ames, Athletic Committee to Faculty of Arts and Sciences, February 25, 1894, Charles Eliot Papers, Box 100, Folder 4; James Barr Ames to Corporation, March 25, 1894, Box 264, Folder "January–March 1895"; "Report to the Overseers, Presidents and Fellows," March 25, 1895, Series II, U.A. II, 10.7.2; Charles W. Eliot, *Report of the President of Harvard College, 1894–1895,* 13–14, Harvard University Archives.

28. Harvard Athletic Committee Minutes, February 16, March 9, June 5, and November 16, 1903, Harvard University Archives.

29. Records of the Overseers of Harvard College, May 9, 1906, Harvard University Archives; *Harvard Crimson,* May 10, 1906, p. 1.

30. "Report of the Joint Committee on the Regulation of Athletic Sports," 644–45.

31. *Northwestern University President's Annual Report, 1895–1896* (Evanston, IL: Northwestern University, 1896), 24.

32. Burt G. Wilder to the Faculty, February 1, 1895, Burt G. Wilder Papers, Box 1, 14/26/95, Cornell University Archives; William F. Atkinson and 648 students, to the President and Faculty, ca. June 1895, Cornell University Faculty Minutes, June 14, 1895.

33. Dartmouth College Records of the Trustees, February 1892 and September 30, 1905, Dartmouth College Archives.

34. "Memorandum," ca. spring 1906, President Tucker Papers, #1, "Athletics, A–H," Dartmouth College Archives.

35. Veblen, "Summary and Trial Balance," *The Higher Learning in America.*

36. Meiklejohn, "The Evils of College Athletics," 1752.

Chapter 3. Early Interinstitutional Reform Efforts

1. For a general discussion of the failure of interinstitutional control of athletics by faculty, see Smith, *Sports and Freedom,* 134–46.

2. Charles W. Eliot to college presidents, September 11, 1882, as quoted in Warren, "The Charles W. Eliot Centennial," 24, and Dartmouth Faculty Records, September 18, 1882, Dartmouth College Archives.

3. Yale University Faculty Minutes, October 11, 1882, Yale University Archives.

4. *Harvard Crimson,* February 14, 1884, p. 1; February 22, 1884, p. 1; and February 23, 1884, p. 1; and John W. White, W. S. Chaplin, and A. B. Hart, "Athletic Report," June 12, 1888, HUD 8388.3B, Harvard University Archives.

5. *Harvard Crimson,* February 26, 1884, p. 1.

6. Harvard Athletic Committee Minutes, March 7, 1884, Harvard University Archives; White, "Athletic Report."

7. *Harvard Crimson,* February 22, 1884, p. 1; February 26, 1884, p. 1; March 6, 1884, p. 1; March 12, 1884, p. 1; and E. L. Richards to W. M. Sloane, February 18, 1884, as quoted in the *Harvard Crimson,* February 21, 1884, p. 1.

8. As quoted in the *Harvard Crimson,* March 1, 1884, p. 2.

9. *The* [Brown College] *Brunonian,* December 18, 1886, pp. 114, 125; Leslie, "The Response of Four Colleges to the Rise of Intercollegiate Athletics," 216.

10. Walter Camp to the editor, *New York Times,* February 27, 1884, p. 3. Camp argued that "by their management of college organizations in their dealings with outside parties the students learn best how to look after their interests in a business-like and self-reliant manner." Camp was arguing strenuously against faculty interference in things such as hiring professional coaches, which he thought was not successful in producing winners, and playing against professionals.

11. Barton, "The College Conference of the Middle West," 42–52; Roberts, *The Big Nine,* 14–16.

12. Frederic J. Turner, "Speech at Alumni Banquet, 21 January 1906," Turner Papers, Box 2, Folder "Athletics," Wis/Mss/Al, State Historical Society of Wisconsin Archives.

13. Wilson and Brondfield, *The Big Ten,* 74.

14. Davis, *Football the American Intercollegiate Game,* 451–53; Behee, *Fielding Yost's Legacy,* 19–23. Davis, a graduate of Princeton, was coaching Lafayette at the time, and another Princeton graduate, Doggie Trenchard, was the West Virginia football coach.

15. Rydjord, *A History of Fairmount College,* 168.

16. *Seattle Daily Times,* October 24, 1931, clipping in 37/5/1495, Cornell University Archives.

17. *Brown Daily Herald,* February 18, 1898, p. 1. Representatives from the three groups were present except that Cornell had no student representative.

18. http://www.brown.edu/administration/news_bureau/databases/encyclopedia/search .php?serial=MO430 (accessed December 14, 2007).

19. "Conference on Intercollegiate Athletics, 1898," early draft, Brown University Archives.

20. Wilfred H. Munro (Brown University), Benjamin I. Wheeler (University of California representing Cornell University), James F. Kemp (Columbia University), Louis M. Dennis (Cornell University), Ira N. Hollis (Harvard University), George S. Patterson (University of Pennsylvania), and Henry B. Fine (Princeton University), "Report on Intercollegiate Sports," ca. April 1898, Brown University Archives.

21. Ibid.

22. Guy M. Lewis, "America's First Intercollegiate Sport," 642.

23. Charles W. Eliot, "Inaugural Address," October 19, 1869, Harvard University Archives.

24. As quoted in Harvard Athletic Committee Minutes, December 10, 1883, Harvard University Archives.

25. Santayana, "Philosophy on the Bleachers," 181–90.

26. "Conference on Intercollegiate Athletics, 1898," early draft, Brown University Archives.

27. For an essay on winning and excellence, see Smith, "Winning and a Theory of Competitive Athletics," 44–50.

28. See Kemp, "History of Faculty Control at Columbia," 39–40; Eliot, "President Eliot's Report," 452; and March, *Athletics at Lafayette College,* 152.

29. Hemenway, Bacon, and Roosevelt, "Important Suggestions in Athletics," 195–96; emphasis added.

Chapter 4. Presidents: Promoters or Reformers?

1. Ade, *The College Widow,* 36. The play was staged in New York City at the Tremont for at least thirty-eight weeks in 1904–5; see *Boston Globe,* August 27, 1905, p. 25, and *New York Times,* September 21, 1904, p. 9, for the opening performance at the Garden Theatre.

2. Canby, *Alma Mater,* 236.

3. Blanchard, *The H Book of Harvard Athletics, 1852–1922,* 166–72. The captain of the 1868 Harvard baseball team was James Ames, who would later become dean of the Harvard Law School and head of the Harvard Athletic Committee.

4. *New York Clipper,* September 4, 1869, p. 170; "The International Boat Race," 409; Blaikie, "The International Rowing-Match," 50; Mathews, "The First Harvard-Oxford Boat Race," 74–82.

5. Blanchard, *The H Book,* 170.

6. "From a Graduate's Window," 222.

7. Roosevelt, "The Law of Civilization and Decay," 371.

8. A number of studies have shown the call for manly sports in the latter years of the nineteenth century. Stearns, *Be a Man!* and Putney, *Muscular Christianity,* are two of the most helpful.

9. *Report of the President of Harvard College, 1887–1888,* 10; *Report of the President of Harvard College, 1892–1893,* 14–15; *Report of the President of Harvard College, 1901–1902,* 4; *Report of the President of Harvard College, 1904–1905,* 46, Harvard University Archives.

10. Veysey, "Letter to the Editor," 44.

11. Pritchett, "Progress of the State Universities," 108.

12. For presidents who lost their positions in the 1980s and 1990s for taking unpopular stands relative to big-time college athletics, see Oriard, *Bowled Over,* 278–79.

13. *New York Daily Tribune,* July 22, 1874, p. 8.

14. Dwight, "Intercollegiate Regattas, Hurdle-Races and Prize Contests," 256; "Diaries," Vol. 14, July 14, 1875, Andrew D. White Papers, Cornell University Archives.

15. Bishop, *A History of Cornell,* 142; Sargendorph, *Michigan: The Story of the University,* 150.

16. James Bryce, the insightful Englishman who wrote the classic *The American Commonwealth,* noted that the president of an American university is much more prominent than those of Oxford and Cambridge in England or universities in Scotland and Germany. He concluded that alumni elected to governing boards made the institutions responsive to the larger society; Bryce, *The American Commonwealth,* 48; see also Geiger, *To Advance Knowledge,* 16, 48, 54, 121.

17. As quoted in Guy M. Lewis's dissertation, "The American Intercollegiate Football Spectacle, 1869–1917," 84. For manliness and Christianity, see Patton, *Religion in College,* 6.

18. Chaffin, *Trinity College, 1839–1892,* 443–46.

19. Havighurst, *The Miami Years, 1809–1959,* 150.

20. As quoted in Lewis, "The American Intercollegiate Football Spectacle," 181.

21. Lester, *Stagg's University,* 2–19.

22. Stagg and Stout, *Touchdown!* 203.

23. Thwing, "A Game of Hearts," 1260–61; Thwing, "Football: Is the Game Worth Saving?" 1167–74.

24. As quoted in Whitney, "Is Football Worthwhile?" 25.

25. As quoted in Somers, *The Rise of Sports in New Orleans, 1850–1900,* 259, 261.

26. Slosson, *Great American Universities,* 309, 503–5.

27. President McCosh was shocked when an athlete told a Princeton professor that he had come to Princeton in the early 1880s to "play football, not to study"; Wertenbaker, *Princeton, 1746–1896,* 329.

28. Chase, "Play," 334.

29. Sumner, "John Franklin Crowell, Methodism, and the Football Controversy at Trinity College, 1887–1894," 5–20.

30. As quoted in Sears, "The Moral Threat of Intercollegiate Sports," 211.

31. Ibid., 216–22.

32. Ibid., 224–26.

33. Watterson, *College Football,* 48–49.

Chapter 5. Football, Progressive Reform, and the Creation of the NCAA

1. Henry M. MacCracken, telegram to Charles W. Eliot, 10:29 P.M., November 25, 1905, President Eliot Papers, Box 227, Folder "Henry M. MacCracken," Harvard University Archives. Harold Moore, star halfback with Union College, died of a cerebral hemorrhage after diving in to stop one of New York University's mass plays. Moore had a head injury from a previous game with Wesleyan, but it was thought to have healed. *New York Daily Tribune,* November 26, 1905, p. 1.

2. Charles W. Eliot, telegram to Henry M. MacCracken, November 26, 1905, in "Call for Conference," *New York Daily Tribune,* November 29, 1905, p. 2.

3. Morton and Phyllis Keller in *Making Harvard Modern,* 14, point out that President Eliot believed in educational laissez-faire, reflecting the Gilded Age, while the next president, A. Lawrence Lowell, was for planning and control, a Progressive Age ideal.

4. Needham, "The College Athlete," 115–28, 260–73; Tarbell, "John D. Rockefeller, A Character Study," 226–49; Steffens, "Ohio: A Tale of Two Cities," 293–311. Michael Oriard's *Reading Football: How the Popular Press Created an American Spectacle* explains the rise of college football through popular newspaper and periodical publications; see, for instance, Oriard, *Reading Football,* 169–75.

5. Endicott Peabody to Theodore Roosevelt, September 21, 1905, Theodore Roosevelt Collection, Letters Received, Vol. 97, Library of Congress, in Lewis, "The American Intercollegiate Football Spectacle, 1869–1917," 223–24; see also Theodore Roosevelt to Walter Camp, November 24, 1905, in Morison, *The Letters of Theodore Roosevelt,* vol. 5, 94.

6. Roosevelt, "The Functions of a Great University," vol. 16, 324–25.

7. Theodore Roosevelt to Henry Beech Needham, July 19, 1905, in Morison, *The Letters of Theodore Roosevelt*, vol. 5, 94.

8. Wiebe, *The Search for Order: 1877–1920,* 192.

9. Endicott Peabody to Theodore Roosevelt, September 16, 1905, as quoted in Lewis, "The American Intercollegiate Football Spectacle," 223.

10. Smith, *Big-Time Football at Harvard, 1905,* 193–95.

11. *New York Herald,* October 12, 1905, p. 1; emphasis added.

12. Quoting Karl F. Brill, newspaper clipping, Fall 1905, HUD 10905, Harvard University Archives.

13. Smith, *Big-Time Football at Harvard,* 265–66, 270–72.

14. Ibid., 266.

15. William Reid Jr., undated "Handwritten manuscript," Reid correspondence, HUD 8010, Harvard University Archives.

16. Paul J. Dashiell to Theodore Roosevelt, December 7, 1905, Charles W. Eliot Papers, Box 244, Folder "Theodore Roosevelt"; and William Reid Jr., "Handwritten manuscript," Reid Correspondence, HUD 8010, Harvard University Archives.

17. *New York Daily Tribune,* December 29, 1905, p. 2.

18. *Boston Globe,* November 29, 1905, p. 8.

19. For a more complete account of the Columbia banning, see Smith, "Harvard and Columbia and a Reconsideration of the 1905–06 Football Crisis," 5–19.

20. *New York Times,* December 7, 1905, p. 7.

21. *Columbia Spectator,* December 11, 1905, p. 1. Fordham, Haverford, Lafayette, Rutgers, Swarthmore, and Syracuse joined West Point and Wesleyan in the vote.

22. Other members of the New Rules Committee were E. K. Hall (Dartmouth), Charley Daly (West Point), James Babbitt (Haverford), C. W. Savage (Oberlin), James Lees (Nebraska), and F. H. Curtis (Texas). Charley Daly had played at Harvard with Bill Reid and was in his mid-twenties while coaching at West Point. *New York Times,* December 29, 1905, p. 7.

23. Ibid. Initially the conference was called the National Intercollegiate Football Conference, soon changed to the Intercollegiate Athletic Association of the United States, and in 1910 changed to the NCAA; see "National Intercollegiate Football Collegiate Conference," National College Conference, letter to American colleges, ca. January 1, 1906, Harvard University Archives.

24. *New York Times,* December 29 and 30, 1905, and *New York Sun,* December 29, 1905, in Columbia University Football Scrapbook, Columbiana Collection, Columbia University Archives; "National Intercollegiate Football Conference," National College Conference, letter to American Colleges, ca. January 1, 1906, Harvard University Archives.

25. W. T. Reid Jr. to Walter Camp, January 10, 1906, Walter Camp Papers, Box 20, Folder 272, Yale University Archives.

26. Arthur Hadley to Walter Camp, February 2, 1906, Walter Camp Papers, Box 49, Folder 1906, Yale University Archives; *New York Times,* January 13, 1906, p. 7.

27. *Boston Herald,* October 17, 1926, sec. E., p. 7. Only after two decades did Reid give this account. It appears to be an accurate account.

28. Wm. T. Reid ms., sent to H. E. von Kersburg, ca. August 1948, in William Reid Papers,

Correspondence Folder, 17–18, HUD 8010, Harvard University Archives; Records of Overseers, January 10, 1906, Harvard University Archives; *New York Times,* January 16, 1906, p. 8.

29. Deming, "Money Power in College Athletics," 569–72; Yale Faculty Records, January 13 and 20, 1906, Yale University Archives.

30. *New York Times,* February 25, 1906, p. 11; Davis, *Football the American Intercollegiate Game,* 495–97; Bill Reid, "A Discussion of the New Football Rules," ms., p. 13, William Reid Papers, General Folder, HUD 8010, Harvard University Archives.

Chapter 6. The NCAA: A Faculty Debating Society for Amateurism

1. Intercollegiate Athletic Association of the United States [NCAA] *Proceedings,* December 29, 1906, 4–6. Only thirty-nine institutions were members of the NCAA at the time of the first annual conference, while sixty-eight institutions had met the previous year to create the NCAA and move toward football reform rules.

2. As quoted in Link, *The Papers of Woodrow Wilson,* vol. 16, 370.

3. Intercollegiate Athletic Association of the United States [NCAA] *Proceedings,* December 28, 1908, 28. Possibly the first time the term *Home Rule* was used at an NCAA meeting was in 1909 when President Palmer Pierce stated: "Let me emphasize again the necessity of keeping in mind the fact that this is a home-rule organization, based on a belief in the honesty of purpose of one another"; Intercollegiate Athletic Association of the United States [NCAA] *Proceedings,* December 28, 1909, 34.

4. "Constitution and By-Laws," Intercollegiate Athletic Association of the United States [NCAA] *Proceedings,* December 29, 1906, 29, 33; emphasis added.

5. Ibid., 29–37.

6. Bryce, "America Revisited," 735.

7. Intercollegiate Athletic Association of the United States [NCAA] *Proceedings,* December 28, 1907, 25.

8. Intercollegiate Athletic Association of the United States [NCAA] *Proceedings,* December 29, 1906, 11.

9. Ibid., 29.

10. Ibid., 33.

11. Ibid., 34–35.

12. Intercollegiate Athletic Association of the United States [NCAA] *Proceedings,* December 19, 1906, passim; Intercollegiate Athletic Association of the United States [NCAA] *Proceedings,* December 28, 1907, passim.

13. Intercollegiate Athletic Association of the United States [NCAA] *Proceedings,* December 29, 1906, 16.

14. The most complete account of summer baseball is McQuilkin, "Summer Baseball and the NCAA," 18–42.

15. Smith, "The Rise of College Baseball," 33.

16. As quoted in a newspaper clipping ca. November 1889, Moses Taylor Pyne Scrapbook, Vol. 8, p. 74, Princeton University Archives.

17. T. S. Woolsey to Walter Camp, December 23, 1901, Walter Camp Papers, Box 22, Folder "Cutts," and H. W. Raymond to Walter Camp, June 12, 1901, Walter Camp Papers, Box 20 Folder 569, Yale University Archives. Caspar Whitney, a promoter of amateurism, claimed

that Clarkson had pitched for a White Mountain hotel team; Whitney, "The Sportsman's View-Point," *Outing* 38 (June 1901): 339.

18. Phillip R. Allen, East Walpole, MA, to Walter Camp, April 30, May 14, and May 21, 1903, Walter Camp Papers, Box 1, Folder 17, Yale University Archives.

19. H. S. White, Harvard Athletic Committee, to Dr. Nichols, baseball advisor, June 11, 1904, Harvard Athletic Committee Minutes, June 13, 1904, Harvard University Archives; "Clarkson a Professional," 2.

20. Whitney, *A Sporting Pilgrimage,* 278; quote in *The* [Brown University] *Brunonian,* October 9, 1897, p. 85.

21. *The Brunonian,* October 9, 1897, p. 86.

22. Intercollegiate Athletic Association of the United States [NCAA] *Proceedings,* December 28, 1907, 23.

23. Hetherington, "Organization and Administration of Athletics," 330–40.

24. Intercollegiate Athletic Association of the United States [NCAA] *Proceedings,* December 28, 1907, 23.

25. See Lester, *Stagg's University,* 20, 28–31, 51–64. There were those who believed Stagg was doing the "heavy pious" at Chicago while at the same time he was recruiting mediocre students but fine athletes to his institution, pleading with professors to retain athletes who were failing students, supporting special makeup exams to maintain eligibility, supplying tutors for football players, providing training tables and athletic dorms, and creating transcontinental bowl games.

26. *New York Daily Tribune,* June 22, 1908, p. 1.

27. Intercollegiate Athletic Association of the United States [NCAA] *Proceedings,* 1908, 55.

28. Intercollegiate Athletic Association of the United States [NCAA] *Proceedings,* December 28, 1911, 20.

29. McQuilkin, "Summer Baseball," 39n36. The vote was 272–65 at Amherst, 119–67 at Wesleyan, and 237–37 at Williams.

30. Possibly the best account of the origin of British amateurism is David C. Young, "The Modern Origins of Amateurism," in his *The Olympic Myth of Greek Amateur Athletics,* 15–27. Historians are in agreement that the ancient Greeks did not have amateur sports and that the concept of Greek amateurism was foisted on the world's psyche by the upper-class British in the nineteenth century for their own social class purposes.

31. Dubeck, "A French View of American Sport," 655.

32. For understanding amateurism as an unworkable concept in American college sport, see Ronald A. Smith, "Amateur College Sport: An Untenable Concept in a Free and Open Society," in his *Sports and Freedom,* 165–74.

33. March, *Athletics at Lafayette College,* 146.

34. "Partial List of Local Leagues," December 15, 1913, President Lowell Papers, 1909–1914, Folder 83, Harvard University Archives; Ruth, "A Study of Selected Conferences in the United States"; Pierce, "History of the Southern Conference"; Kiracofe, "Athletics and Physical Education in the Colleges of Virginia"; Corrie, "A History of the Atlantic Coast Conference"; Fleischer, "A History of the Eastern Collegiate Athletic Conference"; Dougherty, *Educators and Athletes;* Lewis, "Enterprise on the Campus"; "List of College Athletic Conferences,"

Answers.com, http://www.answers.com/topic/list-of-college-athletic-conferences (accessed November 27, 2006).

35. National Collegiate Athletic Association *Proceedings,* December 28, 1916, 13, 44.

36. Ibid., 55.

Chapter 7. The 1920s and the Carnegie Report on College Athletics

1. Three particular histories cover the development of the Carnegie Report on *American College Athletics:* Schmidt, *Shaping College Football,* 217–33; Thelin, *Games Colleges Play,* 13–37; and Watterson, *College Football,* 158–76. I have looked carefully at the Carnegie Report and have a different interpretation than Thelin and Watterson, believing that the entire project included unbalanced research and bias from the beginning. This, in some ways, was similar to the bias of Walter Camp and his attempt to justify football when he led a study to determine the degree of brutality in the game at the time of the flying wedge in 1894. Camp's book *Football Facts and Figures* resulted in rationalizing football for its "marked benefit" both physically and mentally. Camp's bias for football and athletics and the Carnegie Report's condemnation of commercialism and professionalism in college sport reveal an unbalanced and unscientific effort to justify what each wanted to achieve. For one account of *Football Facts and Figures,* see Smith, *Sports and Freedom,* 91–95.

2. Palmer Pierce to NCAA Members, May 25, 1917, President Wilbur Papers, Box 3, Folder 2, Stanford University Archives; Pierce, "The Problem of Athletics in Colleges and Schools under Present War Conditions," 447–49.

3. Frank W. Nicolson to President Ray Lyman Wilbur, Stanford, February 21, 1918, President Wilbur Papers, Box 19, Folder 3, Stanford University Archives.

4. Fred W. Moore to Dean L. B. R. Briggs, Harvard Athletic Committee Chair, November 20, 1918, Committee on the Regulation of Athletic Sports, Folder "Misc. Correspondence," Harvard University Archives.

5. As quoted by Frank W. Nicolson, Wesleyan; James R. Angell, Chicago; and Thomas A. Storey, CCNY, to President Ray Lyman Wilbur, Stanford, May 1, 1919, President Wilbur Papers, Box 27, Folder 4, Stanford University Archives.

6. NCAA *Proceedings,* December 29, 1920, 91.

7. Ibid., 40–41.

8. NCAA *Proceedings,* December 28, 1916, 53. The definition was taken from the Athletic Research Society, a group of individuals, mostly physical educators, more interested in Muscular Morality than in scientific research relative to physical activity; see Brown, "Report of the Committee on Definition of an Amateur," 301–8. For a study of Muscular Morality of physical educators, see Smith, "A Historical Look at Enhancement of Performance in Sport," 2–11.

9. NCAA *Proceedings,* December 28, 1922, 65–66. These principles have been called the "10-Point Code," but the tenth point was to convince colleges of the NCAA to accept the first nine; see Falla, *NCAA: The Voice of College Sports,* 128–29; Crowley, *In the Arena,* 44.

10. NCAA *Proceedings,* December 29, 1921, 51–52; *New York Times,* June 19, 1921, p. 89.

11. The first two decades of NCAA sponsorship of tournaments were track and field (1921), swimming (1924), wrestling (1928), boxing (1937), gymnastics (1938), tennis (1938), cross-country (1938), and basketball (1939); Lewis, "Enterprise on the Campus," 65.

12. Smith, "Commercialized Intercollegiate Athletics and the 1903 Harvard Stadium," 26–48.

13. Needham, "The College Athlete," 268.

14. The universities of California, Illinois, Indiana, Minnesota, Nebraska, and Washington all had memorial stadiums built in the 1920s.

15. "Agreement between Stanford and California, 31 December 1920," SC 506, Box 1, Folder 2, Stanford University Special Collections.

16. "Stanford Stadium," paper presented to San Francisco Section, American Social Civil Engineers, April 18, 1922, by Baker and Carpenter, SC 31, Cutler Papers, File # 14, Stanford University Special Collections.

17. *New York Times,* November 19, 1933, p. SM9.

18. Frank Angel to President Ray Lyman Wilbur, December 19, 1918, SC 506, Box 1, Folder 3, Stanford University Special Collections.

19. *New York Clipper,* August 6, 1864, p. 130; *New York Times,* July 30, 1864, p. 3.

20. Needham, "The College Athlete," 118; Harvard Athletic Committee Minutes, February 17, 1905, Harvard University Archives; "Athletics," *Harvard Graduates' Magazine,* 682.

21. John Heisman Contract, Athletic Association Collection, 1903–1974, Box 3, Folder "Heisman Contracts," Georgia Tech Archives; Pope, *Football's Greatest Coaches,* 119, 128.

22. Behee, "College Football's Oldest Rivalry," 88.

23. Chairman of the Faculty Board of Control of Athletics to Knute Rockne, March 7, 1925, Vice President M. A. Mulcaire Records, UVMU, Box 2, Folder "Rockne," University of Notre Dame Archives.

24. Sperber, *Shake Down the Thunder,* 203. Other estimates found in the presidential files at Notre Dame include $20,000 for three years and $15,000, $17,500, and $20,000 over three years; President Matthew Walsh General Correspondence, UPWL, Box 53, Folder "Rockne-Columbia," University of Notre Dame Archives. What is most likely is that Rockne signed a three-year contract for $17,500 per year with an additional $7,500 to be subscribed by a chemical company; see *New York Times,* December 14, 1925, p. 7.

25. *New York Times,* December 14, 1925, p. 7.

26. President Ray Lyman Wilbur to Glenn Warner, January 26, 1922; Warner to Wilbur, December 30, 1921, Box 51, Folder 13; and Wilbur to William Peterson, Logan, Utah, January 10, 1922, Box 57, Folder 9, Stanford University Special Collections. Salaries at Stanford ranged from $1,800 for instructors to $7,500 for full professors.

27. Dean L. B. R. Briggs, Harvard, to President A. Lawrence Lowell, July 22, 1922, A. L. Lowell Papers, 1919–22, Folder 96, Harvard University Archives; Amos Alonzo Stagg, Chicago, to H. O. Crisler, Earlville, IL, July 26, 1921, A. A. Stagg Papers, Box 77, Folder 8, University of Chicago Archives. At Harvard in 1922, President Lowell's salary was $8,000 with an additional $3,560 in other funds. The Law School's Roscoe Pound received $10,500 and Felix Frankfurter $7,500, while historian Frederick Jackson Turner was at $8,000; Harvard Corporation Minutes, September 25, 1922, Harvard University Archives.

28. "Report to the President and Fellows of Harvard University by the Committee on the Regulation of Athletic Sports, Statement of Policy," October 10, 1925, President Lowell Papers, Folder 72, Harvard University Archives.

29. Harvard Athletic Committee Minutes, October 25, 1920, and January 7, 1925; Henry

Pennypacker, Athletic Committee, to A. L. Lowell, January 9, 1925, President Lowell Papers, 1922–25, Folder 6B; "Agreements between Harvard, Yale, and Princeton in Force 1925," Lowell Papers, Folder 72, Harvard University Archives.

30. Makin, "Science or Athletics?" 527.

31. Fauver, "The Place of Intercollegiate Athletics in Physical Education Programs," 4.

32. Savage, *Fruit of an Impulse,* 155–56; Thelin, *Games Colleges Play,* 22.

33. Bascom, "Athletics," 13. Harvard's President Charles Eliot agreed, stating in 1888 that athletic training requires "many months of monotonous and stupid labor of the treadmill sort"; *Report of the President of Harvard College, 1888–1889,* 12. That college athletics is work, not enjoyable play, is a theme that has existed for a century and a half, far different than the attitude found in that period of intercollegiate athletics at Oxford and Cambridge.

34. Carroll, *Red Grange and the Rise of Modern Football,* 77–96.

35. Ibid., 99.

36. Ibid., 97–106. Carroll devotes a chapter, "The Great Debate," to the opposition to Grange turning to pro football and dropping out of the University of Illinois.

37. *New York Times,* December 6, 1925, pp. S2, S6.

38. NCAA *Proceedings* (December 29, 1921), 89; *New York Times,* December 28, 1921, p. 13.

39. NCAA *Proceedings* (December 30, 1925), 12.

40. *New York Times,* March 30, 1925, p. 6. The annual Carnegie Foundation Report had just been released.

41. *New York Times,* May 24, 1926, p. 10. Pritchett had condemned professional-commercial college athletics at a Lehigh graduation ceremony in June 1925.

42. Savage et al., *American College Athletics,* xxi.

43. Ibid., 102, 213.

44. Ibid., 183–84.

45. Ibid., 172–74.

46. It is not likely that these schools were "clean" relative to subsidization. For instance, Grange was given preferential treatment by his fraternity house while at Illinois, and Amos Alonzo Stagg obtained jobs for special athletes at the University of Chicago; Carroll, *Red Grange,* 51–53; Lester, *Stagg's University,* 109–12. Yale had been recruiting and subsidizing athletes since the 1800s, and the U.S. Military Academy paid everyone to attend, including its recruited athletes, a number of whom had already played at other colleges.

47. Savage et al., *American College Athletics,* 240–65.

48. Ibid., 265.

Chapter 8. Individual Presidential Reform: Gates, Hutchins, and Bowman

1. Behee, *Fielding Yost's Legacy,* 107–9; *New York Times,* January 24, 1930, p. 34.

2. *New York Times,* October 24, 1929, p. 2; *New York Times,* January 14, 1931, p. 19.

3. Raymond Schmidt, *Shaping College Football,* 229.

4. Executive Board of Pennsylvania Board of Trustees Minutes, May 28, 1928, University of Pennsylvania Archives.

5. *New York Times,* December 11, 1930, p. 30; *New York Times,* December 21, 1930, p. 136.

6. *New York Times,* November 8, 1930, p. 6.

7. *New York Times,* January 6, 1931, p. 34.

8. "A Statement by Thomas S. Gates, President of the University of Pennsylvania, 3 February 1931"; Gates, Statement to the Press, February 3, 1931, Papers of the Office of the President, 1950–55, Box 53, Folder "Intercollegiate Athletic Policy," University of Pennsylvania Archives; *New York Times,* February 3, 1931, p. 1; *New York Times,* February 4, 1931, p. 6; *New York Times,* February 15, 1931, p. 79.

9. *New York Times,* February 15, 1931, p. 79.

10. "A Statement by Thomas S. Gates, 3 February 1931," Papers of the Office of the President, 1950–55, Box 53, Folder "Intercollegiate Athletic Policy," University of Pennsylvania Archives.

11. *New York Times,* February 6, 1931, p. 28.

12. Hawkins, *Banding Together,* 16–20.

13. President Robert G. Sproul, California, to Dean Thomas M. Putham, California, February 23, 1932, Presidents Correspondence and Papers, 1932, Folder 435, University of California Archives; *New York Times,* January 22, 1932, p. 22.

14. For example, in 1895 the Harvard faculty voted to ban football, but the Harvard Athletic Committee voted to continue the game. The conflict went to the Harvard Corporation, which sided with the Athletic Committee, and football continued. During the 1905–6 football crisis, the Harvard faculty voted to ban football, but the Harvard Corporation voted to continue the game; "Report to the Overseers, Presidents and Fellows," March 25, 1895, Series II, U.A. II, 10.7.1, Harvard University Archives; "Report of the Joint Committee on the Regulation of Athletic Sports," 648. Dartmouth College faculty petitioned the Trustees to return the control of athletics to the faculty and away from the alumni in 1905. The Trustees sided with the Alumni Committee on Athletics, not surprisingly because President William Tucker had been an original member of the Alumni Committee on Athletics; Dartmouth College Records of the Trustees, September 30, 1905, June 25, 1906; "Memorandum," ca. spring 1906, President Tucker Papers, # 1, "Athletics, A–H," Dartmouth College Archives.

15. *New York Times,* January 19, 1934, p. 26.

16. *New York Times,* January 18, 1936, p. 17.

17. Ibid.

18. Hutchins, "Gate Receipts and Glory," 23, 73.

19. Lester, *Stagg's University,* 184–86.

20. Harold H. Swift to President Harry Pratt Judson, March 18, 1922, Harold Swift Papers, Box 113, Folder 12, University of Chicago Archives.

21. As quoted in Lester, *Stagg's University,* 183. Lester's history of football at Chicago is probably the best institutional sport history written. His discussion of the decline and fall of football at Chicago, pp. 125–86, is superb.

22. As quoted in Lester, *Stagg's University,* 189.

23. Levine, *The American College and the Culture of Aspiration, 1915–1940,* 113–23.

24. Alberts, *Pitt,* 79, 129. Bowman cut his own salary during the Great Depression to $31,500. Sinclair's comments are found in Wallace, "Test Case at Pitt," 47.

25. Wallace, "Test Case at Pitt," 51.

26. Alberts, *Pitt,* 161–62.

27. Foley, "The Elimination of Athletic Subsidies at the University of Pittsburgh, 1936–39."

28. Dr. N. C. Ochenschirt to Chancellor Bowman, November 17, 1938, as quoted in Foley, "The Elimination of Athletic Subsidies at the University of Pittsburgh, 1936–39."

29. *New York Times,* December 29, 1938, p. 22.

30. *New York Times,* March 6, 1939, p. 19; *New York Times,* March 7, 1939, p. 29; *New York Times,* March 11, 1939, p. 4.

31. "Education: Boot for Bowman," *Time Magazine,* October 2, 1939, http://www.time.com/time/magazine/article/0,9171,789020,00.html (accessed February 13, 2008).

32. Alberts, *Pitt,* 170–78.

33. Ibid., 179.

34. Ibid., 168.

Chapter 9. Presidential Conference Reform: The 1930s Graham Plan Failure

1. Ashby, *Frank Porter Graham,* 5–93. While president, Graham backed a socialist professor of English to preserve academic freedom, backed a Jew's admittance to the Medical School, worked to prevent a Japanese student from being deported, supported social security and unemployment compensation, was honorary president of the leftist Southern Conference that backed integration, and bailed out a jailed textile strike worker.

2. Flexner had offered a position to Hutchins in 1927 to study European higher education as well as universities in America, however Hutchins decided to continue in the Yale Law School. Flexner decided to do the study himself, which resulted in the book on higher education three years later; see Dzuback, *Robert M. Hutchins,* 66.

3. Flexner, *Universities.*

4. Flexner, *Abraham Flexner,* 232–35.

5. Flexner, *Universities,* 69, 190.

6. Ashby, *Frank Porter Graham,* 131–32.

7. Hawkins, *Banding Together,* 35–36.

8. Frank Porter Graham to President W. P. Few, Duke University, November 25, 1935, Frank P. Graham Files, 1/1/4, Box 3, Folder "November 1935," University of North Carolina Archives.

9. Lumpkin, "The Graham Plan," 4.

10. Greensboro newspaper clipping, December 12, 1935, W. P. Few Papers, Subject Files, "Southern Conference," Duke University Archives.

11. K. P. Lewis to Frank P. Graham, December 14, 1935, President Graham Files, 1/1/4, Folder "December 1935," University of North Carolina Archives.

12. J. F. Patterson, New Bern, NC, to Frank P. Graham, December 17, 1935, Frank P. Graham Files, 1/1/4, Box 3, Folder "December 1935," University of North Carolina Archives.

13. Frank P. Graham to Howard J. Savage, December 21, 1935; Graham to Jonathan Daniels, *Raleigh News and Observer,* December 30, 1935, President Graham Files, 1/1/4, Box 3, Folder "December 1935"; and Savage to Graham, January 2, 1936, President Graham Files, 1/1/4, Box 3, Folder "January 1936," University of North Carolina Archives.

14. Frank P. Graham to Norton Prichett, Virginia Athletic Director, December 27, 1935,

President Graham Files, 1/1/4, Box 3, Folder "December 1935," University of North Carolina Archives.

15. Frank W. Nicolson to Frank P. Graham, October 28, 1935, Frank P. Graham Files, 1/1/4, Box 3, Folder "November 1935," University of North Carolina Archives.

16. W. P. Few to President J. L. Newcomb and all Southern Conference presidents, January 6, 1936, President Graham Files, 1/1/4, Box 3, Folder "January 1936," University of North Carolina Archives.

17. Stone, "The Graham Plan of 1935," 278.

18. *New York Times,* December 14, 1935, p. 20. Vanderbilt University was the only SEC member to vote against financial aid to athletes.

19. Frank P. Graham to W. P. Grier, Gastonia City Schools Superintendent, December 11, 1933; W. T. Whitsett to Frank P. Graham, December 11, 1933, President Graham Files, 2/2/3, Box 20, Folder "Football: Coach Collins Controversy, 1933–34," University of North Carolina Archives.

20. Frank P. Graham to Dean A. W. Hobbs, Athletic Committee Chair, February 1, 1935, President Graham Files, 2/2/6, Folder "Athletic Committee 1935," University of North Carolina Archives.

21. Frank P. Graham to James R. Angell, January 21, 1936, President Graham Files, 1/1/4, Box 3, Folder "January 1936," University of North Carolina Archives.

22. "Resolution of the High Point Chapter of the Alumni Association of the University of North Carolina," January 31, 1936; "University of North Carolina Alumni of New Hanover County, Wilmington, NC," January 28, 1936; "Montgomery County Alumni Association of UNC Resolution," January 28, 1936, President Graham Files, 1/1/4, Box 3, Folder "January 1936," University of North Carolina Archives.

23. Josephus Daniels to Frank P. Graham, February 7, 1935, President Graham Files, 1/1/4, Box 3, Folder "February 1936," University of North Carolina Archives.

24. James R. Angell to Frank P. Graham, January 21, 1936; January 29, 1936, President Graham Files, 1/1/4, Box 3, Folder "January 1936," University of North Carolina Archives.

25. H. G. Connor Jr. to Frank P. Graham, February 3, 1936, President Graham Files, 1/1/4, Box 3, Folder "February 1936," University of North Carolina Archives.

26. Charles W. Tillett Jr. to R. B. House, Dean of Admissions, President Graham Files, 1/1/4, Box 3, Folder "January 1936," University of North Carolina Archives.

27. John M. Booker to Frank P. Graham, January 29, 1936, President Graham Files, 1/1/4, Box 3, Folder "January 1936," University of North Carolina Archives.

28. The successful Carolina football coach, Carl Snavely, resigned in the spring of 1936 to take a position at Cornell University, where he coached three Ivy League champion teams, before returning to the Carolina Tar Heels in 1945 to coach for eight seasons and participate in the Sugar and Cotton Bowls; Porter, *Biographical Dictionary of American Sports: Football,* 558–59.

29. President J. L. Newcomb, Virginia, telegram to Forest Fletcher, November 10, 1936, President Newcomb Papers, II, Box 5, Folder "Athletics," University of Virginia Archives; "Memo, Office of the President, undated, ca. December 1936," President Newcomb Papers, II, Box 4, Folder "Athletics," University of Virginia Archives; *New York Times,* November

26, 1936, p. 41; *New York Times,* December 12, 1936, p. 22; *New York Times,* December 15, 1936, p. 33; Ashby, *Frank Porter Graham,* 134–36. Virginia withdrew from the conference to become an independent, and it remained so until it joined the Atlantic Coast Conference soon after it was formed in 1953.

30. Stone, "The Graham Plan," 280.

31. Ibid., 290.

32. Frank P. Graham to Prof. Guy A. Cardwell, Tulane University, November 25, 1940, President Graham Files, 2/2/3, Box 120, Folder "General 1939–47," University of North Carolina Archives; Ashby, *Frank Porter Graham,* 136.

33. Frank P. Graham to Dr. W. R. Stanford, Durham, NC, February 15, 1937, President Graham Files, 1/1/4, Box 3, Folder "February 1937," University of North Carolina Archives.

Chapter 10. The NCAA and the Sanity Code: A National Reform Gone Wrong

1. Woodrow Wilson to President A. Lawrence Lowell, Harvard, December 6, 1909, President Lowell Papers, 1901–14, Folder 88, Harvard University Archives. During the second football crisis, 1909–10, following the crisis of 1905–6, Woodrow Wilson said, "The presidents of Harvard, Yale, and Princeton could, if they were to agree upon a principle of action and insist upon it, very largely and perhaps completely control the methods of the game of football."

2. As quoted by the president of the American Football Coaches Association, Harvey J. Harman, at the January 1949 NCAA convention; NCAA *Proceedings,* January 7, 1949, 99.

3. NCAA *Proceedings,* December 27, 1934, 107.

4. Ibid., 77, 78, 115.

5. Ibid., 70–71; for a long discussion on recruiting and subsidizing, see 101–16.

6. NCAA *Proceedings,* December 28, 1939, 34–35.

7. NCAA *Proceedings,* December 30, 1939, 103.

8. Ibid., 104.

9. Ibid., "President's Address," 101.

10. NCAA *Proceedings,* December 28, 1939, 38.

11. Ibid., 119.

12. C. L. Eckel, Chair, Senate Committee on Athletics, to President Robert L. Stearns, University of Colorado, President's Office, Series I, Box 29, Folder "Athletics 1927–53," University of Colorado at Boulder Archives.

13. NCAA *Proceedings,* December 31, 1940, 151.

14. Ibid., 28, 128–30.

15. NCAA *Proceedings,* December 31, 1941, 142–45.

16. NCAA *Proceedings,* January 5, 1944, 22, 38, 46. The V-5 programs were naval flight preparatory schools, and the V-12 programs included general naval training of officers. Many college athletic programs were strongly influenced by the athletes in these two programs. For a summary of the impact of the war on college athletics, see a discussion by Ralph Furey of Columbia University on "Intercollegiate Eligibility Provisions" in NCAA *Proceedings,* January 7, 1947, 121–25.

17. Walter Camp proposed barring every first-year man from sport participation in 1893 in an effort to reduce the intense recruiting of subfreshmen; see Camp, "Undergraduate

Limitation in College Sports," 143. For a lengthy history of eligibility rules, including the freshman rule, see Smith and Helman, "A History of Eligibility Rules among Big-Time Athletic Institutions."

18. NCAA *Proceedings,* December 30, 1941, 136–41; NCAA *Proceedings,* December 30, 1942, 63, 74, 76, 77, 78, 80.

19. NCAA *Proceedings,* January 5, 1944, 47 (the 1941 results were published); NCAA *Proceedings,* January 9, 1946, 76.

20. NCAA *Proceedings,* January 5, 1944, 24, 35.

21. NCAA *Proceedings,* January 12, 1945, 142–43.

22. Ibid., 145–48, 154–56. The GI Bill provided $50 per month up to $450 per year and $75 per month for those who were married. From 1944 to 1951, 2.3 million veterans attended college on the GI Bill; see Schugurensky, "History of Education."

23. NCAA *Proceedings,* January 12, 1945, 28, 36.

24. NCAA *Proceedings,* January 9, 1946, 70.

25. Ibid., 65. The committee members were H. C. Willett, University of Southern California, chair; E. Leroy Mercer, University of Pennsylvania; Robert Fetzer, University of North Carolina; Z. G. Clevenger, Indiana University; and Harry Carlson, University of Pittsburgh.

26. *New York Times,* July 24, 1946, p. 31; *New York Times,* July 25, 1946, p. 28.

27. NCAA *Proceedings,* January 8, 1947, 77–87. The vote was 76–33.

28. *New York Times,* January 9, 1947, p. 30.

29. *New York Times,* January 21, 1947, p. 19.

30. Karl E. Leib, who evidently coined the term *Sanity Code,* used the term as early as November 1947; see Leib to NCAA members, November 19, 1947, President Wilbur Papers, Box 135, Folder "Athletics-General," Stanford University Archives. Tug Wilson, commissioner of the Big Ten, credited Leib with the term *Sanity Code* as a substitute for Purity Code, which he said was used by some as an "epitaph" for the reform effort.

31. *New York Times,* April 19, 1947, p. 19.

32. *New York Times,* August 11, 1947, p. 12; Fred C. Frey, LSU, to Rufus C. Harris, August 4, 1947; H. L. Donavan, Kentucky, to Rufus C. Harris, August 18, 1947; C. M. Sarratt, Vanderbilt, to Rufus C. Harris, August 6, 1947; Ralph E. Adams, Alabama, to Rufus C. Harris, July 31, 1947, President Rufus C. Harris Papers, Box 1, Folder "NCAA 1937–50," Tulane University Archives.

33. "College 'Purity Code' in Athletics Certain to Fail, Experts Believe," *New York Times,* December 19, 1947, p. 36.

34. Karl E. Leib to NCAA members, November 19, 1947, President Wilbur Papers, Box 135, Folder "Athletics-General," Stanford University Archives.

35. NCAA *Proceedings,* January 9, 1948, 94–95.

36. Hawkins, *Banding Together,* 20–24, 62–67.

37. "Dr. George Zook," NCAA *Proceedings,* January 9, 1948, 98–109.

38. NCAA *Proceedings,* January 10, 1948, 188–189; emphasis added. Andrew Zimbalist argues in *Unpaid Professionals,* 10, that the Sanity Code was not an effort to hold back commercialism and professionalism, but rather was "an insidious conspiracy to reduce costs and enlarge profits." Historically, there is no evidence for Zimbalist's statement, though in retrospect it and later legislation held back payment to athletes to very limited financial

benefits while money to coaches and athletic administrators soared. In opposition to Zimbalist's conclusions, many of those who opposed the Sanity Code wanted to make increased payments to athletes, including room and board. The Sanity Code was created to bring about a level playing field, attempting to eliminate illegal benefits to athletes, not as a conspiracy to reduce costs and enlarge profits. The Sanity Code promoters were reformers for amateur sport, not promoters of commercialism and professionalism. Nevertheless, by accepting limited financial aid to athletes in the Sanity Code, doors were opened officially to allow legal athletic scholarships and the professional spirit to expand. In other ways, Zimbalist's volume is a well-documented condemnation of big-time intercollegiate athletics. Allen Sack and Ellen Staurowsky in *College Athletes for Hire*, 40–46, call the Sanity Code the beginning of NCAA-sponsored professionalism. While there is some truth to that, the intent was to put controls on subsidization to create a more level playing field on a national basis.

39. "Recommended NCAA Football Television Plan for 1968 and 1969," Walter Byers Papers, Vol. 48, Folder "TV: General 8/67–9/67," NCAA Headquarters, Indianapolis, IN.

40. The most scholarly account of the myth of Greek amateurism and of elitism of British amateurism is Young, *The Olympic Myth of Greek Amateur Athletics*.

41. For one approach to the failure of amateurism in college sport, see Ronald A. Smith, "Amateur Sport: An Untenable Concept in a Free and Open Society," in his *Sports and Freedom*, 165–74.

42. The application of the Federal Admission Tax of 1932 to college athletics was challenged by the NCAA several times; see, for instance, NCAA *Proceedings*, July 29, 1932, 18–32; NCAA *Proceedings*, December 27, 1934, 68–69. Tax-exempt bonds to build arenas and stadiums were also benefactors for college athletics; see Zimbalist, *Unpaid Professionals*, 127. The Revenue Act of 1950 allowed a tax on unrelated business income of tax-exempt organizations. Obviously, gate receipts and income from telecasts of college sports could come under this law if athletics were not an *integral* part of education. As late as 1974, a memo at the NCAA headquarters stated that a purpose of amateurism in higher education is "to maintain intercollegiate athletics as an *integral* part of the educational program and the athlete as an *integral* part of the student body"; "Internal Revenue Service National Office Technical Advice Memorandum Regarding Tax Payer NCAA," File at NCAA, April 11, 1974, Walter Byers Papers, Vol. 109, Folder "Legal: 1/77–6/77," NCAA Headquarters, Indianapolis, IN; emphasis added. NCAA legal advice for the "integral" argument in 1977 noted: "The tax-exempt purpose of a university is the education of students. That purpose is carried out both through the academic curriculum and through athletic activities provided for the students"; "Memo Draft from John Bates, Cox, Langford & Brown, 5 August 1977," Walter Byers Papers, Vol. 119, Folder: "Legal: 1/77–6/77," NCAA Headquarters, Indianapolis, IN.

43. NCAA *Proceedings*, January 9, 1948, 115.

44. The College All-Stars beat the NFL champions in 1937, 1938, 1943, 1946, and 1947. After 1958, the NFL dominated play, losing only in 1963, until 1976, when the last game was played. The all-time record was nine wins, thirty-one losses, and two ties; Schmidt, *Football's Stars of Summer* 277–78.

45. *New York Times*, April 10, 1948, p. 19.

46. President Blake R. Van Leer, Georgia Tech, to Presidents of the Southern, Southeastern, and Southwest Conferences, January 25, 1949, Records of the Office of the President,

1949–66, Box 16, Folder "NCAA Regional Conference, May 28, 1949," Georgia Tech Archives; "Joint Meeting of the Southern, Southeastern, and Southwest Conferences," May 28, 1949, Unprocessed Athletic Department Papers, Folder "Correspondence—President SEC," University of Alabama Archives.

47. University of Virginia Board of Visitors Minutes, July 21, 1949, University of Virginia Archives; *New York Times,* May 29, 1949, sec. 5, p. 6; *New York Times,* June 10, 1949, p. 39; *New York Times,* July 7, 1949, p. 32; *New York Times,* December 25, 1949, pp. S1, S5. The $5,000 was the same amount the NCAA TV committee was given to carry out a study of the effect of TV on football attendance, a study that eventually led to the NCAA voting to control telecasting of college football and the first effective enforcement of any NCAA regulation in its history in 1951.

48. University of Virginia Board of Visitors Minutes, July 9, 1948, Oct 14, 1949, and December 2, 1949, University of Virginia Archives. The Virginia Board of Visitors in a 1948 unanimous vote offered athletic scholarships through the Alumni Association in opposition to the NCAA Sanity Code.

49. *New York Herald Tribune,* June 15, 1950, clipping in the N. W. Dougherty Collection, Box 20, Folder 3, University of Tennessee Archives; *New York Times,* January 15, 1950, sec. 5, pp. 1, 3; NCAA *Proceedings,* January 14, 1950, 207. The reformers were upset but undaunted. The new NCAA president, Hugh Willett of the University of Southern California, and Tug Wilson, NCAA secretary-treasurer, sent a memorandum to all NCAA members saying the seven violators of the NCAA were "not in good standing" and therefore could not participate in NCAA tournaments or be scheduled athletically by members in good standing. President Harry C. "Curly" Byrd of the University of Maryland, who fought the expulsion of the seven institutions probably more than any other, claimed that the president and secretary-treasurer had no authority to indicate what NCAA policy would be, for that belonged to the NCAA Council, the Executive Committee, and the Compliance Committee. The Virginia athletic director, Norton Pritchett, called the action "undemocratic." And of course it was; see N. W. Dougherty, NCAA Executive Committee, to Hugh C. Willett, January 24, 1950, N. W. Dougherty Collection, Box 20, Folder 3, University of Tennessee Archives; *New York Times,* January 18, 1950, p. 37. Soon, the Virginia governing board set athletic scholarship limits to room, board, tuition, and fees, something similar to limits imposed by many other institutions that had been breaking the Sanity Code; University of Virginia Board of Visitors Minutes, February 10, 1950, University of Virginia Archives.

50. Byers, *Unsportsmanlike Conduct,* 68. Byers was executive director of the NCAA from 1951 to 1987.

51. Cohane, "Let's Take the Hypocrisy Out of College Football," 62.

52. *New York Times,* January 9, 1951, p. 32.

Chapter 11. Ivy League Presidential Reform

1. The tradition of planting ivy along college buildings had been started before the first intercollegiate contest, a crew meet between Harvard and Yale in 1852; see *Yale Literary Magazine,* 18 (November 1852): 56. Harvard first planted ivy around its new stadium, built in 1903, in 1906, when the Harvard Athletic Committee authorized the planting; Harvard Athletic Committee Minutes, November 13, 1906, Harvard University Archives. Mark Bern-

stein, author of a history of Ivy League football, attempted to find the origin of "Ivy League" and accepts the general belief that a sports writer of the *New York Herald Tribune,* Stanley Woodward, coined the term in 1933. The *New York Times* noted the "so-called Eastern 'Ivy League'" on December 6, 1935, p. 35. The *New York Times* headlined "Immediate Formation of Ivy League Advocated at Seven Eastern Colleges" on December 3, 1936, p. 22. Later, in 1937, another writer complained about having to report on a dull Penn-Columbia game and other similar games, watching the ivy grow every fall Saturday afternoon, but this complaint about "Ivy League" games came several years after the term was often used relative to a conference that did not exist, except in people's minds; see Bernstein, *Football: The Ivy League Origins of an American Obsession,* xi–xii.

2. *Harvard Crimson,* February 15, 1906, p. 1; Bellow, "The New Eligibility Rules," 694. These rules were evidently applied to the four major sports—football, baseball, crew, and track and field—but not to basketball and hockey and the lesser sports; see "Tentative Rules Agreed Upon by Harvard, Yale, and Princeton," ca. February 1906, Walter Camp Papers, Box 8, Folder 278, Yale University Archives. Wrote attorney Samuel J. Elder to Walter Camp on January 13, 1906: "Yale will get a savage black eye in the papers and from the public if Harvard adopts [the eligibility rules] and we do not at the same time, and it will be all the worse if Princeton and some other colleges unite with Harvard"; Camp Papers, Box 10, Folder 265, Yale University Archives.

3. H. B. Fine to Walter Camp, January 16, 1906, Walter Camp Papers, Box 8, Folder 278, Yale University Archives.

4. Harvard Athletic Committee Minutes, February 25, 1919, Harvard University Archives.

5. "Harvard-Yale-Princeton Athletic Agreement, Effective 1 January 1923," President Lowell Papers, 1922–25, Folder 6A, Harvard University Archives.

6. Synnott, "The 'Big Three' and the Harvard-Princeton Break, 1926–34," 190; Bernstein, *Football,* 136–37.

7. Bernstein, *Football,* 112–13.

8. *Harvard Crimson,* December 3, 1936.

9. *New York Times,* December 5, 1936, p. 10; *New York Times,* December 16, 1936, p. 37.

10. *New York Times,* January 12, 1937, p. 26.

11. Howard J. Savage to President James B. Conant, Harvard, January 18, 1937, President Conant Papers, 1936–37, Box 2, Folder "Athletic Board of Review," Harvard University Archives; *New York Times,* January 9, 1937, p. 15. All members of the Executive Committee of the Carnegie Foundation for the Advancement of Teaching were presidents of eastern colleges, including Brown, Columbia, Hamilton, Penn, and Smith.

12. James B. Conant to President James R. Angell, Yale, January 23, 1937, President Conant Papers, 1936–37, Box 2, Folder "Athletic Board of Review," Harvard University Archives.

13. H. W. Dodds to James B. Conant, February 8, 1937, President Conant Papers, 1936–37, Box 2, Folder "Athletic Board of Review," Harvard University Archives.

14. Browder and Smith, *Independent,* 19–23, 48, 82, 119.

15. Ernest M. Hopkins to James B. Conant, November 9, 1937, President Conant Papers, 1937–38, Box 3, Folder "Athletic Association," Harvard University Archives.

16. James B. Conant to Ernest M. Hopkins, November 13, 1937, President Conant Papers, 1937–38, Box 3, Folder "Athletic Association," Harvard University Archives.

17. *New York Times,* December 1, 1938, p. 30.

18. "Agreement between Harvard, Yale, and Princeton," October 1939, Harvard Athletic Committee Minutes, November 6, 1939, Harvard University Archives.

19. As quoted in Bernstein, *Football,* 177.

20. Ibid., 177–80.

21. "Ivy Group Presidents' Agreement, 20 November 1945," Papers of the Office of the President, 1950–55, Box 53, Folder "Intercollegiate Athletics IV," University of Pennsylvania Archives.

22. Bernstein, *Football,* 179.

23. *NCAA Proceedings,* January 9, 1946, 27. Professor A. W. Hobbs of the University of North Carolina was not convinced that leadership regarding recruiting and subsidization of athletes would come from the Ivy League.

24. "Poem," Papers of the Office of the President—University of Pennsylvania, 1950–54, Box 54, Folder "Intercollegiate Athletics VII," University of Pennsylvania Archives.

25. The first sport telecast in America was a baseball game between Columbia and Princeton on May 17, 1939, with Bill Stern as the announcer. The first football telecast was between Fordham University and Waynesburgh College on September 20, 1939, two weeks after Nazi Germany invaded Poland, igniting World War II. The University of Pennsylvania and the Philco Radio and Television Corporation telecast all Penn home football games in 1940 and continued to do so, with the exception of one year during World War II; see Smith, *Play-by-Play,* 49–53.

26. "A List of Penn Football Players on Scholarship," Papers of the Office of the President, 1950–55, Box 53, Folder "Intercollegiate Athletics IX," University of Pennsylvania Archives.

27. Smith, *Play-by-Play,* 68–70; Harold E. Stassen, telegram to Robert E. Kintner, ABC, New York City, August 23, 1950, Papers of the Office of the President, Box 54, Folder "Intercollegiate Athletics, TV-I," University of Pennsylvania Archives.

28. University of Pennsylvania Trustee Minutes, June 4, 1951, University of Pennsylvania Archives.

29. Cohen, *The Game They Played,* 119–64; Blackwell, *On Brave Old Army Team,* 258–344; Smith, "The William and Mary Athletic Scandal of 1951," 353–73; Lucas and Smith, *Saga of American Sport,* 392–93.

30. "Ivy Group Agreement," Draft of May 9, 1952, General Athletics, Box 1, Princeton University Archives.

31. "Proposed Action of Ivy League President, January 1952," Papers of the Office of the President, 1950–55, Box 53, Folder "Intercollegiate Athletics Ivy IV," University of Pennsylvania Archives; Bernstein, *Football,* 193–205.

32. Ivy League Coaches, telegram to all Ivy League Group Presidents, ca. February 1952, Papers of the Office of the President, 1950–55, Box 53, Folder "Intercollegiate Athletics Ivy V," University of Pennsylvania Archives. The Yale coach, Herman Hickman, abstained from signing the telegram because Yale's president had already banned spring practice.

33. Harold Dodds to President Gaylord Harnwell, Pennsylvania, March 30, 1954, Papers of the Office of the President, 1950–55, Box 53, Folder "Intercollegiate Athletics Franklin Field II," University of Pennsylvania Archives.

34. Bowen and Levin, *Reclaiming the Game*, 2–3, 179. Bowen was president of Princeton University (1972–88) and president of the Andrew W. Mellon Foundation (1988–2006); see also Shulman and Bowen, *The Game of Life*.

35. Bowen and Levin, *Reclaiming the Game*, 59.

36. John Watterson, in *College Football*, 256–59, might consider a group of small midwestern colleges downsizing their football programs after the 1951 scandal as a reform, but I consider it more in line with Marquette University and some others that dropped football as a financial exigency rather than reform. It is likely that had schools, such as Western Reserve, Baldwin Wallace, and John Carroll University, which formed the Presidents' Athletic Conference in the 1950s, been able to play big-time football profitably, they would have continued to do so for the prestige that it would have brought to those institutions. The University of Chicago is about the only big-time school to drop football for reform reasons.

37. Quoted in Footlick, "The Ivy League: Where Athletics Don't Endanger Academic Standards," 11.

38. Bernstein, *Football,* passim; Footlick, "Ivy League"; Smith and Helman, "A History of the Freshman Rule"; "History of the Ivy League," http://www.ivysport.com/history.php (accessed April 18, 2008); Lambert, "The Professionalization of Ivy League Sports"; "Ivy League Timeline," http://www.ivyleaguesports.com/whatisivy/history.asp (accessed April 12, 2010). The Ivy League tried telecasting its football games in 1984, but the ratings were so low they could not be accurately measured. In the early 2000s, the Yankees Entertainment and Sports Network telecast several Ivy League football games; see "Old College Try," *New York Times,* September 20, 1985, p. B13; *Sports Business News,* September 12, 2002.

Chapter 12. Scandals and the ACE Reform Effort in the 1950s

1. Smith, "A History of Basketball for Women in College," 351–79; Smith, "Women's Control of American College Sport," 103–20; Cahn, *Coming on Strong,* 55–82; Naismith, *Basketball.*

2. Durso, *Madison Square Garden,* 155–60.

3. Rosen, *The Wizard of Odds,* 35, 51.

4. Camp, "Undergraduate Limitation in College Sports," 143.

5. *New York Times,* March 12, 1945, p. 1; *New York Times,* March 28, 1945, p. 22; Rosen, *Scandals of '51,* 29–30; Cohen, *The Game They Played,* 60–61.

6. NCAA *Proceedings,* January 12, 1945, 27–28.

7. J. L. Morrill, Address at NCAA, January 7, 1947, Box 5 Supplement, Folder "J.L. Morrill—President," Department of Intercollegiate Athletics Papers, University of Minnesota Archives.

8. Eastern Collegiate Athletic Conference Minutes, December 11, 1948, ECAC Headquarters and "Pacific Conference Report of Acting Commissioner," June 1945, President Wilbur Papers, Box 135, Folder "Pacific Coast Athletic Conference," Stanford University Archives. Acting Commissioner Victor Schmidt warned the conference of the bribing of New York City basketball players and the larger threat to his conference.

9. Cohen, *The Game They Played,* 63–67.

10. *New York Times,* April 20, 1950, p. 41.

11. Cohen, *The Game They Played,* 79.

12. Ibid., 146.

13. Figone, "Gambling and College Basketball," 56–57.

14. *New York Times,* April 30, 1952, p. 1.

15. Rosen, *Scandals of '51,* 202, 215.

16. Blackwell, *On Brave Old Army Team,* 259–64, 299, 316–17, 333–35.

17. *New York Times,* August 4, 1951, p. 5; *New York Times,* August 5, 1951, p. 1; *New York Times,* August 7, 1951, p. 17.

18. Blackwell, *On Brave Old Army Team,* 343–44.

19. Nelson Marshall to John Pomfret, April 20, 1951, in Appendix to William and Mary Faculty Minutes, September 14, 1951, College of William and Mary Archives.

20. William and Mary Board of Visitors Minutes, October 12, 1946, William and Mary Archives; emphasis added.

21. Smith, "The William and Mary Athletic Scandal of 1951," 353–73.

22. William and Mary Board of Visitors Minutes, May 26, 1951, William and Mary Archives.

23. "A Statement by the Faculty of the College of William and Mary," September 17, 1951, in Executive Committee of the Board of Visitors Minutes, September 18, 1951, William and Mary Archives.

24. For a comparison of gift giving, see *The Alumni Gazette* 19 (March 1951): 12; *The Alumni Gazette* 20 (September 1952): 11.

25. Bernstein, *Football,* 53, 228, 292n35.

26. In 1949, Bright rushed for 975 yards in nine games; in 1950, 1,232 yards rushing and 1,168 yards passing in nine games; and in 1951, 1,025 yards rushing and 1,349 yards passing in seven games. Hailing from Fort Wayne, Indiana, he was not recruited by Purdue, all-white Notre Dame ignored him, and Indiana indicated that it had enough black backs; Wyatt, "Johnny Bright—America's Loss."

27. *New York Times,* December 14, 1947, p. S4.

28. "Caught by the Camera," *Life Magazine* 31 (November 5, 1951): 121–34; *New York Times,* October 22, 1951, p. 28; *New York Times,* October 25, 1951, p. 40.

29. *New York Times,* November 25, 1951, p. 182.

30. The eleven presidents were Raymond Ballen, Washington; John J. Cavanaugh, Notre Dame; John A. Hannah, Michigan State; A. Whitney Griswold, Yale; R. G. Gustavson, Nebraska; Umphrey Lee, Southern Methodist; John S. Millis, Western Reserve; John L. Plyler, Furman; Ray Olpin, Utah; John D. Williams, Mississippi; and H. C. Willett, Southern California.

31. Two years after Hannah's ACE Report, the NCAA put Michigan State College on probation for athletic aid violations and giving illegal tryouts to prospective athletes—with the knowledge of the administration; NCAA *Proceedings,* January 6, 1954, 125.

32. Shapiro, "John Hannah and the Growth of Big-Time Intercollegiate Athletics at Michigan State University," 26–40.

33. *New York Times,* November 21, 1951, p. 17.

34. "Report of the Special Committee on Athletic Policy of the American Council on Education," February 12, 1952. By eliminating free substitution, substantial financial savings

could be obtained by fewer scholarships, lower travel expenses, and cheaper training tables, and fewer coaches would be required.

35. The sixth accrediting organization, the Western Association, was not created until 1962. New England was created in 1885; North Central, 1887; Middle States and Southern, 1895; and Northwest, 1917.

36. Hawkins, *Banding Together,* 90–95, 213–15.

37. Ibid., 94.

38. M. Pattilo, NCA, to President F. Middlebush, Missouri, September 23, 1952, Central Administration, President's Office I-29-1 and "Report of Directors of Intercollegiate Athletics, MVIAA, May 1952, President's Office, Series I, Box 29, Folder "Athletics 1927–53," University of Colorado at Boulder Archives.

39. As quoted by Harry Carlson, Director of Physical Education, Colorado, to President R. Stearns, Colorado, November 29, 1952, President's Office, Series I, Box 29, Folder "Athletics 1927–53," University of Colorado at Boulder Archives.

40. Harry Carlson to R. Stearns, May 18, 1953, President's Office, Series I, Box 29, Folder "Athletics 1927–53," University of Colorado at Boulder Archives.

41. NCAA *Proceedings,* January 10, 1952, 117.

42. NCAA *Proceedings,* January 11, 1952, 200. The vote was 164–55. President Hesburgh of the University of Notre Dame strongly opposed the constitutional change, for he did not want the NCAA to control football telecasting. At the same NCAA meeting, it voted overwhelmingly, 163–8, to restrict football telecasting for 1952; NCAA *Proceedings,* January 11, 1952, 214.

43. Byers, *Unsportsmanlike Conduct,* 56–63. The hiring of Walter Byers was not similar to professional baseball hiring a powerful commissioner, Kenesaw Mountain Landis, following the baseball "Black Sox" scandal of 1919. Bernie Moore of the NCAA stated emphatically that Byers was "in no sense a 'national commissioner'" when he was hired and began his lengthy stay as executive director on October 1, 1951; see *NCAA Proceedings,* January 10, 1952, 100. One must remember that the NCAA had Home Rule, not national rule, for most of its first half century of existence.

Chapter 13. Lowly Standards: Chaos in the Sports Yards

1. For a discussion of college life and the desire for social status, see Levine, *The American College and the Culture of Aspiration, 1915–1940.*

2. To better understand the impact of radio and TV on college sport, see Smith, *Play-by-Play.*

3. The dean of Admissions and Financial Aid at Harvard University, Wilber Bender, felt that recruiting practices at both the Big Ten and the Pacific Coast Conference were stricter than those in the Ivy League, though the "Ivy League tends to look down our noses at" the two big conferences. Bender condemned the Ivy presidents, calling for a public announcement that would give him "great pleasure to put some of these hypocritical presidents on the spot publicly"; Letter in the Harvard Athletic Committee Minutes, April 6 1953, Harvard University Archives. For the many paradoxes and hypocrisy of Ivy League policies and practices, see Bernstein, *Football.*

4. "Constitution of the National Collegiate Athletic Association," NCAA *Proceedings,* January 11, 1956, 3–4.

5. As quoted in Byers, *Unsportsmanlike Conduct,* 73.

6. "Report of a Special Committee [of the Big Ten], 4 August 1956"; "Interim Report on Proposed Financial Aid Program for Conference Athletes, 27 September 1956"; Kenneth L. Wilson, Big Ten Commissioner, to Faculty Representatives and Athletic Directors of the Big Ten, October 16, 1956; Fred Harvey Harrington, memo to President E. B. Fred, University of Wisconsin, November 3, 1956; Minutes of the Intercollegiate Conference of Faculty Representatives, February 22, 1957, President E. B. Fred General Correspondence, 1956–57, Box 274, Folder "Athletic Scholarships," Series 4/16/1, University of Wisconsin Archives. The four institutions opposing need-based scholarships were Iowa, Minnesota, Northwestern, and Ohio State.

7. Justin L. Morrill to John A. Hannah, Michigan State University, January 29, 1957, President E. B. Fred General Correspondence, 1956–57, Box 274, Folder "Athletic Scholarships," Series 4/16/1, University of Wisconsin Archives.

8. For discussions of amateurism and professionalism in Britain, see Holt, *Sport and the British,* 74–117; Dunning and Sheard, *Barbarians, Gentlemen and Players.*

9. Virgil M. Hancher to Big Ten Presidents, Athletic Directors, and Conference Commissioner, February 11, 1957, President E. B. Fred General Correspondence File, 1956–57, Box 274, Folder "Athletic Scholarships," Series 4/16/1, University of Wisconsin Archives.

10. Lewis, "Enterprise on the Campus," 64; Ruth, "A Study of Selected Conferences in the United States," 32.

11. "Pacific Coast Intercollegiate Athletic Conference Report of Commissioner, June 1949," Presidential Correspondence and Papers, 1949, Folder 370, University of California Archives; Larry A. Kimpton, Stanford Faculty Athletic Representative, to President J. E. W. Sterling, Stanford, December 16, 1949, President Wilbur Papers, Box 135, Folder "Athletic-General," Stanford University Archives; Watterson, *College Football,* 279.

12. As quoted in Thelin, *Games Colleges Play,* 132. Thelin's chapter on "The Pacific Coast Conference, 1946 to 1959" is particularly strong on revealing the slush funds and the dissolution of the conference.

13. "1956 Action on Major Rules Violations," Box "Athletic Board of Control Minutes, ca. 1908–1960," Folder "USC-Athletics," University of Southern California Archives.

14. "Consequences of SC's Unilateral Withdrawal from Pacific Coast Conference," August 1956, Box "Athletic Board of Control Minutes, ca. 1908–1960," Folder "USC-Athletics," University of Southern California Archives.

15. *New York Times,* October 15, 1955, p. 10; *New York Times,* September 25, 1956, p. 36; Watterson, *College Football,* 279–80.

16. *New York Times,* May 22, 1956, p. 38; *New York Times,* September 25, 1956, p. 36.

17. Walter Byers gives a firsthand account of Vic Schmidt and the Pacific Coast Conference in his *Unsportsmanlike Conduct,* 114–17.

18. *New York Times,* May 22, 1956, p. 38. Later, the PAC-8 added the University of Arizona and Arizona State University, to become the PAC-10.

19. For a positive view of Bob Neyland, see Cohane, *Great College Football Coaches of the Twenties and Thirties,* 148–54.

20. President Cloide Brehm, "Meeting with Administrative Group," January 20, 1955, President Brehm Papers, Box 2, Folder "Employment of Bowden Wyatt," University of Ten-

nessee Archives. The seventeen-page transcript of the several-hour meeting documents the dilemma in which President Brehm found himself. This document and the 1905 diary of coach Bill Reid at Harvard University are the two most revealing sources of a negative nature that this researcher discovered over four decades of college archival research; see Smith, *Big-Time Football at Harvard, 1905*.

21. Brehm, "Meeting with Administrative Group." General Neyland continued to be a heroic figure for another half century and for several decades was the most important individual on the University of Tennessee campus.

22. NCAA *Proceedings*, January 11, 1956, 288.

23. See the Big Ten "Report of a Special Committee," August 4, 1956, stating that academically "Athletic teams should be genuinely representative of student bodies," President E. B. Fred General Correspondence Files, 1956–57, Series 4/16/1, Box 274, Folder "Athletic Scholarships," University of Wisconsin Archives.

24. NCAA *Proceedings*, January 7, 1959, 156–59.

25. As the ACC drew up more stringent eligibility rules, basketball teams within the ACC were involved in another point-shaving scandal that began in the late 1950s. A decade after the 1951 gambling scandals, the same New York City District Attorney, Frank Hogan, broke a point-shaving scheme in which fifty players from twenty-seven institutions, including North Carolina State and the University of North Carolina, were involved in forty-four fixed games from 1956 to 1961. William Friday, president of both institutions, would later cohead the Knight Foundation Commission to attempt to reform college athletics in the late 1980s and early 1990s; see Beezley, "The 1961 Scandal at North Carolina State and the End of the Dixie Classic," 81–99. The two chancellors and President Friday concluded that "if you could hire a boy to shoot baskets, someone else could hire him to miss them"; Beezley, "The 1961 Scandal at North Carolina State and the End of the Dixie Classic," 87).

26. Memo, President Robert C. Edwards Correspondence, 1966–70, Series 12, Folder 24, Clemson University Special Collections; President Robert C. Edwards to Dewey E. Dodds, Office for Civil Rights, Atlanta, GA, May 21, 1970, President Edwards Correspondence, 1966–70, Series 12, Folder 23, Clemson University Special Collection; Nancy Thompson, ACC Executive Secretary, Notes, ACC Headquarters, Greensboro, NC, January 5, 1988. The Big Ten had an academic progress rule in place for a number of years so that by the end of the freshman year, a 1.7 GPA would be reached for eligibility, a 1.8 by the end of the sophomore year, and a 1.9 by the end of the junior year; NCAA *Proceedings*, January 8, 1963, 214.

27. The ACC dropped its 800 SAT requirement after two Clemson students challenged the ACC in a class action suit claiming a violation of the Fourteenth Amendment to the U.S. Constitution—no state may deprive any person of life, liberty, or property, without due process of the law. Later, the NCAA's Proposition 48 eligibility rule was challenged on the same basis; see "Report of the Faculty Committee on Athletics to the Faculty Council," February 1973, Chancellor Taylor Series, Box 27, Folder "Standing Committee Athletic, 1973–74," University of North Carolina Archives.

28. NCAA *Proceedings*, January 7, 1963, 212; NCAA *Proceedings*, January 13, 1965, 327, and By-Laws, 37.

29. The 1966 Duke study showed that ten of its thirty-seven white freshman football players fell below the 1.600 GPA and five of sixteen white basketball players failed at that

level; Robert L. Dickens to E. M. Cameron, Duke AD, November 29, 1966, E. M. Cameron Papers, Box 3, Folder "NCAA 1.600 Rule," Duke University Archives.

30. Robert F. Goheen to President Everett D. Barnes, NCAA, April 13, 1966, O. C. Aderhold Papers, Series # 4, Box 1, Folder "Athletic Association," University of Georgia Archives; see also Coval and Barr, "The Ties That Bind," 425–26.

31. The NCAA probably reflected the racist nature of American society at midcentury, for race was almost never discussed in any form at NCAA meetings. In the mid-1950s, Mack Greene, athletic director at Central State College of Wilberforce, Ohio, spoke to the NCAA executive committee and asked that the NCAA conduct a study of racial discrimination in colleges. He wanted a statement from the NCAA to encourage members not to practice discrimination, for, he said, it is both "undemocratic and un-American." Greene's suggestions went unanswered; NCAA *Proceedings*, February 7, 1954, 108.

32. In South Carolina in 1965, 93 percent of blacks scored below 800 and 82 percent scored below 700 on the SAT test, while 32 percent of whites scored below 800 and 14 percent scored below 700; "The State Summary of SAT Scores in S. Carolina in 1965," President Robert Edwards Correspondence, 1966–70, Series 12, Folder 23, Clemson University Special Collection.

33. Charles Morgan Jr., Southern Regional Office, ACLU, to Harold Howe II, Commissioner of Education, Washington, DC, May 12, 1966, O. C. Aderhold Papers, Series # 4, Box 1, Folder "Athletic Association," University of Georgia Archives.

34. Eastern Collegiate Athletic Conference Minutes, September 22, 1970, ECAC Headquarters.

35. NCAA *Proceedings*, January 13, 1971, 108.

36. NCAA *Proceedings*, January 8, 1972, 172.

37. Ibid., 166–168. Both freshman basketball and football eligibility were approved by a mere show of hands.

38. Ibid., 167.

39. NCAA *Proceedings*, January 13, 1973, 146.

40. Ibid., 146–47.

41. Byers, *Unsportsmanlike Conduct,* 165.

42. NCAA *Proceedings*, January 13, 1973, 149.

Chapter 14. The Hanford Report, Rejected Reform, and Proposition 48

1. NCAA *Proceedings*, January 13, 1973, 123 and A-20 of the appendix. The action was approved by hand vote and no discussion, though plenty of discussion had occurred prior to the 1973 convention. In 1967, the NCAA had voted 214–13 to take away athletic scholarships if the athlete "voluntarily renders himself ineligible for intercollegiate competition"; NCAA *Proceedings*, January 11, 1967, 122.

2. Michael Oriard, in *Bowled Over,* 127–41, makes a strong case for the one-year athletic scholarship being a major factor in the loss of athletes' freedom and for allowing coaches to make increasing demands on athletes' time as well as the more obvious ability to remove "dead wood" from the teams. Oriard states that "the one-year scholarship changed nothing and changed everything. In some ways it seems more symbolic than actual, though powerfully symbolic" (140). Oriard has one very good suggestion: publish scholarship renewal

statistics so that athletes know what the records of individual coaches are with regard to eliminating "dead wood." We might then know if the one-year athletic scholarship has been significantly misused by unethical coaches. We simply do not know if college athletes fear the one-year rule being used against them, nor do we have good evidence that it is often used or threatened to be used.

3. Free substitution or two-platoon football logically led to the need for more coaches, larger squads, increased recruiting, higher travel costs, more expensive training tables, and more athletic dorms, which all cost more to the athletic departments.

4. Byers, *Unsportsmanlike Conduct,* 165.

5. Hanford, *An Inquiry into the Need for and Feasibility of a National Study of Intercollegiate Athletics.*

6. Hanford, "We Should Speak the 'Awful Truth' about College Sports."

7. Ibid.

8. Hanford, *An Inquiry,* 63, 74, 7, 82, for example.

9. Ibid., 142, 30.

10. Ibid., 55–62.

11. Hanford, "We Should Speak the 'Awful Truth.'

12. Hanford, *An Inquiry into the Need for and Feasibility of a National Study of Intercollegiate Athletics,* 91–92.

13. Hanford, "We Should Speak the 'Awful Truth' about College Sports."

14. Byers, *Unsportsmanlike Conduct,* 167.

15. Randolph, "Dexter Manley's Incredible Story."

16. "Eliminating Illiteracy," 164–71.

17. "Outside the Lines: Unable to Read"; *Kevin Ross v. Creighton University,* 957 F.2d 410 (7th Cir. 1992).

18. Brubaker, "Dear Chris," 120–36.

19. Golenbock, *Personal Fouls,* 42; emphasis in the original.

20. *New York Times,* January 12, 1989, p. D24; Golenbock, *Personal Fouls,* 35–41.

21. Golenbock, *Personal Fouls,* 5.

22. "Noting the Passing of Jan Kemp, UGA Athletics Whistleblower," December 8, 2008, http://feministlawprofs.law.sc.edu/?p=4414 (accessed April 12, 2010).

23. Pratt, *We Shall Not be Moved,* 140–45; *Washington Post,* January 3, 1989.

24. Two decades later, the University of Georgia was embroiled in another scandal. One course at the University of Georgia was taught by assistant basketball coach Jim Harrick Jr., son of the head coach, in which the one test in the 2001 course on basketball included such questions as "How many goals are there on a basketball court?" "How many players for one team are on the court at one time?" and "How many points are counted for a 3-point shot?" "Jock Test," *Grouchy Old Cripple in Atlanta,* March 5, 2004, http://www.grouchyold-cripple.com/archives/000830.html (accessed September 20, 2008).

25. Theodore Hesburgh to Douglas Mills, Illinois Athletic Director, October 6, 1952, President Theodore Hesburgh Files, UPHS, Box 94, University of Notre Dame Archives.

26. NCAA *Proceedings,* Special Convention, August 14–15, 1975, 59.

27. "Interim Report of the Commissioner to the Council of Ten," July 24, 1975, Presi-

dent Enarson Papers, 3/j/16/17, Folder "Council of Ten, 1973–76," Ohio State University Archives.

28. For a short history of the relationship of the CFA to television, see Smith, *Play-by-Play,* 143–52.

29. Robin W. Fleming to President Fred Davison, Georgia, President Davison Papers, Box 19, Folder "CFA, June 16–8, 1976," University of Georgia Archives.

30. Fred C. Davison, "History of College Football Association," June 11, 1980, President Banowsky Papers, Box 74, Folder 13, University of Oklahoma Archives.

31. Ibid.

32. Fred Davison to Joe Paterno, April 13, 1977, President Davison Papers, Box 19, Folder "CFA, June 15–16, 1977," University of Georgia Archives.

33. Minutes of the Second Annual Meeting of the CFA, June 16–17, 1978, President Davison Papers, Box 19, Folder "CFA, June 16–18, 1978," University of Georgia Archives; Tom Osborne to Barry Switzer, Oklahoma football coach and other Big 8 coaches, June 19, 1978, Chancellors Central Files, Box 227, Folder "CFA 1977–80," University of Nebraska Archives.

34. College Football Association Committee on Academic Standards "Report," May 20, 1982, President Banowsky Papers, Box 119, Folder 26, University of Oklahoma Archives.

35. For a fuller account of the CFA challenge to the NCAA, see Smith, *Play-by-Play,* 152–68.

36. NCAA *Proceedings,* January 11, 1983, 110.

37. Ibid., 104.

38. Ibid., 124, appendix A-35.

39. Ibid., 124–25.

40. Bock, "The Easy Way Most Often Turns Out to Be Unfair," 2.

41. The executive vice president of the American Council on Education, Robert Atwell, confirmed the controversy over standardized test scores and the impact upon black athletes, as expressed by presidents of historically black institutions, soon after the passage of Proposition 48; Atwell to Ace Committee on Division One Intercollegiate Athletics, March 10, 1983, Walter Byers Papers, Box "Special Convention," Folder "Select Committee on American Concerns in Higher Education," NCAA Headquarters, Indianapolis, IN.

Chapter 15. Title IX and Governmental Reform in Women's Athletics

1. Sandler, "'Too Strong for a Woman.'"

2. Ibid.

3. Elizabeth L. Bishop Scrapbook, Vassar College Archives.

4. Scoville, "Athletic Vassar," 18. Some of the times reported by Scoville for the women differ from the official times seen in Elizabeth L. Bishop Scrapbook, Vassar College Archives.

5. Much has been written on college women and controlled sport, but a strong volume is Cahn, *Coming on Strong,* 24, 55–82.

6. Hult, "The Story of Women's Athletics," 93; see also Cahn, *Coming on Strong,* 249.

7. Even the Amateur Athletic Union (AAU) criticized women in colleges for the lack of competition and for not producing women coaches, "leaving the field completely open to

men." An AAU study on women's sport concluded: "For the most part the women of our educational institutions have chosen to sit on the sidelines and criticize the efforts of those men who have filled the gap"; Amateur Athletic Union, *A.A.U. Study of Effect of Athletic Competition on Girls and Women,* 9.

8. "Intercollegiate and Interscholastic Sports for Women," Mary Yost Unprocessed Papers, c. 84/94, Box 8, "Mary Yost: Women's Athletics: Competition Information," Ohio State University Archives.

9. Hult, "The Saga of Competition," 230.

10. For an analysis of the negative aspect of women physical educators' control limiting the opportunities for skilled athletes, see Smith, "Women's Control of American College Sport," 103–20.

11. NCAA *Proceedings,* January 12, 1962, 205.

12. See Ying Wushanley's significant "The Olympics, Cold War, and the Reconstruction of the U.S. Women's Athletics," 119–26.

13. The DGWS was a very conservative group relative to giving good athletes an opportunity to compete. Linda Estes, an advocate for real competitive sports, stated the DGWS stood for "Don't Give Women Sports," and as a result she was shunned by her peers in the DGWS; see Maloney, "The Impact of Title IX on Women's Intercollegiate Athletics," 97.

14. Flath, *A History of Relations between the National Collegiate Athletic Association and the Amateur Athletic Union of the United States, 1905–1963;* Smith, "Amateur Athletic Union," 157; Koorsgaard, "A History of the Amateur Athletic Union of the United States."

15. For a more complete analysis of the AAU-NCAA battle influencing women's athletics, see Wushanley, "The Impact of the AAU-NCAA Power Struggle on Women's Athletics," in his *Playing Nice and Losing,* 29–32.

16. Long Range Planning Committee Minutes, March 1, 1965, Folder "Women's Athletics," Walter Byers Papers, NCAA Headquarters.

17. For extensive discussions of Title IX, see Suggs, *A Place on the Team;* Carpenter and Acosta, *Title IX;* Gavora, *Tilting the Playing Field;* Cahn, *Coming on Strong;* Fields, *Female Gladiators;* and Wushanley, *Playing Nice and Losing.*

18. Gavora, *Tilting the Playing Field,* argues that feminists have used Title IX to win victories detrimental to men's sports and have attributed gains made by women specifically to Title IX, when other forces were at work; see, for instance, chapter 1 in *Tilting the Playing Field,* "The Numbers Game," 11–42.

19. John A. Fuzak, memorandum to NCAA members, February 13, 1976, Walter Byers Papers, Vol. CXVIII, Folder "Legal, 1/76–5/76," NCAA Headquarters.

20. Margaret Dunkle, "College Athletics," 114.

21. One should point out that the women's educational model was one of noblesse oblige to the women athletes. When the AIAW began in 1972, there were no student representatives on its "democratic" Executive Board. If sport was for the "good of those who play," one might have expected that athletes would have a voice in determining what was "good." The NCAA commercial model also lacked athlete involvement for most of its history; see Hult, "The Legacy of AIAW," 286.

22. Su, "Collegiate Women's Sport and a Guide to Collecting and Identifying Archival Materials," 104–6; Wushanley, *Playing Nice and Losing,* 64.

23. Donna Mae Miller and Mary Roby, University of Arizona, to Betty Hartman and Mary Rekstad, DGWS, and Carole Oglesby, AIAW President, March 12, 1973, Folder "Special Meeting AIAW, March 25–27, 1973," Box 67, AIAW Papers, University of Maryland Archives.

24. June P. Galloway to Elizabeth Hoyt, March 15, 1973, Folder "Special Meeting AIAW, March 25–27, 1973," Box 67, AIAW Papers, University of Maryland Archives.

25. Harold B. Falls, Southwest Missouri State College, to Carole Oglesby, March 20, 1973, Folder "Votes-Suit," Box 67, AIAW Papers, University of Maryland Archives.

26. Hult, "The Story of Women's Athletics," 83–106; Wushanley, *Winning Nice and Losing*, 62–75; see also *Fern Kellmeyer, et al. v. National Education Association, et al.*, U.S. District Court, Southern District of Florida, no. 73, 21 Civ NCR, January 17, 1973.

27. Sarah Fields in her *Female Gladiators* has shown that while Title IX had massive social and psychological significance for achieving greater equity for women in sport and triggered numerous lawsuits, it was especially the legal cases using the Fourteenth Amendment's equal protection clause that brought access to the most popular American contact sports of baseball, basketball, and football.

28. Wushanley, *Winning Nice and Losing*, 87–88.

29. Ibid., 91.

30. NCAA *Proceedings*, January 8, 1975, 144–50, A82–A83; NCAA *Proceedings*, January 6, 1975, 58–63.

31. NCAA *Proceedings*, January 6, 1975, 60.

32. "A Legal Opinion, 12 November 1975," 3/j/27/9, NCAA Minutes and Reports: 1975–76, President Enarson Papers, Ohio State University Archives.

33. Hult, "The Legacy of AIAW," 302.

34. Wushanley, *Winning Nice and Losing*, 126–35.

35. NCAA *Proceedings*, January 13, 1981, 177. The vote to reconsider its earlier vote against Division I championships for women was 137–117.

36. Wushanley, *Playing Nice and Losing*, 118.

37. Ibid., 142–52.

38. "Chief Executive Officers Big Eight Conference Minutes, 3 June 1980," Folder "Big 8 Conference 1978–80," Box 222, Chancellors' Central Files, University of Nebraska Archives.

39. Guttmann, *Women's Sports: A History*, 221–22; Cahn, *Coming on Strong*, 256–57.

40. Gavora, *Tilting the Playing Field*, 35–38.

41. *Cohen v. Brown University*, 991 F.2d 888 (1st Cir. 1993). At about the same time as the Brown case, of the 108 NCAA Division I-A institutions, only nine met the proportionality test of Title IX, and three of those were the three military academies, where the percentage of female students was 15 percent or less; see Plyley, "The AIAW vs. the NCAA," 129–30. For a sound analysis of *Brown v. Cohen* and the impact of Title IX on intercollegiate athletics, see Thelin, "Good Sports?" 391–410.

42. See "If You Build It, They Will Come," in Gavora, *Tilting the Playing Field*, 70–90; Blum, "Brown Loses Bias Case," A37–A38.

Chapter 16. African Americans, Freshman Eligibility, and Forced Reform

1. Paine, *Thomas Nast*, 411.

2. Statement of Richard E. Lapchick, "Intercollegiate Sports," Hearings before the Sub-

committee on Commerce, Consumer Protection, and Competitiveness of the Committee on Energy and Commerce, 129.

3. For a greater explanation of the Jan Kemp case at the University of Georgia, see chapter 14.

4. Zang, *Fleet Walker's Divided Heart,* 26–47; Pennington, *Breaking the Ice,* 1. Fleet Walker played against the University of Wisconsin in 1882, and a teammate commented that Walker was "the whitest man on our team. He certainly was a star player, a fine fellow and popular with us." Michigan, at the same time, was accused by Wisconsin of playing nonstudents; "Trip to Play Racine and Wisconsin," May 1882, Richard M. Dott Papers, Michigan Historical Collection, Bentley Historical Library, University of Michigan; see also Wigginton, *The Strange Career of the Black Athlete,* 29–30.

5. Smith, "The Paul Robeson—Jackie Robinson Saga and a Political Collision," 8–9.

6. Writing in 1956, John Hope Franklin stated that in mid-twentieth-century America "the wall of segregation had become so formidable, so impenetrable, apparently, that the entire weight of American tradition of equality and all the strength of the American constitutional system had to be brought to bear in order to make even the slightest crack in it; Franklin, "History of Racial Segregation in the United States," 9.

7. "Armageddon to Go," 24; Wesberry, "Football Spoils Georgia Rumpus," 1504–5; *New York Times,* January 3, 1956, p. 33.

8. The movement of black women into college sport was much slower in the 1960s and 1970s. When the first National Intercollegiate Basketball Tournament for Women was held in 1969, representing the dominant women's sport in most colleges, there were only 3 African Americans of the 180 players on sixteen teams. Blacks, if they were prominent, were mostly track participants; see Washington, "Black Women in Sports," 42.

9. President Lyndon B. Johnson gave his first inaugural address on January 8, 1964, following John F. Kennedy's assassination, beginning his "war on poverty." The Educational Opportunity Grant Program and College Work Study Program were two results. Unfortunately, the Educational Opportunities Program (EOP) often resulted in subsidizing the economically needy who were principally athletes, supplementing the athletic department, and producing winners on the field of play rather than winners in education; see, for example, "History of EOP," California State University, http://www.calstate.edu/sas/eop/various/history.shtml (accessed September 9, 2008).

10. Haskins and Wetzel, *Glory Road.* Texas Western became the University of Texas at El Paso in 1967.

11. Jacobs, *Across the Line,* xiv.

12. Pennington, *The Heisman,* 158–73, 334.

13. Stuart Rojstaczer, a geology professor at Duke University, studied grade inflation from the 1960s to the early 2000s. While the data came from a variety of sources, it showed rapid grade inflation from 1967 to 1975, which then leveled off until the 1980s, when it rose again into the early 2000s, though not as rapidly as it had in the late 1960s and into the 1970s; see Rojstaczer, "Grade Inflation at American Colleges and Universities." Rojstaczer did not believe that grade inflation occurred because of better teachers or smarter and better-prepared students. Affirmative action, professors avoiding offending victimized groups, and the Vietnam War were possible sources of grade inflation in the earlier period,

whereas in the period from the 1980s there was the belief that universities had become consumer institutions with the consumer (student) paying higher tuition and demanding a higher GPA, thus contributing to higher grades. This, along with the self-esteem movement and the movement for student course evaluations, probably caused grade inflation; see also Mansfield, "Grade Inflation."

14. Rojstaczer, "Grade Inflation at American Colleges and Universities."

15. "Study of Freshman Eligibility Standards: Executive Summary," Submitted to the NCAA, August 15, 1984, NCAA Headquarters.

16. Tom Osborne to Larry K. Andrews, Assistant to the Chancellor, University of Nebraska, May 25, 1982, Chancellors' Central Files, Box 217, Folder "Athletics 1982," University of Nebraska Archives.

17. Link, *William Friday,* 381.

18. NCAA *Proceedings,* February 7, 1954, 108. Mack Greene of Wilberforce asked the NCAA to do a study of discrimination in colleges on March 22, 1953, and to include a Negro representative on the NCAA Council.

19. NCAA *Proceedings,* January 11, 1983, 104.

20. Ibid., 108–9.

21. Ibid., 114–7.

22. Ibid., A35.

23. Ibid., A39.

24. The two studies were Bartell et al., "Study of Freshman Eligibility Standards"; and American College Testing Program and Educational Testing Service, *Athletics and Academics in the Freshman Year.*

25. American College Testing Program and Educational Testing Service, *Athletics and Academics in the Freshman Year,* chapter 2, p. 10. The study counted "Minorities," and I am interpreting this to mean "Blacks."

26. Ibid., chapter 1, pp. 8–9.

27. Ibid., chapter 1, p. 10.

28. Edwards, "Crisis of Black Athletes on the Eve of the Twenty-First Century," 347.

29. Hanford, "Proposition 48," 371.

30. Edwards, "Educating Black Athletes," 378; emphasis in original.

31. As quoted in Moore, "The Eternal Example: Arthur Ashe," 25.

32. *New York Times,* September 9, 1988, p. A25.

33. "Squeeze Play: Prop 48 Left Frank between Two Worlds."

34. For more details on Ross, Washburn, and Manley, see chapter 14.

35. *NCAA Proceedings,* January 13, 1986, 74.

36. Coval and Barr, "The Ties That Bind, 436–37.

37. NCAA *Proceedings,* January 11, 1989, 247–48, 281, A29.

38. *New York Times,* January 20, 1989, p. A25; Coval and Barr, "The Ties That Bind," 314; NCAA *Proceedings,* January 13, 1986, 67.

39. Coval and Barr, "The Ties That Bind," 440.

40. Byers, *Unsportsmanlike Conduct,* 314–15.

41. Lapchick testimony, "Intercollegiate Sports," Hearings before the Subcommittee on Commerce, Consumer Protection, and Competitiveness of the Committee on Energy and

Commerce, House of Representatives, 128. Lapchick said the sorry state was in part due to the lack of support for black athletes, lack of black faculty, the small percentage of blacks in the total student body, and few blacks in athletic administrative positions.

42. Ibid., 1, 118. Senator Bill Bradley from New Jersey, a collegiate and professional basketball player in addition to being a Rhodes Scholar, was also strongly involved in attempting to reform college athletics.

43. McMillen, *Out of Bounds,* 92–94.

44. NCAA *Proceedings,* January 8, 1989, 62; NCAA *Proceedings,* January 9, 1990, 262–63, 267, A19.

45. Robert H. Atwell to Representative William D. Ford, Chair, Subcommittee on Postsecondary Education, Committee on Education and Labor, U.S. House of Representatives, Washington, D.C., May 30, 1991, "National College Athletics Accountability Act," Hearings.

46. Ibid.

47. The thirteen core course requirement passed the NCAA in 1991, 312–6, and Prop 16 passed 249–72 the following year; see Coval and Barr, "The Ties That Bind," 442–43.

48. "Legislator Challenges Research Group," *NCAA News* (December 22, 1993), 1, 28. For a condemnation of Beyondism, see Mehler, "Beyondism," 153–63. Cattell, the founder of Beyondism, encouraged his smart graduate students to have more children, thus propagating their genes, but not the same for physically strong basketball and football players who scored low on standardized tests; see also Paul, *The Cult of Personality,* 181.

49. For an insightful interpretation of Prop 16, Beyondism, and the Black Coaches Association, see Crowley, *In the Arena,* 197–201. Crowley at the time was president of both the University of Nevada and the NCAA.

50. Rosner and Shropshire, *The Business of Sports,* 510.

51. Crowley, *In the Arena,* 198–201.

52. *Cureton v. NCAA,* 37 F. Supp. 2d 687, 690 (E.D. Pa 1999).

53. Buckwalter was overruled not because the Appeals Court thought the reasoning was wrong, but because no federal funds went to the NCAA and therefore there was no violation of Title VI of the Civil Rights Act of 1964.

54. *Pryor v. NCAA,* 288 F.3d 548 (3rd Cir. May 6, 2002).

55. "NCAA Freshman-Eligibility Standards Quick Reference Sheet."

Chapter 17. Presidential Control, Minor Reform, and the Knight Commission

1. NCAA *Proceedings,* January 9, 1948, 170.

2. *New York Times,* November 21, 1951, p. 55.

3. NCAA *Proceedings,* January 12, 1977, 171–72, A74.

4. As examples of the news media discussing scandals around 1980, see Underwood, "Student-Athletes," 36–73; Sanoff, "Behind Scandals in Big-Time College Sports," 61–62.

5. *New York Times,* October 15, 1980, pp. B7–B8.

6. Byers, *Unsportsmanlike Conduct,* 188–91; *New York Times,* September 8, 1980, p. C3; *New York Times,* May 1, 1981, p. A23.

7. A number of university presidents resigned under pressure or were fired for trying to reform athletics at their institutions. Or as a former University of Michigan president has

stated: "Presidents are frequently placed in harm's way by athletics"; see Duderstadt, *Intercollegiate Athletics and the American University,* 123. A couple of well-known examples are Paul Hardin at Southern Methodist University (1972–74) and John DiBiaggio at Michigan State (1985–92), both of whom were driven from their jobs over athletics.

8. *New York Times,* November 30, 1981, p. C6; *New York Times,* November 23, 1982, p. B9; *New York Times,* December 12, 1982, p. S2; *New York Times,* March 3, 1985, p. S4; *New York Times,* June 11, 1986, p. D27, D30.

9. Asher, "Abuses in College Athletics," 16; *New York Times,* January 20, 1981, p. 77; *New York Times,* February 12, 1981, p. D18; *New York Times,* November 18, 1981, p. B8; *New York Times,* February 6, 1982, p. 17; Hill, "How I Put the Fix In," 14–21.

10. *New York Times,* March 27, 1985, p. B11; *New York Times,* April 5, 1985, p. A1; *New York Times,* April 8, 1985, p. C11; *New York Times,* April 14, 1985, p. S3.

11. *New York Times,* July 31, 1982, p. 15.

12. Bok, "Presidents Need Power within the NCAA to Preserve Academic Standards and Institutional Integrity," 208.

13. Crowley, *In the Arena,* 117. Crowley was president of the University of Nevada, Reno for twenty-three years and served the NCAA in a variety of roles, including president, member of the Council, and the Presidents Commission.

14. NCAA *Proceedings,* January 10, 1984, 92–112, specifically 99.

15. "'In' Box," *Chronicle of Higher Education,* January 4, 1989, A13.

16. NCAA *Proceedings,* Special Convention, June 21, 1985, 62–76.

17. Ibid., 69–71. Donna Lopiano of the University of Texas, Austin asked that the NCAA refine its investigatory and due process mechanism for accused violators with open disclosure of evidence. The convention referred this question to the Presidents Commission and NCAA Council.

18. NCAA *Proceedings,* June 30, 1987, 117, A47, 86–88, 116, A45–A46.

19. Ibid., 161.

20. Ibid., 45.

21. Ibid., 81; "Presidents Commission Intercollegiate Athletics—Agenda for Reform, 5 May 1987," Walter Byers Papers, Box "Special Convention," Folder "Special Convention 1987," NCAA Headquarters.

22. *New York Times,* September 23, 1984, p. D26; *New York Times,* September 23, 1984, p. S3; *New York Times,* October 14, 1984, p. S1.

23. Pratt, *We Shall Not Be Moved,* 140–45; *Washington Post,* January 3, 1989, http://www.uga.edu/ao/kemp.html (accessed September 20, 2008).

24. "J. P. Comer Recollection," Faculty Recollections, Folder 1, Southern Methodist University Archives.

25. Thomas, *Southern Methodist University,* 86.

26. Southwest Conference Investigation Committee, letter to Ray Morrison, SMU football coach, December 21, 1922, File "1922 Athletic Controversy"; *Houston Chronicle,* December 8, 1922, newspaper clipping, File "1922 Athletic Controversy"; "George F. Thomas Recollections," Faculty Recollections, Folder 1, Southern Methodist University Archives.

27. Whitford, *A Payroll to Meet,* 113–35. For a thorough account of the SMU scandal, see

Watterson, "Sudden Death at SMU: Football Scandals in the 1980s," in his *College Football*, 353–78. Possibly the best inside story of the SMU scandal is Byers, "The Governor and the 'Death Penalty,'" in his *Unsportsmanlike Conduct*, 17–36.

28. Byers, *Unsportsmanlike Conduct*, 17.

29. Friday and Hesburgh, *Keeping Faith with the Student-Athlete*, v.

30. The members were Lamar Alexander, president, University of Tennessee; Creed C. Black, president, Knight Foundation; Douglas S. Dibbert, University of North Carolina Alumni Association; John A. DiBiaggio, president, Michigan State University; William C. Friday, president emeritus, University of North Carolina; Thomas K. Hearn Jr., president, Wake Forest University; Theodore M. Hesburgh, president emeritus, University of Notre Dame; J. Lloyd Huck, Board of Trustees, Penn State University; Bryce Jordan, president emeritus, Penn State University; Richard W. Kazmaier, president, Kazmaier Associates; Donald R. Keough, president, Coca-Cola; Martin A. Massengale, president, University of Nebraska; Tom McMillen, U.S. House of Representatives; Chase N. Peterson, president, University of Utah; Jane C. Pfeiffer, former chair, NBC; A. Kenneth Pye, president, Southern Methodist University; Richard D. Schultz, executive director, NCAA; Donna E. Shalala, chancellor, University of Wisconsin; LeRoy T. Walker, treasurer, U.S. Olympic Committee; James J. Whalen, president, Ithaca College; Clifton R. Wharton, chairman, TIAA-CREF; and Charles E. Young, chancellor, University of California, Los Angeles.

31. Friday and Hesburgh, *Keeping Faith with the Student-Athlete*, vii, 25.

32. Ibid., 16.

33. See Timothy V. Franklin "Knight Commission Beginnings: Contextual History, Stakeholders, and Formation," in his dissertation "An Educational Reform Commission and Institutional Change," 186–209. Franklin shows that Creed Black of the Knight Foundation was in early talks with North Carolina's Bill Friday and the ACE's Bob Atwell for an independent evaluation of intercollegiate athletics. The Knight Commission was highly rationalized, with a professional hired to write the report, a public relations firm to publicize it, a poll by Lou Harris to show the need for reform, and a handpicked commission by Black, Friday, and Hesburgh, most of whom had connections with the ACE, the Association of Governing Boards, the National Association of Alumni Executives, the National Association of State Universities and Land Grant Colleges, the American Association of Universities, the National Association of Independent Colleges and Universities, the Presidents Commission of the NCAA, and other NCAA leadership; see Franklin, "An Educational Reform Commission and Institutional Change," 216. The fact that no university faculty members were on the Knight Commission was likely a major problem for this or any other effective reform. This was not an oversight, but it did reflect the past half century and more of faculty, not president-selected faculty, being left out of reform equations.

34. Friday and Hesburgh, *Keeping Faith with the Student-Athlete*, 25.

35. Later research by Shulman and Bowen, *The Game of Life*, 44, indicated that a large gap existed in 1989 between athletes and nonathletes in SAT scores at all NCAA division levels.

36. Friday and Hesburgh, *Keeping Faith with the Student-Athlete*, 16.

37. Ibid., 18–21.

38. Ibid., 21.

39. Ibid., 21–22.

40. "Walter Byers Former NCAA Executive Director," *NCAA News,* January 2, 1991, p. 4.

Chapter 18. NCAA Reorganization, the Board of Presidents' Reform, and the APR

1. Friday and Hesburgh, *Keeping Faith with the Student-Athlete,* vii.

2. Eliot, telegram to Chancellor Henry MacCracken, New York University, as quoted in the *Boston Globe,* November 29, 1905, p. 3.

3. *New York Times,* January 1, 1990, p. 25.

4. Ibid.

5. Economist Andrew Zimbalist discussed this and other commercial ventures in his important book *Unpaid Professionals,* 148 and elsewhere.

6. Rawlings, "Why Did We Take So Long," 72.

7. As quoted in Lederman, "Despite Adoptions of Sweeping Reforms, NCAA Continues to Face Pressure from Lawmakers and other 'Outsiders,'" A31–A32.

8. "Walter Byers Former NCAA Executive Director," *NCAA News,* January 2, 1991, p. 4.

9. "Intercollegiate Sports," Hearings before the Subcommittee on Commerce, Consumer Protection, and Competitiveness of the Committee on Energy and Commerce, 76.

10. As quoted in Blum, "Athletics: The Big Scramble," A37. In just two months in 1994, the SEC announced it would leave the College Football Association, the Big East got a TV deal from CBS, the ACC negotiated a TV contract with ABC, the Big 8 added four Texas institutions to become the Big 12, and the Big East was reconstituted.

11. Patberg, "Presidential Involvement in NCAA Division I Governance Related Issues," 63–69.

12. NCAA *Proceedings,* January 8, 1996, http://web1.ncaa.org/conventionArchive/1996/files/ncaa-1996-proceedings-division-business-session-002.htm (accessed May 6, 2010).

13. For example, in the first decade of the twenty-first century, lawyers among big-time conference commissioners were Jim Delany of the Big Ten, Dan Beebe of the Big 12, Britton Banowsky of Conference USA, and Mike Slive of the Southeastern Conference.

14. NCAA *Proceedings,* January 13, 1997, http://web1.ncaa.org/conventionArchive/1997/files/ncaa-1997-proceedings-general-business-session-003.htm (accessed May 6, 2010).

15. Knight Foundation Commission on Intercollegiate Athletics, *A Call to Action,* 6, 13.

16. Ibid., 14, 17, 19.

17. Ibid., 23.

18. Ibid., 26–33.

19. An important U.S. Supreme Court decision in 1975, *Goldfarb v. Virginia State Bar,* 421 U.S. 773 (1975), ruled that educational institutions were not entitled to blanket immunity from antitrust laws that higher education had previously enjoyed. As Carl L. Reisner noted in the *Yale Law Review,* "After Goldfarb the NCAA's anticompetitive practices are susceptible to antitrust attack"; Reisner, "Tackling Intercollegiate Athletics," 658. The NCAA had seriously considered asking the U.S. Congress for an antitrust exemption for its television TV plan in 1983 at the time the College Football Association (CFA) was taking the NCAA to court over the NCAA monopoly. Two leaders of the American Council on Education (ACE), Jack Peltason and Robert Atwell, met with NCAA Executive Director Walter Byers in 1983

to discuss possible antitrust exemption legislation. The ACE leaders discouraged the NCAA from going to Congress. Head of the CFA, Charles Neinas, commented: "Presidents of many major universities are hesitant to support any antitrust exemption for college football. Apparently the college presidents believe that they need to save their ammunition to secure favorable consideration of other proposals that may be more important to higher education than college football"; Charles M. Neinas to Andy Coats, University of Oklahoma Counsel, April 26, 1983, Ralph Beaird Papers, Box "U. of OK & GA v. NCAA," University of Georgia Archives. Walter Byers agreed with the assessment of his enemy, Neinas, when he wrote, "Peltason and Atwell expressed concern regarding a possible antitrust exemption for televising college football"; Byers to John L. Toner, University of Connecticut, May 13, 1983, Walter Byers Papers, Box "Special Convention," Folder "Select Committee on Athletic Concerns in Education," NCAA Headquarters.

20. Smith, *Play-by-Play,* 167.

21. Zimbalist, *Unpaid Professionals,* 184–86; *Law v. NCAA,* 5 F. Supp. 2nd 921 (D. Kan. 1998). Zimbalist pointed out the irony of restricting the third assistant coach while the head coaching salaries were escalating to unprecedented heights. The amount of penalty could have been around $75 million, but through mediation it was lowered to $54.4 million in 1998; see "NCAA to Pay Coaches $54.5 M," CBS Sportsline, http://www.cbsnews.com/stories/1999/03/09/sports/main38197.shtml (accessed February 25, 2009).

22. *NCAA v. Board of Regents of the University of Oklahoma,* 468 U.S. 85 (1984). As an example of questionable decisions, one might look at *Hennessey v. NCAA,* 564 F.2d 1136 (5th Cir. 1997), in which the circuit court found that there was no unreasonable restraint of trade in limiting the number of coaches any institution may employ in football and basketball. This case was decided before the important 1984 TV case in which a restraint of trade was applied against the NCAA. Had it been decided after 1984, the decision might have been different. In 1986, the NCAA had been considering for several years a national basketball TV contract and the possible need for a federal law exempting the NCAA from antitrust action. Both Robert Atwell of the American Council on Education (ACE) and Walter Byers of the NCAA opposed seeking antitrust exemption; see Robert Atwell to ACE Committee on Division One Intercollegiate Athletics, March 10, 1983, Walter Byers Papers, Box "Special Convention," Folder "Select Committee on American Concerns in Higher Education," NCAA Headquarters; Walter Byers to J. Davis, NCAA President, May 23, 1986, Walter Byers Papers, Box "TV, FB, 1986," Folder "TV, FB, 1986," NCAA Headquarters. Byers wrote: "I do not believe the NCAA should take a leadership or participatory role in seeking an antitrust exemption" and that he did not think antitrust exemption would be achieved regardless of who undertook the task.

23. See note 19.

24. Garrett and Hochberg, "Sports Broadcasting and the Law," n135.

25. Byers, *Unsportsmanlike Conduct,* 392. Byers stated that "state and federal challenges to these artificial restraints will be necessary" to bring about human equity and individual freedom to the athletes.

26. As quoted in Zimbalist, *Unpaid Professionals,* 19.

27. Ericson, "Remarks Before the Knight Commission on Intercollegiate Athletics."

28. Suggs, "NCAA Board Rejects Idea of Creating Outside Group to Push for Reform," A59.

29. "Sidelines," A56. Kirwan would later become a member of the Knight Commission in 2006 and take the position of cochair the following year.

30. This statement is found in Article I of the NCAA constitution.

31. The Knight Foundation Commission on Intercollegiate Athletics called the graduation rates for football and men's basketball "abysmal"; Knight Foundation Commission on Intercollegiate Athletics, *A Call to Action: Reconnecting College Sports to Higher Education,* 15. Seven teams in the 2001 NCAA basketball tourney had graduation rates of 0 percent. Football teams at the Rose, Orange, Fiesta, Citrus, Gator, Cotton, Outback, Peach, Liberty, and ten other bowls following the 2001 football season had graduation rates lower than 50 percent; see *Sports Business News,* January 3, 2002.

32. "The Will to Act Project."

33. "NCAA Board of Directors Adopts Landmark Academic Reform Package," April 29, 2004, http://ncaabbs.com/showthread.php?tid=25750 (accessed April 14, 2010).

34. *New York Times,* April 29, 2004, p. D1. Bensel-Meyers was an athletic-academic whistle-blower at the University of Tennessee and ostracized because she blew the whistle on academic fraud at the university. She became president of the Drake Group, a collection of faculty members who criticized big-time intercollegiate athletics.

35. "Presidential Task Force on the Future of Division I Athletics."

36. *USA Today,* November 19, 2008, pp. 1–2.

37. Amalie Nase, "Kinesiology Reserves Slots for Michigan Athletes," *Ann Arbor News,* March 16–17, 2008, http://www.mlive.com/wolverines/academics/stories/index.ssf/2008/03/kinesiology_reserves_slots_for.html (accessed February 14, 2009).

38. "Cut and Run Athletics." Other lesser-known institutions given APR penalties after four years of operation were Georgia State University, Indiana University-Purdue University Indianapolis, Kent State University, Nichols State University, Southeastern Louisiana University, University of North Texas, University of Tennessee, Martin, and Western Carolina University; see "Teams Subject to Penalties 2008–09 by Institution," NCAA, July 30, 2009, http://www.ncaa.org/wps/portal/ncaahome?WCM_GLOBAL_CONTEXT=/ncaa/ncaa/academics+and+athletes/education+and+research/academic+reform/apr/2009/2008–09_penalty_list_by_institution_y7txijra.html (accessed April 4, 2010).

39. "National and Sport-Group APR Averages, Trends and Penalties."

40. Steve Wieberg, "NCAA Hands Down Postseason Bans over Poor APR Scores," *USA Today,* May 7, 2009, http://www.usatoday.com/sports/college/2009–05–06-apr-report-postseason-bans_N.htm (accessed July 16, 2009).

41. Knight Commission on Intercollegiate Athletics, *A Call to Action,* 23.

42. NCAA *Proceedings,* January 11, 1999, 87.

43. "The Faculty Athletics Representatives: A Survey of Membership."

44. Bok, *Universities in the Marketplace,* 35–56, 123, 189.

45. Duderstadt, *The View from the Helm,* 320, 325.

46. "NCAA Presidential Task Force on the Future of Division I Athletics: Subcommittee on the Implementation of Academic Values and Standards."

Chapter 19. Faculty Reform Efforts: CARE, the Drake Group, and COIA

1. John W. White, W. S. Chaplin, and A. B. Hart, "Athletic Report," June 12, 1888, HUD 8388.3B, Harvard University Archives.

2. Frederick J. Turner, "Speech at Alumni Banquet, 31 January 1906," Turner Papers, Box 2, "Athletics," Wis/Mss/AL, State Historical Society of Wisconsin Archives.

3. "Faculty Resolution," December 2, 1907, Turner Papers, Box 2, "Athletics," Wis/Mss/AL, State Historical Society of Wisconsin Archives.

4. Veblen, "Summary and Trial Balance," in his *The Higher Learning in America*, http://www.ditext.com/veblen/veb8.html (accessed July 18, 2009). Veblen had taught at the University of Chicago, Stanford University, and the University of Missouri prior to publishing *The Higher Learning*.

5. See chapter 12.

6. *New York Times*, November 29, 1961, p. 48; *New York Times*, December 3, 1961, p. S1; Schmidt, *The Rose Bowl*, 8.

7. For a lengthy and persuasive account of the impact of the Cold War on the faculty's decision to oppose the Rose Bowl invitation and to raise the image of Ohio State University as an academic institution, see Kemper, *College Football and American Culture in the Cold War*, 47–79.

8. Bennett, "An Analysis of Why Ohio State Did Not Go to the Rose Bowl in 1962," 73–74; Odenkirk, "The Eighth Wonder of the World," 389–95. A decade and a half before, the Big Ten Faculty Representatives voted 7–3 not to allow Ohio State to represent the Big Ten in the 1945 Rose Bowl, during the last year of World War II; Intercollegiate Conference of Faculty Representatives Minutes, November 26, 1944, Senate Athletic Committee Chairman and Faculty Representative's File, 1907–68, Box 2, Folder "Conference Minutes 1944–45," University of Illinois Archives. One might note that the Harvard faculty voted 37–16 not to go to the 1920 Rose Bowl but were overruled. President Lawrence Lowell allowed the game to be played for "the cancellation of the Rose Bowl trip would destroy Harvard's prestige and with it the endowment fund"; P. W. K. Johnson, President Harvard Club of Southern California, telegram to President A. Lawrence Lowell, December 8, 1919, Lowell Papers, 1919–22, Folder 96, Harvard University Archives.

9. Odenkirk, "The Eighth Wonder of the World," 393.

10. Sack, *Counterfeit Amateurs*, 79–80. In the book, Sack probably gives the best historical account of CARE, 84–96.

11. Dave Anderson, "Sports of the Times," *New York Times*, October 1, 1981, p. B16.

12. *New York Times*, February 3, 1982, p. B7.

13. *New York Times*, September 27, 1981, p. S2. The CFA negotiated a tentative four-year $18-million deal with NBC while the NCAA's contract called for four years, $263.5 million, and additional money from Turner Broadcasting; see Smith, *Play-by-Play*, 160–61.

14. Byers, *Unsportsmanlike Conduct*, 342.

15. Sack, *Counterfeit Amateurs*, 96.

16. *Chicago Tribune*, May 17, 1992, sec. 3, p. 1; *San Antonio Express News*, November 1, 1992, C2.

17. Sperber, *Beer and Circus*, 130–31.

18. Sack, *Counterfeit Amateurs,* 151.

19. Jay Weiner, "College Athletic Reformers Find It's a Daunting Task," *Minneapolis Star Tribune,* October 23, 1999; Marc Hansen, "Faculty Athletic Reformers Should Target Disclosure," *Des Moines Register,* October 24, 1999; see also http://thedrakegroup.org/ (accessed February 17, 2006).

20. Tom Witosky, "Reform Group Sends a Message: Critics of Major College Sports Search for Way to Clean Up Athletics," *Des Moines Register,* October 24, 1999; see also http://thedrakegroup.org/ (accessed February 17, 2006).

21. Myles Brand, "In Athletics, Level Field Must Begin in Classroom," *New York Times,* May 9, 2004, p. SP10.

22. *New York Times,* May 16, 2004, p. SP11.

23. "The Drake Group Proposals," http://www.thedrakegroup.org/proposals.html (accessed July 24, 2009).

24. Earl, "The Faculty's Role in Reforming College Sports."

25. Wells, "CIC History."

26. Bob Eno, email to Ronald Smith, August 21, 2009. A number of the ideas included in later COIA proposed reforms were first introduced to the CIC faculty senate group in a document of "best practices" created by Penn State University Faculty Representative Scott Kretchmar.

27. The six conferences were the Atlantic Coast, Big 12, Big East, Big Ten, PAC-10, and Southeastern. Soon the other conference senates in Division I were invited to join, including Conference USA, Mid-America, Mountain West, and Sun Belt.

28. Coalition on Intercollegiate Athletics (COIA). "Charter of the Coalition on Intercollegiate Athletics."

29. Earl, "The Faculty Coalition's Role in Intercollegiate Athletics Reform."

30. Coalition on Intercollegiate Athletics (COIA), "Academic Integrity in Intercollegiate Athletics: Principles, Rules, and Best Practices." The 2005 document discussed five areas: admissions, athletic scholarships, curricular integrity, practice time and game schedules, and academic advising. Three recommendations would require NCAA constitutional changes: creating five-year scholarships, collecting data on athletes' academic performance, and eliminating divided fall-spring seasons.

31. Presidential admits are considered those athletes admitted to the institution who do not meet regular admittance requirements.

32. Coalition on Intercollegiate Athletics (COIA), "A Report to the NCAA Presidential Task Force."

33. NCAA Presidential Task Force on the Future of Division I Intercollegiate Athletics, "The Second-Century Imperatives."

34. NCAA Presidential Task Force on the Future of Division I Intercollegiate Athletics, "Executive Summary."

35. Ibid.; Palaima, "NCAA Panel Disses the Faculty."

36. NCAA Presidential Task Force on the Future of Division I Intercollegiate Athletics, "The Second-Century Imperatives."

37. Tublitz, "Putting the Student Back into the Student-Athlete."

38. Brand, "Faculty Members' Constructive Engagement in Intercollegiate Athletics."

39. Coalition on Intercollegiate Athletics (COIA), "Framing the Future: Reforming Intercollegiate Athletics."

40. *New York Times,* March 12, 2004, p. D1; emphasis added.

41. Brand, letter to William Thomas, November 13, 2006.

42. Splitt et al., "A Commentary on NCAA President Myles Brand's November 13, 2006, Reply to the Honorable William Thomas's Letter of October 2, 2006."

Chapter 20. The Freshman Rule: A Nearly Forgotten Reform

1. Rutgers Faculty Minutes, November 5, 1869, November 12, 1869, December 21, 1869, February 22, 1870, and May 21, 1872; *Rutgers Targum,* December 1869, pp. 3–4; *Rutgers Targum,* December 1870, p. 1; *Rutgers Targum,* May 1871, p. 7; *Rutgers Targum,* October 1871, p. 2; *Rutgers Targum,* November 1871, p. 2.

2. *Report of the President of Harvard College, 1897–1898,* 16–17, Harvard University Archives.

3. Camp, "Undergraduate Limitation in College Sports," 143.

4. Harvard Athletic Committee Minutes, February 20, 1899, Harvard University Archives.

5. Conference Minutes, March 10, 1906, Frederick Jackson Turner Files, Box 1, University of Wisconsin-Madison Archives.

6. Samuel J. Elder, Boston, to Walter Camp, Yale, January 17, 1906, Walter Camp Papers, Box 10, Folder 265, Yale University Archives.

7. NCAA *Proceedings,* December 29, 1906, 29.

8. William J. Tucker to Edward Cowles, Boston, May 7, 1906, President Tucker Papers, # 1, Folder "Athletics (A–H)," Dartmouth College Archives.

9. "Observation," *The Harvard Bulletin,* March 17, 1909, p. 4.

10. NCAA *Proceedings,* December 28, 1916, 46.

11. John Rydjord, *A History of Fairmount College,* 172; Corrie, "A History of the Atlantic Coast Conference," 60. Corrie noted that the Southern Intercollegiate Athletic Association in 1914 allowed colleges with fewer than 400 male students to play freshmen.

12. Palmer E. Pierce to NCAA membership, August 14, 1917, General Athletics, Box 1, Princeton University Archives.

13. Knute Rockne, "Notre Dame Sports—1918," CJWC, Box 12, Folder "Letters from Rockne," University of Notre Dame Archives.

14. Ray Lyman Wilbur to Leland Cutler, August 13 and August 27, 1917, President Wilbur Papers, Box 19, Folder 3, Stanford University Archives.

15. Leland Cutler to R. L. Wilbur, August 13, 1917, President Wilbur Papers, Box 19, Folder 3, Stanford University Archives.

16. Benjamin I. Wheeler to R. L. Wilbur, January 30, 1919, Board of Athletic Control, Box 3 Miscellaneous Papers, Stanford University Archives.

17. For instance, the Southern Intercollegiate Athletic Association in 1915 had a serious controversy over freshman eligibility, the larger schools favoring no freshman eligibility and the smaller schools desiring their eligibility. The result was that the eight larger schools formed the Southern Intercollegiate Conference, which in 1932 became the powerful Southeastern Conference; see Saylor, "Southern Intercollegiate Conference, 1921–1932."

18. Savage et al., *American College Athletics,* 84, 120.

19. Ralph Aigler, University of Michigan Board in Control of Athletics, 1933–34, Michigan Historical Collection, University of Michigan Archives.

20. *New York Times,* May 5, 1936, p. 28. NCAA championship competition was limited to three years for both transfer students and freshmen, beginning in 1936–37.

21. NCAA *Proceedings,* December 31, 1941, 29, 136–41; NCAA *Proceedings,* January 6, 1944, 34. See also Dean A. B. Moore, Faculty Chair of Athletics, Alabama, to Commissioner Mike S. Conner, Southeastern Conference, February 23, 1942, Unprocessed Athletic Department Papers, Folder "Transfer Rule," University of Alabama Archives; President A. W. Hobbs, Southern Conference, to Presidents and Faculty Chairmen of Southern Conference institutions, October 1, 1942, President Graham Files, Box 20, Folder "General 1939–47," University of North Carolina Archives; President Wilbur Papers, Box 135, Folder "Stanford Athletic Council," Stanford University Archives. Fritz Crisler, football coach and athletic director at Michigan, stated shortly after American involvement in World War II, "I hope we don't have to play freshmen. It would lend itself to and invite proselyting to a degree unknown at the present time"; *New York Times,* June 27, 1942, p. 27.

22. NCAA Council Minutes, November 19, 1951, NCAA Headquarters, Indianapolis, IN.

23. "Ivy Group Agreement Draft," May 9, 1952, General Athletics, Box 1, Princeton University Archives; Letter to Faculty Representatives of the SWC, January 31, 1951, Southwest Conference Papers, Folder "Votes on Eligibility," Southern Methodist University Archives.

24. Ruth, "A Study of Selected Conferences in the United States," 62.

25. President Gordon Gray, University of North Carolina, to Kept D. Battle, Rocky Mount, NC, October 21, 1952, President Gray Files, Box 10, Folder "General, 1952," University of North Carolina Archives; Minutes of the Southern Conference, May 8, 1953, and President Tribble, Wake Forest, to President Edens, Duke, May 26, 1953, A Hollis Edens Papers, Duke University Archives.

26. American Council on Education, *Report of the Special Committee on Athletic Policy,* 2.

27. NCAA *Proceedings,* January 10, 1967, 85–95; NCAA *Proceedings,* January 10, 1968, 82–86. A 1965 survey of NCAA institutions indicated that nearly two-thirds of the institutions favored freshman eligibility; Crowley, *In the Arena,* 91.

28. NCAA *Proceedings,* January 10, 1968, 84.

29. No vote count was recorded in 1972.

30. Alan Wieder, "NCAA Rule 48: Origins and Reactions," 42.

31. NCAA *Proceedings,* January 11, 1983, 103.

32. Ibid., 124.

33. NCAA *Proceedings,* January 13, 1988, 91.

34. Lederman, "U. of Iowa Sparks a Firestorm with Challenge to NCAA to Bar Freshmen from Sports within 3 Years," A1, A34.

35. This includes modifications of Prop 48 with Prop 42 in 1989, Prop 16 in 1992, and modifications of Prop 16 in 2003 by raising the number of high school core courses required to fourteen and in 2005 to sixteen beginning in 2008.

36. Leatherman, "High-School Students Found Taking More Core-Curriculum Courses," A2.

37. CFA Committee on Academic Standards, May 3, 1982, President Davison Papers, Box

18, "College Football Association," University of Georgia Archives; Hanford, "Proposition 48," 371; NCAA *Proceedings,* January 14, 1981, 187; NCAA *Proceedings,* June 29, 1987, 49; NCAA *Proceedings,* January 9, 1989, 113; Edward T. Foote II to James H. Wharton, Louisiana State University, April 23, 1982, President Davison Papers, Box 18, Folder "CFA-3," University of Georgia Archives; Bok, *Universities in the Marketplace,* 120; "National Symposium on Athletic Reform"; Tom Osborne to Martin Massengale, Chancellor, University of Nebraska, November 17, 1986, Chancellor's Central Files, Box 299, Folder 20, University of Nebraska Archives; "Intercollegiate Sports," Hearings before the Subcommittee on Commerce, Consumer Protection, and Competitiveness of the Committee on Energy and Commerce, 133; Smith, *The Carolina Way,* 107.

38. Franklin, "An Educational Reform Commission and Institutional Change," 134, 254–57.

39. The closest the NCAA came to consensus on freshman eligibility came in 1995, when a vote for freshman ineligibility was defeated, 311–17. One of the reasons given for opposing freshman ineligibility was that to support women's athletics, institutions needed as much money as possible, and freshman ineligibility would likely lead to greater costs; NCAA *Proceedings,* January 9, 1995, 255–56. A number of selective liberal arts colleges favored freshman ineligibility because of the "opportunity cost" of assigning many places to recruited athletes in the freshman class and thus turning away more educationally prepared individuals who would likely take greater advantage of their educational opportunities; see William G. Bowen to Willis Regier, University of Illinois Press, September 8, 2009, in the author's possession.

Afterword

1. Virgil Hancher, president of the University of Iowa in the 1950s, used this argument as part of his justification for allowing athletic scholarships in American universities. For a brilliant defense of athletic scholarships, see Hancher to President John A. Hannah, Michigan State University, February 11, 1957, President E. B. Fred General Correspondence File, 1956–57, Series 4/16/1, Box 274, Folder "Athletic Scholarships," University of Wisconsin Archives.

2. This general proposition of athletes fitting the general student population profile was shown to be not true for elite institutions as well as nonelite colleges, large and small, by Shulman and Bowen, *The Game of Life.*

3. Whitney, "The Sportsman's View-Point," 220.

4. Thelin, "Academics on Athletics: Review Essay," 410.

5. Brand, "Sustaining the Collegiate Model of Athletics."

6. Homer, "The Funeral and the Games," 419–36.

7. Louise Lincoln, Brookline, MA, to Christine Reid, Belmont, CA, November 1, 1903, Thomas Stetson Personal Collection and *New York Times,* November 1, 1903, p. 13. Warner had used the play previously in an 1897 game against Penn State; Bishop, *A History of Cornell,* 345.

8. "Final Drive. Missouri. 1990. 5th Down." http://www.youtube.com/watch?v=ZQJT8q0MMwQ (accessed March 29, 2010).

9. Kyle, "Winning at Olympia."

10. Wikipedia, "Death Penalty (NCAA)," http://en.wikipedia.org/wiki/Death_penalty_ (NCAA) (accessed August 11, 2009). One could also consider the 1952 ban against playing Kentucky in basketball as the first successful death penalty; NCAA, *Proceedings* January 8, 1953, pp. 122–23, 270.

11. Attorney Gary Roberts, in testimony before the U.S. Congress, indicated that the NCAA would need antitrust exemption for such significant reforms as (1) limiting coaching salaries, (2) capping athletic expenditures, (3) limiting television revenues and number of appearances, and (4) sharing revenues more equitably; "2004 Due Process and the NCAA Hearings Before the Subcommittee on the Constitution of the Committee on the Judiciary," House of Representatives, 108th Congress, 2nd Session, September 14, 2004.

12. The NCAA seriously considered asking for an antitrust exemption at the time of the U.S. Supreme Court's decision to break up the NCAA TV monopoly in football in 1984, as the National Football League successfully did a generation before.

13. "Statement and Resignation of President John W. Abercrombie of the University of Alabama," 1911, Unprocessed Papers, University of Alabama Archives.

14. It is obvious that coaches and athletic directors must be listened to, but reform efforts logically would focus on academic issues first, and the policy-making governing boards, chief administrators, faculty representatives, and participants should be in the legislative mix.

15. The FERPA question is addressed by Salzwedel and Ericson, "Cleaning up Buckley."

Bibliography

Works on Sport and College Sport

A.A.U. *A.A.U. Study of Effect of Athletic Competition on Girls and Women*. New York: Amateur Athletic Union, 1953.

Ade, George. *The College Widow*. New York: Samuel French, 1924, originally published in 1904.

American Association for Health, Physical Education, and Recreation. *Athletics in Education*. Washington, DC: AAHPER, 1963.

Andre, Judith, and David N. James, eds. *Rethinking College Athletics*. Philadelphia: Temple University Press, 1991.

Atwell, Robert H., et al. *The Money Game: Financing of Collegiate Athletics*. Washington, DC: American Council on Education, 1980.

Bailey, Wilford S. *Athletics and Academe: An Anatomy of Abuses and Prescriptions for Reform*. New York: American Council on Education, Macmillan, 1991.

Baker, L. H. *Football: Facts and Figures*. New York: Farrar & Rinehart, 1945.

Behee, John R. *Fielding Yost's Legacy*. Ann Arbor, MI: privately printed, 1971.

Bergin, Thomas G. *The Game: The Harvard-Yale Football Rivalry, 1875–1983*. New Haven, CT: Yale University Press, 1984.

Bernstein, Mark F. *Football: The Ivy League Origins of an American Obsession*. Philadelphia: University of Pennsylvania Press, 2001.

Betts, John R. *America's Sporting Heritage, 1850–1950*. Reading, MA: Addison-Wesley, 1974.

Blackwell, James. *On Brave Old Army Team: The Cheating Scandal That Rocked the Nation: West Point, 1951*. Navato, CA: Presidio, 1996.

Blanchard, John A., ed. *The H Book of Harvard Athletics: 1852–1922*. Cambridge, MA: Harvard Varsity Club, 1923.

Byers, Walter. *Unsportsmanlike Conduct: Exploiting College Athletes*. Ann Arbor: University of Michigan Press, 1995.

Cady, Edwin H. *The Big Game: College Sports and American Life*. Knoxville: University of Tennessee Press, 1978.

Cahn, Susan K. *Coming on Strong: Gender and Sexuality in Twentieth-Century Women's Sport*. New York: Free Press, 1994.

Camp, Walter. *Football Facts and Figures: A Symposium of Expert Opinions on the Game's Place in American College Athletics*. New York: Harper & Brothers, 1894.

Carnegie Foundation for the Advancement of Teaching. *College Athletes and Scholarship*. Boston: Merrymount Press, 1927.

Carpenter, Linda Jean, and R. Vivian Acosta. *Title IX*. Champaign, IL: Human Kinetics, 2005.

Carroll, John M. *Fritz Pollard: Pioneer in Racial Advancement*. Urbana: University of Illinois Press, 1992.

Carroll, John M. *Red Grange and the Rise of Modern Football*. Urbana: University of Illinois Press, 1999.

Cavallo, Dominick. *Muscles and Morals: Organized Playgrounds and Urban Reform, 1880–1920*. Philadelphia: University of Pennsylvania Press, 1981.

Christenson, Ade. *The Verdict of the Scoreboard: A Study of the Value and Practices Underlying College Athletics Today*. New York: American Press, 1958.

Chu, Donald, Jeffrey O. Segrave, and Beverly J. Becker, eds. *Sport and Higher Education*. Champaign, IL: Human Kinetics, 1985.

Cohane, Tim. *Great College Football Coaches of the Twenties and Thirties*. New Rochelle, NY: Arlington House, 1973.

Cohen, Stanley. *The Game They Played*. New York: Carroll & Graf, 2001.

Cozillio, Michael J., and Robert L. Hayman Jr. *Sports and Inequality*. Durham, NC: Carolina Academic Press, 2005.

Cozillio, Michael J., et al. *Sports Law: Cases and Materials*. Durham, NC: Carolina Academic Press, 2007.

Crawford, Albert Beecher. *Football Y Men, 1872–1919*. New Haven, CT: Yale University, 1962.

Crowley, Joseph N. *In the Arena: The NCAA's First Century*. Indianapolis, IN: National Collegiate Athletic Association, 2006.

Crowmartie, Bill. *Alabama vs. Auburn: Braggin' Rights*. West Point, NY: Leisure Press, 1982.

Cutting, George R. *Student Life at Amherst*. Amherst, MA: Hatch & Williams, 1871.

Davies, Richard O. *American Obsession: Sports and Society Since 1945*. Fort Worth, TX: Harcourt Brace, 1994.

Davies, Richard O. *Sports in American Life*. Malden, MA: Blackwell, 2007.

Davis, Parke H. *Football the American Intercollegiate Game*. New York: Charles Scribner's Sons. 1911.

Dealy, Francis X. Jr. *Win at Any Cost: The Sell Out of College Athletics*. New York: Birch Lane, 1990.

Denlinger, Kenneth, and Leonard Shapiro. *Athletes for Sale*. New York: Crowell, 1975.

Dizikes, John. *Sportsmen and Gamesmen*. Boston: Houghton Mifflin, 1971.

Dowling, William C. *Confessions of a Spoilsport: My Life and Hard Times Fighting Sports Corruption at an Old Eastern University*. University Park: Penn State University Press, 2007.

Duderstadt, James J. *Intercollegiate Athletics and the American University: A University President's Perspective*. Ann Arbor: University of Michigan Press, 2000, 2003.

Dunnavant, Keith. *The Fifty-Year Seduction*. New York: Thomas Dunne Books, 2004.

Dunning, Eric, and K. Sheard. *Barbarians, Gentlemen and Players*. London: Martin Robertson, 1979.

Durso, Joseph. *Madison Square Garden: 100 Years of History*. New York: Simon & Schuster, 1979.

Durso, Joseph. *The Sports Factory: An Investigation into College Sports*. New York: Quadrangle, 1975.

Eitzen, D. Stanley. *Fair and Foul: Beyond the Myths and Paradoxes of Sport.* Lanham, MD: Rowman & Littlefield, 1999.

Evans, J. Robert. *Blowing the Whistle on Intercollegiate Sports.* Chicago: Nelson-Hall, 1974.

Falla, Jack. *NCAA: The Voice of College Sports.* Mission, KS: National Collegiate Athletic Association, 1981.

Feinstein, John. *The Last Amateurs: Playing for Glory and Honor in Division I College Basketball.* Boston: Little, Brown, 2000.

Festal, Mary Jo. *Playing Nice: Politics and Apologies in Women's Sports.* New York: Columbia University Press, 1996.

Fields, Sarah K. *Female Gladiators: Gender, Law, and Contact Sport in America.* Urbana: University of Illinois Press, 2005.

Fitzpatrick, Frank. *And the Walls Came Tumbling Down: Kentucky, Texas Western, and the Game That Changed American Sports.* New York: Simon & Schuster, 1999.

Fizel, J., and R. Fort, eds. *Economics of College Sports: An Overview.* Westport, CT: Greenwood, 2004.

Flath, Arnold. *A History of Relations between the National Collegiate Athletic Association and the Athletic Union of the United States (1905–1963).* Champaign, IL: Stipes, 1964.

Fleisher, Arthur A. III, Brian L. Goff, and Robert D. Tollison. *The National Collegiate Athletic Association: A Study in Cartel Behavior.* Chicago: University of Chicago Press, 1992.

Frey, James, ed. *The Governance of Intercollegiate Athletics.* West Point, NY: Leisure Press, 1982.

Fulks, Daniel L. *Revenues and Expenses of Division I and II Intercollegiate Athletics Programs: Financial Trends and Relationships—2001.* Indianapolis, IN: National Collegiate Athletic Association, 2001.

Funk, Gary D. *Major Violations: The Unbalanced Priorities in Athletics and Academics.* Champaign, IL: Leisure Press, 1991.

Gavora, Jessica. *Tilting the Playing Field: Schools, Sports, Sex and Title IX.* San Francisco: Encounter Books, 2002.

Gems, Gerald. *For Pride, Profit, and Patriarchy: Football and the Incorporation of American Cultural Values.* Lanham, MD: Scarecrow Press, 2000.

Gerdy, John R. *Air Ball: American Education's Failed Experiment with Elite Athletics.* Jackson: University Press of Mississippi, 2006.

Gerdy, John. *Sports: The All-American Addiction.* Jackson: University of Mississippi Press, 2002.

Golenbock, Peter. *Personal Fouls.* New York: Carroll & Graf, 1989.

Gorn, Elliott J., and Warren Goldstein. *A Brief History of American Sports.* Urbana: University of Illinois Press, 2004.

Graham, Archibald H. Jr. *Cricket at the University of Pennsylvania.* Printed privately, 1930.

Graham, Tom, and Rachel Graham Cody. *Getting Open: The Unknown Story of Bill Garrett and the Integration of College Basketball.* Bloomington: Indiana University Press, 2006.

Grant, Randy R., John Leadley, and Zenon Zygmont. *The Economics of Intercollegiate Sports.* Hackensack, NJ: World Scientific, 2008.

Guttmann, Allen. *From Ritual to Record: The Nature of Modern Sports.* New York: Columbia University Press, 1978.

Guttmann, Allen. *A Whole New Ball Game: An Interpretation of American Sport.* Chapel Hill: University of North Carolina Press, 1988.

Guttmann, Allen. *Women's Sports: A History.* New York: Columbia University Press, 1991.

Haskins, Don, and Dan Wetzel. *Glory Road.* New York: Hyperion, 2006.

Hawkins, Billy. *The New Plantations: The Internal Colonization of Black Student-Athletes.* Winterville, GA: Sadiki Press, 2001.

Holt, Richard. *Sport and the British: A Modern History.* Oxford: Oxford University Press, 1989.

Hurd, Richard M. *A History of Yale Athletics: 1840–1888.* New Haven, CT: privately printed, 1888.

Jacobs, Barry. *Across the Line: Tales of the First Black Players in the ACC and SEC.* Guilford, CT: Lyons Press, 2008.

Kemper, Kurt E. *College Football and American Culture in the Cold War Era.* Urbana: University of Illinois Press, 2009.

Kennedy, Charles W. *College Athletics.* Princeton, NJ: Princeton University Press, 1925.

Lawrence, Paul R. *Unsportsmanlike Conduct: The National Collegiate Athletic Association and the Business of College Football.* Westport, CT: Praeger, 1987.

Lester, Robin. *Stagg's University: The Rise, Decline, and Fall of Big-Time Football at Chicago.* Urbana: University of Illinois Press, 1995.

Lomax, Michael E., ed. *Sports and the Racial Divide: African American and Latino Experience in an Era of Change.* Jackson: University Press of Mississippi, 2008.

Lucas, John. *The Amateur Athletic Union of the United States: 1888–1988.* Privately printed, 1998.

Lucas, John A., and Ronald A. Smith. *Saga of American Sport.* Philadelphia: Lea & Febiger, 1978.

Mangan, J. A., and James Walvin, eds. *Manliness and Morality: Middle-Class Masculinity in Britain and America, 1800–1940.* Manchester, England: Manchester University Press, 1987.

March, Francis A. Jr. *Athletics at Lafayette College.* Easton, PA: Lafayette College, 1923.

McCallum, John D. *Big Ten Football Since 1895.* Radnor, PA: Chilton Book, 1976.

McCarty, Bernie. *All-America: The Complete Roster of Football's Heroes.* University Park, IL: printed privately, 1991.

McMillen, Tom, with Paul Coggins. *Out of Bounds: How the American Sports Establishment Is Being Driven by Greed and Hypocrisy and What Needs to Be Done About It.* New York: Simon & Schuster, 1992.

Michener, James. *Sports in America.* New York: Random House, 1976.

Miller, Patrick, ed. *The Sporting World of the Modern South.* Urbana: University of Illinois Press, 2002.

Miracle, A. W., and Roger C. Rees. *Lessons of the Locker Room: The Myth of School Sports.* Amherst, NY: Prometheus Books, 1994.

Naismith, James. *Basketball's Origins: Creative Problem Solving in the Gilded Age.* Cambridge, NY: Bear Publications, 1976.

Naismith, James. *Basketball: Its Origin and Development*. New York: Associated Press of New York City, 1941.

Nelson, David M. *Anatomy of a Game: Football, the Rules, and the Men Who Made the Game*. Newark: University of Delaware Press, 1994.

Ogden, David C., and Joel Nathan Rosen, eds. *Reconstructing Fame: Sport, Race, and Evolving Reputations*. Jackson: University Press of Mississippi, 2008.

Olson, Jack. *The Black Athlete: A Shameful Story. The Myth of Integration in American Sport*. New York: Time-Life Books, 1968.

Oriard, Michael. *Bowled Over: Big-Time College Football from the Sixties to the BCS Era*. Chapel Hill: University of North Carolina Press, 2009.

Oriard, Michael. *The End of Autumn: Reflections on My Life in Football*. Urbana: University of Illinois Press, 2009.

Oriard, Michael. *Reading Football: How the Popular Press Created an American Spectacle*. Chapel Hill: University of North Carolina Press, 1993.

Orton, George W. *A History of Athletics at Pennsylvania, 1873–1896*. Philadelphia: privately printed, ca. 1896.

Pennington, Bill. *The Heisman: Great American Stories of the Men Who Won*. New York: Regan Books, 2004.

Pennington, Richard. *Breaking the Ice: The Racial Integration of Southwest Conference Football*. Jefferson, NC: McFarland, 1987.

Pitt, Larry. *Football at Rutgers: A History, 1869–1969*. New Brunswick, NJ: Rutgers University Press, 1972.

Pittman, Andrew T., John O. Spengler, and Sarah J. Young. *Case Studies in Sport Law*. Champaign, IL: Human Kinetics, 2008.

Pope, Edwin. *Football's Greatest Coaches*. Atlanta: Tupper and Love, 1955.

Porter, David L., ed., *Biographical Dictionary of American Sports*. 4 vols. Westport, CT: Greenwood Press, 1987–88.

Porto, Brian L. *A New Season: Using Title IX to Reform College Sports*. Westport, CT: Praeger, 2003.

Presbrey, Frank, and James Moffatt. *Athletics at Princeton*. New York: Frank Presbrey, 1901.

Pritchard, George H. *Intercollegiate Athletics: From the Viewpoint of College and University Presidents and Deans*. Cape Girardeau, MO: State Teachers College, ca. 1928.

Putney, Clifford. *Muscular Christianity: Manhood and Sports in Protestant America, 1880–1920*. Cambridge, MA: Harvard University Press, 2001.

Rader, Benjamin G. *American Sports: From the Age of Folk Games to the Age of Televised Sports*. Upper Saddle River, NJ: Prentice-Hall, 1999.

Rhoden, William C. *The $40 Million Slaves: The Rise, Fall, and Redemption of the Black Athlete*. New York: Crown, 2006.

Roberts, Howard. *The Big Nine: Story of Football in the Western Conference*. New York: G. P. Putnam's Sons, 1948.

Roberts, Randy, and James Olson. *Winning Is the Only Thing: Sports in America Since 1945*. Baltimore: Johns Hopkins University Press, 1989.

Rooney, James F. Jr. *The Recruiting Game*. Lincoln: University of Nebraska Press, 1980.

Rosen, Charles. *Scandals of '51: How the Gamblers Almost Killed College Basketball*. New York: Holt, Rinehart & Winston, 1978.

Rosen, Charles. *The Wizard of Odds: How Jack Molinas Almost Destroyed the Game of Basketball*. New York: Seven Stories Press, 2001.

Rosner, Scott, and Kenneth L. Shropshire. *The Business of Sports*. New York: Jones & Bartlett, 2004.

Ross, Gordon. *The Boat Race*. London: Hodder & Stoughton, 1954.

Sack, Allen L. *Counterfeit Amateurs: An Athlete's Journey through the Sixties to the Age of Academic Capitalism*. University Park: Penn State University Press, 2008.

Sack, Allen L., and Ellen J. Staurowsky. *College Athletes for Hire: The Evolution and Legacy of the NCAA's Amateur Myth*. Westport, CT: Praeger, 1998.

Schmidt, Raymond. *Football's Stars of Summer: A History of the College All-Star Football Game Series of 1934–1976*. Lanham, MD: Scarecrow Press, 2001.

Schmidt, Raymond. *The Rose Bowl: A Modern History, 1960–2008*. Haworth, NJ: St. Johann Press, 2008.

Schmidt, Raymond. *Shaping College Football: The Transformation of an American Sport*. Syracuse, NY: Syracuse University Press, 2007.

Schugurensky, Daniel, ed. "History of Education: Selected Moments of the 20th Century." http://www.oise.utoronto.ca/research/edu20/moments/1944gibill.html (accessed April 11, 2010).

Scott, Jack. *The Athletic Revolution*. New York: Free Press, 1971.

Shropshire, Kenneth L. *Agents of Opportunity: Sports Agents and Corruption in Collegiate Sports*. Philadelphia: University of Pennsylvania Press, 1990.

Shropshire, Kenneth L. *Black and White: Race and Sports in America*. Jackson: University Press of Mississippi, 2004.

Smith, C. Fraser. *Lenny, Lefty, and the Chancellor: The Len Bias Tragedy and the Search for Reform in Big-Time College Basketball*. Baltimore: Bancroft Press, 1992.

Smith, Dean. *The Carolina Way: Leadership Lessons from a Life in Coaching*. New York: Penguin Press, 2004.

Smith, Melvin L. *Early American & Canadian 'Football': Beginnings through 1883/84*. Bloomington, IN: privately printed, 2003.

Smith, Ronald A., ed. *Big-Time Football at Harvard, 1905: The Diary of Coach Bill Reid*. Urbana: University of Illinois Press, 1994.

Smith, Ronald A. *Play-by-Play: Radio, Television, and Big-Time College Sport*. Baltimore: Johns Hopkins University Press, 2001.

Smith, Ronald A. *Sports and Freedom: The Rise of Big-Time College Athletics*. New York: Oxford University Press, 1988.

Somers, Dale A. *The Rise of Sports in New Orleans, 1850–1900*. Baton Rouge: Louisiana State University Press, 1972.

Sperber, Murray. *Beer and Circus: How Big-time College Sports Is Crippling Undergraduate Education*. New York: Henry Holt, 2000.

Sperber, Murray. *College Sports, Inc.: The Athletic Department vs. the University*. New York: Henry Holt, 1990.

Sperber, Murray. *Onward to Victory: The Crises That Shaped College Sport*. New York: Henry Holt, 1998.

Sperber, Murray. *Shake Down the Thunder: The Creation of Notre Dame Football*. New York: Henry Holt, 1993.

Stagg, Amos Alonzo, and Wesley Winans Stout. *Touchdown!* New York: Longmans, Green, 1927.

Steiner, Celestin J. *College Football: Asset or Liability*. Detroit: Press of the University of Detroit, 1951.

Suggs, Welch. *A Place on the Team: The Triumph and Tragedy of Title IX*. Princeton, NJ: Princeton University Press, 2005.

Telander, Rick. *The One Hundred Yard Lie: The Corruption of College Football and What We Should Do About It*. New York: Simon & Schuster, 1989.

Thelin, John R. *Games Colleges Play: Scandal and Reform in Intercollegiate Athletics*. Baltimore: Johns Hopkins University Press, 1994.

Thelin, John R., and Lawrence L. Wiseman. *The Old College Try: Balancing Academics and Athletics in Higher Education*. Washington, DC: School of Education and Human Development, George Washington University, 1989.

Thoma, J. Douglas. *Football U: Spectator Sports in the Life of the American University*. Ann Arbor: University of Michigan Press, 2003.

Torr, James D., ed. *Sports and Athletes: Opposing Viewpoints*. Detroit: Greenhaven Press, 2005.

Underwood, Clarence. *The Student Athlete: Eligibility and Academic Integrity*. East Lancing: Michigan State University Press, 1984.

Underwood, John. *Death of an American Game*. Boston: Little, Brown, 1979.

Voltmer, Carl D. *A Brief History of the Intercollegiate Conference of Faculty Representatives with Special Consideration of Athletic Problems*. Menasha, WI: George Banta, 1935.

Walsh, Christopher J. *Where Football Is King: A History of the SEC*. Lanham, MD: Taylor, 2006.

Ware, Susan, ed. *Title IX: A Brief History with Documents*. Boston: Bedford/St. Martins, 2007.

Watterson, John S. *College Football: History, Spectacle, Controversy*. Baltimore: Johns Hopkins University Press, 2000.

Watts, Tim J. *The Regulation of College Sports: A Bibliography*. Monticello, IL: Vance Bibliographies, 1991.

Welch, Lewis B., and Walter Camp. *YALE: Her Campus, Classrooms, and Athletics*. Boston: L. C. Page, 1899.

Wheeler, Lonnie. *Blue Yonder: Kentucky: The United State of Basketball*. Wilmington, OH: Orange Frazer Press, 1998.

Whitford, David. *A Payroll to Meet: A Story of Greed, Corruption and Football at SMU*. New York: Macmillan, 1989.

Whitney, Caspar. *A Sporting Pilgrimage*. New York: Harper & Brothers, 1895.

Wiggins, David K. *Glory Bound: Black Athletes in a White America*. Syracuse, NY: Syracuse University Press, 1997.

Wigginton, Russell Thomas. *The Strange Career of the Black Athlete*. Westport, CT: Praeger, 2006.

Wigglesworth, Neil. *The Evolution of English Sport*. London: Frank Cass, 1996.

Wilson, Kenneth L. (Tug), and Jerry Brondfield. *The Big Ten*. Englewood Cliffs, NJ: Prentice-Hall, 1967.

Worsnop, Richard L. *College Sports: Will Reform Efforts Help or Hurt Student Athletes?* Washington, DC: Congressional Quarterly, 1994.

Wushanley, Ying. *Playing Nice and Losing: The Struggle for Control of Women's Intercollegiate Athletics, 1960–2000*. Syracuse, NY: Syracuse University Press, 2004.

Yaeger, Don. *Undue Process: The NCAA's Injustice to All*. Champaign, IL: Sagamore, 1991.

Yost, Mark. *Varsity Green: A Behind the Scenes Look at Culture and Corruption in College Athletics*. Stanford, CA: Stanford University Press, 2009.

Young, David C. *The Olympic Myth of Greek Amateur Athletics*. Chicago: Ares, 1985.

Zang, David W. *Fleet Walker's Divided Heart: The Life of Baseball's First Black Major Leaguer*. Lincoln: University of Nebraska Press, 1995.

Zang, David W. *SportsWars: Athletes in the Age of Aquarius*. Fayetteville: University of Arkansas Press, 2001.

Zimbalist, Andrew. *Unpaid Professionals: Commercialism and Conflict in Big-Time College Sports*. Princeton, NJ: Princeton University Press, 1999.

Histories, Including Educational Histories

Alberts, Robert C. *Pitt: The Story of the University of Pittsburgh, 1787–1987*. Pittsburgh: University of Pittsburgh Press, 1986.

Ashby, Warren. *Frank Porter Graham: A Southern Liberal*. Winston-Salem, NC: John F. Blair, 1980.

Bagg, Lyman. *Four Years at Yale*. New York: Henry Holt, 1871.

Bergeria, Gary J., and Ronald Priddis. *Brigham Young University: A House of Faith*. Salt Lake City, UT: Signature Books, 1985.

Bishop, Morris. *A History of Cornell*. Ithaca, NY: Cornell University Press, 1962.

The Black Book, or Book of Misdemeanors in King's College, New York, 1771–1775. New York: Columbia University Press, 1931.

Bledstein, Burton J. *The Culture of Professionalism*. New York: W. W. Norton, 1976.

Bok, Derek. *Universities in the Marketplace: The Commercialization of Higher Education*. Princeton, NJ: Princeton University Press, 2003.

Bowen, William G., and Derek Bok. *The Shape of the River: Long-Term Consequences of Considering Race in College and University Admissions*. Princeton, NJ: Princeton University Press, 2000.

Bowen, William G., and Sarah A. Levin. *Reclaiming the Game: College Sports and Educational Values*. Princeton, NJ: Princeton University Press, 2003.

Browder, Robert Paul, and Thomas G. Smith. *Independent: A Biography of Lewis W. Douglas*. New York: Alfred A. Knopf, 1986.

Bryce, James. *The American Commonwealth*. 3 vols. Chicago: Charles H. Sergel, 1891.

Burgan, Mary. *What Ever Happened to the Faculty? Drift and Decision in Higher Education*. Baltimore: Johns Hopkins University Press, 2006.

Canby, Henry Seidel. *Alma Mater: The Gothic Age of American College*. New York: Farrar and Rinehart, 1936.

Carey, James C. *Kansas State University*. Lawrence: Regents Press of Kansas, 1977.

Chaffin, Nora C. *Trinity College, 1839–1892: The Beginnings of Duke University*. Durham, NC: Duke University Press, 1950.

Cheyney, Edward P. *History of the University of Pennsylvania, 1740–1940*. Philadelphia: University of Pennsylvania Press, 1940.

Corbin, John. *An American at Oxford*. London: A. P. Watt and Sons, 1902.

Croome, A. C. M., ed. *Fifty Years of Sport at Oxford, Cambridge, and the Great Public Schools*. Vol. 1. London: Walter Southwood, 1913.

Curti, Merle, and Vernon C. Carstensen. *The University of Wisconsin: A History, 1848–1925*. 2 vols. Madison: University of Wisconsin Press, 1949.

Dabney, Virginia. *Mr. Jefferson's University*. Charlottesville: University of Virginia, 1981.

Damerest, William H. S. *History of Rutgers College*. New Brunswick, NJ: Rutgers College, 1924.

Dougherty, Nathan W. *Educators and Athletics*. Knoxville: Department of Athletics, University of Tennessee, 1976.

Duderstadt, James J. *The View from the Helm: Leading the American University During an Era of Change*. Ann Arbor: University of Michigan Press, 2007.

Dyer, Thomas G. *The University of Georgia: A Bicentennial History, 1785–1985*. Athens: University of Georgia Press, 1985.

Dzuback, Mary Ann. *Robert M. Hutchins: Portrait of an Educator*. Chicago: University of Chicago Press, 1991.

Fine, Sidney. *Laissez Faire and the General-Welfare State: A Study of Conflict in American Thought, 1865–1901*. Ann Arbor: University of Michigan Press, 1956.

Flexner, Abraham. *Abraham Flexner: An Autobiography*. New York: Simon and Schuster, 1960.

Flexner, Abraham. *I Remember: The Autobiography of Abraham Flexner*. New York: Simon & Schuster, 1940.

Flexner, Abraham. *Universities: American, English, German*. New York: Teachers College Press, 1967, originally published in 1930.

Flower, John A. *Downstairs, Upstairs: The Changed Spirit and Face of College Life in America*. Akron, OH: University of Akron Press, 2003.

Friday, William C. *Frank Porter Graham and Human Rights*. Chapel Hill, NC: privately printed, 1983.

Geiger, Roger L. *To Advance Knowledge*. New York: Oxford University Press, 1986.

Geiger, Roger L., ed. *The American College in the Nineteenth Century*. Nashville, TN: Vanderbilt University Press, 2000.

Geiger, Roger L., ed. *Future of the American Public Research University*. Rotterdam, Netherlands: Sense, 2007.

Geiger, Roger L. *Knowledge and Money: Research Universities and the Paradox of the Market Place*. Stanford, CA: Stanford University Press, 2004.

Glide, Christian. *Higher Education: Open for Business*. Lanham, MD: Lexington Books, 2007.

Godson, Susan H., et al. *The College of William & Mary: A History*. 2 vols. Williamsburg: College of William and Mary in Virginia, 1993.

Goodspeed, Thomas Wakefield. *William Rainey Harper*. Chicago: University of Chicago Press, 1928.

Grant, Gerald, and David Riesman. *The Perpetual Dream: Reform and Experiment in the American College*. Chicago: University of Chicago Press, 1978.

Handlin, Oscar, and Mary F. Handlin. *The American College and American Culture*. New York: McGraw-Hill, 1970.

Haskins, Charles Homer. *The Rise of Universities*. Ithaca, NY: Cornell University Press, 1957.

Havighurst, Walter. *The Miami Years: 1809–1959*. New York: Putnam, 1958.

Hawkins, Hugh. *Banding Together: The Rise of National Associations in American Higher Education, 1887–1950*. Baltimore: Johns Hopkins University Press, 1992.

Hawkins, Hugh. *Between Harvard and America: The Educational Leadership of Charles W. Eliot*. New York: Oxford University Press, 1972.

Hesburgh, Theodore M. *God, Country, Notre Dame*. New York: Doubleday, 1990.

Hofstadter, Richard, and Wilson Smith, eds. *American Higher Education: A Documentary History*. Vol. 2. Chicago: University of Chicago Press, 1961.

Homer. "The Funeral and the Games." *Iliad,* Book XXIII. Translated by E. V. Riew. Baltimore: Penguin Books, 1966.

Horowitz, Helen Lefkowitz. *Campus Life: Undergraduate Cultures from the End of the Eighteenth Century to the Present*. Chicago: University of Chicago Press, 1988.

Hutchins, Robert Maynard. *The New College Plan*. Chicago: University of Chicago Press, 1931.

Jencks, Christopher, and David Riesman. *The Academic Revolution*. Garden City, NY: Doubleday, 1968.

Keller, Morton, and Phyllis Keller. *Making Harvard Modern: The Rise of America's University*. New York: Oxford University Press, 2001.

Kerr, Clark. *The Uses of the University*. Cambridge, MA: Harvard University Press, 1995.

Kett, Joseph F. *Rites and Passages*. New York: Basic Books, 1977.

LaVaque-Manty, Mike. *The Playing Fields of Eton: Equality and Excellence in Modern Meritocracy*. Ann Arbor: University of Michigan Press, 2009.

The Laws of Yale-College. New Haven, CT: Thomas and Samuel Green, 1774.

Leslie, W. Bruce. *Gentlemen and Scholars: College and Community in the "Age of the University."* University Park: Penn State University Press, 1992.

Levine, David O. *The American College and the Culture of Aspiration, 1915–1940*. Ithaca, NY: Cornell University Press, 1986.

Link, Arthur S., ed. *The Papers of Woodrow Wilson*. Princeton, NJ: Princeton University Press, 1973.

Link, William A. *William Friday: Power, Purpose, and American Higher Education*. Chapel Hill: University of North Carolina Press, 1995.

Manley, Robert N. *Centennial History of the University of Nebraska*. Vol. 1. Lincoln: University of Nebraska Press, 1969.

Mattingly, Paul H. *The Classless Profession*. New York: New York University Press, 1975.

Mayer, Milton. *Robert Maynard Hutchins: A Memoir*. Berkeley: University of California Press, 1993.

McMath, Robert C. Jr., et al. *Engineering the New South: Georgia Tech, 1885–1985*. Athens: University of Georgia Press, 1985.

McNeill, William H. *Hutchins' University: A Memoir of the University of Chicago, 1929–1950*. Chicago: University of Chicago Press, 1991.

Mitchell, J. Pearce. *Stanford University, 1916–1941*. Palo Alto, CA: Stanford University, 1958.

Morison, Elting E., ed. *The Letters of Theodore Roosevelt*. Cambridge, MA: Harvard University Press, 1952.

Morison, Samuel Eliot, ed. *The Development of Harvard University, 1869–1929*. Cambridge, MA: Harvard University Press, 1930.

Munro, Walter L. *The Old Back Campus at Brown*. Providence, RI: Haley & Sykes, 1929.

Northwestern University President's Annual Report, 1895–1896. Evanston, IL: Northwestern University, 1896.

Paine, Albert B. *Thomas Nast*. New York: Macmillan, 1904.

Patton, Francis L. *Religion in College*. Princeton, NJ: Princeton University Press, 1889.

Paul, Annie Murphy. *The Cult of Personality*. New York: Free Press, 2004.

Porter, Earl W. *Trinity and Duke, 1892–1924*. Durham, NC: Duke University Press, 1964.

Pratt, Robert A. *We Shall Not Be Moved: The Triumphant Story of Horace Wallace, Charlayne Hunter, and Hamilton Holmes*. Athens: University of Georgia Press, 2002.

Putney, Clifford. *Muscular Christianity: Manhood and Sports in Protestant America: 1880–1920*. Cambridge, MA: Harvard University Press, 2001.

Reuben, Julie E. *The Making of the Modern University: Intellectual Transformation and the Marginalization of Morality*. Chicago: University of Chicago Press, 1996.

Richardson, Leon B. *History of Dartmouth College*. 2 vols. Hanover, NH: Dartmouth College Publications, 1932.

Rodgers, Daniel T. *The Work Ethic in Industrial America, 1850–1920*. Chicago: University of Chicago Press, 1978.

Rogers, Walter P. *Andrew White and the Modern University*. Ithaca, NY: Cornell University Press, 1962.

Rudolph, Frederick. *The American College and University*. New York: Vintage Books, 1962.

Rydjord, John. *A History of Fairmount College*. Lawrence: Regents Press of Kansas, 1977.

Sargendorph, Kent. *Michigan: The Story of the University*. New York: E. P. Dutton, 1948.

Savage, Howard. *Fruit of an Impulse: Forty-Five Years of the Carnegie Foundation, 1905–1950*. New York: Harcourt, Brace, 1953.

Schmidt, George P. *The Liberal Arts College*. New Brunswick, NJ: Rutgers University Press, 1957.

Sharpless, Isaac. *The American College*. New York: Doubleday, Page, 1915.

Sheldon, Sheldon D. *Student Life and Customs*. New York: D. Appleton, 1901.

Shulman, James L., and William G. Bowen. *The Game of Life: College Sports and Educational Values*. Princeton, NJ: Princeton University Press, 2001.

Slosson, Edwin E. *Great American Universities*. New York: Macmillan, 1910.

Solberg, Winton U. *The University of Illinois, 1867–1894*. Urbana: University of Illinois Press, 1968.

Solomon, Barbara. *In the Company of Educated Women: A History of Higher Education in America*. New Haven, CT: Yale University Press, 1985.

Stearns, Peter N. *Be a Man! Males in Modern Society*. New York: Holmes & Meier, 1979.

Stein, Donald G. *Buying In or Selling Out?: The Commercialism of the American Research University*. New Brunswick, NJ: Rutgers University Press, 2004.

Storr, Richard J. *Harper's University: The Beginnings*. Chicago: University of Chicago Press, 1966.

Thelin, John R. *The Cultivation of Ivy: A Saga of the College in America*. Cambridge, MA: Schenkman, 1976.

Thelin, John R. *History of American Higher Education*. Baltimore: Johns Hopkins University Press, 2004.

Thomas, David A. *Michigan State College: John Hannah and the Creation of a World University, 1926–1969*. East Lancing: Michigan State University Press, 2008.

Thomas, Mary Martha. *Southern Methodist University: Founding and Early Years*. Dallas: Southern Methodist University Press, 1974.

Trachtenberg, Stephen Joel, with Tansy Blumer. *Big Man on Campus: A University President Speaks Out on Higher Education*. New York: Touchstone, 2008.

Vaille, F. O., and H. A. Clark, eds. *The Harvard Book*. Cambridge, MA: Welch, Bigelow, 1875.

Veblen, Thorstein. *The Higher Learning in America: A Memorandum on the Conduct of Universities by Business Men*. New York: Viking Press, 1935 [1918].

Veysey, Laurence R. *The Emergence of the American University*. Chicago: University of Chicago Press, 1965.

Welter, Rush. *The Mind of America, 1820–1860*. New York: Columbia University Press, 1975.

Wertenbaker, Thomas J. *Princeton, 1746–1896*. Princeton, NJ: Princeton University Press, 1946.

Wiebe, Robert H. *The Search for Order: 1877–1900*. New York: Hill & Wang, 1967.

Wiebe, Robert H. *The Segmented Society*. New York: Oxford University Press, 1975.

Reports, Documents, Lawsuits, and Studies on College Sport

"Agreement between Harvard, Yale, and Princeton." October 1939, Harvard Athletic Committee Minutes, November 6, 1939, Harvard University Archives.

"Agreements between Harvard, Yale, and Princeton in Force 1925." President Lowell Papers, Folder 72, Harvard University Archives.

American Association of University Professors. "The Role of Faculty in the Governance of College Athletics: A Report of the Special Committee on Athletics." *Academe* 76 (January–February 1990): 43–47.

American Association of University Professors Committee on Athletic Problems. "The Faculty Role in the Reform of Intercollegiate Athletics: Principles and Recommended Practices." *Academe* 89 (January–February 2003): 64–70.

American Association of University Professors Special Committee on Athletics. "The Role of the Faculty in the Governance of College Athletics." December 1989. http://www.aaup.org/aaup/comm/rep/athgov.htm (accessed September 1, 2008).

American College Testing Program and Educational Testing Service. *Athletics and Academics in the Freshman Year: A Study of the Academic Effects of Freshman Participation in Varsity Athletics.* Washington, DC: American Association of Collegiate Registrars and Admissions Officers, December 1984.

American Council on Education. "Report of the Special Committee on Athletic Policy." Washington, DC: American Council on Education, February 16, 1952.

"Appeals Court Temporarily Keeps NCAA 'Prop 16' Intact." March 29, 1999. http://www .sportslawnews.com (accessed March 30, 2010).

"Athletic Committee Minutes [Harvard Graduates' Athletic Association Specific Rules]." *Harvard Graduates' Magazine* 14 (March 1906): 486–88.

"Athletics Recruiting and Academic Values: Enhancing Transparency, Spreading Risk, and Improving Practice." Roundtable on Intercollegiate Athletics and Higher Education, University of Georgia, Institute of Higher Education. Fall 2006. http://www.knightcom-mission.org/images/pdfs/recruitingessayknight.pdf (accessed May 6, 2009).

Bakker, Doug. "NCAA Initial Eligibility Requirements: The Case Law Behind the Changes." http://www.law.depaul.edu/students/organizations_journals/student_orgs/lawslj/ Volume%203,%20Issue%202%20Current%20Issue/NCAA%20eligibility%20by%20Bakker .pdf (accessed March 30, 2010).

Bartell, Ted, et al. "Study of Freshman Eligibility Standards: Technical Report." August 25, 1984. NCAA Headquarters.

"Benefits of NCAA Division II Membership Classification," November 9, 2009. http://www .ncaa.org/wps/wcm/connect/e400d180408092dda1d6b96292/c9519/d2+membership +benefits_revis (accessed April 9, 2010).

Board of Trustees Athletics Subcommittee. "Intercollegiate Athletics at Rice." April 2004. http://professor.rice.edu/images/professor/report.pdf (accessed August 30, 2008).

Brand, Myles. "Faculty Members' Constructive Engagement in Intercollegiate Athletics." *The Montana Professor.* October 2006. http://coia.comm.psu.edu/News%20of%20interest/ Brand%20The%20Montana%20Professor%20Oct%2006.pdf (accessed March 30, 2010).

Brand, Myles. Letter to William Thomas, Chair, House Committee on Ways and Means, November 13, 2006. http://www.ncaa.org/wps/wcm/connect/2fa84c004e0d90aea0caf01a d6fc8b25/20061115_response_to_housecommitteeonwaysandmeans.pdf?MOD=AJPERES &CACHEID=2fa84c004e0d90aea0caf01ad6fc8b25 (accessed May 6, 2010).

Coalition on Intercollegiate Athletics (COIA). "Academic Integrity in Intercollegiate Athletics: Principles, Rules, and Best Practices." April 1, 2005. http://coia.comm.psu.edu/ AID.html (accessed March 30, 2010).

Coalition on Intercollegiate Athletics (COIA). "Charter of the Coalition on Intercollegiate Athletics." March 2003. http://coia.comm.psu.edu/Charter.html (accessed March 30, 2010).

Coalition on Intercollegiate Athletics (COIA). "Framing the Future: Reforming Intercollegiate Athletics." June 15, 2007. http://coia.comm.psu.edu/FTF/FTFproposals.pdf (accessed March 30, 2010).

Coalition on Intercollegiate Athletics (COIA). "A Report to the NCAA Presidential Task Force." December 23, 2005. http://coia.comm.psu.edu/PTF%20report%20%20Dec%2005.htm (accessed March 30, 2010).

Cohen v. Brown. 991 F.2d 888 (1st Cir. 1993).

College Football Association Committee on Academic Standards. "Report." May 20, 1982. President Banowsky Papers, Box 119, Folder 26, University of Oklahoma Archives.

Collins, Cardiss. "Letter to NCAA from Congresswoman Cardiss Collins." http://www.ferris.edu .htmls/othersrv/isar/institut/ncaa/collins/letter/html (accessed February 18, 2009).

"Collins Releases Findings from Independent Scientific Conference on NCAA Propositions 48 and 16," August 9, 1994. http://www.ferris.edu.htmls/othersrv/ISAR/institut/NCAA/ findings/htm (accessed April 9, 2010).

Colombo, John D. "The NCAA, Tax Exemption and College Athletics." Illinois Public Law Research Paper No. 08–08, May 27, 2009. http://ssrn.com/abstract=1336727 (accessed September 2, 2009).

Committee on the Regulation of Athletic Sports. "Report of Governing Boards to Athletic Sports." 1907. Harvard University Archives.

"Competition in College Athletic Conferences and Antitrust Aspects of the Bowl Championship Series." Hearings Before the Committee on the Judiciary, House of Representatives 108th Congress, First Session, September 4, 2003.

Congressional Budget Office Paper. "Tax Preferences for Collegiate Sports." May 2009. http:// www.cbo.gov/doc.cfm?index=10055 (accessed March 30, 2010).

"Constitutional Compliance Committee Report of the NCAA, November 28, 1950." President's Papers–1950, Box 3, Folder "NCAA-1950," University of Virginia Archives.

Cureton v. NCAA. 198 F.3d 107 (3d Cir. 1999).

Cureton v. NCAA. 37 F. Supp. 2d 687 (E.D. Pa 1999).

Cureton v. NCAA. U.S. Court of Appeals for 3rd Circuit, No. 99–102.

"Drake Group Proposals, The." http://www.thedrakegroup.org/proposals.html (accessed July 24, 2009).

Davison, Fred C. "History of College Football Association." June 11, 1980. President Banowsky Papers, Box 74, Folder 13, University of Oklahoma Archives.

Earl, James W. "The Faculty Coalition's Role in Intercollegiate Athletics Reform." http:// www.sc.edu/faculty/PDF/JimEarl.Indy.pdf (accessed March 30, 2010).

Eastern College Athletic Conference. "Report of the Special Committee on the Improvement of Intercollegiate Athletics." November 18, 1951, Eastern Collegiate Athletic Conference Headquarters, Centerville, MA.

"Eliminating Illiteracy." CIS-NO: 89-S541–47, Committee on Labor and Human Resources, U.S. Senate, Doc-type: Hearing, Doc-No:S.Hrg.101–260, May 18, 1989, 164–71.

Eliot, Charles W. "Inaugural Address, 19 October 1869." Harvard University Archives.

Frank, Robert A. "Challenging the Myth: A Review of the Links among College Athletic Success, Student Quality, and Donations." May 2004. http://www.knightfoundation.org/ dotAsset/131763.pdf (accessed March 30, 2010).

Friday, William C., Theodore M. Hesburgh, et al. "A Call to Action: Reconnecting College Sports and Higher Education." June 2001. http://www.knightfoundation.org/research_ publications/detail.dot?id=178173 (accessed March 25, 2010).

Friday, William C., and Theodore M. Hesburgh, eds. *A Call to Action: Reconnecting College Sports and Higher Education.* Charlotte, NC: Knight Foundation Commission on Intercollegiate Athletics, June 18, 2001.

Friday, William C., and Theodore M. Hesburgh, eds. *Keeping Faith with the Student-Athlete: A New Model for Intercollegiate Athletics.* Charlotte, NC: Knight Foundation Commission on Intercollegiate Athletics, March 1991.

Friday, William C., and Theodore M. Hesburgh. *A Solid Start: A Report on Reform of Intercollegiate Athletics.* Miami, FL: Knight Foundation Commission on Intercollegiate Athletics, 2002.

Fulks, Daniel L. "The Faculty Athletics Representatives: A Survey of Membership." Spring 2008. http://www.farawebsite.org/documents/FARA2008SurveyReport.pdf (accessed July 13, 2009).

Fullinwider, Robert K. "Academic Standards and the NCAA." Institute for Philosophy and Public Policy. http://www.publicpolicy.umd.edu/IPPP/spring (accessed August 25, 2008).

Gates, Thomas S. "A Statement by Thomas S. Gates, President of the University of Pennsylvania, 3 February 1931 [Gates Plan]." Papers of the Office of the President, 1950–55, Box 53, Folder "Intercollegiate Athletics Policy," University of Pennsylvania Archives.

"Grade Inflation at American Colleges and Universities." http://www.gradeinflation.com/ (accessed December 16, 2008).

Goldfarb v. Virginia State Bar. 421 U.S. 773 (1975).

Hanford, George H. *An Inquiry into the Need for and Feasibility of a National Study of Intercollegiate Athletics: A Report to the American Council on Education.* Washington, DC: American Council on Education, March 22, 1974.

Harris, Louis. "Poll." Study No. 891202, June 2, 1989. http://arc.irss.unc.edu.ezaccess.libraries.psu.edu/dvn/faces/study (accessed April 16, 2009).

Hennessey v. NCAA. 564F.2d 1136 (5th Cir. 1997).

"The History of Intercollegiate Sports in America, 1900–2005: An Eclectic Bibliography, Draft, August 2005." http://courses.umass.edu/lombardi (accessed August 29, 2008).

Hubert H. Humphrey Institute of Public Affairs Center for School Change. "A Call for Reform." August 30, 2007. http://www.centerforschoolchange.org/ncaa-challenge/a-call-for-reform.html (accessed August 18, 2008).

"Intercollegiate Sports." Hearings Before the Subcommittee on Commerce, Consumer Protection, and Competitiveness of the Committee on Energy and Commerce, House of Representatives, 102nd Congress, First Session, June 19, July 25, and September 12, 1991.

"Interim Report of the Commissioner to the Council of Ten." July 24, 1975. President Enarson Papers, 3/j/16/17, Folder "Council of Ten, 1973–76," Ohio State University Archives.

"Interim Report on Proposed Financial Aid Program for Conference Athletes, 27 September 1956." President E. B. Fred General Correspondence, 1956–57, Box 274, Folder "Athletic Scholarships," Series 4/16/1, University of Wisconsin Archives.

"Ivy Group Agreement." February 11, 1954. Papers of the Office of the President, 1950–55, Box 53, "Intercollegiate Athletics Ivy IX," Folder "UPA4," University of Pennsylvania Archives.

"Ivy Group Agreement, Amended as of 7 May 1952." Papers of the Office of the President, 1950–55, Box 53, Folder "Intercollegiate Athletics VI," University of Pennsylvania Archives.

"Ivy Group Presidents' Agreement, 20 November 1945." Papers of the Office of the President, 1950–55, Box 53, Folder "Intercollegiate Athletics IV," University of Pennsylvania Archives.

"A Joint Meeting of the Southern, Southeastern, and Southwest Conferences, 28 May 1949." Records of the Office of the President, 1946–1966, Box 16, Folder "NCAA Regional Conference, 28 May 1949," Georgia Tech University Archives.

"Joint Statement of Scholarship Policy by the Presidents of Harvard, Yale, and Princeton Universities." October 22, 1951. General Athletics, Box 1, Princeton University Archives.

Kevin Ross v. Creighton University. 957 F.2d 410 (7th Cir. 1992).

"Knight Commission Announces Summit on the Collegiate Athlete Experiences in 2006." November 8, 2005. http://www.knightcommission.org/index.php?option=com_content&view=article&id=340:november-8-2005-knight-commission-announces-summit-on-the-collegiate-athlete-experience&catid=22:press-room&Itemid=12 (accessed March 30, 2010).

Knight Commission on Intercollegiate Athletics. *College Sports 101: A Primer on Money, Athletics, and Higher Education.* Miami, FL: Knight Foundation, October 2009. http://www.knightcommission.org (accessed October 28, 2009).

Knight Commission on Intercollegiate Athletics. *Quantitative and Qualitative Research with Football Bowl Subdivision University Presidents on the Costs and Financing of Intercollegiate Athletics: Report of Findings and Implications.* Miami, FL: Knight Foundation, October 2009. http://www.knightcommissionmedia.org/images/President_Survey_FINAL.pdf (accessed October 28, 2009).

Knight Foundation Commission on Intercollegiate Athletics. *A Call to Action: Reconnecting College Sports to Higher Education.* Miami, FL: Knight Foundation, June 2001.

Law v. NCAA. 5 F. Supp. 2nd 921 (D. Kan. 1998).

Lawrence, Janet H., et al. "Faculty Perception of Intercollegiate Athletics: A National Study of Faculty at NCAA Division I Football Bowl Subdivision Universities." October 15, 2009. http://208.86.5/knightcommission/joomla/images/pdfs/faculty_perceptions_final.pdf. (accessed April 8, 2010).

Munro, Wilfred H., et al. "Report on Intercollegiate Sport" [Brown Conference Report], ca. April 1898, Brown University Archives.

"National College Athletics Accountability Act." 101st Congress, 2nd Session, HR 4232, March 8, 1990. http://thomas.loc.gov/cgi-bin/query/z?c101:h.r.4232.IH (accessed April 8, 2010).

National Collegiate Athletic Association *Proceedings.* 1906–2009.

"National Symposium on Athletic Reform." New Orleans, LA, November 11, 2003. http://coalition.tulane.edu (accessed April 8, 2010).

"NCAA Division I Board of Directors Gives Final Approval to New Academic Standards." http://www.ncaa.org/release/divi/2002103101dl.htm (accessed October 30, 2003).

"NCAA Independent Auditor's Report." http://web1.ncaa.org/web_video/membership_report/Content/pdf/610ncaafinancialstatement (accessed August 20, 2008).

"NCAA Passes Landmark Academic Reform Plan." *Black Issues in Higher Education.* January 27, 2005. http://findarticles.com/p/articles/mi_mOXK/is_25/ai_n13246330/ (accessed April 9, 2010). "NCAA Presidential Task Force of the Future of Division I Intercollegiate Athletics Student-Athlete Well-Being Subcommittee, 19 January 2006." http://www.ncaa.org/wps/portal/ncaahome?WCM_GLOBAL_CONTEXT=/ncaa/ncaa/legislation+and+governance/c (accessed April 9, 2010).

NCAA Presidential Task Force on the Future of Division I Intercollegiate Athletics. "Executive Summary." October 2006. http://coia.comm.psu.edu/NCAA%20Presidential%20Task%20 Force%20Executive%20Summary%20Oct%2006.pdf (accessed March 30, 2010).

NCAA Presidential Task Force on the Future of Division I Intercollegiate Athletics. "The Second-Century Imperatives: Presidential Leadership—Institutional Accountability." October 2006. http://www.ncaapublications.com/productdownloads/PTF092.pdf (accessed March 30, 2010).

"NCAA to Pay Coaches $54.5 M." CBS Sportsline. http://www.cbsnews.com/stories/1999/03/09/ sports/main38197.shtml (accessed May 7, 2009).

NCAA v. Board of Regents of the University of Oklahoma. 468 U.S. 85 (1984).

"1996 NCAA Division I Graduation-Rates Summary." June 1996. National Collegiate Athletic Association Headquarters.

Nyquest, Ewald B., et al. *Final Report: The Commission on Collegiate Athletics.* Washington, DC: American Council on Education, 1979.

O'Bannon v. National Collegiate Athletic Association, F.Supp2d (N.D. Cal).

O'Connor, Eugene P. "NCAA Governance, Its Past and Future," Canisius College Richard J. Wehle School of Business Working Paper Series, November 2006. http://www.canisius .edu/images/userImages/wsbweb/Page_9979/NCAA.doc (accessed July 7, 2008).

Oliva, L. Jay. *What Trustees Should Know about Intercollegiate Athletics: AGB Special Report.* Washington, DC: Association of Governing Boards of Universities and Colleges, 1989.

"Outside the Lines: Unable to Read." ESPN Transcript, March 17, 2002. http://sports.espn .go.com/page2/tvlistings/show103transcript.html (accessed September 15, 2008).

"Overseers Athletic Abuses Committee Report, 1888." HUD8388.5, Harvard University Archives.

"Participation 1981–82—2007–08: NCAA Sports Sponsorship and Participation Rates Report." April 2009. http://www.ncaapublications.com/productdownloads/PR2009.pdf (accessed March 30, 2010).

"Presidential Task Force on the Future of Division I Athletics." October 2006. http://docs.google .com/viewer?1=v&q=cache:zRJOPx5cLNAJ:vcafa.org/support_bulletin/2007/2007–2 .pdf+ncaa (accessed April 9, 2010).

Pritchett, Henry S. "Progress of the State Universities." *Carnegie Foundation for the Advancement of Teaching, Annual Report* 6 (1911): 108.

Pryor v. NCAA. 2888 F.3d 548 (3rd Cir. May 6, 2002).

Raiborn, Mitchell. *Financial Reporting and Control for Intercollegiate Athletics.* Shawnee Mission, KS: National Collegiate Athletics Association, 1974.

"Recommendations of the Presidents of Six Member Institutions of the Southern Conference for Consideration at the Next Meeting of the Southern Conference." January 10, 1936. Frank P. Graham Files, Box 3, "January 1936," Folder 1/1/4, University of North Carolina Archives.

"Regulations of the Committee on Eligibility of the Ivy Group." October 2, 1952. Papers of the Office of the President, 1950–55, Box 55, Folder "Intercollegiate Athletics Ivy VII," University of Pennsylvania Archives.

"Report of Conference on Intercollegiate Athletics, 1898." Brown University Archives.

"Report of the Joint Committee on the Regulation of Athletic Sports." *Harvard Graduates' Magazine* 15 (June 1907): 642–66.

"Report of the National Collegiate Athletic Association Division I Infractions Appeal Committee, January 5, 2010, Report No. 294, Florida State University." http://www.ncaa.org/wps/wcm/connect/81f3900ce5e166807ba7dzzbaesaf/fsu (accessed January 7, 2010).

"Report: Exemptions Benefit Athletes." Associated Press, December 30, 2009. http://sports.espn.go.com/ncf/news/story?id=4781264 (accessed January 5, 2010).

"Report to the President and Fellows of Harvard University by the Committee on the Regulation of Athletic Sports, Statement of Policy, 10 October 1925." President Lowell Papers, Folder 72, Harvard University Archives.

"A Report of the Recruiting Situation in the Intercollegiate Conference." March 7, 1927. Harold H. Swift Papers, Box 114, University of Chicago Archives.

"Report of the Special Committee on Athletic Policy of the American Council on Education." Washington, DC: American Council on Education, February 16, 1952.

"Report of a Special Committee [of the Big Ten], 4 August 1956." President E. B. Fred General Correspondence, 1956–57, Box 274, Folder "Athletic Scholarships." Series 4/16/1, University of Wisconsin Archives.

"Report of Special Committee of ECAC Policies and Principles." ca. May 17, 1950, ECAC Binder "November 18, 1948," Eastern Collegiate Athletic Conference Headquarters, Centerville, MA.

"Report of the Sub-Committee on the Athletic Program to the Faculty Committee on Athletic Eligibility." June 5, 1940, General Athletics, Box 1, Princeton University Archives.

"Rules and Regulations of the Committee on the Regulation of Athletics Sports [Big Three], 1926." President Lowell Papers, 1925–28, Folder 563, Harvard University Archives.

Sandler, Bernice R. "'Too Strong for a Woman'—The Five Words That Created Title IX," http://www.bernicesandler.com/id44.htm (accessed March 30, 2010).

Savage, Howard J., et al. *American College Athletics* [Bulletin No. 23]. New York: Carnegie Foundation for the Advancement of Teaching, 1929.

Savage, Howard J., et al. *Current Developments in American College Sport* [Bulletin No. 26]. New York: Carnegie Foundation for the Advancement of Teaching, 1931.

Savage, Howard J. *Games and Sports in British Schools and Universities* [Bulletin No. 22]. New York: Carnegie Foundation for the Advancement of Teaching, 1927.

Saylor, Roger. "Southern Intercollegiate Conference, 1921–1932." http://www.la84foundation.org/SportsLibrary/CFHSN/CFHSNv06/CFHSNv06n4c.pdf (accessed March 30, 2010).

Schofield, Susan W. "PAC-10 Athletics Resolution." May 10, 2001. http://www.stanford.edu/dept/facultysenate/2000_2001/reports/SenD5217_PAC10_athletic_res.pdf (accessed March 30, 2010).

Siegfried, John J., and Molly Gardner Burba. "The College Football Association Television Broadcast Cartel." Working Paper No. 03-W20, September 2003. http://www.vanderbilt.edu/econ/wparchive/workpaper/vu03-w20.pdf (accessed March 30, 2010).

Smith, Ronald A. "NCAA Division I-A Football Playoff." Report to the National Collegiate Athletic Association, 1995.

Smith, Ronald A. "NCAA-AAU Cold War Time-Line: W.W.II–1990s." Report to the National Collegiate Athletic Association, 1991.

Smith, Ronald A. "Presidents Can't Punt, at Least Not Straight: Who Has Controlled and Who Should Control College Athletics." October 1989. Unpublished paper in writer's possession.

Smith, Ronald A., and Jay W. Helman. "A History of Eligibility Rules among Big-Time Athletic Institutions." Report to the National Collegiate Athletic Association, 1990.

Smith, Ronald A., and Jay W. Helman. "A History of the Freshman Rule." Report to the National Collegiate Athletic Association, 1987.

Splitt, Frank G. "Reclaiming Academic Primacy in Higher Education: New Hope for the Future." March 2009. http://www.thedrakegroup.org/splitt_new_hope.pdf (accessed April 9, 2010).

Splitt, Frank, et al. "A Commentary on NCAA President Myles Brand's November 13, 2006, Reply to the Honorable William Thomas's Letter of October 2, 2006." April 9, 2007. http://coia.comm.psu.edu/News%20of%20interest/The%20Drake%20Group%20reply%20to%20NCAA%20response%20to%20House%20Ways%20and%20Means%20letter%2010%20Apr%2007.pdf (accessed March 30, 2010).

"Squeeze Play: Prop 48 Left Frank Between Two Worlds." *Champion* (Winter 2008): 36. http://www.tabpi.org/2009/f14.pdf (accessed March 30, 2010).

"Study of Freshman Eligibility Standards: Executive Summary." Submitted to the NCAA, August 15, 1984. NCAA Headquarters.

"The Supreme Court Decision in 'NCAA v. University of Oklahoma.'" Hearings, Committee on the Judiciary of the U.S. Senate, 98th Congress, 2nd Session, November 19, 1984.

"Televised College Football." *Hearings, Subcommittee on Oversights and Investigations of the Committee on Energy and Commerce, House of Representatives.* 98th Congress, 2nd Session, July 31, 1984. Washington, DC: U.S. Government Printing Office, 1984.

Toma, J. Douglas, and Welch Suggs. "Athletics Recruiting and Academic Values: Enhancing Transparency, Spreading Risk, and Improving Practice." Fall 2006. Roundtable on Intercollegiate Athletics in Higher Education, University of Georgia Institute of Higher Education. http://www.uga.edu/ihe/research/toma/recruitingessayfinal.pdf (accessed March 30, 2010).

"Transfer, Academic Outcomes and the APR." Faculty Athletic Representatives Association, November 2007. http://farawebsite.org/files/faraannualmeeting/transferacademicoutcomesandtheAPR.pdf (accessed April 9, 2010).

"2004 Due Process and the NCAA Hearings Before the Subcommittee on the Constitution of the Committee on the Judiciary," House of Representatives, 108th Congress, 2nd Session, September 14, 2004.

U. S. Congress, House Committee on Education and Labor. *Hearings Before the Subcommittee on Postsecondary Education of the Committee on Education and Labor.* 101st Congress, 1st Session, Serial 101–22. Washington, DC: U.S. Government Printing Office, 1989.

U.S. Department of Education. *Revenues and Expenditures in Intercollegiate Athletics: The Feasibility of Collecting National Data by Sport.* Washington, DC: Office of Educational Research and Improvement, U.S. Department of Education, October 1992.

Waller, Jeffrey M. "A Necessary Evil: Proposition 16 and Its Impact on Academics and Athletics in the NCAA." *DePaul Journal of Sports Law and Contemporary Problems* 1, no. 2 (2003):

189–206. http://www.law.depaul.edu/students/organizations_journals/student_orgs/lawslj/Volume%201,%20Issue%202/waller.pdf (accessed March 30, 2010).

Wells, Herman B. "CIC History." 1967. http://www.cic.net/Libraries/News-Pub/HistoryOfCIC.sflb (accessed March 30, 2010).

White, John W. "Annual Report, 1889–1890 to President C. W. Eliot." UAI.5.150, Box 262, Folder "1891, January–May," Harvard University Archives.

White, John W., W. S. Chaplin, and A. B. Hart. "Athletic Report." June 12, 1888. HUD 8388.3B, Harvard University Archives.

White v. NCAA. C.D. Cal. Case NO. C V 06 0999 VBF, August 4, 2008.

"Who Can Play? An Examination of NCAA Proposition 16." National Center for Education Statistics, August 1995. http://nces.ed.gov/pubsearch/pubsinfo.asp?pubid=95763 (accessed March 30, 2010).

"The Will to Act Project." September 16, 2002. http://www.ncaapublications.com/product-downloads/WTA02.pdf (accessed April 9, 2010).

Young, Charles E. *Report to the NCAA Special Committee to Study a Division I-A Football Championship.* Overland Park, KS: National Collegiate Athletic Association, 1994.

Reform Articles and Book Chapters

Adams, Charles K. "Moral Aspects of College Life." *Forum* 8 (February 1890): 665–75.

Amato, Louis H., et al. "The Impact of Proposition 48 on the Relationship between Football Success and Football Player Graduation Rates." *Journal of Sports Economics* 2, no. 2 (2001): 101–12.

"Armageddon to Go." *Time* 66 (December 12, 1955): 24.

Armstrong, J. E., et al. "The Question of School and College Athletics." *School Review* 10 (January 1902): 4–8.

Asher, Mark. "Abuses in College Athletics." In *Fractured Focus: Sports as a Reflection of Society,* ed. Richard E. Lapchick. Lexington, MA: Lexington Books, 1986.

"Assessing the Faculty Role in Sports Oversight." *Inside Higher Ed,* October 16, 2007. http://www.insidehighered.com/news/2007/10/16/knight (accessed March 25, 2010).

"Athletics." *Harvard Graduates' Magazine* 13 (June 1905): 682.

"Athletics, Antitrust, and Amateurism." *Inside Higher Ed,* May 13 2009. http://insidehighered.com/news/2009/05/13/knight (accessed September 2, 2009).

Atwell, Robert H. "Some Reflections on Collegiate Athletics." *Educational Record* 60 (Fall 1979): 367–73.

Austin, Brad. "Protecting Athletics and the American Way: Defense of Intercollegiate Athletics at Ohio State and the Big Ten during the Great Depression." *Journal of Sport History* 27 (Summer 2000): 247–70.

Axhelm, Peter. "The Shame of College Sports." *Newsweek* (September 22, 1980): 54–59.

"Ball's in the NCAA Court." *Inside Higher Ed,* October 6, 2006. http://www.insidehighered.com/news/2006/10/06/ncaa (accessed October 18, 2007).

Barton, Herbert I. "The College Conference of the Middle West." *Educational Review* 27 (January 1904): 42–52.

Bascom, John. "Athletics." *Williams Alumni Review* 2 (October 1910): 13.

Basten, J. "Air Ball: American Education's Failed Experiment with Elite Athletics." *Review of Higher Education* 1, no. 4 (2007): 472–73.

Bates, Arlo. "The Negative Side of Modern Athletics." *Forum* 31 (1901): 287–97.

Beehe, John. "College Football's Oldest Rivalry—Commercialism Versus Education." In *Sport in American Education: History and Perspective,* ed. Wayne M. Ladd and Angela Lumpkin, 84–98. Washington, DC: American Alliance for Health, Physical Education, and Recreation, 1979.

Beezley, William H. "The 1961 Scandal at North Carolina State and the End of the Dixie Classic." In *Sport in Higher Education,* ed. Donald Chu et al., 81–99. Champaign, IL: Human Kinetics, 1985.

Bellow, H. A. "The New Eligibility Rules." *Harvard Graduates' Magazine* 14 (June 1906): 694.

Benford, Robert D. "The College Sports Reform Movement: Reframing the 'Edutainment' Industry." *Sociological Quarterly* 48 (January 2007): 1–28.

Bennett, Bruce. "An Analysis of Why Ohio State Did Not Go to the Rose Bowl in 1962." North American Society for Sport History *Proceedings* (1994): 73–74.

Berg, Rick. "Retooling the NCAA." *Athletic Business* 4 (April 1990): 12–13.

Berryman, Jack. "Historical Roots of the Collegiate Dilemma." *National College Physical Education Association for Men Proceedings* (1976): 141–54.

Blaikie, William. "The International Rowing-Match." *Harper's Monthly* 40 (December 1870): 50–66.

Blum, Debra A. "Athletics: The Big Scramble," *Chronicle of Higher Education* (March 16, 1994): A37.

Blum, Debra A. "Brown Loses Bias Case." *Chronicle of Higher Education* (April 7, 1995): A37–A38.

Bock, Hal. "The Easy Way Most Often Turns Out to Be Unfair." *NCAA News* (January 22, 1986): 2.

Bok, Derek. "Presidents Need Power within the NCAA to Preserve Academic Standards and Institutional Integrity." In *Sport and Higher Education,* ed. Donald Chu et al., 207–10. Champaign, IL: Human Kinetics, 1985.

Bowen, W. P. "The Evolution of Athletic Evils." *American Physical Education Review* 14 (March 1909): 151–56.

Brand, Myles. "Faculty Members' Constructive Engagement in Intercollegiate Athletics." *The Montana Professor* 17, no. 2 (Spring 2007). http://mtprof.msun.edu (accessed August 29, 2008).

Brickman, W. W. "Professionalized Sports and Higher Education." *School and Society* 86 (March 1, 1958): 114–15.

Briggs, L. B. R. "Athletic Sports." *Harvard Graduates' Magazine* 17 (June 1909): 697–700.

Briggs, L. B. R. "Intercollegiate Athletics and the War." *Atlantic Monthly* 122 (September 1918): 304–9.

Brown, Gary. "Smith Scholar Sees Football Playoff as Economic Tonic." *NCAA News* (January 13, 2010). http://www.ncaa.org/wps/portal/ncaahome?WCM_GLOBAL_CONTEXT=/ncaa/ncaa/ncaa+news/ncaa+news+online/2010/association-wide/smith+scholar+sees+football+playoff+as+economic+tonic (accessed February 3, 2010.)

Brown, John Jr. "Report of the Committee on Definition of an Amateur." *American Physical Education Review* 21 (May 1916): 301–8.

Brown, Rollo W. "An Idealist in Athletics." In *Dean Briggs,* 168–207. New York: Harper, 1926.

Brownell, Clifford Lee. "College Presidents and Athletic Reform." *Phi Delta Kappan* 19 (February–March 1937): 152–55.

Brubaker, Bill. "Dear Chris." *Sports Illustrated* (November 26, 1984): 120–36.

Bryce, James. "America Revisited: The Changes of a Quarter Century." *Outlook* 79 (March 25, 1905): 25.

Bullock, Clifford A. "Fired by Conscience: The Black 14 Incident at the University of Wyoming and Black Protest in the Western Athletic Conference." Ca. 1991. http://uwacadweb .uwyo.edu/robertshistory/fired_by_conscience.htm (accessed December 22, 2009).

Burns, N. "Recommended Changes in Athletic Policies." *School Review* 60 (December 1952): 509–18.

Camp, Walter. "Call for a High Standard in College Athletics." *Harper's Weekly* 44 (January 8, 1898): 46.

Camp, Walter. "College Athletics." *Harvard Graduates' Magazine* 2 (September 1895): 139.

Camp, Walter. "College Athletics." *New Englander* 44 (January 1885): 139.

Camp, Walter. "The Two Problems of Amateur Athletics: The Spectator and the Professional." *Outing* 19 (December 1891): 197–200.

Camp, Walter. "Undergraduate Limitation in College Sports." *Harper's Weekly* 37 (February 11, 1893): 143.

Camp, Walter. "The Yale Side of the Athletic Question." *Harper's Weekly* 37 (April 8, 1893): 339.

Carlson, William S. "A Protest against the Bowls." *Colliers* (December 31, 1949): 12–13, 70.

Carpenter, Linda A. "Worker's Compensation and the Scholarship Athlete." *Journal of Higher Education* 53 (July–August 1982): 448–59.

Carter, W. B. "The Age of Innocence: The First 25 Years of the National Collegiate Athletic Association, 1906–1931." *Vanderbilt Journal of Entertainment and Technology Law* 8 (2006): 211–91.

Caughron, R. L. "A Historical Perspective of Reform in Intercollegiate Athletics." *International Sports Journal* 5, no. 1 (2001): 1–16.

"Caught by the Camera." *Life Magazine* 31 (November 5, 1951): 121–34.

Cave, Ray. "A Ruse Flushes Some Eager Recruiters." *Sports Illustrated* 14 (May 29, 1961): 20–23.

Chase, Stuart. "Play." In *Whither Mankind,* ed. Charles A. Beard. New York: Longsman Green, 1928.

Ciccolella, Margaret E., et al. "Good Faith and Fair Dealing: The Implied Duty to Meaningful Education of the College Athlete." *Entertainment and Sport Law Journal* 6 (June 2008). http://www2.warwick.ac.uk/fac/soc/law/elj/eslj/issues/volume6/number1/cicolella (accessed April 9, 2010).

Clark, Vernon L., Floyd Horton, and Robert L. Alford. "NCAA Rule 48: Racism or Reform?" *Journal of Negro Education* 55 (Spring 1986): 162–70.

"Clarkson a Professional." *The Harvard Bulletin* (June 15, 1904): 2.

Clement, Rufus E. "Racial Integration in the Field of Sports." *Journal of Negro Education* 23 (1954): 222–30.

Coakley, Jay, ed. "Research on Intercollegiate Sports: A Working Bibliography, 2008." *Journal of Intercollegiate Sport* 1 (2008): 147–69.

Cohane, Tim. "Inside the West Coast Football Scandal." *Look* 20 (August 7, 1956): 72–80.

Cohane, Tim. "Let's Take the Hypocrisy Out of College Football." *Look* (December 1950): 60–63.

"Colleges in a Moral Fog." *Christian Century* (February 1, 1950): 135–37.

Columbo, John D. "The NCAA, Tax Exemption, and College Athletics." *University of Illinois Law Review* no. 1 (2010): 109–63.

Commager, Henry Steele. "Give the Games Back to the Students." *New York Times Magazine* (April 16, 1961): 27, 120–21.

"Commercialism in College Athletics." *School and Society* 24 (June 24, 1922): 681–86, and 16 (July 1, 1922): 7–11.

Conant, James B. "Athletics, the Poison Ivy in Our Schools." *Look* 25 (January 17, 1961): 56–60.

Cook, T. "Some Tendencies of Modern Sport." *Quarterly Review* 199 (January 1904): 127–52.

Corbin, John. "English and American University Athletics." *Outing* 39 (October 1901): 31–38.

Coval, Dan, and Carol A. Barr. "The Ties That Bind: Presidential Involvement with the Development of NCAA Division I Initial Eligibility Legislation." *Journal of Higher Education* 72 (July–August 2001): 414–52.

Cozzillio, M. J. "The Athletic Scholarship and the College National Letter of Intent: A Contract by Any Other Name." *Wayne Law Review* 35 (1989): 1275.

Cramer, Jerome. "Winning or Learning? Athletes and Academics in America." *Phi Delta Kappan* 67 (May 1986): K1–K9.

Craughron, Rodney. "An Historical Perspective of Reform in Intercollegiate Athletics." *International Sports Journal* 5 (2001): 1–16.

Cullen, Francis T., et al. "Scandal and Reform in Collegiate Athletics: Implications from a National Survey of Head Football Coaches." *Journal of Higher Education* 61 (January–February 1990): 50–64.

"Cut and Run Athletics." *Inside Higher Education,* May 1, 2009. http://www.insidehighered.com/news/2009/05/01/apr (accessed April 9, 2010).

Danzig, Allison. "Ivy League Agreement against Abuses in College Sports." *New York Times* March 22, 1954, p. 30; March 23, 1954, p. 30; March 24, 1954, p. 34.

Dashiell, Alfred. "The National Religion of Football." *Forum* 76 (November 1926): 680–89.

Davis, Andrew M. F. "College Athletics." *Atlantic Monthly* 51 (1883): 677–84.

Davis, Parke. "What Woodrow Wilson Did for American Football." *St. Nicholas* 40 (November 1912): 13–19.

Davis, R. N. "Athletic Reform: Missing the Bases in University Athletics." *Capital University Law Review* 20 (1991): 597–610.

Davis, William E. "The President's Role in Athletics: Leader or Figurehead?" *Educational Record* 60 (Fall 1979): 420–30.

Dawidoff, Nicholas. "The Best Little Ballpark in Texas." *Sports Illustrated* 71 (July 31, 1989): 58–70.

Dawkins, Pete. "We Play to Win, They Play for Fun." *New York Times Magazine* (April 24, 1960): 34, 36.

Demas, Lane. "Beyond Jackie Robinson: Racial Integration in American College Football and New Directions in Sport History." *History Compass* 5 (February 2007): 675–90.

Demas, Lane. "'On the Threshold of Broad and Rich Football Pastures': Integrated College Football at UCLA, 1938–1941." In *Horsehide, Pigskin, Oval Tracks and Apple Pie: Essays on Sports and American Culture,* ed. James A. Vlasich, 86–103. Jefferson, NC: McFarland, 2006.

Deming, Clarence. "Money Power in College Athletics." *Outlook* 80 (July 1905): 569–72.

Dempsey, Cedric. "Title IX: An Opportunity for Women: A Solution for Men." *Title IX: Moving Toward Implementation,* 14–20. NAPECW and NCPEAM, 1975.

Doyle, Andrew. "Causes Won, Not Lost: College Football and the Modernization of the American South." *International Journal of the History of Sport* 11 (August 1994): 231–51.

Doyle, Andrew. "Foolish and Useless Sport: The Southern Evangelical Crusade against Intercollegiate Football." *Journal of Sport History* 24 (Fall 1997): 317–40.

Doyle, Andrew. "Turning the Tide: College Football and Southern Progressivism." *Southern Cultures* 3 (Fall 1997): 28–51.

Dubeck, Lucien. "A French View of American Sport." *Living Age* 339 (February 1921): 655–56.

Duderstadt, James J. "An Epilogue to the Paperback Edition of Intercollegiate Athletics and the American University, March 2003." http://Milproj.ummu.umich.edu/publications/epilogue_athletics/download/sports_book_epilogue.pdf (accessed October 4, 2007).

Duer, A. O. "Basic Issues of Intercollegiate Athletics." *Journal of Health, Physical Education and Recreation* 31 (January 1960): 22–24.

Dunkle, Margaret. "College Athletics: Tug-of-War for the Purse Strings." *Ms. Magazine* 3 (September 1974): 114, 117.

Dwight, Benjamin W. "Intercollegiate College Regattas, Hurdle-Races, and Prize Contests." *New Englander* 35 (April 1876): 251–79.

Dyreson, Mark. "The Emergence of Consumer Culture and the Transformation of Physical Culture: American Sport in the 1920s." *Journal of Sport History* 16 (1989): 262–81.

Dyreson, Mark. "Reading Football History: New Vistas in the Landscape of American Sport." *Journal of Sport History* 29 (Summer 2002): 203–20.

Earl, James W. "The Faculty's Role in Reforming College Sports." *Academe Online,* September–October 2004. http://www.aaup.org/AAUP/pubsres/academe/2004/SO/Feat/earl.htm (accessed October 29, 2007).

Edwards, Harry. "The Black 'Dumb Jock': An American Sports Tragedy." *The College Board Review* 131 (Spring 1984): 8–13.

Edwards, Harry. "The Collegiate Athletic Arms Race: Origins and Implications of the 'Rule 48' Controversy." In *Fractured Focus: Sport as a Reflection of Society,* ed. Richard E. Lapchick, 21–43. Lexington, MA: Lexington Books, 1986.

Edwards, Harry. "Crisis of Black Athletes on the Eve of the Twenty-First Century." In *Sport and the Color Line,* ed. Patrick B. Miller and David K. Wiggins, 345–50. New York: Routledge, 2003.

Edwards, Harry. "Educating Black Athletes." In *Sport in Higher Education,* ed. Donald Chu et al., 373–84. Champaign, IL: Human Kinetics, 1985.

Ehler, George W. "The Regulation of Intercollegiate Sports." *American Physical Education Review* 19 (April 1904): 284–91.

Eliot, Charles W. "Athletics Still Exaggerated." *Harvard Graduates' Magazine* 16 (June 1908): 624–27.

Eliot, Charles W. "The Evils of Football." *Harvard Graduates' Magazine* 13 (March 1905): 383–87.

Eliot, Charles W. "President Eliot's Report." *Harvard Graduates' Magazine* 9 (March 1901): 452.

Eliot, Charles W. "President Eliot's Report, Athletics." *Harvard Graduates' Magazine* 2 (March 1894): 376–83.

Eliot, Charles W. "The Value of Athletics." *Mind and Body* 7 (1900): 141–42.

Emmons, Robert W. II. "Needed Football Reforms." *Harvard Graduates' Magazine* 3 (March 1895): 318–22.

"The Faculty Role in Sports Reform." *Inside Higher Ed,* November 9, 2005. http://www .insidehighered.com/news/2005/11/09/knight (accessed October 18, 2007).

Farrand, Wilson. "Scholarships for Athletics: Position of the Association of Colleges and Secondary Schools of the Middle States." *School and Society* 40 (July 7, 1934): 6–7.

Farrell, Charles S. "Colleges Must Clean Up Their Athletics Programs or Face Professionalism." *Chronicle of Higher Education* (May 27, 1987): 27–28.

Faunce, William H. P. "Character in Athletics." *National Education Association Proceedings* 43 (1904): 558–64.

Fauver, Edgar. "The Place of Intercollegiate Athletics in a Physical Education Program." *American Physical Education Review* 27 (June 1922): 1–5.

Figone, Albert J. "Gambling and College Basketball: The Scandal of 1951." *Journal of Sport History* 16 (Spring 1989): 44–61.

Fitt, Virginia A. "The NCAA's Lost Cause and the Legal Ease of Redefining Amateurism." *Duke Law Journal* 59 (2009): 555–93.

"Football Reform by Abolition," *Nation* 81 (November 30, 1905): 437–38.

Footlick, Jerrold K. "The Ivy League: Where Athletics Don't Endanger Academic Standards." *Columbia: The Magazine of Columbia University* 6 (Spring 1981): 11.

Foster, William T. "An Indictment of Intercollegiate Athletics." *Atlantic Monthly* 116 (November 1915): 577–88.

Franklin, John Hope. "History of Racial Segregation in the United States." *Annals of the American Academy of Political and Social Science* 304 (March 1956): 1–9.

"A French View of English Sport." *Living Age* 339 (February 1921): 655.

Frey, James H. "Boosterism, Scarce Resources, and Institutional Control: The Future of American Intercollegiate Athletics." *International Review for the Sociology of Sport* 17, no. 2 (1982): 53–70.

Frey, James H. "The Coming Demise of Intercollegiate Athletics." *Arena Review* 3, no. 3 (1979): 34–43.

Frey, James H. "Institutional Control of Athletics: An Analysis of the Role Played by Presidents, Trustees, Alumni, and the NCAA." *Journal of Sport and Social Issues* 11, no. 1 (1987): 49–59.

Fried, Barbara H. "Punting Our Future: College Athletics and Admissions." *Change,* May/June 2007. http://www.changemag.org/Archives/Back%20Issues/May-June%202007/full-punting-our-future.html (accessed March 30, 2010).

"From a Graduate's Window." *Harvard Graduates' Magazine* 14 (December 1905): 216–23.

Gardner, Frank N. "The Place of Intercollegiate Athletics in Higher Education: Hold That Tiger!" *Journal of Higher Education* 31 (1960): 364–68.

Garrett, Robert Alan, and Philip R. Hochberg. "Sports Broadcasting and the Law." Reprinted from *Indiana Law Journal* 59 (1984).

Gerber, Ellen W. "The Controlled Development of College Sports for Women, 1923–1936." *Journal of Sport History* 2 (Spring 1975): 1–18.

Gerber, Ellen W. "The Legal Basis for the Regulation of Intercollegiate Sport." *Educational Record* 60 (Fall 1979): 467–81.

Gerdy, John. "Facing Up to the Conflict between Athletics and Academics." *Priorities* 16 (Summer 2001): 1–15.

Giddens, Paul. H. "Scramble for College Athletics: Increasing Professionalism." *Atlantic Monthly* 216 (December 1965): 49–52.

Glazer, Nathan. "Regulating Business and Universities: One Problem or Two? *The Public Interest* (Summer 1979): 42–65.

Godkin, E. L. "Athletic Craze." *Nation* 57 (December 7, 1893): 422–23.

Godkin, E. L. "The Future of Football." *Nation* 51 (November 20, 1890): 395.

Goldfield, David. "College Entrance Requirements for Athletes Are Fair." In *Sports and Athletes,* ed. James D. Torr, 77–82. Detroit: Greenhaven Press, 2005.

Goplerud, C. Peter III. "Pay for Play for College Athletics: Now More than Ever." *South Texas Law Review* 38 (1997): 1081–95.

Green, George W. "Athletics in Colleges." *New Englander* 35 (July 1876): 548–60.

Green, Robin J. "Does the NCAA Play Fair? A Due Process Analysis of NCAA Enforcement Regulations." *Duke Law Journal* 42 (October 1992): 99–144.

Griffith, John L. "The Carnegie Reports." *Journal of Higher Education* 1 (June 1930): 325–50.

Grundman, Adolph H. "The Image of Intercollegiate Sports and the Civil Rights Movement: A Historian's View." In *Fractured Focus: Sport as a Reflection of Society,* ed. Richard E. Lapchick, 77–85. Lexington, MA: Lexington Books, 1986.

Guttmann, Allen. "The Anomaly of Intercollegiate Athletics." In *Rethinking College Athletics,* ed. Judith Andre and David N. James, 17–30. Philadelphia: Temple University Press, 1991.

Hall, G. Stanley. "Student Customs." *American Antiquarian Society Proceedings* 14 (October 1900): 83–124.

Hamilton, Brutus. "Can College Athletics Be Saved?" *Christian Century* (March 28, 1951): 397–98.

Hanford, George H. "Controversies in College Sports." *Educational Record* 60 (Fall 1979): 351–66.

Hanford, George H. "Intercollegiate Athletics Today and Tomorrow: The President's Challenge." *Educational Record* 58 (Fall 1977): 232–35.

Hanford, George H. "Proposition 48." In *Sport in Higher Education,* ed. Donald Chu et al., 367–72. Champaign, IL: Human Kinetics, 1985.

Hanford, George H. "We Should Speak the 'Awful Truth' about College Sports." *Chronicle of Higher Education,* May 30, 2003. http://chronicle.com/article/we-should-speak-the-awful/15514/ (accessed April 9, 2010).

Hart, Albert B. "Harvard's Athletic Policy." *Harvard Graduates' Magazine* 4 (December 1895): 209–14.

Hart, Albert B. "The Status of Athletics in American Colleges." *Atlantic Monthly* 66 (July 1890): 63–71.

Heck, Robert H., and Robin Takahashi. "Examining the Impact of Proposition 48 on Graduation Rates in Division IA Football and Program Recruiting Behavior." *Educational Policy* 20, no. 4 (2006): 587–614.

Hemenway, August, Robert Bacon, and Theodore Roosevelt. "Important Suggestions in Athletics." *Harvard Graduates' Magazine* 6 (December 1897): 195–96.

Henderson, R. J. "The 1963 Mississippi State University Basketball Controversy and the Repeal of the Unwritten Law: 'Something More than the Game Will Be Lost.'" *Journal of Southern History* 63, no. 4 (1997): 827–54.

Hetherington, Clark W. "Organization and Administration of Athletics." *National Education Association Proceedings* (1907): 330–40.

Hill, Henry, with Douglas S. Looney. "How I Put the Fix In." *Sports Illustrated* (February 16, 1981): 14–21.

"A History of Academic Legislation." *NCAA News* (December 15, 1980): 2–3.

Hitchcock, Edward. "Athletics in American Colleges." *Journal of Social Science* 20 (June 1885): 27–44.

Hoger, Marc. "Basketball and Athletic Control at Oberlin College, 1896–1915." *Journal of Sport History* 23 (Fall 1996): 256–83.

Hollis, Ira H. "Intercollegiate Athletics." *Atlantic Monthly* 90 (1902): 534–44.

Howe, L. T. "Academics and Athletics at SMU: A View from a Swaying Bridge." *Academe* 73 (1987): 18–24.

Howell, Reet A., and Maxwell L. Howell. "The Myth of 'Pop Warner': Carlisle Revisited." *Quest,* Monograph 30 (Summer 1978): 19–27.

Huckle, Patricia. "Back to the Starting Line: Title IX and Women's Intercollegiate Athletics." *American Behavioral Scientist* 21 (January/February 1978): 379–92.

Huie, William B. "How to Keep Football Stars in College." *Collier's* (January 4, 1941): 18–20, 48–49.

Hult, Joan S. "The Legacy of AIAW." In *A Century of Women's Basketball: From Frailty to Final Four,* ed. Joan S. Hult and Marianna Trekell, 281–307. Reston, VA: National Association for Girls and Women's Sport, 1991.

Hult, Joan S. "The Role of Sport Governing Bodies in College Athletics." *National Association for Physical Education in Higher Education* (June 5–8, 1980): 18–26.

Hult, Joan S. "The Saga of Competition: Basketball Battles and Governance War." In *A Century of Women's Basketball: From Frailty to Final Four,* ed. Joan S. Hult and Marianna Trekell, 223–48. Reston, VA: National Association for Girls and Women's Sport, 1991.

Hult, Joan S. "The Story of Women's Athletics: Manipulating a Dream, 1890–1985." In *Women and Sport: Interdisciplinary Perspectives,* ed. D. Margaret Costa and Sharon R. Guthrie, 83–106. Champaign, IL: Human Kinetics, 1994.

Hutchins, Robert M. "Gate Receipts and Glory." *Saturday Evening Post* 211 (December 3, 1938): 23, 73–74, 76–77.

Hutchinson, R. C. "Football: Symbol of College Unity." *Christian Century* 69 (April 16, 1952): 461–63.

"'In' Box." *Chronicle of Higher Education,* January 4, 1989, A13.

"Intercollegiate Football, Report by Committee G." *American Association of University Professors Bulletin* 12 (April 1926): 218, 234.

"The International Boat Race." *Frank Leslie's Illustrated* 29 (September 11, 1869): 409.

Jackson, Allen. "Too Much Football." *Atlantic Monthly* 188 (October 1951): 27–33.

Jackson, N. L. "Professionalism and Sport." *Fortnightly Review* 47 (January 1906): 154–61.

"The James Brooks Illiteracy Scandal." *Black Issues,* January 6, 2000. http://diverseeducation.com/article/432/1.php (accessed February 3, 2010).

Jenkins, Dan. "It's One Point Six, Pick Up Sticks." *Sports Illustrated* (March 21, 1966): 30–31.

Jenkins, Sally. "Sorry State." *Sports Illustrated* 77 (November 16, 1992): 70–76.

Jones, Oliver S. "Morality in College Athletics." *North American Review* 160 (May 1895): 638–40.

Jordan, Edward S. "Buying Football Victories." *Collier's* 36 (November 11, 1905): 19–20, 23; (November 18, 1905), 22–23; (November 25, 1905), 21–22, 24; (December 2, 1905), 19–20, 23.

"Judge Rules against NCAA Freshman Eligibility Requirements." *Black Issues in Higher Education,* March 18, 1999. http://findarticles.com/p/articles/mi_m0DXK/is_2_16/ai_54296832/?tag=content;col1 (accessed March 30, 2010).

Kaliss, Gregory J. "Un-Civil Discourse: Charlie Scott, the Integration of College Basketball, and the 'Progressive Mystique.'" *Journal of Sport History* 35 (Spring 2008): 99–117.

Kemp, James F. "History of Faculty Control at Columbia." *Columbia University Quarterly* 4 (December 1901): 39–40.

Kemp, James F. "History of Faculty Regulation of Athletics at Columbia." *Columbia University Quarterly* 4 (March 1902): 168–75.

Kemper, Kurt Edward. "The Smell of Roses and the Color of the Players: College Football and the Expansion of the Civil Rights Movement in the West." *Journal of Sport History* 31 (Fall 2004): 317–39.

Keppel, Frederick P. "Athletic Sports." In *Columbia.* New York: Oxford University Press, American Branch, 1914.

Kirshenbaum, Jerry. "A Question of Authority." *Sports Illustrated* 62 (March 11, 1985): 13.

Knight, Edgar W. "Athletics." In *What College Presidents Say,* 162–203. Chapel Hill: University of North Carolina Press, 1940.

Kyle, Donald G. "Winning at Olympia." *Archeology,* April 6, 2004. http://www.archaeology.org/online/features/olympics/olympia.html (accessed August 11, 2009).

Laing, J. W., and W. W. Bolton. "Faculty Control of Athletics at the English Universities." *Outing* 27 (March 1896): 490–92.

Lambert, Craig. "The Professionalization of Ivy League Sports." *Harvard Magazine* 100 (September–October 1997): 36–39, 96–98.

Lawrence, Janet, Molly Ott, and Lori Hendricks. "Athletics, Reform and Faculty Perceptions." *New Directions for Higher Education* 148 (Winter 2009): 73–81.

Lawson, Hal, and Alan G. Ingham. "Conflicting Ideologies Concerning the University and Intercollegiate Athletics: Harper and Hutchins at Chicago, 1892–1940." *Journal of Sport History* 7 (Winter 1980): 37–67.

Lazaroff, Daniel E. "The NCAA in Its Second Century: Defender of Amateurism or Anti-trust Recidivist?" *Oregon Law Review* 86 (2007): 329–71.

Leatherman, Courtney. "High-School Students Found Taking More Core-Curriculum Courses." *Chronicle of Higher Education* (August 2, 1989): A2.

Lederman, Douglas. "College Football Association at Annual Meeting Rejects Some Reforms Proposed by the NCAA and Attacks the NFL for Interfering with Students." *Chronicle of Higher Education* (June 13, 1999): A44.

Lederman, Douglas. "Despite Adoptions of Sweeping Reforms, NCAA Continues to Face Pressure from Lawmakers and Other 'Outsiders.'" *Chronicle of Higher Education* (January 23, 1991): A31–A32.

Lederman, Douglas, "Irked by Sluggish Pace of Sports Reform, Some Presidents Move to Speed Change." *Chronicle of Higher Education* (July 26, 1989): A1, A30.

Lederman, Douglas. "Rift among Presidents Perils Drive to Reform Big-Time College Sports." *Chronicle of Higher Education* (September 2, 1987): A92–A97.

Lederman, Douglas. "U. of Iowa Sparks a Firestorm with Challenge to NCAA to Bar Freshmen from Sports within 3 Years." *Chronicle of Higher Education* (April 19, 1989): A1, A34.

"Legislator Challenges Research Group." *NCAA News* (December 22, 1993): 1, 28.

Leslie, Bruce. "The Response of Four Colleges to the Rise of Intercollegiate Athletics." *Journal of Sport History* 3 (Winter 1976): 213–22.

Lewis, Guy M. "Adoption of the Sports Program, 1906–1929: The Role of Accommodation in the Transformation of Physical Education." *Quest* 12 (May 1969): 34–46.

Lewis, Guy M. "America's First Intercollegiate Sport: Regattas from 1852–1875." *Research Quarterly* 38 (December 1967): 637–47.

Lewis, Guy M. "Beginnings of Organized Sport." *American Quarterly* 22 (Summer 1970): 222–29.

Lewis, Guy M. "Enterprise on the Campus: Developments in Intercollegiate Sport and Higher Education, 1875–1930." In *The History of Physical Education and Sport,* ed. Bruce L. Bennett, 53–66. Chicago: Athletic Institute, 1972.

Lewis, Guy M. "Sport and the Making of American Higher Education: The Early Years, 1783–1875." *National College Physical Education Association for Men Proceedings* (1971): 208–13.

Lewis, Guy M. "Theodore Roosevelt's Role in the 1905 Football Controversy." *Research Quarterly* 40 (December 1969): 717–24.

Lowell, Cym H. "The Law and Collegiate Athletics in Public Institutions." *Educational Record* 60 (Fall 1979): 482–98.

MacCambridge, Michael. "End the Tug of War." *Inside Sports* 20 (January 1998): 66–74.

Makin, E. G. "Science or Athletics?" *Science* 55 (May 19, 1922): 527.

Mansfield, Harvey. "Grade Inflation: It's Time to Face the Facts." *Chronicle of Higher Education*, April 6, 2001. http://chronicle.com/free/v47/i30/30b02401.htm (accessed December 16, 2008).

Marcello, Ronald E. "The Integration of Intercollegiate Athletics in Texas: North Texas State as a Test Case." *Journal of Sport History* 14 (Winter 1987): 286–316.

Marco, S. M. "The Place of Intercollegiate Athletics in Higher Education." *Journal of Higher Education* 31 (1960): 422–27.

Marmion, Harry A., ed. "On Collegiate Athletics." *Educational Record* 60 (Fall 1979): 343–44.

Martin, Charles H. "Commentary: Beer, Parking, and Football." *Journal of Sport History* 34 (Fall 2007): 397–404.

Martin, Charles H. "Integrated New Year's Day: The Racial Politics of College Bowl Games in the American South." *Journal of Sport History* 24 (1997): 358–77.

Marullo, Ronald E. "The Integration of Intercollegiate Athletics in Texas: North Texas State College as a Test Case." *Journal of Sport History* 14 (1987): 286–316.

Mathews, Joseph J. "The First Harvard-Oxford Boat Race." *New England Quarterly* 33 (March 1960): 74–82.

McCormick, Amy C., and Robert A. McCormick. "The Emperor's New Clothes: Lifting the NCAA's Veil of Amateurism." *San Diego Law Review* 45 (2008): 495–545.

McCormick, Robert E., and Maurice Tinsley. "Athletics versus Academics? Evidence from SAT Scores." *Journal of Political Economy* 95 (1987): 1103–16.

McKenzie, Richard B., and Dwight R. Lee. "The NCAA: A Case Study of the Misuse of the Monopsony and Monopoly Models." In *In Defense of Monopoly: How Market Power Fosters Creative Production*, 143–72. Ann Arbor: University of Michigan Press, 2008.

McQuilkin, Scott A. "Summer Baseball and the NCAA: The Second 'Vexation.'" *Journal of Sport History* 25 (Spring 1998): 18–42.

McQuilkin, Scott A., and Ronald A. Smith. "The Rise and Fall of the Flying Wedge: Football's Most Controversial Play." *Journal of Sport History* 20 (Spring 1993): 57–64.

Mehler, Barry. "Beyondism: Raymond B. Cattell and the New Eugenics." *Genetica* 99 (1997): 153–63. http://www.ferris.edu/isar/bios/cattell/genetica.htm (accessed February 18, 2009).

Meiklejohn, Alexander. "The Evils of College Athletics." *Harper's Weekly* (December 2, 1905): 1751–52.

Meiklejohn, Alexander. "What Are College Games For?" *Atlantic Monthly* 130 (1922): 663–71.

Mencken, H. L. "The Striated Muscle Fetish." *American Mercury* 23 (June 1931): 156–58.

Merriman, R. B. "The Athletic Situation." *Harvard Graduates' Magazine* 16 (June 1908): 665–68.

Merriman, R. B. "Football Reform." *Harvard Graduates' Magazine* 14 (March 1906): 426–27.

Meylan, George L. "Athletics." *American Physical Education Review* 10 (June 1905): 157–63.

Miller, Patrick. "The Manly, the Moral, and the Proficient: College Sports in the New South." *Journal of Sport History* 24 (Summer 1997): 285–316.

Moore, John H. "Football's Ugly Decades, 1893–1913." *Smithsonian Magazine of History* 2 (Fall 1967): 49–63.

Moore, Kenny. "The Eternal Example: Arthur Ashe." *Sports Illustrated* 77 (December 21, 1992): 16–27.

Nack, William. "This Case Was One for the Books." *Sports Illustrated* 64 (February 24, 1986): 34–42.

Nathan, Daniel A. "Of Grades and Glory: Rethinking Intercollegiate Athletics." *American Quarterly* 54 (March 2002): 139–47.

"National and Sport-Group APR Averages, Trends and Penalties." NCAA Research, May 6, 2009. http://www.ncaa.org/wps/wcm/connect/6851f7004e0dae9ea486f41ad6fc8b25/ Four-Year+APR+Averages.pdf?MOD=AJPERES&CACHEID=6851f7004e0dae9ea486f41ad6f c8b25 (accessed March 30, 2010).

"NCAA Board of Directors Adopts Landmark Academic Reform Package." April 29, 2004. http://ncaabbs.com/showthread.php?tid=25750 (accessed April 14, 2010).

"NCAA Passes Landmark Academic Reform Plan." *Black Issues in Higher Education*, January 27, 2005. http://findarticles.com/p/articles/mi_m0DXK/is_25_21/ai_n13246330/ (accessed March 30, 2010).

"NCAA Reform: The Vandy Plan." *Sports Illustrated* (June 21, 1999): 30–32.

Needham, Henry B. "The College Athlete." *McClure's Magazine* 25 (June/July 1905): 115–28, 260–73.

Nelli, Humbert S. "The Kentucky Basketball Survey of 1945." *Journal of Sport History* 16 (Summer 1989): 186–93.

Neuberger, Richard L. "Gridiron G-Men." *Collier's* (November 1938): 74–81.

"Observation." *The Harvard Bulletin* (March 17, 1909), 4.

Odenkirk, James E. "The Eighth Wonder of the World: Ohio State University's Rejection of a Rose Bowl Bid in 1961." *Journal of Sport History* 34 (Fall 2007): 389–95.

Odenkirk, James E. "Intercollegiate Athletics—A Malignancy on Campus!" *National Association for Physical Education in Higher Education Proceedings* (June 5–8, 1980): 27–34.

"Overseers, Not Athletes, Reap Benefits." *NCAA News* (June 15, 1994).

Paine, Ralph D. "The Spirit of School and College Sport: American and English Rowing." *Century* 70 (August 1905): 484–503.

Palaima, Tom. "NCAA Panel Disses the Faculty." *Inside Higher Ed,* November 27, 2006. http:// www.insidehighered.com/views/2006/11/27/palaima (accessed April 9, 2010).

Park, Roberta. "From Football to Rugby—and Back, 1906–1919: The University of California-Stanford University Response to the 'Football Crisis of 1905.'" *Journal of Sport History* 11 (Winter 1984): 5–40.

Park, Roberta. "Muscle, Mind, and 'Agon': Intercollegiate Debating and Athletics at Harvard and Yale, 1892–1909." *Journal of Sport History* 14 (1987): 263–85.

Peabody, Rev. Endicott. "The Ideals of Sport in England and America." *American Physical Education Review* 19 (1914): 277–83.

Pennington, Bill. "Unusual Alliance Forming to Rein in College Sports." *New York Times,* January 17, 2003, p. D1.

Pepper, George W. "Faculty and Alumni Control of College Athletics." *National Education Association Proceedings* (1894): 808–15.

Pierce, Palmer E. "The Problem of Athletics in Colleges and Schools under Present War Conditions." *American Physical Education Review* 22 (October 1917): 447–49.

Pittman, Marvin S. "Football, Sport or Spoils?" *School and Society* 48 (August 13, 1938): 213–17.

"The Place of Intercollegiate Athletics in Higher Education: The Responsibility of the Faculty." *Journal of Higher Education* 31 (1960): 422–27.

Plant, Marcus L. "The Place of Intercollegiate Athletics in Higher Education." *Journal of Higher Education* 32 (1961): 1–8.

Randolph, Laura B. "Dexter Manley's Incredible Story." *Ebony,* October 1989. http://findarticles.com/p/articles/mi_m1077/is_n12_v44/ai_8010811/ (accessed September 16, 2008).

Rascher, D. A., and A. D. Schwarz. "Neither Reasonable Nor Necessary: 'Amateurism' in Big-Time College Sports." *Antitrust* 14 (2000): 51–56.

Rawlings, Hunter R. III. "Why Did We Take So Long?: Reform, Says a College President, Was Overdue." *Sports Illustrated* 74 (January 21, 1991): 72.

Raycroft, J. E. "Educational Value of Athletics in Schools and Colleges." *School and Society* 3 (February 26, 1916): 295–300.

"Recruiting High-School Athletes: Code of the Committee of Sixty." *School and Society* 25 (June 11, 1927): 687.

"The Regulation of Intercollegiate Sports." *Columbia University Quarterly* 3 (December 1900): 16–25.

Reid, William T. Jr. "The Football Situation." *Harvard Graduates' Magazine* 13 (June 1905): 601–5.

Reisner, Carl L. "Tackling Intercollegiate Athletics: An Antitrust Analysis." *Yale Law Review* 87 (January 1978): 655–79.

Richards, Eugene L. "College Athletics." *Popular Science Monthly* 24 (1884): 446–53, 587–97.

Richards, Eugene L. "The Football Situation." *Popular Science Monthly* 45 (October 1894): 721–33.

Richards, Eugene L. "Intercollegiate Athletics and Faculty Control." *Outing* 26 (July 1895): 328.

Riche, Patrick J. "Reexamination of How Athletic Success Impacts Graduation Rates: Comparing Student Athletes to All Other Undergraduates." *American Journal of Economics and Sociology* 62 (2003): 407–27.

Ridpath, Bradley David. "Can the Faculty Reform Intercollegiate Athletics? A Past, Present, and Future Perspective." *Journal of Issues in Intercollegiate Athletics* 1 (2008): 11–25.

Riesman, David, and Reuel Denney. "Football in America: A Study in Culture Diffusion." *American Quarterly* 3 (1951): 309–25.

Ripley, Alfred L. "Gentlemanliness in College Athletics." *New Englander* 44 (January 1885): 141.

Rojstaczer, Stuart. "Grade Inflation at American Colleges and Universities." http://www.gradeinflation.com/ (accessed December 16, 2008).

Roosevelt, Theodore. "The Law of Civilization and Decay." In *American Ideals.* New York: G. P. Putnam's Sons, 1897.

Ryan, W. Carson. "The Literature of American School and College Athletics." In *Bulletin Number Twenty-four of the Carnegie Foundation for the Advancement of Teaching.* Boston: Merrymount Press, 1929.

Sack, Allen L. "Are 'Improper Benefits' Really Improper? A Study of College Athlete's Views Concerning Amateurism." *Journal of Sport and Social Issues* 12, no. 1 (1988): 1–16.

Sack, Allen L. "Big-Time Athletics vs. Academic Values: It's a Rout." *Chronicle of Higher Education* (January 26, 2001).

Sack, Allen L. "College Sport and the Student-Athlete." *Journal of Sport and Social Issues* 11, no. 1–2 (1987): 31–48.

Sack, Allen L. "Proposition 48: A Masterpiece in Public Relations." *Journal of Sport and Social Issues* 8 (1984): 1–3.

Sailes, Gary A. "The Case against NCAA Proposition 48." In *African Americans in Sport*, 133–44. Piscataway, NJ: Transaction, 1998.

Salzwedel, Matthew R., and Jon Ericson. "Cleaning Up Buckley: How the Family Educational Rights and Privacy Act Shields Academic Corruption in College Athletics." *Wisconsin Law Review* 6 (2003): 1053–113.

Sanoff, A. P. "Behind Scandals in Big-Time College Sports." *U.S. News and World Report* (February 11, 1980): 61–62.

Santayana, George. "Philosophy on the Bleachers." *Harvard Monthly* 17 (July 1894): 181–90.

Sargent, Dudley A. "Evils of the Professional Tendencies of Modern Athletics." *Journal of Social Science* 20 (1885): 90.

Sargent, Dudley A. "History of the Administration of Intercollegiate Athletics in the United States." *American Physical Education Review* 15 (1910): 252–61.

Schindler, Steven. "Case 65: Balancing the Power of College Sports: The Knight Commission on Intercollegiate Athletics." In *The Foundation: A Great American Secret: How Private Wealth Is Changing the World,* ed. Joel L. Fleishman, J. Scott Kohler, and Steven Schindler, 189–91. New York: Public Affairs, 2007.

Schmidt, Raymond. "The 1929 Iowa Football Scandal: Paying Tribute to the Carnegie Report." *Journal of Sport History* 34 (Fall 2007): 343–51.

Schofield, Susan W. "PAC-10 Athletics Resolution." Letter to Stanford University Senate, May 10, 2001. http://www.stanford.edu/dept/facultysenate/2000_2001/reports/SenD5217_PAC10_athletic_res.pdf (accessed March 30, 2010).

Scott, Harry A. "New Directions in Intercollegiate Athletics." *Teachers College Record* 58 (October–May 1957): 29–37.

Scoville, S. "Athletic Vassar," *Outlook* 54 (July 4, 1896): 18.

Sears, Hal D. "The Moral Threat of Intercollegiate Sports: An 1893 Poll of Ten College Presidents, and the End of 'The Champion Football Team of the Great West.'" *Journal of Sport History* 19 (Winter 1992): 211–26.

Sellers, Robert M., and Tabbye Chavous. "Motivation vs. Structure: Factors in the Academic Performance of African American College Athletes." http://www.rcgd.isr.umich.edu/prba/perspectives/winter1997/rsellers.pdf (accessed April 9, 2010).

Shaler, N. S. "The Athletic Problem in Education." *Atlantic Monthly* 63 (1889): 79–88.

"Shall Intercollegiate Football Be Abolished?" *Literary Digest* 87 (October 10, 1925): 68–76.

Shapiro, Beth J. "John Hannah and the Growth of Big-Time Intercollegiate Athletics at Michigan State University." *Journal of Sport History* 10 (Winter 1983): 26–40.

"Sidelines." *Chronicle of Higher Education* (November 2, 2001): A56.

Smith, Judson. "College Intercollegiate Contests." *New Englander* 34 (July 1875): 518–29.

Smith, Ronald A. "Amateur Athletic Union." In *Encyclopedia USA,* vol. 2, ed. Donald W. Wisenhunt, 157–59. Gulf Breeze, FL: Academic International, 1983.

Smith, Ronald A. "Amateurism in Late Nineteenth-Century College Sports." In *Major Problems in American Sport History,* ed. Steven A. Riess, 121–28. Boston: Houghton-Mifflin, 1997.

Smith, Ronald A. "Commercialized Intercollegiate Athletics and the 1903 Harvard Stadium." *New England Quarterly* 78 (March 2005): 26–48.

Smith, Ronald A. "A Failure of Elitism: The Harvard-Yale Dual League Plan of the 1890s." *New England Quarterly* 59 (June 1988): 201–13.

Smith, Ronald A. "Harvard and Columbia and a Reconsideration of the 1905–06 Football Crisis." *Journal of Sport History* 8 (Winter 1981): 5–19.

Smith, Ronald A. "A Historical Look at Enhancement of Performance in Sport: Muscular Moralists versus Muscular Scientists." *American Academy of Physical Education Papers No. 25* (April 2–3, 1991): 2–11.

Smith, Ronald A. "History of Amateurism in Men's Intercollegiate Athletics: The Continuance of a 19th Century Anachronism in America." *Quest* 45 (November 1993): 430–47.

Smith, Ronald A. "A History of Basketball for Women in Colleges." In *The American Sporting Experience: A Historical Anthology of Sport in America,* ed. Steven A. Riess, 351–79. West Point, NY: Leisure Press, 1984.

Smith, Ronald A. "Intercollegiate Athletics/Football History at the Dawn of a New Century." *Journal of Sport History* 29 (Summer 2002): 229–39.

Smith, Ronald A. "The Lost Battle for Gentlemanly Sport, 1869–1909." In *The Rock, the Curse, and the HUB: A Random History of Boston Sports,* ed. Randy Roberts, 160–77. Cambridge, MA: Harvard University Press, 2005.

Smith, Ronald A. "The Paul Robeson—Jackie Robinson Saga and a Political Collision." *Journal of Sport History* 6 (Summer 1979): 5–27.

Smith, Ronald A. "Preludes to the NCAA: Early Failures of Faculty Intercollegiate Athletic Control." In *Sport in America. From Wicked Amusement to National Obsession,* ed. David K. Wiggins, 151–62. Champaign, IL: Human Kinetics, 1995.

Smith, Ronald A. "Reaction to 'Historical Roots of the Collegiate Dilemma.'" *National College Physical Education Association for Men Proceedings* (1976): 154–62.

Smith, Ronald A. "The Rise of College Baseball." *Baseball History* 1 (Spring 1986): 23–41.

Smith, Ronald A. "The William and Mary Athletic Scandal of 1951: Governance and the Battle for Academic and Athletic Integrity." *Journal of Sport History* 34 (Fall 2007): 353–73.

Smith, Ronald A. "Winning and a Theory of Competitive Athletics." In *Sport and the Humanities: A Collection of Original Essays,* ed. William J. Morgan, 44–50. Knoxville: Bureau of Education Research, University of Tennessee, 1980.

Smith, Ronald A. "Women's Control of American College Sport: The Good of Those Who Played or an Exploitation by Those Who Controlled It?" *Sport History Review* 29 (May 1998): 103–20.

Sojka, Gregory S. "Evolution of the Student-Athlete in America." *Journal of Popular Culture* 16 (Spring 1983): 54–62.

Sowell, Thomas. "The New Racism on Campus." *Fortune* (February 13, 1989): 115–16.

Sperber, Murray. "In Praise of 'Student-Athletes': The NCAA Is Haunted by Its Past." *Chronicle of Higher Education* (January 8, 1999): A76.

Spivey, Donald. "End Jim Crow in Sports: The Protest at New York University, 1940–1941." *Journal of Sport History* 15 (1988): 282–303.

"Squeeze Play: Prop 48 Left Frank Between Two Worlds." *Champion* (Winter 2008): 36. http://www.tabpi.org/2009/f14.pdf (accessed March 30, 2010).

Srinivasan, Srikanth. "Sherman Act Invalidation of the NCAA Amateurism Rules." *Harvard Law Review* 105, no. 6 (April 1992): 1299–1318.

Star, Jack, and Clark Mollenhoff. "Football Scandal Hits the Big Ten." *Look* 20 (August 21, 1956): 19–25.

Steffens, Joseph Lincoln. "Ohio: A Tale of Two Cities," *McClure's Magazine* 25 (June/July 1905): 293–311.

Stern, Carol Simpson. "The Faculty Report in the Reform of Intercollegiate Athletics." *Academe* 89 (January/February 2003): 64–70.

Stewart, C. A. "Athletics and the College." *Atlantic Monthly* 113 (February 1914): 153–60.

Stoke, Harold W. "College Athletics: Education or Show Business." *Atlantic Monthly* 193 (March 1954): 46–50.

Stone, Richard. "The Graham Plan of 1935: An Aborted Crusade to De-emphasize College Athletics." *North Carolina Historical Review* 64 (July 1987): 274–93.

Suggs, Welch. "Can Anyone Do Anything About College Sports?" *Chronicle of Higher Education* (February 23, 2001): A50–A52.

Suggs, Welch. "NCAA Adopts Rules Changes Aimed at Curbing Abuses in Men's Basketball." *Chronicle of Higher Education* (May 12, 2000): A54.

Suggs, Welch. "NCAA Board Rejects Idea of Creating Outside Group to Push for Reform." *Chronicle of Higher Education* (September 7, 2001): A59.

Suggs, Welch. "Proposed NCAA Study of Football Rubs the Sports Powerhouse the Wrong Way." *Chronicle of Higher Education* (August 18, 2000): A44.

Sumner, Jim L. "John Franklin Crowell, Methodism, and the Football Controversy at Trinity College, 1887–1994." *Journal of Sport History* 17 (Spring 1990): 5–20.

Sutter, Daniel. "NCAA Scholarship Limits and Competitive Balance in College Football." *Journal of Sports Economics* 4, no. 1 (2003): 3–18.

Synnott, Marcia G. "The 'Big Three' and the Harvard-Princeton Break, 1926–1934." *Journal of Sport History* 3 (Summer 1976): 188–202.

Tarbell, Ida M. "John D. Rockefeller, A Character Study." *McClure's Magazine* 25 (June/July 1905): 226–49.

"Teaching in American Colleges." *Nation* 35 (November 30, 1882): 458.

Thelin, John R. "Academics on Athletics: Review Essay." *Journal of Higher Education* 73 (May/June 2002): 409–19.

Thelin, John R. "Good Sports? Historical Perspective on the Political Economy of Intercollegiate Athletics in the Era of Title IX, 1972–1997." *Journal of Higher Education* 71 (July–August, 2000): 391–410.

Thwing, Charles W. "Football: Is the Game Worth Saving?" *Independent* 54 (May 15, 1902): 1167–74.

Thwing, Charles W. "A Game of Hearts." *Independent* 10 (November 3, 1898): 1260–61.

Toma, J. Douglas, and Dennis A. Kramer II, eds. "The Uses of Intercollegiate Athletics: Opportunities and Challenges for the University." *New Directions for Higher Education* 148 (Winter 2009): 1–116.

Tublitz, Nathan. "Putting the Student Back into the Student-Athlete." 2007 NCAA Convention, January 6, 2007. http://coia.comm.psu.edu/Tublitz%20NCAA%20Convention%20%20talk%20Jan%202007.pdf (accessed March 30, 2010).

Tucker, William H. "The Racist Past of American Psychology." *Journal of Blacks in Higher Education* 41 (2005): 108–12.

Tunis, John R. "The Great God Football." *Harper's Magazine* 157 (1928): 742–52.

Tunis, John R. "More Pay for College Football Stars." *American Mercury* 39 (November 1936): 267–72.

Tunis, John R. "What Price College Football?" *American Mercury* 47 (October 1939): 129–42.

Turpie, David. "From Broadway to Hollywood: The Image of the 1939 University of Tennessee Football Team and the Americanization of the South." *Journal of Sport History* 35 (Spring 2008): 119–40.

Uehling, B. S. Athletics and Academe: Creative Divorce or Reconciliation?" *Educational Record* 64 (Summer 1983): 13–15.

Underwood, Arthur W. "The Right and Wrong of Athletics." *The Sunset Club Yearbook, 1893–,* 213–32. Chicago: Privately printed, 1895.

Underwood, John. "The Desperate Coach." *Sports Illustrated* 31 (August 25, 1969): 70–80.

Underwood, John. "Student-Athletes: The Sham and the Shame." *Sports Illustrated* 52 (May 19, 1980): 36–73.

Van Dyne, Larry. "Presidents Trying to Gain Power in the NCAA." *Chronicle of Higher Education* (January 24, 1977): 7.

Veysey, Lawrence. "Letter to the Editor." *New York Review of Books,* March 4, 1982, 44.

Walker, Francis A. "College Athletics." *Harvard Graduates' Magazine* 2 (September 1893): 1–18.

Wallace, Francis. "Test Case at Pitt: The Facts about College Football for Pay." *Saturday Evening Post* 212 (October 28, 1939): 14–25, 47–49, 51–52, and (November 4, 1939): 20–21, 80, 82, 85–86.

Waller, Jeffrey M. "A Necessary Evil: Proposition 16 and Its Impact on Academics and Athletics in the NCAA." *DePaul Law Journal* 1, no. 2 (2003): 189–206.

"Walter Byers Former NCAA Executive Director." *NCAA News* (January 2, 1991): 4.

Warren, Luther W. "The Charles W. Eliot Centennial." *Journal of Physical Education* 5 (March 1934): 24.

Washington, Marian E. "Black Women in Sports: Can We Get Off the Track?" National College Physical Education Association for Men *Proceedings* (December 26–29, 1973): 42–44.

Washington, Marvin. "Field Approaches to Institutional Change: The Evolution of the National Collegiate Athletic Association 1906–1995." *Organization Studies* 25, no. 3 (2004): 393–414.

Watterson, John S. III. "The Death of Archer Christian: College Presidents and the Reform of College Football." *Journal of Sport History* 22 (Summer 1995): 149–67.

Watterson, John S. III. "Football at the University of Virginia, 1951–1961." *Journal of Sport History* 34 (Fall 2007): 375–87.

Watterson, John S. III. "The Football Crisis of 1909–1910: The Response of the Eastern 'Big Three.'" *Journal of Sport History* 8 (Spring 1981): 5–19.

Watterson, John S. III. "The Gridiron Crisis of 1905: Was It Really a Crisis?" *Journal of Sport History* 27 (Summer 2000): 291–98.

Watterson, John S. III. "Out of Baseball's Shadow: The Paradox of College Football Scholarship." *Journal of Sport History* 29 (Summer 2002): 221–28.

Weber, Ellen. "The Title IX Controversy." *WomenSports* 1 (June 1974): 74–77.

Weistart, John C. "College Sports Reform: Where Are the Faculty?" *Academe* 73 (July–August, 1987): 12–17.

Weistart, John C. "The Role of Faculty in the Governance of College Athletics: A Report of the Special Committee on Athletics." *Academe* 76 (January–February 1998): 43–47.

Wertheim, L. J., and Douglas Yeager. "The Passing Game." *Sports Illustrated* (June 14, 1989): 92–102.

Wesberry, James P. "Football Spoils Georgia Rumpus." *Christian Century* 52 (December 21, 1955): 1504–5.

Westby, David L., and Allen Sack. "The Commercialization and Functional Rationalization of College Football: The Origins." *Journal of Higher Education* 47 (1976): 625–47.

"What Football Players Are Earning this Fall." *Literary Digest* 107 (November 15, 1930): 28, 33.

Whigham, H. J. "American Sport from an English Point of View." *Outlook* 93 (November 1909): 738–44.

White, John W. "The Constitution, Authority, and Policy of the Committee on the Regulation of Athletic Sports." *Harvard Graduates' Magazine* 1 (January 1893): 209–31.

Whitney, Caspar W. "Amateur Sports." *Harper's Weekly* 39 (November 23, 1895): 1123–24.

Whitney, Caspar W. "The Guiding Hand of Faculty in College Sports." *Outing* 40 (July 1902): 497.

Whitney, Caspar W. "Is Football Worthwhile?" *Collier's* 45 (December 18, 1909): 13, 24–25.

Whitney, Caspar W. "The Sportsman's View-Point." *Outing* 37 (January 1901): 461–78.

Whitney, Caspar W. "The Sportsman's View-Point." *Outing* 38 (June 1901): 329–43.

Whitney, Caspar W. "The Sportsman's View-Point." *Outing* 38 (May 1901): 219–26.

Whitney, Caspar W. "Who Is Responsible for the Commercialism in College Sports?" *Outing* 46 (July 1905): 485–87.

Whiton, James. "The First Harvard-Yale Regatta (1852)." *Outlook* 68 (June 1901): 286–89.

"Who Plays?" Online NewsHour with Jim Lehrer Transcript. March 12, 1999. http://www.pbs .org/newshour/bb/sports/jan-june99/ncaa_3-12.html (accessed March 30, 2010).

Wieder, Alan. "NCAA Rule 48: Origins and Reactions." *Proteus* 3 (Spring 1986): 41–51.

Wiggins, David K. "'The Future of College Athletics Is at Stake': Black Athletes and Racial Turmoil on Three Predominately White University Campuses, 1968-1972." *Journal of Sport History* 15 (Winter 1988): 304–33.

Williams, Alexander Jr. "The Impact of Rule 48 upon the Black Student Athlete: A Comment." *Journal of Negro Education* 52 (Summer 1983): 362–73.

Wilson, Woodrow. "What Is a College For?" *Scribner's Magazine* 46 (November 1909): 570–77.

Wolverton, Brad. "The Athletics Department of the Future." *Chronicle of Higher Education* 53 (July 20, 2007): A28.

Wu, Ying. "Early NCAA Attempts at the Governance of Women's Intercollegiate Athletics, 1968–1973." *Journal of Sport History* 26 (Fall 1999): 585–601.

Wu, Ying. "Margot Polivy, Legal Costs, and the Demise of the Association for Intercollegiate Athletics for Women." *Sport History Review* 30 (November 1999): 119–39.

Wushanley, Ying. "The Olympics, Cold War, and the Reconstruction of U.S. Women's Athletics." *Fifth International Symposium for Olympic Research* (2000): 119–26.

Young, C. A. "College Athletic Sports." *Forum* 2 (October 1886): 142–52.

Young, C. V. P. "Intercollegiate Athletics and the Professional Coach." *American Physical Education Review* 19 (May 1914): 331–38.

Zimbalist, Andrew. "College Athletic Budgets Are Bulging but Their Profits Are Slim to None." *Sports Business Journal* (June 18, 2007): 26.

Zingg, P. J. "No Simple Solution: Proposition 48 and the Possibilities of Reform." *Educational Record* 64 (Summer 1983): 6–12.

Speeches and Unpublished Works

Bergstrom, Art. "Unedited Draft NCAA Chronology." ca. 1974. Ursula Walsh Files, NCAA Headquarters, Indianapolis, IN. October 18, 2007.

Brand, Myles. "A Crossroads in College Sport." Speech to the AAUP, October 9, 2003. http://www.sc.edu/faculty/PDF/MylesBrand.pdf (accessed May 7, 2010).

Brand, Myles. "Presidents Have Cause, Means to Reduce Arms." *NCAA News* (February 12, 2001). http://coia.comm.psu.edu/pac10.html (accessed April 9, 2010).

Brand, Myles. "Speech to National Press Club." October 20, 2006. http://www2.ncaa.org/portal/legislation_and_governance/committees/future_task_force/pressclub.pdf (accessed August 20, 2008).

Brand, Myles. "Sustaining the Collegiate Model of Athletics." Keynote address, National Symposium on Athletics Reform, November 11, 2003. http:/symposium.tulane.edu/keynote.txt (accessed August 14, 2009).

Brehm, President Cloide E. "Meeting with Administrative Group." Transcript, January 29, 1955. President Brehm Papers, Box 2, Folder "Employment of Bowden Wyatt," University of Tennessee Archives.

Bullock, Clifford A. "Fired by Conscience: The Black 14 Incident at the University of Wyoming and Black Protest in the Western Athletic Conference." http://uwacadweb.uwyo.edu/robertshistory/fired_by_conscience.htm (accessed May 6, 2010.)

Burnett, Cecil J. "The Tradition of Athletics: The University of Pennsylvania." Unpublished manuscript, 1956. UPA4, Box 89, Folder "Intercollegiate Athletics—History of Athletics," University of Pennsylvania Archives.

Canham, Don. "College Presidents Have Failed College Sports." Readers Report, November 10, 2003. http://www.businessweek.com/magazine/content/03_45/c3857049_mz004.htm#B3857051 (accessed March 30, 2010).

Coalition on Intercollegiate Athletics (COIA). "Framing the Future: Reforming Intercollegiate

Athletics." June 15, 2007. http://coia.comm.psu.edu/FTF/FTFproposals.pdf (accessed March 30, 2010).

COIA Press Release. "Statement on the NCAA's Academic Progress Rate." July 21, 2008. http://www.neuro.uoregon.edu/~tublitz/coia/index.html (accessed August 20, 2008).

Dott, Richard M. "[Michigan] Trip to Play Harvard, Yale, Princeton." Fall 1881. Richard M. Dott Papers, Michigan Historical Collection, Bentley Historical Library, University of Michigan.

Edwards, Amanda. "Why Sport?: The Development of Sport as a Policy Issue in Title IX of Education Amendments of 1972." Paper presented at the Midwest Political Science Association, Chicago, April 15, 2004. http://www.allacademic.com/meta/p83807_index.html (accessed April 9, 2010).

Eliot, Charles W. "Inaugural Address." October 19, 1869.

Ericson, Jon. "Remarks before the Knight Commission on Intercollegiate Athletics." October 18, 2000, http://www.thedrakegroup.org/Ericson_KC_Remarks_2000.pdf (accessed April 14, 2010).

Hawes, Kaye. "The History of Intercollegiate Athletics and the NCAA." http://worldscibooks.com/etextbook/6172/6172_chap0l.pdf (accessed April 9, 2010).

Hubert H. Humphrey Institute of Public Affairs Center for School Change. "A Call for Reform." August 30, 2007. http://www.centerforschoolchange.org/ncaa-challenge/a-call-for-reform/html (accessed August 18, 2008).

Joyce, Rev. Edmund P. "Speech at College Football Association, 30 May 1980." President Banowsky Papers, Box 74, Folder 13, University of Oklahoma Archives.

Lederman, Doug. "Due Process and the NCAA." *Insidehighered.com,* June 13, 2006. http://www.insidehighered.com/news/2006/06/13/ncaa (accessed September 4, 2008).

Lederman, Doug. "A (Money) Losing Proposition." *Insidehighered.com,* May 16, 2008. http://www.insidehighered.com/news/2008/05/16/ncaa (accessed August 17, 2008).

Leland, Ted. "Speech at the FARA Annual Meeting." November 9, 2007. http://www.farawebsite.org/files/Faraannualmeeting/Leland_presentation_FARAAnnualMeeting112007.pdf (accessed April 9, 2010).

"The Literature of American School and College Athletics." May 2008. http://lombardi.lsu.edu/his09/bib.html (accessed April 10, 2010).

Lumpkin, Angela. "The Graham Plan—An Early Attempt to Achieve Sanity in Sport." Paper presented at the AAHPERD Convention, Anaheim, CA, March 30, 1984.

MacCracken, H. M. "Speech before the Third Annual Convention of the Intercollegiate Athletic Association of the United States." *National Collegiate Athletic Association Proceedings* 3 (1909): 6.

Moses Taylor Pyne Scrapbook. Vol. 8, Princeton University Archives.

"NCAA Freshman-Eligibility Standards Quick Reference Sheet." https://web1.ncaa.org/eligibilitycenter/hs/d1_standards.pdf (accessed March 30, 2010).

Neinas, Charles M. "Where Have We Been and Where Are We Going." Speech at College Football Association meeting, May 30, 1980, President Banowsky Papers, Box 74, Folder 13, University of Oklahoma Archives.

"The New Division I Governance Structure." November 9, 2007. http://www.farawebsite.org/annualmeetingpresentations.asp (accessed April 9, 2010).

"Noting the Passing of Jan Kemp, UGA Athletics Whistleblower." http://feministlawprofs
.law.sc.edu/?p=4414 (accessed May 7, 2010).

Orszag, Jonathan, and Peter R. Orszag. "The Empirical Effects of Collegiate Athletics: An
Update." April 2005. http://www.ncaa.org/wps/wcm/connect/97483e804e0dabfa9f32f
f1ad6fc8b25/empirical_effects_of_collegiate_athletics_update.pdf?MOD=AJPERES&CAC
HEID=97483e804e0dabfa9f32ff1ad6fc8b25. (accessed May 7, 2010).

Roosevelt, Theodore. "The Functions of a Great University." Address at Harvard University,
June 28, 1905. In *The Works of Theodore Roosevelt*. New York: Charles Scribner's Sons,
1926.

Sandler, Bernice R. "'Too Strong for a Woman'—The Five Words That Created Title IX." http://
www.bernicesandler.com/id44.htm (accessed October 29, 2008).

Smith, Ronald A. "College Athletics: Has Anyone Been at the Helm?" Speech at the First
Wenner-Wingate Memorial Lecture on History and Literature of Sport, Western Maryland
College, March 1990.

Smith, Ronald A. "Intercollegiate Athletic Reform: An Historical View of Presidents, Governing Boards, and Faculty." Plenary Session presentation, North American Society for Sport
History Conference, California State University, Long Beach, May 1995.

Smith, Ronald A. "Presidents Can't Punt, at Least Not Straight: Who Has Controlled Big-
Time College Athletics." Presentation at the University of California Center for Studies
in Higher Education Seminar, University of California–Berkeley, October 1989.

Smith, Ronald A. "Women's and Men's Models of College Sport from the Nineteenth Century
to Title IX: Maternalism and Paternalism." Raymond Weiss Lecture, Research Consortium
and American Academy of Kinesiology and Physical Education at the American Association
for Health, Physical Education, and Recreation Convention, Atlanta, GA, April 1996.

Stevenson, William E. "Amateurism in Athletics." Address at Metropolitan AAU Gold Medal
Dinner, New York City. April 29, 1957, Papers of the Office of President, Box 89, Folder
"IVY Group, President-II," University of Pennsylvania Archives.

"Story of a Graduate Manager." Transcript, September 1, 1925, President Lowell Papers,
1922–25, Folder 6B, Harvard University Archives.

"The Student-Athlete Experience: Findings from the NCAA Goals and Score Study." November 9, 2007. http://www.farawebsite.org/files/Faraannualmeeting/fara_goals_report_
nov0707.pdf (accessed May 7, 2010).

"Transfer, Academic Outcomes and the ARP." November 2007. Faculty Athletic Representatives Association. http://www.farawebsite.org/files/Faraannualmeeting/TransferAca-
demicOUtcomesandtheAPR.pdf (accessed May 7, 2010).

Tublitz, Nathan. "Putting the Student Back into the Student-Athlete." 2007 NCAA Convention, January 6, 2007. http://coia.comm.psu.edu/Tublitz%20NCAA%20Convention%20
%20talk%20Jan%2007.pdf (accessed March 30, 2010).

Turner, Frederick Jackson. "Speech at Alumni Banquet, University of Wisconsin, Madison,
January 31, 1906." Wis/Mss/Al, Box 2, Turner Papers, "Athletics," Wisconsin State Historical Society.

"What's Wrong with Proposition 48 and 16?" *Fairtest: The National Center for Fair and Open
Testing*, August 20, 2007. http://www.fairtest.org/whats-wrong-proposition-48-and-16
(accessed August 17, 2008).

Wyatt, Hugh. "Johnny Bright—America's Loss." 2000. http://www.coachwyatt.com/johnnybright.html (accessed April 12, 2010).

Dissertations, Theses, and Undergraduate Papers

Borkowski, Richard P. "The Life and Contributions of Walter Camp to American Football." EdD dissertation, Temple University, 1979.

Castle, David B. "The Pacific Coast Conference, 1915–1959: The Limits of Intercollegiate Athletic Reform." MA thesis, University of Oregon, 1984.

Cohen, Steven D. "More than Fun and Games: A Comparative Study of the Roles of Sport in English and American Society at the Turn of the Century." PhD dissertation, Brandeis University, 1980.

Corrie, Bruce. "A History of the Athletic Coast Conference." PED dissertation, Indiana University, 1970.

Demas, Lane. "Integrating the Gridiron: Civil Rights and American College Football, 1935–1970." PhD dissertation, University of California, Irvine, 2008.

Engstrand, Gary. "Faculty Control of Athletics: A Case Study of the University of Minnesota." PhD dissertation, University of Minnesota, 1995.

Epling, Robert T. "Seasons of Change: Football Desegregation at the University of Tennessee and the Transformation of the Southeastern Conference, 1963–1967." PhD dissertation, University of Tennessee, 1994.

Fleischer, Michael M. "A History of the Eastern Collegiate Athletic Conference." EdD dissertation, Teachers College, Columbia University, 1959.

Foley, Nancy C. "The Elimination of Athletic Subsidies at the University of Pittsburgh, 1936–1939." Exercise and Sport Science 444 Paper, Penn State University, April 27, 1987, Penn State University Archives.

Forbes, Theodore W. "The N.C.A.A. since 1942." DEd dissertation, Teachers College, Columbia University, 1955.

Franklin, Timothy V. "An Educational Reform Commission and Institutional Change: Case Study of the Policies, Politics, and Processes of the Knight Foundation Commission on Intercollegiate Athletics." PhD dissertation, Virginia Polytechnic University, 1992.

Helman, Jay. "History of Intercollegiate Athletic Eligibility: Educational Compromises to Competitive Interests." PhD dissertation, Penn State University, 1990.

Highes, Raymond. "Desegregating the Holy Day: Football, Blacks, and the Southeastern Conference." PhD dissertation, Ohio State University, 1991.

Hunt, Virginia. "Governance of Woman's Intercollegiate Athletics: An Historical Perspective." EdD dissertation, University of North Carolina at Greensboro, 1976.

Kaliss, Gregory J. "Everyone's All-Americans: Race, Men's College Athletics, and the Ideal of Equal Opportunity." PhD dissertation, University of North Carolina, Chapel Hill, 2008.

Kiracofe, Edgar S. "Athletics and Physical Education in the Colleges of Virginia." PhD dissertation, University of Virginia, 1932.

Koorsgaard, Robert. "A History of the Amateur Athletic Union of the United States." EdD dissertation, Columbia University Teachers College, 1952.

Lester, Robin. "The Rise, Decline, and Fall of Intercollegiate Football at the University of Chicago, 1890–1940." PhD dissertation, University of Chicago, 1974.

Lewis, Guy M. "The American Intercollegiate Football Spectacle, 1869–1917." PhD dissertation, University of Maryland, 1964.

Maloney, Gail F. "The Impact of Title IX on Women's Intercollegiate Athletics." PhD dissertation, State University of New York, Buffalo, 1994.

Marino, Rob. "Development of the Knight Foundation Commission on Intercollegiate Athletics and Its Impact on College Sports, 1989–2001." MA thesis, University of Florida, 2002.

McQuilkin, Scott A. "A History of Intercollegiate Athletic Reform during the Progressive Era, 1890–1920." PhD dissertation, Penn State University, 1995.

Miller, Patrick B. "Athletes in Academe: College Sports and American Culture, 1850–1920." PhD dissertation, University of California, 1987.

Patberg, Kurt. "Presidential Involvement in NCAA Division I Governance Related Issues." PhD dissertation, University of Minnesota, 2002.

Pierce, Jester L. "History of the Southern Conference." PhD dissertation, University of North Carolina, Chapel Hill, 1954.

Plyley, Dale E. "The AIAW vs. the NCAA: A Struggle for Power to Govern Women's Athletics in American Institutions of Higher Education, 1972–1982." MA thesis, University of Western Ontario, 1997.

Roberts, Gerald F. "The Strenuous Life: The Cult of Manliness in the Era of Theodore Roosevelt." PhD dissertation, Michigan State University, 1970.

Ruth, Earl B. "A Study of Selected Conferences in the United States." PhD dissertation, University of North Carolina, Chapel Hill, 1954.

Sack, Allen. "The Commercialization and Rationalization of Intercollegiate Football: A Comparative Analysis of the Development of Football at Yale and Harvard in the Latter Nineteenth Century." PhD dissertation, Penn State University, 1974.

Smith, Ronald A. "From Normal School to State University: A History of the Wisconsin State University Conference." PhD dissertation, University of Wisconsin, Madison, 1969.

Solow, R. "Faculty Athletic Committees as a Source of Intercollegiate Athletic Authority." PhD dissertation, University of Georgia, 1998.

Sparhawk, Ruth M. "A Study of the Life and Contributions of Amos Alonzo Stagg to Intercollegiate Football." DPE dissertation, Springfield College, 1968.

Sponberg, Adryn L. "The Evolution of Athletic Subsidization in the Intercollegiate Conference of Faculty Representatives (Big Ten)." PhD dissertation, University of Michigan, 1968.

Su, Mila. "Collegiate Women's Sport and a Guide to Collecting and Identifying Archival Materials." MS thesis, Penn State University, 2002.

Wu, Ying. "The Demise of the AIAW and Women's Control of Intercollegiate Athletics for Women: The Sex Separatist Policy in the Reality of the NCAA, Cold War, and Title IX." PhD dissertation, Penn State University, 1997.

Index

Ronald A. Smith is a professor
of history, emeritus, at
Pennsylvania State University.

Sport and Society

Global Games   *Maarten Van Bottenburg*
The Sporting World of the Modern South   *Edited by Patrick B. Miller*
The End of Baseball As We Knew It: The Players Union, 1960–81   *Charles P. Korr*
Rocky Marciano: The Rock of His Times   *Russell Sullivan*
Saying It's So: A Cultural History of the Black Sox Scandal   *Daniel A. Nathan*
The Nazi Olympics: Sport, Politics, and Appeasement in the 1930s   *Edited by*
   Arnd Krüger and William Murray
The Unlevel Playing Field: A Documentary History of the African American
   Experience in Sport   *David K. Wiggins and Patrick B. Miller*
Sports in Zion: Mormon Recreation, 1890–1940   *Richard Ian Kimball*
Sweet William: The Life of Billy Conn   *Andrew O'Toole*
Sports in Chicago   *Edited by Elliot J. Gorn*
The Chicago Sports Reader   *Edited by Steven A. Riess and Gerald R. Gems*
College Football and American Culture in the Cold War Era   *Kurt Edward Kemper*
The End of Amateurism in American Track and Field   *Joseph M. Turrini*
Benching Jim Crow: The Rise and Fall of the Color Line in Southern College Sports,
   1890–1980   *Charles H. Martin*
Pay for Play: A History of Big-Time College Athletic Reform   *Ronald A. Smith*

Reprint Editions

The Nazi Olympics   *Richard D. Mandell*
Sports in the Western World (2d ed.)   *William J. Baker*
Jesse Owens: An American Life   *William J. Baker*

The University of Illinois Press
is a founding member of the
Association of American University Presses.

Designed by Kelly Gray
Composed in 9.75/14 ITC Officina Serif
with ITC Officina Sans display
by Jim Proefrock
at the University of Illinois Press
Manufactured by Sheridan Books, Inc.
University of Illinois Press
1325 South Oak Street
Champaign, IL 61820-6903
www.press.uillinois.edu